Irene C. Fountas **&** Gay Su Pinnell

The Reading
Minilessons
Book

Your Every Day Guide for Literacy Teaching

KINDERGARTEN

HEINEMANN
Portsmouth, NH

Heinemann
361 Hanover Street
Portsmouth, NH 03801–3912
www.heinemann.com

Offices and agents throughout the world

The authors and publisher wish to thank those who have generously given permission to reprint borrowed material: Please see the Credits section at the back of the book, starting on page 445.

Library of Congress Cataloging-in-Publication Data is on file at the Library of Congress.
ISBN: 978-0-325-09861-6

Editor: Sue Paro
Production: Cindy Strowman
Cover and interior designs: Ellery Harvey
Illustrator: Will Sweeney
Typesetter: Ed Stevens Design
Manufacturing: Deanna Richardson

Printed in the United States of America on acid-free paper

22 21 20 19 18   LSC   1 2 3 4 5 6

CONTENTS

2   Literary Analysis

Fiction and Nonfiction

General

Book and Print Features

Fiction

Setting

Plot

Character

Illustrations

3 Strategies and Skills

4 Writing About Reading

GOAL OF READING:
is the joyful, independent, and meaningful processing of meaningful text.

Chapter **1** **The Role of Reading Minilessons in Early Literacy Learning**

THE GOAL OF ALL READING is the joyful, independent, and meaningful processing of a written text. As a competent reader, you become immersed in a fiction or nonfiction text; you read for a purpose; you become highly engaged with the plot and characters or the content. Focused on the experience of reading the text, you are largely unconscious of the thousands of actions happening in your brain that support the construction of meaning from the print that represents language. And, this is true whether the print is on a piece of paper or an electronic device. Your purpose may be to have vicarious experiences via works of fiction that take you to places far distant in time and space—even to worlds that do not and cannot exist! Or, your purpose may be to gather fuel for thinking (by using fiction or nonfiction) or it may simply be to enjoy the sounds of human language via literature and poetry. Most of us engage in the reading of multiple texts every day— some for work, some for pleasure, and some for practical guidance—but what we all have in common as readers is the ability to independently and simultaneously apply in-the-head systems of strategic actions that enable us to act on written texts.

we all read for different purposes...

Young readers are on a journey toward efficient processing of any texts they might like to attempt, and it is important every step of the way that they have successful experiences in reading independently those texts that are available at each point in time. In a literacy-rich classroom with a

MUST HAVE Successful Experiences! (reading independently)

1

multitext approach, readers have the opportunity to hear written texts read aloud through interactive read-aloud, and so they build a rich treasure chest of known stories and nonfiction books that they can share as a classroom community. They understand and talk about these shared texts in ways that extend comprehension, vocabulary, and knowledge of the ways written texts are presented and organized. They participate with their classmates in the shared reading of a common text so that they understand more and know how to act on written language. They experience tailored instruction in small guided reading groups using leveled texts precisely matched to their current abilities and needs for challenge. They stretch their thinking as they discuss a variety of complex texts in book clubs. They process fiction and nonfiction books with expert teacher support—always moving in the direction of more complex texts that will lift their reading abilities. *But it is in independent reading that they apply everything they have learned across all of those instructional contexts.* So the goal of all the reading instruction is to enable the young reader to engage in effective, efficient, and joyful independent and meaningful processing of written text *every day* in the classroom. This is what it means to grow up literate in our schools.

Independent reading involves choice based on interests and tastes. Competent, independent readers are eager to talk and write about the books they have read for themselves. They are gaining awareness of themselves as readers with favorite authors, illustrators, genres, and topics; their capacity for self-regulation is growing. The key to this kind of independent reading is making an explicit connection between all other instructional contexts— interactive read-aloud, shared reading, guided reading, and book clubs—and the reader's own independent work. Making these explicit links is the goal of minilessons. All teaching, support, and confirmation lead to the individual's successful, independent reading.

Making Learning Visible Through Minilessons

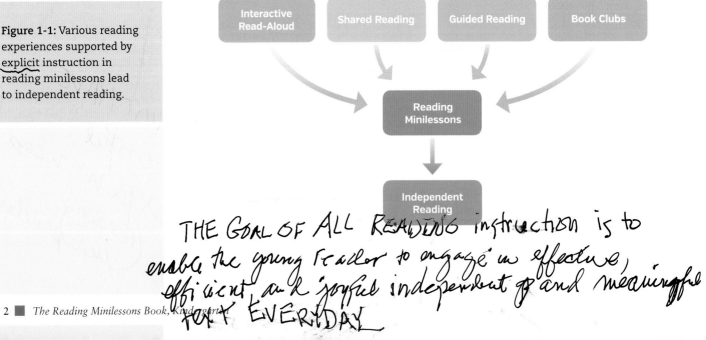

Figure 1-1: Various reading experiences supported by explicit instruction in reading minilessons lead to independent reading.

What Is a Reading Minilesson?

A reading minilesson is a concise and focused lesson on any aspect of effective reading or classroom reading work that is important for children to explicitly understand at a particular point in time. It is an opportunity to build on all of the children's literacy experiences, make one important understanding visible, and hold the children accountable for applying it consistently in reading. Minilessons place a strong instructional frame around independent reading.

A minilesson takes only a few minutes and usually involves the whole class. It builds on shared literary experiences the children in your class have experienced prior to the lesson. You can quickly bring these shared texts to mind as powerful examples. Usually, you will teach only one focused lesson each day, but minilessons will be logically organized and build on each other. Each minilesson engages your children in an inquiry process that leads to the discovery and understanding of a general principle. Most of the time interactive read-aloud books and shared reading texts that children have already heard serve as mentor texts from which they generalize the understanding. The reading minilesson provides the link between students' previous experience with texts to their own independent reading (see Figure 1-1). The reading minilesson plays a key role in systematic, coherent teaching, which is directed toward each reader's developing competencies.

built on each other in logical order

To help children connect ideas and develop deep knowledge and broad application of principles, related reading minilessons are grouped under "umbrella" concepts (see Chapter 3). An umbrella is the broad category within which several lessons are linked to each other and all of which contribute to the understanding of the umbrella concept. Within each umbrella, the lessons build on each other (see Figure 1-2). In each lesson, you create an "anchor chart" with the children. This visual representation of the principle will be a useful reference tool as young children learn new routines, encounter new texts, and draw and write about their reading in a reader's notebook.

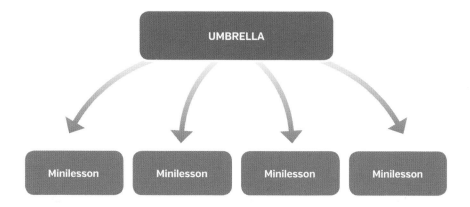

Figure 1-2: Each minilesson focuses on a different aspect of the larger umbrella concept.

Four Types of Reading Minilessons

In this book, you will find 150 minilessons that are organized into four types:

Management	Page 69
Literary Analysis	Page 119
Strategies and Skills	Page 321
Writing About Reading	Page 357

Figure 1-3: The minilessons in this book are organized into four sections.

Management Minilessons. These lessons include routines that are essential to the smooth functioning of the classroom and student-centered, independent literacy learning. The management minilessons are designed to support children's development of independence and self-regulatory behavior. Most of your minilessons at the beginning of the school year will focus on management. You will want to repeat any of the lessons as needed across the year. A guiding principle: teach a minilesson on anything that prevents the classroom from running smoothly.

Literary Analysis Minilessons. These lessons build children's awareness of the characteristics of various genres and of the elements of fiction and nonfiction texts. The books that you read during interactive read-aloud and shared reading serve as mentor texts when applying the principles of literary analysis. Through these lessons, children learn how to apply new thinking to their independent reading and how to share their thinking with others.

Strategies and Skills Minilessons. Young readers need to develop a robust body of in-the-head strategic actions for the efficient processing of texts. For example, they need to monitor their reading for accuracy and understanding, solve words (simple and complex), read fluently with phrasing, and constantly construct meaning. Teaching related to processing texts will best take place in guided reading and shared reading; these general lessons reinforce broad principles that every reader in your class may need to be reminded of from time to time.

Writing About Reading Minilessons. Throughout the kindergarten year, children will have opportunities to respond to what they read in a reader's notebook in the forms of drawing and writing. These lessons introduce the *Reader's Notebook: Primary* (Fountas and Pinnell 2014) and help children use this important tool for independent literacy learning. Kindergarteners will usually create drawings in response to the text, but as the year progresses, they will increasingly use writing, along with drawing.

The goal of all minilessons is to help children to think and act like readers and to build effective processing strategies while reading continuous text independently. Whether you are teaching management lessons, literary analysis lessons, strategies and skills lessons, or writing about reading lessons, the characteristics of effective minilessons, listed in Figure 1-4, apply.

Characteristics of Effective Minilessons

Effective Minilessons . . .

- have a **clear rationale and a goal** to focus meaningful teaching
- are **relevant to the specific needs of readers** so that your teaching connects with the learners
- are **brief, concise, and to the point** for immediate application
- use **clear and specific language** to avoid talk that clutters learning
- stay **focused on a single idea** so students can apply the learning and build on it day after day
- **build one understanding on another** across several days instead of single isolated lessons
- use an **inquiry approach** whenever possible to support constructive learning
- often include **shared, high-quality mentor texts** that can be used as examples
- are **well paced** to engage and hold students' interest
- are **grouped into umbrellas** to provide depth and coherence
- provide time for children to **"try out" the new concept** before independent application
- engage students in **summarizing the new learning** and thinking about its application to their own work
- build **academic vocabulary** appropriate to the grade level
- help students become **better readers and writers**
- **foster community** through the development of shared language
- **can be assessed** as you observe students in authentic literacy activities to provide feedback on your teaching
- help **students understand what they are learning** how to do and how it helps them as readers

Figure 1-4: Characteristics of effective minilessons

Constructing Anchor Charts
for Effective Minilessons

Anchor charts are an essential part of each minilesson in this book (see Figure 1-5). They provide a way for you to capture the children's thinking during the lesson and reflect on the learning at the end. When you think about a chart, it helps you think through the big, important ideas and the language you will use in the minilesson. It helps you think about the sequence and your efficiency in getting down what is important.

Each minilesson in this book provides guidance for adding information to the chart. Read through lessons carefully to know whether any parts of the chart should be prepared ahead or whether the chart is constructed during the lesson or left until the end. After the lesson, the charts become a resource for your students to use as a reference throughout the day. They provide a visual resource for children who need to not only hear but also see the information. They can revisit these charts as they apply the principle in reading, talking, and writing about books, or as they try out new routines in the classroom. You can refer to them during interactive read-aloud, shared reading, reading conferences, guided reading, and book clubs.

Though your charts will be unique because they are built from the ideas your students share, you will want to consider some of the common characteristics among the charts we have included in this book. We have created one example in each lesson, but vary it as you see fit. When you create charts with children, consider the following:

> **Make your charts simple, clear, and organized.** The charts you create with your students should be clearly organized. It is particularly important in kindergarten to keep them simple without a lot of dense text. Provide white space and print neatly in dark, easy-to-read colors. You will notice that some of the sample charts are more conceptual. The idea is conveyed through a few words and a visual representation. Others use a grid to show how the principle is applied specifically across several texts.

> **Make your charts visually appealing and useful.** All of the minilesson charts for kindergarten contain visual support. For example, you will see book covers, symbols, and drawings throughout the lesson charts to support kindergarteners in reading the words on the chart and in understanding the concept. The drawings are intentionally simple to give you a quick model to draw yourself. These visuals are particularly supportive for English language learners, who might need to rely heavily on a graphic representation of the principle ideas. You might find it helpful to prepare these drawings on separate pieces of paper or sticky notes ahead of the lesson and tape or glue them on the chart as the students construct their understandings. This time-saving tip can also make the charts look more interesting and colorful, because certain parts stand out for the children.

When you teach English language learners, you must adjust your teaching–not more teaching, but different teaching–to teach effectively. Look for this symbol to see ways to support English language learners.

ELL CONNECTION

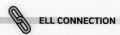
▶ **Make your charts colorful.** Though the sample minilesson charts are colorful for the purpose of engagement or organization, be careful about the amount and types of color that you use. You may want to use color for a purpose. Color can help you point out particular parts of the chart. For example, "Look at the purple word on the chart." Color can support English language learners by providing a visual link to certain words or ideas. However, color can also be distracting if overused. Be thoughtful about when you choose to use colors to highlight an idea or a word on a chart so that children are supported in reading continuous text. Text that is broken up by a lot of different colors can be very distracting for beginning readers who are just getting used to the distinguishing characteristics of letters. You will notice that the minilesson principle is usually written in black or a dark color across the top of the chart so that it stands out and is easily recognized as the focus of the lesson.

Anchor charts support language growth in all students, and especially in English language learners. Conversation about the minilesson develops oral language and then connects that oral language to print when you write words on the chart and provide picture support. By constructing an anchor chart with your students, you provide print that is immediately accessible to them because they helped create it and have ownership of the language. After a chart is finished, revisit it as often as needed to reinforce not only the ideas but also the printed words.

Figure 1-5: Constructing anchor charts with your students provides verbal and visual support for all learners.

Using Reading Minilessons with Kindergarten Children

A minilesson brings to children's conscious attention a focused principle that will assist them in developing an effective, independent literacy processing system. It provides an opportunity for students to do the following:

▶ Respond to and act on a variety texts

▶ Become aware of and be able to articulate understandings about texts

▶ Engage in further inquiry to investigate the characteristics of texts

▶ Search for and learn to recognize patterns and characteristics of written texts

▶ Build new ideas on known ideas

▶ Learn how to think about effective actions as they process texts

▶ Learn to manage their own reading lives

▶ Learn how to work together well in the classroom

▶ Learn to talk to others about their thinking about books

▶ Learn how to use and care for books and materials

Reading minilessons help readers build in-the-head processing systems. In the following chapters, you will explore how minilessons support children in using integrated systems of strategic actions for thinking *within*, *beyond*, and *about* many different kinds of texts and also how to use minilessons to build a community of readers who demonstrate a sense of agency and responsibility. You will also look in more depth at how minilessons fit within a design for literacy learning and within a multitext approach.

We conclude this chapter with some key terms we will use as we describe minilessons in the next chapters (see Figure 1-6). Keep these in mind so we can develop a common language to talk about the minilessons you teach.

Figure 1-6: Important terms used in *The Reading Minilessons Book*

Key Terms When Talking About Reading Minilessons

Umbrella	A group of minilessons, all of which are directed at different aspects of the same larger understanding.
Principle	A concise statement of the understanding children will need to learn and apply.
Mentor Text	A fiction or nonfiction text that offers a clear example of the principle toward which the minilesson is directed. Students will have previously heard and discussed the text.
Text Set	A group of fiction or nonfiction or a combination of fiction and nonfiction texts that, taken together, support a theme or exemplify a genre. Students will have previously heard all the texts referenced in a minilesson and had opportunities to make connections between them.
Anchor Chart	A visual representation of the lesson concept, using a combination of words and images. It is constructed by the teacher and students to summarize the learning and is used as a reference tool by the children.

2

Using *The Literacy Continuum* to Guide the Teaching of Reading Minilessons

WE BELIEVE SCHOOLS SHOULD BE places where students read, think, talk, and write every day about relevant content that engages their hearts and minds. Learning deepens when students engage in thinking, talking, reading, and writing about texts across many different instructional contexts and in whole-group, small-group, and individual instruction. Students who live a literate life in their classrooms have access to multiple experiences with texts throughout a day. As they participate in interactive read-aloud, shared reading, guided reading, book clubs, and independent reading, they engage in the real work of reading and writing. They build a network of systems of strategic actions that allow them to think deeply within, beyond, and about text.

The networks of in-the-head strategic actions are inferred from observations of proficient readers, writers, and speakers. We have described these networks in *The Fountas & Pinnell Literacy Continuum: A Tool for Assessment, Planning, and Teaching* (Fountas and Pinnell 2017c). This volume presents detailed text characteristics and behaviors and understandings to notice, teach for, and support for prekindergarten through middle school, across eight instructional reading, writing, and language contexts. In sum, *The Literacy Continuum* describes proficiency in reading, writing, and language as it changes over grades and over levels.

Figure 2-1: Minilesson principles are drawn from the observable behaviors of proficient students as listed in *The Literacy Continuum*.

	INSTRUCTIONAL CONTEXT	BRIEF DEFINITION	DESCRIPTION OF THE CONTINUUM
1	Interactive Read-Aloud and Literature Discussion	Students engage in discussion with one another about a text that they have heard read aloud or one they have read independently.	• Year by year, grades PreK–8 • Genres appropriate to grades PreK–8 • Specific behaviors and understandings that are evidence of thinking within, beyond, and about the text
2	Shared and Performance Reading	Students read together or take roles in reading a shared text. They reflect the meaning of the text with their voices.	• Year by year, grades PreK–8 • Genres appropriate to grades PreK–8 • Specific behaviors and understandings that are evidence of thinking within, beyond, and about the text
3	Writing About Reading	Students extend their understanding of a text through a variety of writing genres and sometimes with illustrations.	• Year by year, grades PreK–8 • Genres/forms for writing about reading appropriate to grades PreK–8 • Specific evidence in the writing that reflects thinking within, beyond, and about the text
4	Writing	Students compose and write their own examples of a variety of genres, written for varying purposes and audiences.	• Year by year, grades PreK–8 • Genres/forms for writing appropriate to grades PreK–8 • Aspects of craft, conventions, and process that are evident in students' writing, grades PreK–8
5	Oral and Visual Communication	Students present their ideas through oral discussion and presentation.	• Year by year, grades PreK–8 • Specific behaviors and understandings related to listening and speaking, presentation
6	Technological Communication	Students learn effective ways of communicating and searching for information through technology; they learn to think critically about information and sources.	• Year by year, grades PreK–8 • Specific behaviors and understandings related to effective and ethical uses of technology
7	Phonics, Spelling, and Word Study	Students learn about the relationships of letters to sounds as well as the structure and meaning of words to help them in reading and spelling.	• Year by year, grades PreK–8 • Specific behaviors and understandings related to nine areas of understanding related to letters, sounds, and words, and how they work in reading and spelling
8	Guided Reading	Students read a teacher-selected text in a small group; the teacher provides explicit teaching and support for reading increasingly challenging texts.	• Level by level, A to Z • Genres appropriate to grades PreK–8 • Specific behaviors and understandings that are evidence of thinking within, beyond, and about the text • Specific suggestions for word work (drawn from the phonics and word analysis continuum)

Figure 2-2: From *The Literacy Continuum* (Fountas and Pinnell 2017c, 3)

Systems of Strategic Actions

The systems of strategic actions are represented in the wheel diagram shown in Figure 2-3 and on the inside back cover of this book. This model helps us think about the thousands of in-the-head processes that take place simultaneously and largely unconsciously when a competent reader processes a text. When the reader engages the neural network, he builds a literacy processing system over time that becomes increasingly sophisticated. Teaching in each instructional context is directed toward helping every reader expand these in-the-head networks across increasingly complex texts.

Four sections of *The Literacy Continuum* (Fountas and Pinnell 2017c)—Interactive Read-Aloud and Literature Discussion, Shared and Performance Reading, Guided Reading, and Writing About Reading—describe the specific competencies or goals of readers, writers, and language users:

Within the Text   (literal understanding achieved through searching for and using information, monitoring and self-correcting, solving words, maintaining fluency, adjusting, and summarizing) The reader gathers the important information from the fiction or nonfiction text.

Beyond the Text   (predicting, making connections with personal experience, content knowledge and other texts, synthesizing new information, and inferring what is implied but not stated) The reader brings understanding to the processing of a text, reaching for ideas or concepts that are implied but not explicitly stated.

About the Text   (analyzing or critiquing the text) The reader looks at a text to appreciate or evaluate its construction, logic, or literary elements.

The Literacy Continuum is the foundation for all the minilessons. The minilesson principles come largely from the behaviors and understandings in the interactive read-aloud continuum, but some are selected from the shared reading, oral and visual communication, and writing about reading continua. In addition, we have included minilessons related to working together in a classroom community to assure that effective literacy instruction can take place. In most lessons, you will see a direct link to the goals from *The Literacy Continuum* called Continuum Connection.

As you ground your teaching in support of each reader's development of the systems of strategic actions, it is important to remember that these actions are never applied one at a time. A reader who comprehends a text engages these actions rapidly and simultaneously and largely without conscious attention. Your intentional talk and conversations in the various instructional contexts should support students in engaging and building their processing systems while they respond authentically as readers and enjoy the text.

Figure 2-3: All of your teaching will be grounded in support of each reader's development of the systems of strategic actions (see the inside back cover for a larger version of the Systems of Strategic Actions wheel).

Relationship of Intentional Talk to Reading Minilessons

Intentional talk refers to the language you use that is consciously directed toward the goal of instruction. We have used the term *facilitative talk* to refer to the language that supports student learning in specific ways. When you plan for intentional talk in your interactive read-aloud and shared reading experiences, think about the meaning of the text and what your students will need to think about to fully understand and enjoy the story. You might select certain pages where you want to stop and have students turn and talk about their reading so they can engage in sharing their thinking with each other. The interactive read-aloud and shared reading sections of *The Literacy Continuum* can help plan what to talk about. For example, when you read a book like *Miss Bindergarten Goes to Kindergarten,* you would likely invite talk about how the characters feel about their school, notice and discuss the details in the illustrations, and provide opportunities to notice that the book is organized by the ABCs. When you read a text set of cumulative tales, including stories like *The Enormous Potato* and *My Friend Rabbit*, you might invite your students to comment on the funny parts of the story, on the humorous illustrations, on the repetition of language, and on how the events build on one another.

As you talk about texts together, embed brief and specific teaching in your read-aloud and shared reading lessons while maintaining a focus on enjoyment and support for your students in gaining the meaning of the whole text. In preparation, mark a few places with sticky notes and a comment or question to invite thinking. Later, when you teach explicit minilessons about concepts such as character feelings, illustrations, and text organization, your students will already have background knowledge to bring to the minilesson and will be ready to explore how the principle works across multiple texts.

In reading minilessons, you explicitly teach the principles you have already embedded in the students' previous experiences with text in these different instructional contexts. Intentional talk within each context prepares a foundation for this explicit focus. Through each interactive read-aloud and shared reading experience, you build a large body of background knowledge, academic vocabulary, and a library of shared texts to draw on as you explore specific literary principles. You will read more about this multitext approach in Chapter 9.

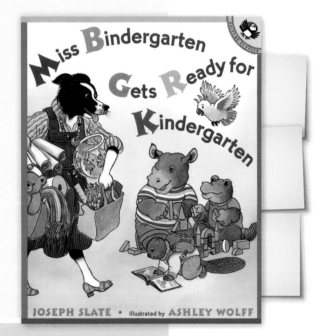

Figure 2-4: Mark a few pages to invite students to think about in the reading minilesson.

Chapter 3

Understanding the Umbrellas and Minilessons

MINILESSONS IN THIS BOOK ARE organized into conceptual groups called "umbrellas," in which a group of principles are explored in sequence, working toward a larger concept. Within each section (Management, Literary Analysis, etc.), the umbrellas are numbered in sequence and are often referred to by *U* plus the number; for example, U1 for the first umbrella. A suggested sequence of umbrellas is presented on pages 51–52 to assist you in planning across the year, but the needs of your students always take priority.

Umbrella Front Page

Each umbrella has an introductory page on which the minilessons in the umbrella are listed and directions are provided to help you prepare to present the minilessons within the umbrella (see Figure 3-1). The introductory page is designed to provide an overview of how the umbrella is organized and the texts from *Fountas & Pinnell Classroom*™ (FPC) *Collections* that are suggested for the lessons. In addition, we provide types of texts you might select if you are not using the *FPC Collections* referenced in the lessons. Understanding how the umbrella is designed and how the minilessons fit together will help you keep your lessons focused, concise, and brief. Using familiar mentor texts that you have read and enjoyed with your children previously will help you streamline the lessons in the umbrella. You will not need to spend a lot of time rereading large sections of the text because the students already know the texts so well.

When you teach lessons in an umbrella, you help children make connections between concepts and texts and help them develop deeper understandings. A rich context such as this one is particularly helpful for English language learners. Grouping lessons into umbrellas supports English language learners in developing shared vocabulary and language around a single and important area of knowledge.

Following the umbrella front page, you will see a series of two-page lesson spreads that include several parts.

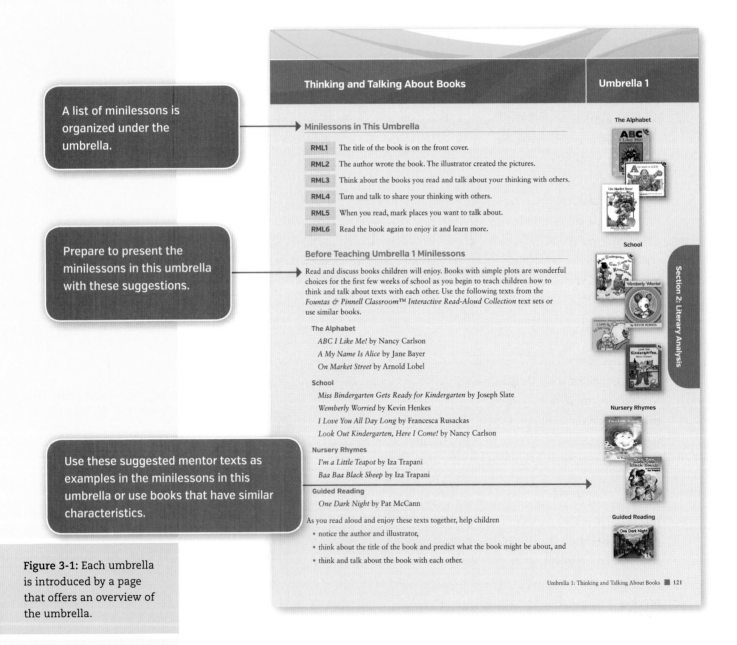

A list of minilessons is organized under the umbrella.

Prepare to present the minilessons in this umbrella with these suggestions.

Use these suggested mentor texts as examples in the minilessons in this umbrella or use books that have similar characteristics.

Figure 3-1: Each umbrella is introduced by a page that offers an overview of the umbrella.

Thinking and Talking About Books   **Umbrella 1**

Minilessons in This Umbrella

RML1	The title of the book is on the front cover.
RML2	The author wrote the book. The illustrator created the pictures.
RML3	Think about the books you read and talk about your thinking with others.
RML4	Turn and talk to share your thinking with others.
RML5	When you read, mark places you want to talk about.
RML6	Read the book again to enjoy it and learn more.

Before Teaching Umbrella 1 Minilessons

Read and discuss books children will enjoy. Books with simple plots are wonderful choices for the first few weeks of school as you begin to teach children how to think and talk about texts with each other. Use the following texts from the *Fountas & Pinnell Classroom™ Interactive Read-Aloud Collection* text sets or use similar books.

The Alphabet
ABC I Like Me! by Nancy Carlson
A My Name Is Alice by Jane Bayer
On Market Street by Arnold Lobel

School
Miss Bindergarten Gets Ready for Kindergarten by Joseph Slate
Wemberly Worried by Kevin Henkes
I Love You All Day Long by Francesca Rusackas
Look Out Kindergarten, Here I Come! by Nancy Carlson

Nursery Rhymes
I'm a Little Teapot by Iza Trapani
Baa Baa Black Sheep by Iza Trapani

Guided Reading
One Dark Night by Pat McCann

As you read aloud and enjoy these texts together, help children
• notice the author and illustrator,
• think about the title of the book and predict what the book might be about, and
• think and talk about the book with each other.

The Alphabet

School

Section 2: Literary Analysis

Nursery Rhymes

Guided Reading

Umbrella 1: Thinking and Talking About Books ■ 121

Two-Page Minilesson Spread

Each minilesson includes a two-page spread that consists of several parts. The section (for example, Literary Analysis), umbrella number (for example, U1), and minilesson number (for example, RML1) are listed at the top to help you locate the lesson you are looking for. For example, the code LA.U1.RML1 identifies the first minilesson in the first umbrella of the Literary Analysis section.

Principle, Goal, Rationale

The **principle** describes the understanding the children will need to learn and apply. The idea of the principle is based on *The Literacy Continuum* (Fountas and Pinnell 2017c), but the language of the principle has been carefully crafted to be precise, focused on a single idea, and accessible to children. We have placed the principle at the top of the lesson on the left-hand page so you have a clear idea of the understanding you will help children construct through the example texts used in the lesson. Although we have crafted the language to make it simple and appropriate for the age group, you may shape the language in a slightly different way to reflect the way your students use language. Be sure that the principle is stated simply and clearly.

The **goal** of the minilesson is stated in the top section of the lesson, as is the **rationale,** to help you understand what this particular minilesson will do and why it may be important for the children in your classroom. In this beginning section, you will also find suggestions for specific behaviors and understandings to observe as you assess children's learning during or after the minilesson.

Minilesson

In the Minilesson section of the lesson, you will find an example lesson for teaching the understanding, or principle. The example includes suggestions for teaching and the use of precise language and open-ended questions to engage students in a brief, focused inquiry. Effective minilessons include, when possible, the process of inquiry so children can actively construct their understanding from concrete examples, because telling is not teaching. Instead of simply being told what they need to know, the children get inside the understanding by engaging in the thinking themselves. In the inquiry process, invite the children to look at a group of texts that were read previously (for example, stories with animals that act like people). Choose the books carefully so they represent the characteristics the children are learning about. They will have knowledge of these texts because they have previously experienced them. Invite them to talk about what they notice across all the books. As children explore the text examples using your

A Closer Look at a Reading Minilesson

The **Goal** of the minilesson is clearly identified, as is the **Rationale**, to support your understanding of what this particular minilesson is and why it may be important for the children in your classroom.

The Reading Minilesson Principle—a brief statement that describes the understanding children will need to learn and apply.

This code identifies this minilesson as the first reading minilesson (RML1) in the first umbrella (U1) in the Literary Analysis (LA) section.

Specific behaviors and understandings to observe as you assess children's learning after presenting the minilesson.

Academic Language and **Important Vocabulary** that children will need to understand in order to access the learning in the minilesson.

Suggested language to use when teaching the minilesson principle.

RML1
LA.U1.RML1

Thinking and Talking About Books

You Will Need

- two or three books with titles that give a clear idea of what the book is about, such as the following from Text Set: School:
  - *I Love You all Day Long* by Francesca Rusackas
  - *Miss Bindergarten Gets Ready for Kindergarten* by Joseph Slate
  - *Wemberly Worried* by Kevin Henkes
- chart paper and markers
- a book for each child

Academic Language / Important Vocabulary

- title
- front cover

 Continuum Connection

- Notice a book's title and its author and illustrator on the cover and title page [p. 29]

Reading Minilesson Principle
The title of the book is on the front cover.

Goal

Identify the title on the front cover of a book and use it to think about what the book might be about.

Rationale

Children begin constructing their understanding of a book when they read or hear the title. When you help them to think about the title before reading the book you support their comprehension. Thinking about titles will help children to select books independently.

Assess Learning

Observe children when they talk about the titles of books they have read or heard. Notice if there is evidence of new learning based on the goal of this minilesson.

- Are children able to identify the title of the books they read independently?
- What evidence do you have that children use the title to predict what the story might be about?
- Do the children use the terms *title* or *front cover* while discussing the books?

Minilesson

To help children think about the minilesson principle, choose familiar texts and examples to provide an inquiry-based lesson about book titles. Here is an example.

- Show the front cover of *I Love You All Day Long*.

  The title of this book is *I Love You All Day Long*. How do you know that is the title of the book?

  How does the title help you remember what the book is about?

- Show the front cover of *Miss Bindergarten Gets Ready for Kindergarten*. Point to the title and read aloud. Record the title on the chart paper.

  What does the title tell you about the book?

- Record the children's responses on the chart.
- Show the front cover of *Wemberly Worried*.

  What's the title of this book?

- Record the title on the chart.

  How does the title help you know what the story is going to be about?

  Before we read the book, you didn't know why Wemberly was worried, but you did know she was worried about something by reading the title.

Figure 3-2: All the parts of a single minilesson are contained on a two-page spread.

Suggestions for children to practice the new thinking from the minilesson, usually with a partner.

Create **anchor charts** as a useful reference tool and reinforcement of the principle for students during independent reading and writing.

RML1
LA.U1.RML1

Have a Try

Invite the children to apply the new thinking about book titles with a partner.

▸ Give a book to each child.

Point to the title of your book and tell your partner how you know it is the title.

What do you think your book will be about from looking at the title and front cover?

▸ Choose a few children to share with the class.

Summarize and Apply

Summarize the learning and remind children to think about the title of the book before they read.

▸ Review the chart with the children. After summarizing the learning, write the principle at the top.

Today you learned that the title of the book is on the front cover, and you can use it to help you think what the book will be about.

When you read today, notice the title on the front cover. Bring your book when we come back together.

Share

Following independent work time, gather children together in the meeting area to talk about the title of the book.

Point to the title of the front cover of your book.

Turn and talk to a partner. Tell your partner the title and what the book is about.

Extend the Lesson (Optional)

After assessing your students' understanding, you might decide to extend the learning over several days.

▸ Continue to add titles to the chart during interactive read-aloud and shared reading. Ask children to think about the title before reading the story. Talk about the fact that sometimes you don't understand a title until the end of the story.

▸ When talking about the title on the front cover, also address the illustrations that the illustrator drew for the cover.

▸ Drawing/Writing About Reading Have children study several book covers to gather ideas for how to make covers for their own stories.

The title of the book is on the front cover.

Title	What the Book Is About
I Love You All Day Long	Mom loves Owen all day when he is at school.
Miss Bindergarten Gets Ready for Kindergarten	A teacher gets ready for school. ABC
Wemberly Worried by KEVIN HENKES	Wemberly is worried about going to school for the first time.

A **summary** of the minilesson principle to help you guide the children to **apply** what they have learned to their independent reading.

After independent literacy work time, it is important for children to have a chance to **share** learning, which gives you feedback on the learning children took on.

Optional suggestions for extending the learning of the minilesson over time or in other contexts.

questions and supportive comments as a guide, co-construct the anchor chart, creating an organized and visual representation of the children's noticings and understandings. (See the section on Anchor Charts in Chapter 1 for more information on chart creation.) From this exploration and the discussion surrounding it, children derive the principle, which is then written at the top of the chart.

Throughout this book, you will find models and examples of the anchor charts you will co-construct with children. Of course, the charts you create with the children will be unique because they reflect your students' thinking. Learning is more powerful and enjoyable for the children when they actively search for the meaning and find patterns. Children need to form networks of understanding around the concepts related to literacy and to be constantly looking for connections for themselves.

ELL CONNECTION

Creating a need to produce language is an important principle in building language, and reading minilessons provide many opportunities for children to express their thoughts in language and to communicate with others. The inquiry approach found in these lessons invites more student talk than teacher talk, and that can be both a challenge and an opportunity for English language learners. In our previous texts, we have written that Marie Clay (1991) urges us to be "strong minded" about holding meaningful conversations even when they are difficult. In *Becoming Literate*, she warns us that it is "misplaced sympathy" to do the talking for those who are developing and learning language. Instead, she recommends "concentrating more sharply, smiling more rewardingly and spending more time in genuine conversation." Building talk routines, such as turn and talk, into your reading minilessons can be very helpful in providing these opportunities for English language learners in a safe and supportive way.

When you ask students to think about the minilesson principle across several texts that they have previously listened to and discussed, they are more engaged and able to participate because they know these texts and can shift their attention to a new way of thinking about them. Using familiar texts is particularly important for English language learners. When you select examples for a reading minilesson, choose texts that you know were particularly engaging for the English language learners in your classroom. Besides choosing accessible, familiar texts, it is important to provide plenty of wait and think time. For example, you might say, "Let's think about that for a minute" before calling for responses.

When working with English language learners, value partially correct responses. Look for what the child knows about the concept instead of focusing on faulty grammar or language errors. Model appropriate language use in your responses, but do not correct a child who is attempting to use language to learn it. You might also provide an oral sentence frame to get the children's response started. Accept variety in pronunciation and intonation, remembering that the more children speak, read, and write, the more they will take on the understanding of grammatical patterns and the complex intonation patterns that reflect meaning in English.

Have a Try

Because children will be asked to apply the new thinking independently during independent literacy work, it is important to give students a chance to apply it with a partner or a small group while still in the whole-group setting. Have a Try is designed to be brief, but it offers you an opportunity to gather information on how well students understand the minilesson principle. In many minilessons, students are asked to apply the new thinking to another concrete example from a familiar book. In management lessons, students quickly practice the new routine that they will be asked to do independently. You will often add further thinking to the chart after the students have had the chance to try out their new learning. On occasion, you will find lessons that do not include Have a Try because children will practice the routine or concept as part of the application. However, in most cases, Have a Try is an important step in reinforcing the principle and moving the students toward independence.

ELL CONNECTION

The Have a Try portion of the reading minilesson is particularly important for English language learners. Besides providing repetition and allowing for the gradual release of responsibility, it gives English language learners a safe place to try out the new idea before sharing it with the whole group. These are a few suggestions for how you might support students during the Have a Try portion of the lesson:

▶ Pair children with specific partners in a way that will allow for a balance of talk between the two.

▶ Spend time teaching students how to turn and talk. (You will find a minilesson in Section Two: Literary Analysis, Umbrella 1: Thinking and Talking About Books, that helps children develop this routine.) Teach children how to provide wait time for one another, invite the other partner into the conversation, and take turns.

▶ Provide concrete examples to discuss so that children are clear about what they need to talk about and are able to stay grounded in the text. English language learners will feel more confident if they are able to talk about a text that they know really well.

▶ Observe partnerships involving English language learners and provide support as needed.

- When necessary, you might find it helpful to provide the oral language structure or language stem for how you want children to share. For example, ask students to start with the phrase "I think the character feels. . . ." Ask children to rehearse the language structure a few times before turning and talking.

Summarize and Apply

This part of the lesson consists of two parts: summarizing the learning and applying the learning to independent reading.

The **summary** is a brief but essential part of the lesson. It provides a time to bring together all of the learning that has taken place through the inquiry and to help children think about its application and relevance to their own learning. It is best to involve the children in constructing the minilesson principle with you. Ask them to reflect on the chart you have created together and talk about what they have learned that day. In simple, clear language, shape the suggestions. Other times, you may decide to help summarize the new learning to keep the lesson short and allow enough time for the children to apply it independently. Whether you state the principle or co-construct it with your students, summarize the learning in a way that makes the principle generative and applicable to future texts the students will read.

After the summary, the students **apply** their new understandings to their independent reading and literacy work in the classroom. If you have literacy centers, they will apply their learning to their independent reading. In addition, let students know what you expect them to discuss or bring for the group sharing session so they can think about it as they read. They know they are accountable for trying out the new thinking in their own books or reflect on their participation because they are expected to share upon their return.

As you will read in Chapter 9, students engaged in independent reading might be reading books from their individual book bags or boxes, their browsing boxes, or the classroom library. When needed, plan to supply independent reading books that will provide opportunities to apply the principle. For example, if you teach the umbrella on exploring animal tales, make sure children have access to animal tales. You will notice that in some of the lessons, children are invited to read from a certain basket of books in the classroom library to ensure that there are opportunities to apply their new learning. In some cases, the texts that provide opportunities for children to apply these concepts are not at their independent or even instructional levels. If this is the case, make sure the texts that you have placed in these baskets are familiar to the children because they have heard them read aloud. Children can also listen to audio recordings of more sophisticated texts and independently apply the minilesson principle to the audiobook.

We know that when students first take on new learning, they often overgeneralize or overapply the new learning at the exclusion of some of the other things they have learned. The best goal when children are reading any book is to enjoy it, process it effectively, and gain its full meaning. Always encourage meaningful and authentic engagement with text. You don't want children so focused and determined to apply the minilesson principle that they make superficial connections to text that actually distract from the understanding of the book. You will likely find the opportunity in many reading conferences, guided reading lessons, or book club meetings to reinforce the minilesson understanding.

In our professional book, *Teaching for Comprehending and Fluency* (Fountas and Pinnell 2006), we write, "Whenever we instruct readers, we mediate (or change) the meaning they derive from their reading. Yet we must offer instruction that helps readers expand their abilities. There is value in drawing readers' attention to important aspects of the text that will enrich their understanding, but we need to understand that using effective reading strategies is not like exercising one muscle. The system must always work together as an integrated whole." The invitation to apply the new learning must be clear enough to have children try out new ways of thinking, but "light" enough to allow room for readers to expand and express their own thinking. The application of the minilesson principle should not be thought of as an exercise or task that needs to completed but instead as an invitation to deeper, more meaningful response to the events or ideas in a text.

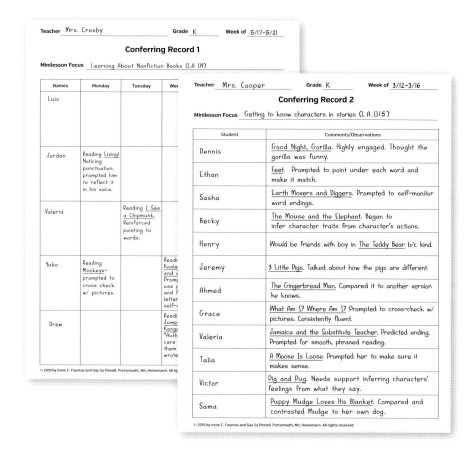

Figure 3-3: Choose one of these downloadable forms to record your observations of students' behaviors and understandings during reading conferences. Visit **resources.fountasandpinnell.com** to download this and all other online resources.

While the children are reading independently, you may be meeting with small groups for guided reading or book clubs, rotating to observe work in literacy centers, or conferring with individuals. If you have a reading conference, you can take the opportunity to reinforce the minilesson principle. We have provided two conferring record sheets (use whichever form suits your purposes) for you to download from the Online Resources (see Figure 3-3) so that you can make notes about your individual conferences with children. You can use your notes to plan the content of future minilessons.

Share

At the end of the independent work time, students come together and have the opportunity to share their learning with the entire group. Group share provides an opportunity for you to revisit, expand, and deepen understanding of the minilesson principle as well as to assess learning. In Figure 3-2, you will notice that in the Share section we provide suggestions for how to have children share their new learning. Often, children are asked to bring a book to share and to explain how they applied the minilesson principle in their independent reading. Sometimes we suggest sharing with the whole group, but other times we suggest that sharing take place among pairs, triads, or quads. As you observe and talk to students engaged in independent reading, shared reading, guided reading, or book clubs, you can assess whether they are easily able to apply the minilesson principle. Use this information to inform how you plan to share. If only a few students were able to apply the minilesson to their reading, you might ask only a few children to share. Whereas if you observe most of the class applying the principle, you might have them share in pairs or small groups.

As a general guideline, in addition to revisiting the reading minilesson principle at the end of independent work time, you might also ask children to share what they did in their independent literacy work that day. For example, a child might share something he noticed in the word study center or another student might tell about an all about book she made in the writing center. The Share is a wonderful way to bring the community of readers and writers back together to expand their understandings and celebrate their learning at the end of the workshop time.

ELL CONNECTION

There are some particular accommodations you might want to consider to support English language learners during the Share:

▶ Ask English language learners to share in pairs before sharing with the whole group.

▶ Use individual conferences and guided reading to help children rehearse the language structure they might use to share their application of the minilesson principle to the text they have read.

▶ Teach the entire class respectful ways to listen to peers and model how to give their peers time to express their thoughts. Many of the minilessons in the Management section will be useful for developing a safe and supportive community of readers and writers.

Extending the Lesson

At the end of each lesson we offer suggestions for extending the learning of the principle. Sometimes extending the learning involves repeating the lesson over time with different examples. Kindergarteners might need to experience some of the concepts more than once before they are able to transfer actions to their independent reading. Using the questions in the Assessment section will help you to determine if you need to repeat the lesson, move on, or revisit the lesson (perhaps in a slightly different way) in the future. Other suggestions for extending the lesson include using songs or games, having students role play, and writing or drawing about reading either independently or through shared or interactive writing. In several cases, the suggestions will reference a reader's notebook. See Chapter 7 for more information about drawing and writing about reading and Section Four: Writing About Reading for minilessons that teach ways to use a reader's notebook.

Umbrella Back Page

Assessment and Link to Writing

Following the minilessons in each umbrella, you will see the final umbrella page that includes **Assessment** and **Link to Writing**. The last page of each umbrella, as shown in Figure 3-4, provides suggestions for assessing the learning that has taken place through the minilessons in the entire umbrella. The information you gain from observing what the children can already do, almost do, and not yet do will help inform the selection of the next umbrella you teach. (See Chapter 8 for more information about assessment and the selection of umbrellas.) For many umbrellas, this last page also provides a Link to Writing. In some cases, this section provides further suggestions for writing/drawing about reading in a reader's notebook. However, in most cases, the Link to Writing provides ideas for how students might try out some of the new learning in their own writing. For example, after learning about text features in nonfiction, you might want to teach children how to include one or more of the features, such as a table of contents or sidebar, in their own nonfiction writing.

Gain important information by **assessing** children's understandings as they apply and share their learning of a minilesson principle. Observe and then follow up with individuals or address the principle during guided reading.

Umbrella 1 | Thinking and Talking About Books

Assessment

After you have taught the minilessons in this umbrella, observe children as they talk and write about their reading across instructional contexts: interactive read-aloud, independent reading and literacy work, guided reading, shared reading, and book club. Use *The Literacy Continuum* (Fountas and Pinnell 2017) to observe children's reading and writing behaviors across instructional contexts.

- What evidence do you have of new understandings relating to thinking and talking about texts?
  - Can children identify the title, author, and illustrator on the front cover of a book?
  - Are children following the guidelines for turn and talk?
  - In what ways are they sharing their thinking about books?
  - Do they use academic language, such as *title, author, illustration, reread, notice,* and *turn and talk?*
- In what other ways, beyond the scope of this umbrella, are they thinking and talking about books?

Use your observations to determine the next umbrella you will teach. You may also consult Minilessons Across the Year (p. 51) for guidance.

Link to Writing

After teaching the minilessons in this umbrella, help children link the new learning to their own writing or drawing:

- If you are using *Reader's Notebook: Primary* (Fountas and Pinnell 2014), introduce the Books I Like to Read section. Children can record their favorite titles and authors and draw and write about an interesting part. If you are using a plain reader's notebook, help children set up a page to record books they have read. See Section Four: Writing About Reading for guidance in how to introduce and use a reader's notebook.

134 ■ *The Reading Minilessons Book, Kindergarten*

Engage children in **response to reading** activities in order to link the new learning to their own writing or drawing.

Figure 3-4: The final page of each umbrella offers suggestions for assessing the learning and, in many umbrellas, a Link to Writing.

Online Resources for Planning

We have provided examples in this book of how to engage your kindergarten children in developing the behaviors and understandings of competent readers, as described in *The Literacy Continuum* (Fountas and Pinnell 2017c). However, you can modify a suggested lesson to fit your students and construct new lessons using the goals of the continuum as needed for your particular students. The form shown in Figure 3-5 will help you plan each part of a new minilesson. For example, you can design a minilesson that uses a different set of example texts from the ones suggested in this book or you can teach a concept in a way that fits the current needs of your students. The form shown in Figure 3-6 will help you plan which minilessons to teach over a period of time so as to address the goals that are important for your students. You can find both forms at **resources.fountasandpinnell.com.**

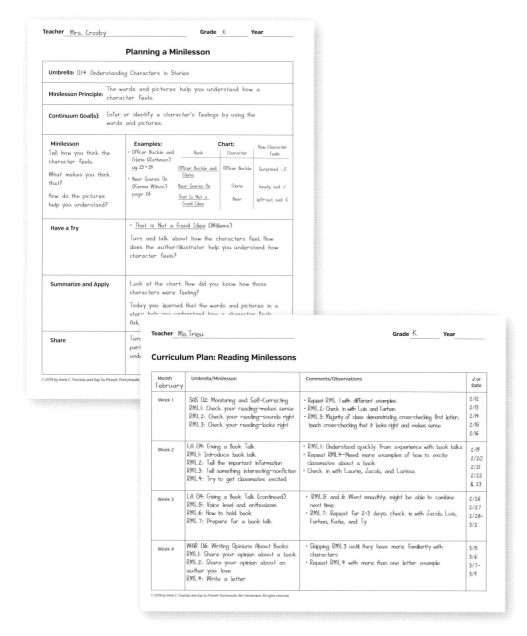

Figure 3-5: Use this downloadable form to plan your own minilessons.

Figure 3-6: Use this downloadable form to make notes about specific minilessons for future planning.

Chapter 4 Management Minilessons: Building a Literacy Community

MANAGEMENT MINILESSONS FOCUS ON ROUTINES for thinking and talking about reading and working together in the classroom. They allow you to teach effectively and efficiently because they create an orderly, busy classroom in which students know what is expected and how to behave responsibly and respectfully in a community of learners. They learn how the classroom library is organized, how to choose books and return them, how to use their voices in the classroom, and how to work in various organized literacy centers. You can use these minilessons to teach your young students how to use a simple list or work board to manage their own time, how to use and return materials, and how to problem solve independently. Classroom management is important in implementing a multitext approach to literacy learning. You want your students to grow in the ability to regulate their own behavior and to sustain reading and writing for increasing periods of time.

Altogether, there are twenty-one management minilessons for your use. Some management minilessons may need to be retaught across the year, especially as students encounter more complex situations and routines (for example, choosing books instead of reading from browsing baskets or individual book bags). Sometimes when there is a schedule change or other disruption in classroom operations, a refresher management minilesson will be needed. Any problem in your classroom should be addressed through a management minilesson.

The Physical Space

Before students enter your classroom, prepare the physical space in a way that provides maximum support for learning. Remember that this relatively small room must support the productive work of some 20 to 30 people, 6 or 7 hours a day, 180+ days a year. Each management umbrella will help your students become acquainted with different parts of the classroom, which will make them feel secure and at home. Make sure that the classroom is:

▶ **Welcoming and Inviting.** Pleasing colors and a variety of furniture will help. There is no need for commercially published posters or slogans, except for standard references such as the Alphabet Linking Chart or colorful poetry posters. The room can be filled with the work that children have produced beginning on day one. They see signs of their learning everywhere—interactive writing, charts, drawings of various kinds, and their names. Be sure that children's names are at various places in the room—the name chart, on desks or tables, the helper's charts, and on some of the charts that you will be making in minilessons. The classroom library should be as inviting as a bookstore or a library. Place books in baskets and tubs on shelves to make the front covers of books visible and accessible for easy browsing. Clear out old, dated, or tattered books that children never choose. Clearly label the tub or basket with the topic, author, series, genre or illustrator. It can be a wonderful learning experience to create these labels with your children using interactive writing (see Figure 4-1).

▶ **Organized for Easy Use.** The first thing you might want to do is to take out everything you do not need. Clutter increases stress and noise. Scattered, hard to find materials increases student dependence on the teacher. Every work area should be clearly organized with necessary, labeled materials and nothing else. The work that takes place in each area should be visible at a glance; all materials needed for the particular activity are available. See Figure 4-2 for a list of some suggested materials to keep accessible in the different work areas, or centers, in your classroom.

▶ **Designed for Whole-Group, Small-Group, and Individual Instruction.** Minilessons are generally provided as whole-class instruction and typically take place at an easel in a meeting space that is comfortable and large enough to accommodate all students in a group or circle. It will be helpful to have a colorful rug with some way of helping students find an individual space to sit where they do not touch others. Often, the meeting space is adjacent to the classroom library so books are handy. The teacher usually has a larger chair or seat next to an easel or two so that he can display the mentor texts, make anchor charts, do interactive or shared writing, or place big books for shared

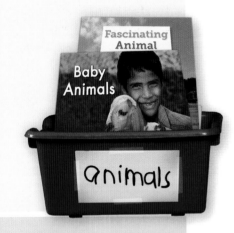

Figure 4-1: Whenever possible, involve the children in making the classroom their own.

reading. This space is available for all whole-group instruction; for example, the children come back to it for group share. In addition to the group meeting space, there should be designated tables and spaces in the classroom for small-group reading instruction. The guided reading table is best located in a quiet corner of the room that allows you the opportunity to scan the room to identify students who may need help staying on task independently. The table (round or horseshoe) should be positioned so the children in the group are turned away from the activity in the classroom. Students also need tables and spaces throughout the classroom where they can work independently and where you can easily set a chair next to a child for a brief, individual conference.

▶ **Respectful of Personal Space.** Kindergarten students do not necessarily need an individual desk, but they do need a place to keep a personal box, including items such as their individual book bags (sealed plastic bags containing their independent reading books) and word study activities to take home. These containers can be placed on a shelf labeled for each student. Reader's notebooks and writing folders may be stored in the same place or in groups by themselves to be retrieved easily. If students have a personal poetry books (growing out of the shared reading of poetry and colorfully decorated by them), they can be placed face out on a rack for easy retrieval. Artifacts like these add considerably to the aesthetic quality of the classroom.

Figure 4-2: Adapted from *Guided Reading: Responsive Teaching Across the Grades* (Fountas and Pinnell 2017d)

Yearlong Literacy Centers	Materials
Independent Reading	Organize books by topic, author, illustrator, genre, and series. Include colored browsing baskets geared to each guided reading group.
Writing Center	Pencils, paper, markers, stapler, scissors, glue, premade blank books for bookmaking, cover-up tape, sticky notes, crayons, and date stamp.
Word Work [ABCs]	Blank word cards, wall of high-frequency words, alphabet linking chart, magnetic letters, games, words to sort, phonogram pattern charts.
Listening Center	Player (e.g., iPod™, iPhone™, tablet), clear set of directions with picture clues, multiple copies of books organized in boxes or plastic bags.
Poetry Center [can be adjacent to the writing center so that supplies can be shared]	Personal poetry book for each student, copies of poems they have read in shared reading, glue, crayons, markers, and decorative stickers. The center may also include large-print poems, poetry cards mounted on stiff paper, small books of poems, and a class book of poems.
Pocket Chart	Pocket chart hanging from a rack or fastened firmly to the wall, sentence strips and individual words in a basket near the chart.

A Peaceable Atmosphere for a Community of Readers and Writers

The minilessons in this book will help you establish a classroom environment where children can become confident, self-determined, and kind members of the community. They are designed to contribute to an ambiance of peaceful activity and shared responsibility in the kindergarten classroom. Through the management minilessons they will learn how to modulate the voice to suit various purposes (silent to outdoor). There are also lessons on keeping supplies in order and on using routines for taking turns, listening to and looking at others, and engaging in conversation. The whole tone of every classroom activity is respectful. Kindergarten children who enter your classroom for the first time have learned ways of interacting that are appropriate for home and neighborhood, but none of them knows how to work with twenty to thirty others in a small room day after day. These minilessons are designed to help you establish the atmosphere you want. Everything in the classroom reflects the children who work there; it is their home for the year.

Getting Started with Independent Work Time

Many of the minilessons in the Management section will be the ones that you address early in the year to establish routines that children will use to work at their best with one another and independently. In the largest umbrella in this section, Umbrella 3: Engaging in Classroom Literacy Work, you will teach children how to work independently on meaningful and productive literacy activities. The minilessons in this umbrella are designed to introduce work activities, or centers, one at a time, allowing children time to practice as a

Figure 4-3: Books in the classroom library are organized in labeled bins.

whole group before being expected to integrate more than one literacy task. It is possible that you will spend several days reviewing one minilesson until you feel students are able to perform the routine independently. For a beginning group of kindergarten children, make independent work time relatively short and circulate around the room to help students select books, draw and write, and stay engaged. As children become more self-directed, you can increase independent work time. When you determine that they can sustain productive independent behavior, you can begin to meet with guided reading groups.

As described in our professional book, *Guided Reading: Responsive Teaching Across the Grades* (Fountas and Pinnell 2017d), we offer two options for managing this classroom literacy work in the early grades: a simple system and a work board system. You might use a combination of these approaches or start with one and then move to the other. Either way, the minilessons in Umbrella 3: Engaging in Classroom Literacy Work, will help you get the children acquainted with the routines and expectations of the literacy activity. Select the minilessons that make sense for your students based on the management system you decide to use. You may decide to introduce different activities throughout the school year. The minilessons in this umbrella do not need to be taught all at once or in consecutive order.

A Simple System: Four Activities a Day

In this system, instead of moving through centers, children work at their desks or tables on the same four or five activities every day during the time set aside for literacy and language. You can decide whether to suggest an order for the activities or allow them to choose. These four activities might include the following:

Read a Book. During this time, children engage in independent reading. This might include reading from their individual book bags (or boxes), from a browsing box, or from the classroom library. In the first minilesson in the

Figure 4-4: A kindergarten classroom accommodates many kinds of literacy activities.

umbrella, you teach students how to use the classroom library or individual book bags for this reading time. In a subsequent lesson, you teach children how to read from browsing boxes since it is likely you will introduce browsing boxes a little later once guided reading is established.

Listen to a Book. Listening to audiobooks is a valuable and meaningful literacy activity. As children listen with a book in hand, they follow along with reading, exposing themselves to high-frequency words, to new vocabulary and language structures, and to a model for fluent reading. The listening center provides another way for children to access higher levels of text across a variety of genres. You might also incorporate writing about reading into this listening time by asking children to write or draw a brief response to the text. The minilesson that introduces the listening center (Umbrella 3: Engaging in Classroom Literacy Work) is used to teach children how to use the audio equipment and sets up the routines and procedures that need to be in place for an efficient, productive listening experience.

Work on Words. The word work center activity will take a little more time to prepare than some of the other activities in this simple system because you will want to connect it to your phonics lessons. See *Phonics, Spelling, and Word Study System, for Kindergarten* (Fountas and Pinnell 2017e) for examples. Children can be engaged in a range of activities from simple work with the alphabet (for example, name puzzles or sorting letters) to more complex word study (for example, games, letter or word sorts). Use the lesson in Umbrella 3: Engaging in Classroom Literacy Work to introduce children to the routines of the word work center, including where to find supplies and visual directions for what to do during word work time and how to clean up.

Figure 4-5: Children gathered in the meeting area for shared reading

Work on Writing. During this time, children can work on a variety of forms of writing—cards, thank-you notes, letters, stories, alphabet books, how-to books, or all about books. They work on pieces they started in writing workshop or you might provide specific directions for writing/drawing about reading in a reader's notebook. Use the minilesson in Umbrella 3: Engaging in Classroom Literacy Work to introduce where to find directions in the writing area or center and how to access, organize, and return supplies. This writing work does not take the place of writers' workshop, in which children begin to learn through writing minilessons and to engage in the writing process.

Using Centers and a Work Board

The other option for managing independent literacy work is to teach children how to use a work board to rotate and work independently in centers. A work board enables each child to work at her own pace. This option allows for more movement and often provides more opportunity for collaboration as children in proximity are working on the same kinds of activities. Group children and post their names in the suggested order of work you would like them to complete. You can also list options or choices for children who complete their work before others. The work board can include a variety of different literacy activities, including the four activities described in the simple system: independent reading, listening to a book, working with words, and working on writing. You will find minilessons for introducing some of the other activities in Umbrella 3: Engaging in Classroom Literacy Work. These lessons include reading and illustrating poetry in a poetry notebook; reading around the room with a pointer; assembling and reading a poem, song, or story in pocket charts; and reading with a partner. The final minilesson in the umbrella teaches children how to work independently using the work board as a tool.

English language learners can productively engage in a series of actions with the support of the work board. Take the time to "act out" each of the actions several times. Give special attention to the icon because it is the children's cue to action. Involve children in the action several times (with your support) until you are sure they can follow the steps independently. Don't just tell; show and do every step. You will find it is well worth the time it takes to do this teaching. You will see students acting with confidence and independence.

Figure 4-6: The four activities in the simple system from *Guided Reading: Responsive Teaching Across the Grades* (Fountas and Pinnell 2017d)

Reading Time

1. Read a book
2. Listen to a book
3. Work on words
4. Work on writing

 ELL CONNECTION

Reference Chapter 22 of our professional book, *Guided Reading: Responsive Teaching Across the Grades* (Fountas and Pinnell 2017d), for more detailed information on managing independent learning in the early grades. Whether you choose to use a simple system or a work board with centers, it is important for children to be engaged in meaningful, authentic reading and writing experiences. Management minilessons provide your readers with the tools and skills they need to make this time productive, collaborative, and enjoyable.

Figure 4-7: When children are learning to use a work board, only one or two activity choices are offered. This work board shows two tasks for each child to complete. Once children understand the routines for several activities and show that they can work independently, more icons are added.

Figure 4-8: This chart from a management minilesson was created as children learned how to follow a work board.

Chapter 5

Literary Analysis Minilessons: Thinking and Talking About Books

LITERARY ANALYSIS MINILESSONS SUPPORT CHILDREN in a growing awareness of the elements of literature and the writer's and illustrator's craft. They help children learn how to think analytically about texts and identify the characteristics of fiction and nonfiction genres. Invite students to notice characters and how they change, identify problems and solutions in stories, and notice how nonfiction writers present and organize information as well as their use of graphics and other nonfiction features. Prior to each literary analysis minilesson, students will have listened to texts read aloud or have experienced them through shared reading. You will have taught specific lessons based on the text that encourage students to discuss and explore concepts and to respond in writing, art, or drama. This prior knowledge will be accessed as they participate in the minilesson and will enable them to make the understanding explicit. They then can apply the concepts to their own reading and share what they have learned with others.

Organization of Literary Analysis Umbrellas and the Link to *The Literacy Continuum*

There are eighty-two literary analysis minilessons in this book. These minilessons are divided into categories according to *The Literacy Continuum* (Fountas and Pinnell 2017c), and the order of presentation in this book follows that of *The Literacy Continuum*. The categories for fiction and nonfiction are listed below:

- ◗ Fiction and Nonfiction:
  - General
  - Genre
  - Messages and Themes
- ◗ Nonfiction:
  - Topic
  - Illustrations/Graphics
  - Book and Print Features
- ◗ Fiction:
  - Setting
  - Plot
  - Character
  - Illustrations

As you can tell from the suggested sequence in Minilessons Across the Year (Figure 8-2), you will want to use simpler concepts (such as book title and author) before more sophisticated concepts (such as character change).

Echoes of the literary analysis minilessons reverberate across all the instruction for the year in instructional contexts for reading (interactive read-aloud, shared reading, guided reading, book clubs, and independent reading) as well as for writing. The children continue to develop their understanding of the characteristics of fiction and nonfiction texts.

Genre Study

Within the Literary Analysis section, you will find two umbrellas that bring children through a process of inquiry-based study of the characteristics of a particular genre. Genre study gives students the tools they need to navigate a variety of texts with deep understanding. When readers understand the characteristics of a genre, they know what to expect when they begin to read a text. They use their knowledge of the predictable elements within a genre as a roadmap to anticipate structures and elements of the text. They make connections between books within the same genre and begin to develop a shared language for talking about genre. In our professional book, *Genre*

Study: Teaching with Fiction and Nonfiction Books (Fountas and Pinnell 2012a), we designed a six-step approach for learning about a variety of genres. The six broad steps are described in Figure 5-1. For this book, we have designed specific minilessons based on our *Genre Study* book to help you engage your students in the powerful process of becoming knowledgeable about a range of genres.

The first two steps of the genre study process take place before and during interactive read-aloud. Steps 3–5 are accomplished through reading minilessons. Step 6 is addressed on the last page of each genre study umbrella. In kindergarten, we suggest two simple genre studies to introduce this process and to help children develop a beginning understanding of genre. The first is a genre study of fiction and nonfiction. This umbrella utilizes a text set of fiction and nonfiction pairs (for example, Ann Morris' nonfiction book, *Hats, Hats, Hats*, and Esphyr Slobodkina's fiction text, *Caps for Sale*) to explore and study the difference between fiction and nonfiction. The second is a genre study of animal tales (for example, *The Three Little Pigs, The Three Bears*, and *The Three Billy Goats Gruff*). Animal tales are popular among kindergartners. Most kindergarten children are able to bring a large amount of background information to the study of animal tales, which makes it a good choice for a genre study in kindergarten.

The first step in the genre study process, **Collect**, involves collecting a set of texts. The genre study minilessons in this book draw on texts sets from the *Fountas & Pinnell Classroom™ Interactive Read-Aloud Collection*. Use these texts if you have them, but we encourage you to collect additional texts

Figure 5-1: Adapted from *Genre Study* (Fountas and Pinnell 2012a)

Steps in the Genre Study Process
1   **Collect** books in a text set that represent good examples of the genre you are studying.
2   **Immerse**. Read aloud each book using the lesson guidelines. The primary goal should be enjoyment and understanding of the book.
3   **Study**. After you have read these mentor texts, have children analyze characteristics or "noticings" that are common to the texts, and list the characteristics on chart paper.
4   **Define**. Use the list of characteristics to create a short working definition of the genre.
5   **Teach** specific minilessons on the important characteristics of the genre.
6   **Read and Revise**. Expand children's understanding by encouraging them to talk about the genre in appropriate instructional contexts (book club, independent reading conferences, guided reading lessons, and shared reading lessons) and revise the definition.

within each genre to immerse your students in as many texts as possible. Children will enjoy additional examples of the genre placed in a bin in the classroom library. You can use the texts listed in the Before Teaching section of each umbrella as a guide to making your own genre text set if you do not have access to the *Interactive Read-Aloud Collection*.

As you engage students in step 2, **Immerse**, of the genre study process, be sure that the children think and talk about the meaning of each text during the interactive read-aloud. The goal is for students to enjoy a wonderful book, so it is important for them to first enjoy and respond to the full meaning of the text before focusing their attention on the specific characteristics of the genre.

After immersing students in the books through interactive read aloud, it is time to teach minilessons in the genre study umbrella. The first minilesson in the genre study umbrella addresses step 3 in the process, **Study.** During this initial minilesson, help children notice what is common across all of the texts. As children discuss and revisit books in the genre, list their noticings on chart paper. Distinguish between what is always true about the genre and what is often true about the genre.

The second minilesson in the genre study umbrellas addresses step 4, **Define**, in the process. Teach a minilesson in which you use shared writing to co-construct a working definition of the genre based on the children's previous noticings. Help children to understand that you will revisit and revise this definition as they learn more about the genre over the next few days.

Next, as part of step 5, **Teach**, provide specific minilessons related to each of your students' noticings about the genre. In each genre study umbrella, we offer minilessons that we think would develop out of most kindergarten-aged children's noticings. Pick and choose the lessons that match your own students' noticings or use these lessons as a model to develop your own minilessons.

At the end of the umbrella, work with the children to **Read and Revise** the class definition of the genre based on the minilessons that have been taught. Using shared or interactive writing, make changes to the definition so it reflects children's understanding of the genre.

Fiction

Noticings:

Always	Often
• The story has made-up characters.	• The characters are animals that act like people.
• The place where the story happens can be made-up or real.	
• The story never really happened.	
• The story has a problem.	
• The problem gets solved.	

Figure 5-2: On this anchor chart, the teacher has recorded what her class noticed was always or often true about several fiction texts that they had heard or read.

Author and Illustrator Studies

Section Two: Literary Analysis also includes an umbrella of minilessons for conducting inquiry-based author and illustrator studies. Author and illustrator studies allow children to make connections to the people behind the books they love. They learn about the craft decisions an author or illustrator makes. For an author or illustrator study, be sure that the children think and talk about the full meaning of each text in interactive read-aloud before identifying characteristics specific to the author or illustrator.

Children will need plenty of opportunity to explore the texts during read-aloud time and on their own or in groups or pairs. As they become more familiar with the steps in an author or illustrator study, they learn how to notice characteristics common to a particular author's or illustrator's work. The steps in an author/illustrator study are described in Figure 5-4.

In the two minilessons in Umbrella 3: Studying Authors and Illustrators, you provide a demonstration of step 3 by working with your students to create a chart of "noticings" about an author or illustrator. In these two lessons, we model a study of Eric Carle and Lois Ehlert from the *Fountas & Pinnell Classroom™ Interactive Read-Aloud Collection*. In kindergarten, we have chosen to study authors who are also the illustrators of their books. You might choose to use these same popular authors or choose authors and illustrators you and your children are familiar with and love. The process described in the minilessons in this umbrella can be used throughout the year to study different authors and illustrators. Simply collect books by a particular author or illustrator and follow the steps listed in Figure 5-4. Use the same language and process modeled in the minilessons in this umbrella but substitute the authors and illustrators of your choice.

Lois Ehlert

Noticings:

Always	Often
• She uses things like cloth, paper, and real toys in her illustrations.	• She uses photos to make her illustrations.
• She cuts or finds shapes and makes pictures with them.	• She adds labels around the illustrations.
• She makes illustrations about animals and nature.	

Figure 5-3: This chart shows what students noticed about the work of illustrator Lois Ehlert.

Figure 5-4: Minilessons address step 3 of an author/illustrator study.

Steps in an Author/Illustrator Study

1. Gather a set of books and read them aloud to the class over several days.

2. Take children on a quick tour of all the books in the set. As you reexamine each book, you might want to have children do a brief turn and talk with a partner about what they notice.

3. Have children analyze the characteristics of the author's or illustrator's work, and record their noticings on chart paper.

4. You may choose to read a few more books by the author and compare them to the books in this set, adding to the noticings as needed.

Chapter 6 Strategies and Skills Minilessons: Teaching for Effective Processing

FOR THE STRATEGIES AND SKILLS lessons, you will usually use enlarged texts that have been created for shared reading because children can see the print and the illustrations easily. These minilessons are most effective after children have begun to process print and to search for and use information from the text, self-monitor their reading, and self-correct their errors. You'll notice the children engaging in these behaviors in your shared reading lessons.

The large print is ideal for problem solving with a common example. Shared reading leads the way for children to apply strategic actions in guided reading lessons. Strategies and skills are taught in every instructional context for reading, but guided reading is the most powerful one. The text is just right to support the learning of all the readers in the group, enabling them to learn how to solve words and engage in the act of problem solving across a whole text.

The strategies and skills minilessons in this book are some general lessons that may serve as reminders and be helpful to the whole class. For example, as students engage in independent reading, they may need to realize that a reader

▶ looks at the illustrations and thinks what would make sense, and

▶ thinks what would make sense and notices whether it fits with the first letter of the word.

The minilessons in Section Three: Strategies and Skills are designed to bring a few important strategies to temporary, conscious attention so that kindergarten children are reminded to think in these ways as they problem solve in independent reading. By the time students participate in these minilessons, they should have engaged these strategic actions successfully in shared or guided reading. In the minilessons, they will recognize the strategic actions; bringing them to brief, focused attention; and think about applying them consistently in independent reading.

Because the children have read continuous text in unison and individually, they have developed an internal sense of actions, like monitoring and checking, searching for and using information, and using multiple sources of information to solve words. They have experienced early foundational concepts of print (such as left-to-right directionality, word-by-word matching) through processing a text. They have a sense of how to put words together to sound like talking. The minilesson, the application, and the share help them better understand what they do and internalize the effective behaviors.

Figure 6-1: Children are able to see and follow print and punctuation when you use an enlarged text, such as a big book or a poetry chart, or project a text.

Chapter 7

Writing About Reading Minilessons: The Reading-Writing Connection

THROUGH DRAWING/WRITING ABOUT READING, children reflect on their understanding of a text. For example, a story might have a captivating character or characters or a humorous sequence of events. A nonfiction text might have interesting information or call for an opinion. There are several kinds of writing about reading that are highly effective with kindergarten students.

▶ **Shared Writing.** In shared writing you offer the highest level of support to the students. You act as scribe while the students participate fully in the composition of the text. You help shape the text, but the students supply the language and context.

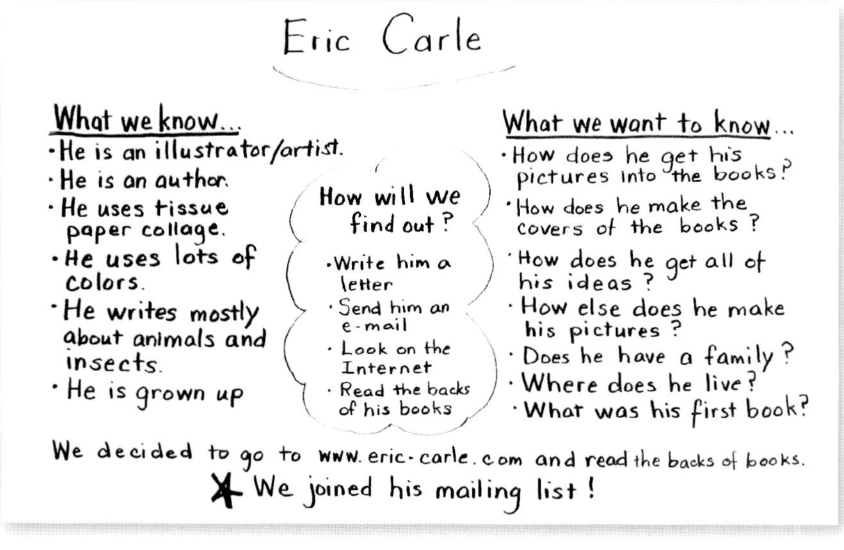

> Eric Carle
>
> **What we know...**
> - He is an illustrator/artist.
> - He is an author.
> - He uses tissue paper collage.
> - He uses lots of colors.
> - He writes mostly about animals and insects.
> - He is grown up
>
> **How will we find out?**
> - Write him a letter
> - Send him an e-mail
> - Look on the Internet
> - Read the backs of his books
>
> **What we want to know...**
> - How does he get his pictures into the books?
> - How does he make the covers of the books?
> - How does he get all of his ideas?
> - How else does he make his pictures?
> - Does he have a family?
> - Where does he live?
> - What was his first book?
>
> We decided to go to www.eric-carle.com and read the backs of books.
> ✱ We joined his mailing list!

Figure 7-1: In shared writing, the teacher acts as scribe.

> **Interactive Writing.** Interactive writing is exactly the same as shared writing in that the students participate actively in the actual composition of the text and you act as scribe. But in interactive writing, you invite students to "share the pen" at points in the text that offer high instructional value. An individual may contribute the first letter of a word, the middle, or last letter of a word. He may contribute a word part like *-ing* or quickly write a high-frequency word that has just been learned. In general, you write words that are too difficult for students to attempt and you write words that everyone knows how to write quickly (so in this case sharing the pen would not result in new learning). It is important to move interactive writing along at a good pace and to make teaching points with precision. Don't try to have students write too much because the lesson can become tedious. Be selective.

Figure 7-2: Interactive writing differs from shared writing only in that the teacher shares the pen with students at points that offer high instructional value.

Bird used a feather to wake up Elephant.

> **Independent Writing.** For kindergarten children, the first response is often drawing, painting or collage. But very soon they like to add print to their works of art. This may involve labels or simple texts with approximated spellings. But soon they will begin to write simple sentences because they are immersed in language through read-aloud, shared reading, and guided reading. Keep good examples of different writing on hand (possibly in a scrapbook) for children to use as models.

In most literary analysis lessons, you will find a suggestion for extending the learning using one of these types of writing. But, at any point in these minilessons, you can choose to use shared, interactive, or independent writing. When children have the opportunity to apply the new thinking through shared writing or interactive writing, they are exposed to different ways of writing about their reading. It is important at some point to encourage students to do their own writing. Of course, the early independent writing of your students will not be entirely standard spelling. They are developing new systems for writing words through approximation, and their risk-taking attempts are critical to their success. If students know some easy high-frequency words, these may be accurately spelled, but you can expect them to try many others using their growing knowledge of how to say words slowly and listen for the sounds and connect them with letters.

Much of the children's independent writing will be in a reader's notebook. The Writing About Reading umbrellas, Umbrella 4: Writing About Fiction Books in a Reader's Notebook and Umbrella 5: Writing About Nonfiction Books in a Reader's Notebook, both provide inquiry-based lessons to help children make this transition to independent writing about reading. Like management minilessons, the lessons in these umbrellas might not be taught consecutively within the umbrella, but instead paired with the literary analysis lessons that support the concept students are being asked to draw or write about. For example, after you have taught a lesson on the feelings of characters, you might first extend learning by providing an interactive writing lesson in which you write about a character's feelings with your students. Once you feel they are ready, you might introduce them to writing or drawing about character feelings in a reader's notebook using the minilessons in Umbrella 4: Writing About Fiction Books in a Reader's Notebook. Through this gradual release of responsibility, children learn how to transition to writing about their reading independently as they learn how to use each section of the notebook. A reader's notebook is an important tool to support student independence and response to books. It becomes a rich collection of thinking across the years.

For English language learners, a reader's notebook is a safe place to practice a new language. It eventually becomes a record of their progress. In kindergarten, all children will do more drawing than writing early in the year. Drawing is key because it provides a way to rehearse ideas. Use this opportunity to ask students to talk about what they have drawn, and then help them compose labels for their artwork so they begin to attach meaning to the English words. Eventually, the students will do more writing, but you can support the writing by providing a chance for them to rehearse their sentences before writing them and encourage students to borrow language from the texts they are writing about. The writing in a reader's notebook is a product they can read because they have written it. It is theirs. They can read and reread it to themselves and to others, thereby developing their confidence in the language.

ELL CONNECTION

Figure 7-3: Through indepedent writing, children develop new systems for writing words.

Using a Reader's Notebook in Kindergarten

A reader's notebook is a place where children can collect their thinking about books. They draw and write to tell about themselves and respond to books. A reader's notebook includes

⟩ a variety of sections for children to tell about themselves,

⟩ a section for children to list and respond to books they have read or listened to,

⟩ a section for children to list words they know, and

⟩ several letter and word resources.

With places where students can draw and write about themselves as well as make a record of their reading and what they think about it a reader's notebook thus represents a rich record of progress. To the child, the notebook represents a year's work to reflect on with pride and share with family. Children keep their notebooks in their personal book boxes, along with their bags of book choices for independent reading time. We provide a series of minilessons in Section Four: Writing About Reading for teaching students how to use a reader's notebook. As we described previously, reading minilessons in the Writing About Reading section focus on drawing and writing in response to reading.

If you do not have access to the preprinted *Reader's Notebook: Primary* (Fountas and Pinnell 2014), simply give each student a blank notebook (bound if possible). Glue in sections and insert tabs yourself to make a neat, professional notebook that can be cherished.

Figure 7-4: Kindergarten children personalize the covers of *Reader's Notebook: Primary*. Inside, they draw and write about themselves and their reading.

Chapter 8

Putting Minilessons into Action: Assessing and Planning

As NOTED IN CHAPTER 2, the minilessons in this book are examples of teaching that address the specific bullets that list the behaviors and understandings to notice, teach for, and support in *The Literacy Continuum* (Fountas and Pinnell 2017c) for kindergarten. We have drawn from the sections on Interactive Read-Aloud, Shared Reading, Guided Reading, *small groups instruction* Writing About Reading, and Oral and Visual Communication to provide a comprehensive vision of what children need to become aware of, understand, and apply to their own literacy and learning. With such a range of important goals, how do you decide what to teach and when?

Deciding Which Reading Minilessons to Teach

To decide which reading minilessons to teach, first look at the students in front of you. Teach within what Vygotsky (1979) called the students' "zone of proximal development"—the zone between what the students can do independently and what they can do with the support of a more expert other. Teach on the cutting edge of children's competencies. Select topics for minilessons that address the needs of the majority of students in your class.

Think about what will be helpful to most readers based on your observations of their reading and writing behaviors. Here are some suggestions and tools to help you think about the students in your classroom:

- **Use *The Literacy Continuum*** (Fountas and Pinnell 2017c) to assess your students and observe how they are thinking, talking, and writing/drawing about books. Think about what they can already do, almost do, and not yet do to select the emphasis for your teaching. Look at the Selecting Goals pages in each section to guide your observations.

- **Use the Interactive Read-Aloud and Literature Discussion section.** Scan the Selecting Goals in this section and think about the ways you have noticed students thinking and talking about books. *[handwritten: → in Continuum]*

- **Use the Writing About Reading section** to analyze how students are responding to texts in their drawing and writing. This analysis will help you determine possible next steps. Talking and writing about reading provides concrete evidence of students' thinking.

- **Use the Oral Language Continuum** to help you think about some of the routines your students might need for better communication between peers. You will find essential listening and speaking competencies to observe and teach.

- **Look for patterns in your anecdotal records.** Review the anecdotal notes you take during reading conferences, shared reading, guided reading, and book clubs to notice trends in students' responses and thinking. Use *The Literacy Continuum* to help you analyze the records and determine strengths and areas for growth across the classroom. Your observations will reveal what children know and what they need to learn next as they build understanding over time. Each goal becomes a possible topic for a minilesson.

- **Consult district and state standards as a resource.** Analyze the suggested skills and areas of knowledge specified in your local and state standards. Align these standards with the minilessons suggested in this text to determine which might be applicable within your frameworks (see **fountasandpinnell.com/resourcelibrary** for an alignment of *The Literacy Continuum* with Common Core Standards).

- **Use the Assessment section after each umbrella.** Take time to assess student learning after the completion of each umbrella. Use the guiding questions on the last page of each umbrella to determine strengths and next steps for your students. This analysis can help you determine what minilessons to reteach if needed and what umbrella to teach next.

A Suggested Sequence

The suggested sequence of umbrellas, Minilessons Across the Year shown in Figure 8-2 (also downloadable from the Online Resources for record keeping), is intended to establish good classroom management early and work toward more sophisticated concepts across the year. Learning in minilessons is applied in many different situations and so is reinforced daily across the curriculum. Minilessons in this sequence are timed so they occur after children have had sufficient opportunities to build some explicit understandings as well as a great deal of implicit knowledge of aspects of written texts through interactive read-aloud and shared reading texts. In the community of readers, they have acted on texts through talk, writing, and extension through writing and art. These experiences have prepared them to fully engage in the reading minilesson and move from this shared experience to the application of the concepts in their independent reading.

The sequence of umbrellas in Minilessons Across the Year follows the suggested sequence of text sets in *Fountas & Pinnell Classroom™ Interactive Read-Aloud Collection*. If you are using this collection, you are invited to follow this sequence of texts. If you are not using it, the first page of each umbrella describes the types of books students will need to read before you teach the minilessons. The text sets are grouped together by theme, topic, author, and genre, not by skill or concept. Thus, in many minilessons, you will use books from several different text sets.

The umbrellas draw examples from text sets that have been read and enjoyed previously. In most cases, the minilessons draw on text sets that are introduced within the same month or at least in close proximity to the umbrella. However, in some cases, minilessons taught later, for example in month 8, might draw on texts introduced earlier in the year.

We have selected the most concrete and instructive examples from the texts available to illustrate the minilesson principle. Most of the time, children will have no problem recalling the events of these early texts because you have read and discussed them thoroughly as a class. However, in some cases, you might want to reread these texts, or a portion of the text, quickly before teaching the umbrella so the books are fresh in the students' minds.

As you begin to work with the minilessons, you may want to follow the suggested sequence, but remember to use the lessons flexibly to meet the needs of the children you teach:

▶ Omit lessons that you think are not necessary for your children (based on assessment and your experiences with them in interactive read-aloud).

▶ Repeat some lessons that you think need more time and instructional attention (based on observation of children across reading contexts).

- Repeat some lessons using different examples for a particularly rich experience.

- Move lessons around to be consistent with the curriculum that is adopted in your school or district.

The minilessons are here for you to choose from according to the instructional needs of your class, so do not be concerned if you do not use them all within the year. Record or check the minilessons you have taught so that you can reflect on the work of the semester and year. You can do this simply by downloading the checklist from Online Resources (Figure 8-1) for your record keeping.

Figure 8-1: Download this record-keeping form to record the minilessons that you have taught. Visit resources.fountasandpinnell.com to download this online resource.

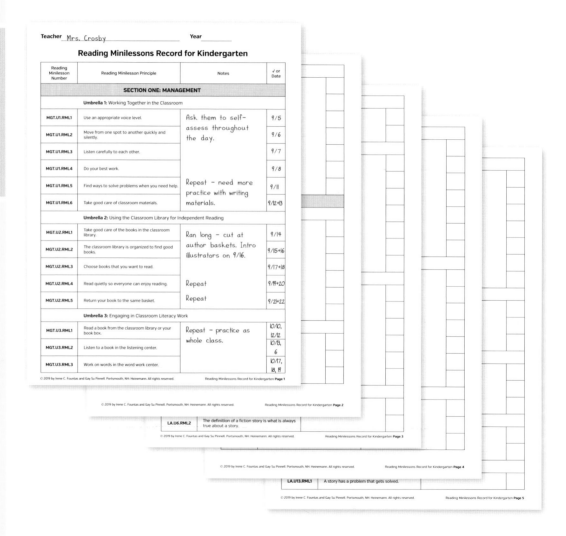

Teacher ___Mrs. Crosby___   Year _____

Reading Minilessons Record for Kindergarten

Reading Minilesson Number	Reading Minilesson Principle	Notes	✓ or Date
SECTION ONE: MANAGEMENT			
Umbrella 1: Working Together in the Classroom			
MGT.U1.RML1	Use an appropriate voice level.	Ask them to self-assess throughout the day.	9/5
MGT.U1.RML2	Move from one spot to another quickly and silently.		9/6
MGT.U1.RML3	Listen carefully to each other.		9/7
MGT.U1.RML4	Do your best work.		9/8
MGT.U1.RML5	Find ways to solve problems when you need help.	Repeat – need more practice with writing materials.	9/11
MGT.U1.RML6	Take good care of classroom materials.		9/12+13
Umbrella 2: Using the Classroom Library for Independent Reading			
MGT.U2.RML1	Take good care of the books in the classroom library.	Ran long – cut at author baskets. Intro illustrators on 9/16.	9/14
MGT.U2.RML2	The classroom library is organized to find good books.		9/15+16
MGT.U2.RML3	Choose books that you want to read.		9/17+18
MGT.U2.RML4	Read quietly so everyone can enjoy reading.	Repeat	9/19+20
MGT.U2.RML5	Return your book to the same basket.	Repeat	9/21+22
Umbrella 3: Engaging in Classroom Literacy Work			
MGT.U3.RML1	Read a book from the classroom library or your book box.	Repeat – practice as whole class.	10/10, 12/12
MGT.U3.RML2	Listen to a book in the listening center.		10/13, 6
MGT.U3.RML3	Work on words in the word work center.		10/17, 18, 19

© 2019 by Irene C. Fountas and Gay Su Pinnell. Portsmouth, NH: Heinemann. All rights reserved.   Reading Minilessons Record for Kindergarten **Page 1**

© 2019 by Irene C. Fountas and Gay Su Pinnell. Portsmouth, NH: Heinemann. All rights reserved.   Reading Minilessons Record for Kindergarten **Page 2**

| LA.U6.RML2 | The definition of a fiction story is what is always true about a story. | | |

© 2019 by Irene C. Fountas and Gay Su Pinnell. Portsmouth, NH: Heinemann. All rights reserved.   Reading Minilessons Record for Kindergarten **Page 3**

© 2019 by Irene C. Fountas and Gay Su Pinnell. Portsmouth, NH: Heinemann. All rights reserved.   Reading Minilessons Record for Kindergarten **Page 4**

| LA.U13.RML1 | A story has a problem that gets solved. | | |

© 2019 by Irene C. Fountas and Gay Su Pinnell. Portsmouth, NH: Heinemann. All rights reserved.   Reading Minilessons Record for Kindergarten **Page 5**

MINILESSONS ACROSS THE YEAR

Month	Recommended Umbrellas	Approximate Time
Month 1	MGT U1: Working Together in the Classroom	1.5 weeks
	MGT U2: Using the Classroom Library for Independent Reading	1 week
	LA U1: Thinking and Talking About Books	1.5 weeks
Month 2	MGT U3: Engaging in Classroom Literacy Work	2.5 weeks
	Note: The first five minilessons in this umbrella will get children started with independent literacy work. RML10 introduces the children to the work board. We recommend introducing the rest of the minilessons in this umbrella as the year progresses. See month 4.	
	LA U14: Understanding Characters in Stories	1 week
Month 3	WAR U1: Introducing a Reader's Notebook	2.5 weeks
	LA U17: Using Pictures in a Book to Tell the Story	1 week
Month 4	LA U5: Getting Started with Book Clubs	1.5 weeks
	MGT U3: Engaging in Classroom Literacy Work	2 weeks
	Note: We suggest introducing the remaining minilessons at the end of month 4 or beginning of month 5. The last minilesson can be repeated if necessary.	
	LA U3: Studying Authors and Illustrators	0.5 week
	Note: We suggest repeating these minilessons whenever you conduct an author or illustrator study (see month 8).	
Month 5	WAR U2: Using a Reader's Notebook	2 weeks
	LA U6: Studying Fiction and Nonfiction	2 weeks
Month 6	SAS U1: Searching for and Using Meaning, Language, and Visual Information	1.5 weeks
	WAR U3: Introducing Writing About Reading in a Reader's Notebook	1 week
	Note: You may instead decide to teach individual minilessons alongside the literacy analysis minilessons that address similar behaviors.	
	LA U7: Studying Animal Tales	2 weeks

KEY			
MGT	Section One	Management Minilessons	
LA	Section Two	Literary Analysis Minilessons	
SAS	Section Three	Strategies and Skills Minilessons	
WAR	Section Four	Writing About Reading Minilessons	

Figure 8-2: Use this chart as a guideline for planning your year with minilessons.

Month	Recommended Umbrellas	Approximate Time
Month 7	SAS U2: Monitoring and Self-Correcting	0.5 week
	LA U4: Giving a Book Talk	1.5 weeks
	WAR U6: Writing Opinions About Books	1.5 weeks
	Note: You may decide to teach individual minilessons in this umbrella alongside literacy analysis minilessons that address similar behaviors.	
	LA U15: Getting to Know the Characters in Stories	2 weeks
Month 8	LA U3: Studying Authors and Illustrators	0.5 week
	Note: The second minilesson focuses on illustrator study. See month 4 for author study.	
	LA U12: Thinking About Where Stories Happen	0.5 week
	SAS U3: Maintaining Fluency	1.5 weeks
	WAR U4: Writing About Fiction Books in a Reader's Notebook	2 weeks
	Note: You may decide to teach individual minilessons in this umbrella alongside literacy analysis minilessons that address similar behaviors.	
Month 9	LA U9: Learning About Nonfiction Books	2 weeks
	LA U18: Looking Closely at Illustrations	1 week
	LA U10: Learning Information from Illustrations/Graphics	0.5 week
	WAR U5: Writing About Nonfiction Books in a Reader's Notebook	1 week
	Note: You may decide to teach the minilessons in this umbrella alongside literacy analysis minilessons that address similar behaviors.	
Month 10	LA U11: Using Text Features to Gain Information	0.5 week
	LA U13: Understanding How Stories Work	1.5 weeks
	LA U16: Understanding Character Change	0.5 week
	LA U8: Thinking About the Author's Message	0.5 week
	LA U2: Noticing How Authors Tell Their Stories	0.5 week

KEY			
MGT	Section One	Management Minilessons
LA	Section Two	Literary Analysis Minilessons
SAS	Section Three	Strategies and Skills Minilessons
WAR	Section Four	Writing About Reading Minilessons

Chapter 9

Reading Minilessons Within a Multitext Approach to Literacy Learning

THIS COLLECTION OF 150 LESSONS for kindergarten is embedded within an integrated set of instructional approaches that build an awareness of classroom routines, literary characteristics, strategies and skills, and ways of writing about written texts. In Figure 9-1, this comprehensive, multitext approach is represented, along with the central role of minilessons. Note that students' processing systems are built across instructional contexts so that students can read increasingly complex texts independently. In this chapter, we will look at how the reading minilessons fit within this multitext approach and provide a balance between implicit and explicit teaching that allows for authentic response and promotes the enjoyment of books.

In Figure 9-1, we describe how to build the shared literary knowledge of your classroom community, embedding implicit and explicit teaching with your use of intentional conversation and specific points of instructional value to set a foundation for explicit teaching in reading minilessons. All of the teaching in minilessons is reinforced in shared reading, guided reading, and book clubs, with all pathways leading to the goal of effective independent reading.

Let's look at the range of research-based instructional contexts that comprise an effective literacy design.

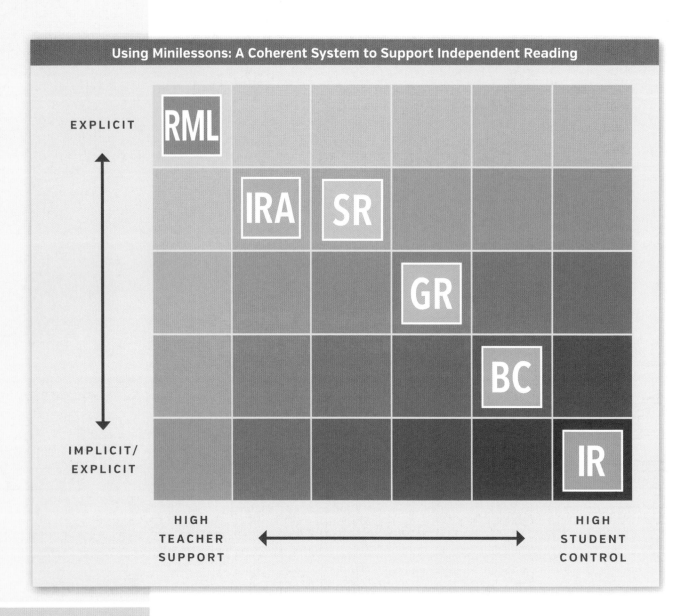

Figure 9-1: Text experiences are supported and developed by implicit and explicit teaching in all instructional contexts, including interactive read-aloud, shared reading, guided reading, book clubs, and independent reading conferences. Reading minilessons provide explicit teaching that makes learning visible and is reinforced in the other contexts.

Interactive Read-Aloud

Interactive read-aloud includes the highest level of teacher support for students as they experience a complex, grade-appropriate text. Carefully select sets of high-quality children's literature, fiction and nonfiction, and read them aloud to students. We use the word *interactive* because talk is a salient characteristic of this instructional context. You do the reading but pause to invite student discussion in pairs, in triads, or as a whole group at selected points. After the reading, students engage in a lively discussion. Finally, you invite students to revisit specific points in the text for deeper learning and may provide further opportunities for responding to the text through writing, drama, movement, or art.

We recommend that you read aloud from high-quality, organized text sets, which you use across the year. A text set contains several titles that are related in some conceptual way, for example:

- Author
- Illustrator
- Genre
- Topic
- Theme or big idea
- Format (such as graphic texts)

When you use books organized in text sets, you can support children in making connections across a related group of texts and in engaging them in deeper thinking about texts. All children benefit from the use of preselected sets, but these connected texts are particularly supportive for English language learners. Text sets allow children to develop vocabulary around a particular theme, genre or topic. This shared collection of familiar texts and the shared vocabulary developed through the talk provides essential background knowledge that all students will be able to apply during subsequent reading minilessons.

ELL CONNECTION

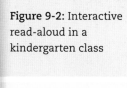
Figure 9-2: Interactive read-aloud in a kindergarten class

The key to success with reading minilessons is providing the intentional instruction in interactive read-aloud that will, first, enable the children to enjoy and come to love books and, second, build a foundation of shared understandings about texts within a community of readers and writers.

If you are using *Fountas & Pinnell Classroom™*, you will notice that we have used examples from *Interactive Read-Aloud Collection* as the mentor texts in the minilessons. If you do not have the texts from *Fountas & Pinnell Classroom™*, select read-aloud texts with the same characteristics (described at the beginning of each umbrella) to read well ahead of the minilessons and use the lessons as organized and presented in this book. Simply substitute the particular texts you selected. You can draw on any texts you have already read and discussed with the children as long as the genre is appropriate for the set of minilessons and the ideas can be connected. For example, if you are going to teach a set of minilessons about characters, pull examples from fiction stories rather than nonfiction books and include engaging characters. If you are reading rich literature in various genres to your children, the chances are high that many of the types of reading behaviors or understandings you are teaching for in reading minilessons can be applied to those texts.

At the beginning of each umbrella (set of related minilessons), you will find a section titled "Before Teaching Minilessons," which offers guidance in the use of interactive read-aloud as a prelude to teaching the explicit minilessons in the umbrella. It is important to note that the texts in a text set can be used for several different umbrellas. In general, text sets are connected with each other in particular ways so children can think about concepts across texts and notice literary characteristics during read-aloud lessons. But the texts have multiple uses. When you complete reading the books in a set, you will have provided children with a rich, connected set of literacy experiences that include both explicit teaching and implicitly

Figure 9-3: Examples of preselected text sets from *Fountas & Pinnell Classroom™ Interactive Read-Aloud Collection*

understood concepts. But, we would not label one text set for the study of illustrations and another for the study of character. Instead, we have often selected examples across sets. Rich, literary texts can be used for multiple types of lessons, so you will see many of the same, familiar texts referenced throughout the reading minilessons across umbrellas. Each time a text is used for a different focus, children have a chance to view it with new eyes and see it differently. Usually, texts are not reread in entirety. They are known from a rich and deep experience, and the result is shared literary knowledge for the class. In minilessons, they are revisited briefly with a particular focus. It is most powerful to select examples from texts that children have heard in their *recent* experience. But you can always revisit favorites that you read at the very beginning of the year, which can be referenced all year long. When texts have been enjoyed and loved in interactive read-aloud, children know them deeply and can remember them over time. Here are some steps to follow for incorporating your own texts into the minilessons:

1. Identify a group of read-aloud texts that will be valuable resources for use in the particular minilesson. (These texts may be from the same text set, but usually they are drawn from several different sets. The key is their value in teaching routines, engaging in literary analysis, building particular strategies and skills, or writing about reading.)

2. The mentor texts you select will usually be some that you have already read to and discussed with the children; but if not, read and discuss them with the goal of enjoyment and understanding. The emphasis in interactive read-aloud is not on the minilesson principle but on enjoying and deeply understanding the text, appreciating the illustrations and design, and constructing an understanding of the deeper messages of the text.

3. Teach the reading minilesson as designed, substituting the texts you have chosen and read to the children.

Interactive read-aloud will greatly benefit your English language learners. In *Fountas & Pinnell Classroom*™, we have selected the texts with English language learners in mind and recommend that you do the same if you are selecting texts from your existing resources. In addition to expanding both listening and speaking vocabularies, interactive read-aloud provides constant exposure to English language syntax. Stories read aloud provide "ear print" for children. Hearing grammatical structures of English over and over helps English language learners form an implicit knowledge of the rules. Here are some other considerations for your English language learners:

 **ELL CONNECTION**

▶ Increase the frequency of your interactive read-alouds.

▶ Choose books that have familiar themes and concepts and take into account the cultural backgrounds of all the students in your classroom.

- Reread texts that your English language learners enjoy. Rereading texts that children especially enjoy will help them acquire and make use of language that goes beyond their current understanding.

- Choose texts that are simple and have high picture support. This will allow you to later revisit concrete examples from these texts during reading minilessons.

- Seat English language learners in places where they can easily see, hear, and participate in the text.

- Preview the text with English language learners by holding a small-group discussion before reading the book to the entire class. As they hear it the second time, they will understand more and will have had the experience of talking. This will encourage the children to participate more actively during the discussion.

When you provide a rich and supportive experience through interactive read-aloud, you prepare English language learners for a successful experience in reading minilessons. They will bring the vocabulary and background knowledge developed in interactive read-aloud to the exploration of the reading minilesson principle. These multiple layers of support will pave the road to successful independent reading.

Shared Reading

In shared reading with kindergarten children, use an enlarged text, either fiction or nonfiction. Read the text to the children and then invite them to read a part of the text or the whole text in unison. Have children reread the text several times until they know it well, and then you have the option of revisiting it for different purposes (for example, to locate high-frequency words, words that start with the same letter, or punctuation) and to extend the meaning through writing, art, or drama.

Like the texts in interactive read-aloud, shared reading texts offer students the opportunity to understand and discuss characters, events, concepts, and ideas. In addition, an enlarged text offers the advantage of making print, layout, and punctuation available to the readers because all can see them clearly.

You will find that some minilessons in this book refer to shared reading examples from *Fountas & Pinnell Classroom*™. If you do not have access to these resources, you can easily use the lessons in this book by collecting your own set of shared reading books and/or using a document camera to show pages of an appropriate book. Simply substitute the texts you select.

At the beginning of each umbrella, you will find a short section titled "Before Teaching Minilessons," which will have suggestions for the teaching needed prior to your use of the umbrella. Here are some steps to follow for incorporating your own shared reading texts into the minilessons:

1. Prior to implementing a lesson, select a group of texts that are appropriate for teaching the principle. Use the examples in the lesson as a guide. The texts may be some that you have previously read and built lessons around.

2. Engage children in a shared reading of each text that is not familiar to them. Shared reading books are designed for repeated readings, so plan to reread each several times. (Use your own judgment. Sometimes two or three readings are sufficient.) Remember, the focus is on understanding and enjoying the text, not on a specific principle.

3. Revisit the text to do some specific teaching toward any of the systems of strategic actions listed in *The Literacy Continuum* (Fountas and Pinnell 2017c). As an option, give children opportunities to respond to the text through writing, art, or drama.

4. Implement the reading minilesson as designed using the texts you have used in teaching.

In lessons using shared reading texts, students have had opportunities to notice print and how it works—the directionality, the use of space, and the way letters are used to spell words. They have located individual words and noticed the use of bold and sound words. They have learned how to use the meaning, language, and print together to process the text fluently. In addition, here, too, they noticed characteristics of the genre, the characters, and the message anchors.

Figure 9-4: Shared reading in a kindergarten class

Shared reading can also be important in reinforcing students' ability to apply understandings from the minilesson. You can revisit the texts to remind children of the minilesson principle and invite them to notice text characteristics or engage strategic actions to process them. When you work across texts, you help children apply understandings in many contexts.

ELL CONNECTION

Shared reading provides a supportive environment for English language learners to both hear and produce English language structures and patterns. Familiar shared reading texts often have repeated or rhythmic text, which is easy to learn. Using shared reading texts to teach strategies and skills minilessons can be particularly supportive for English language learners because they have had the opportunity to develop familiarity with the meaning, the vocabulary, and the language structures of the text. They can focus on exploring the minilesson principle because they are not working so hard to read and understand the text. Shared reading gives them the background and familiarity with text that facilitates the learning of the minilesson principle.

Shared reading is a context that is particularly supportive to English language learners because of the enjoyable repetition and opportunity to "practice" English syntax with the support of the group. Following are some suggestions you can use to support English language learners:

> Select enlarged texts with simple illustrations.

> Select enlarged texts with easy-to-say refrains, often involving rhyme and repeating patterns.

> Reread the book as much as needed to help children become confident in joining in.

> Use some texts that lend themselves to inserting children's names or adding repetitive verses.

> Meet in a small group so learners can get "hands-on" experience pointing to words and pictures.

Guided Reading

Guided reading is small-group instruction using an appropriately selected leveled text that is at students' instructional level. This means that the text is more complex than the students can process independently, so it offers appropriate challenge.

Supportive and precise instruction with the text enables the students to read it with proficiency, and in the process they develop in-the-head strategic actions that they can apply to the reading of other texts. Guided reading involves several steps:

1. Assess students' strengths through the analysis of oral reading behaviors as well as the assessment of comprehension—thinking within, beyond, and about the text. This knowledge enables you to determine an appropriate reading level for instruction.

2. Bring together a small group of students who are approximately at the same level, so it makes sense to teach them together. (Ongoing assessment takes place in the form of running records or reading records so that the information can guide the emphasis in lessons and so that groups may be changed and reformed as needed.)

3. Based on assessment, select a text that is at students' instructional level and offers opportunities for new learning.

4. Introduce the text to the students in a way that will support reading and engage them with the text.

5. Students read the text individually. (In kindergarten, this usually means reading very quietly [whisper reading] while pointing to the words at the early text levels.) Support reading through quick interactions that use precise language to support effective processing.

6. Invite students to engage in an open-ended discussion of the text and use some guiding questions or prompts to help them extend their thinking.

7. Based on previous assessment and observation during reading, select a teaching point.

8. Engage students in quick word work that helps them flexibly apply principles for solving words that that have been selected based on information gained from the analysis of oral reading behaviors and reinforcement of principles explored in phonics minilessons (see *The Fountas & Pinnell Comprehensive Phonics, Spelling, and Word Study Guide* [2017b] and *Phonics, Spelling, and Word Study System, for Kindergarten* [2017e]).

Figure 9-5: Guided reading in a kindergarten class

9. As an option, you may have children engage in drawing and/or writing about the book to extend their understanding, but it is not necessary—or desirable—to write about every book.

Guided reading texts are not usually used as examples in minilessons because they are not texts that are shared by the entire class. You can, however, take the opportunity to reinforce the minilesson principle across the guided reading lesson at one or more points:

- In the introduction to the text, refer to a reading minilesson principle as one of the ways that you support readers before reading a new text.

- In your interactions with children during the reading of the text, remind them of the principle from the reading minilesson.

- In the discussion after the text, reinforce the minilesson principle when appropriate.

- In the teaching point, reinforce a minilesson principle.

In small-group guided reading lessons, students explore aspects of written texts that are similar to the understandings they discuss in interactive read-aloud and shared reading. They notice characters and character change, talk about where the story takes place, talk about the problem in the story and the ending, and discuss the lesson or message of the story. They talk about information they learned and questions they have, they notice genre characteristics, and they develop phonics knowledge and word-solving strategies. So, guided reading also gives readers the opportunity to apply what they have learned in reading minilessons.

ELL CONNECTION

When you support readers in applying the minilesson principle within a guided reading lesson, you give them another opportunity to talk about text with this new thinking in mind. It is particularly helpful to English language learners to have the opportunity to try out this new thinking in a small, safe setting. Guided reading can provide the opportunity to talk about the minilesson principle before the class comes back together to share. Often, they feel more confident to share their new thinking with the whole group because they have had this opportunity to practice talking about their book in the small-group setting.

Book Clubs

For a book club meeting, bring together a small group of students who have chosen the same book to read and discuss with their classmates. The book can be one that you have read to the group or one that the children can either read independently or listen to and understand from an audio recording.

The implementation of book clubs follows these steps:

1. Preselect about four books that offer opportunities for deep discussion. These books may be related in some way (for example, they might be by the same author or feature stories around a theme). Or, they might just be a group of titles that will give children good choices.

2. Give a book talk about each of the books to introduce them to children. A book talk is a short "commercial" for the book.

3. Children read and prepare for the book club discussion. If the child cannot read the book, prepare an audio version that can be used during independent reading time. Each reader marks a place or places that he wants to discuss with a sticky note.

4. Convene the group and facilitate the discussion.

5. The students self-evaluate the discussion.

Kindergarten children have much to learn about participating in a book discussion group. It's likely that this is a new experience for many of them, but you will find that kindergarteners *love* being in a book club; they prepare for it and take it seriously. They are taking the first steps toward deep, enjoyable talk with their classmates about books. In this book, one entire umbrella is devoted to teaching the routines of book clubs (see Umbrella 5: Getting Started with Book Clubs in Section Two: Literary Analysis).

A discussion among four or five diverse kindergarten students can go in many directions, and you want to hear all of their ideas! They are largely focused on using the illustrations to support their responses. *Prompting Guide, Part 2, for Comprehension: Thinking, Talking, and Writing* (Fountas and Pinnell 2016) is a helpful tool, especially the section on book discussions. The section on book discussions contains precise teacher language for getting a discussion started, asking for thinking,

Figure 9-6: Book club in a kindergarten class

affirming thinking, agreeing and disagreeing, changing thinking, clarifying thinking, extending thinking, focusing on the big ideas, making connections, paraphrasing, questioning and hypothesizing, redirecting, seeking evidence, sharing thinking, and summarizing.

To help the students learn how to hold book club discussions, consider using the fishbowl technique. Before you teach the minilesson, prepare one group of children to model the minilesson concept. During the minilesson, seat those children in the center and the rest of the children in a ring around them so that they can see and hear what is going on.

ELL CONNECTION

Book clubs offer English language learners the unique opportunity of entering into conversations about books with other children. Because they are using picture books, the images support their understanding. If they have listened to an audio recording many times, they are gaining more and more exposure to language. The language and content of the book lifts the conversation and gives them something to talk about. They learn the conventions of discourse, which become familiar because they do it many times. They can hear others talk and respond with social language, such as "I agree with_____."

Independent Reading

In independent reading, students have the opportunity to apply all they have learned in minilessons. To support independent reading, assemble a well-organized classroom library with a range of engaging fiction and nonfiction books. Although you will take into account the levels students can read independently to assure a range of options, we do *not* suggest that you arrange the books by level. It is not productive and can be destructive for the students to choose books by "level." Instead, create tubs or baskets by author, topic, genre, and so forth. There are minilessons in Section One: Management to help you teach kindergarten children how to choose books for their own reading (see Umbrella 2: Using the Classroom Library for Independent Reading).

Children may choose books for independent reading from a variety of sources:

▶ **Individual Book Bags or Boxes.** Using clear resealable bags, empty shoeboxes, or cereal boxes, help each child build an individual collection of books they want to read. Children can put their names on the bags or boxes and decorate them. These may include some books previously read in guided reading or books they have selected from the classroom library. Students can keep these individual book bags at a central place and retrieve them during independent reading time.

▶ **Browsing Boxes.** Place guided reading books or small versions of shared reading books that have been previously read, along with other books at lower levels, in a basket or box identified by a color or other means. You may put children's names on the browsing boxes they are assigned to, but these should be temporary. Children select books from the box to read. Children may read several during reading time.

▸ **Classroom Library.** The classroom library is filled with baskets or tubs of books that kindergarten students will love. Early in the year, students may spend their time revisiting books you have read aloud to them even though they cannot read the words. They can still notice the illustrations and "tell" the story or share the information based on their understandings. Shared reading books, too, are good resources in the classroom library. In some minilessons, a teacher might guide children to read from a particular basket in the classroom library so they have the opportunity to apply the reading minilesson to books that include the characteristics addressed in the minilesson. For example, she might have them read from a particular genre or author set.

Becoming independent as a reader is an essential life skill for all students. English language learners need daily opportunities to use their systems of strategic actions on text that is accessible, meaningful, and interesting to them. Here are some suggestions for helping English language learners during independent reading:

ELL CONNECTION

▸ Make sure your classroom library has a good selection of books at a range of levels. If possible, provide books in the first language of your students as well as books with familiar settings and themes.

▸ During individual conferences, help students prepare—and sometimes rehearse—something that they can share with others about the text during group share. When possible, ask them to think about the minilesson principle.

▸ Provide opportunities for English language learners to share with partners before being asked to share with the whole group.

Figure 9-7: Independent reading in a kindergarten class

Combining Implicit and Explicit Teaching for Independent Reading

You are about to embark on a highly productive year of literacy lessons. We have prepared these lessons as tools for your use as you help children engage with texts, making daily shifts in learning. When children participate in a classroom that provides a multitext approach to literacy learning, they are exposed to textual elements in a variety of instructional contexts. As described in Figure 9-1, all of these instructional contexts involve embedding literary and print concepts into authentic and meaningful experiences with text. There is a powerful combination of many concepts that are implicitly understood as children engage with books and the explicit teaching that brings them to conscious awareness and supports students' ability to articulate them using academic language.

In interactive read-aloud, children are invited to respond to text as they turn and talk and participate in lively discussions after a text is read. In interactive read-aloud, you support your students to think within, beyond, and about the text because you will have used *The Literacy Continuum* to identify when you will pause and invite these conversations and how you will ask questions and model comments to support the behaviors you have selected.

In shared reading, students learn from both implicit and explicit teaching. They first read and discuss the text several times, enjoying the book and discussing aspects of the text that support their thinking within, beyond, and about the text. Teachers often revisit the text with an explicit focus that supports thinking within the text (e.g., finding high-frequency words, words with the same initial letters). The embedded, implicit teaching, as well as some of the more explicit teaching that children experience, lays the groundwork for the explicit teaching that takes place in reading minilessons. Reading minilessons become the bridge from these shared and interactive whole-group reading experiences to independent reading.

Figure 9-8: Organize classroom library books in labeled bins so that children can find books they will enjoy reading.

Guided reading and book clubs scaffold the reading process through a combination of implicit and explicit teaching that helps children apply the reading minilesson principles across a variety of instructional-level texts. The group share reinforces the whole process. Reading minilessons do not function in the absence of these other instructional contexts; rather, they all work in concert to build processing systems for students to grow in their ability to independently read increasingly complex texts over time.

The minilessons in this book serve as a guide to a meaningful, systematic approach to joyful, literacy learning across multiple reading contexts. Children acquire a complex range of understandings. Whole-class minilessons form the "glue" that connects all of this learning, makes it explicit, and turns it over to the children to apply it to their own reading and writing. You will find that the talk and learning in those shared experiences will bring your class together as a community with a shared knowledge base. We know that you and your students will enjoy the rich experiences as you engage together in thinking, talking, and responding to a treasure chest of beautiful books. Children deserve these rich opportunities—every child, every day.

Works Cited

Asbjørnson, P. C., and Moe, J. E. 1991. *The Three Billy Goats Gruff.* Boston: Houghton Mifflin Harcourt.

Clay, Marie. 2015 [1991]. *Becoming Literate: The Construction of Inner Control.* Auckland, NZ: Global Education Systems.

Fountas, Irene C., and Gay Su Pinnell. 2006. *Teaching for Comprehending and Fluency.* Portsmouth, NH: Heinemann.

———. 2012a. *Genre Study: Teaching with Fiction and Nonfiction Books.* Portsmouth, NH: Heinemann.

———. 2012b. *Fountas & Pinnell Prompting Guide, Part 1, for Oral Reading and Early Writing.* Portsmouth, NH: Heinemann.

———. 2014. *Reader's Notebook: Primary.* Portsmouth, NH: Heinemann.

———. 2016. *Fountas & Pinnell Prompting Guide, Part 2, for Comprehension: Thinking, Talking, and Writing.* Portsmouth, NH: Heinemann.

———.2017a. *Fountas & Pinnell Classroom™.* Portsmouth, NH: Heinemann.

———. 2017b. *The Fountas & Pinnell Comprehensive Phonics, Spelling, and Word Study Guide.* Portsmouth, NH: Heinemann.

———. 2017c. *The Fountas & Pinnell Literacy Continuum: A Tool for Assessment, Planning, and Teaching.* Portsmouth, NH: Heinemann.

———. 2017d. *Guided Reading: Responsive Teaching Across the Grades.* Portsmouth, NH: Heinemann.

———. 2017e. *Phonics, Spelling, and Word Study System, for Kindergarten.* Portsmouth, NH: Heinemann.

Galdone, Paul. 2000 [1972]. *The Three Bears.* Boston: Houghton Mifflin Harcourt.

Morris, Ann. 1993. *Hats, Hats, Hats.* New York: HarperCollins.

Seibert, Patricia. 2002. *The Three Little Pigs.* Greensboro, NC: Carson-Dellosa.

Slate, Joseph. 2001. *Miss Bindergarten Gets Ready for Kindergarten.* New York: Penguin.

Slobodkina, Esphyr. 1968 [1940]. *Caps for Sale.* New York: HarperCollins.

Vygotsky, Lev. 1979. *Mind in Society: The Development of Higher Psychological Processes.* Cambridge, MA: Harvard University Press.

Section 1 | Management

Management minilessons focus on routines for thinking and talking about reading and working together in the classroom. They allow you to teach effectively and efficiently and are directed toward the creation of an orderly, busy classroom in which students know what is expected and how to behave responsibly and respectfully in a community of learners. Most of the minilessons at the beginning of the school year will focus on management.

1 Management

Minilessons in This Umbrella

RML1 Use an appropriate voice level.

RML2 Move from one spot to another quickly and silently.

RML3 Listen carefully to each other.

RML4 Do your best work.

RML5 Find ways to solve problems when you need help.

RML6 Take good care of classroom materials.

Before Teaching Umbrella 1 Minilessons

This set of minilessons helps you establish a respectful, caring, and organized classroom community (see pages 27–29). In addition to explicitly teaching routines through minilessons, provide regular and frequent times to read aloud and talk about books. Interactive read-aloud is a community-building experience that teaches children to communicate their thinking about books as well as to listen carefully and respond to others in respectful ways. Read from your own library or use books from the *Fountas & Pinnell Classroom™ Interactive Read-Aloud Collection* to discuss what it means to be part of a caring community.

Create a warm and inviting student-centered classroom in which children can take ownership of their own space and materials and do their best work:

▶ Designate a whole-group meeting area where the class gathers to think and learn together. Consider a colorful rug with a spot for each member of the class.

▶ Post a daily schedule so children know what to expect each day.

▶ Find appropriate places throughout the classroom to house materials and supplies.

▶ Place only one type of materials/supplies in each container.

▶ Organize and label both the materials and the shelves so children can access and return supplies independently.

▶ Allow many opportunities for the children to choose books from the classroom library.

▶ Set up a regular time each day for children to read books. Many kindergarten children will be able to "read" the pictures and tell the stories after hearing them read aloud.

Reading Minilesson Principle
Use an appropriate voice level.

Working Together in the Classroom

You Will Need

▶ chart paper
▶ markers
▶ sticky notes

Academic Language / Important Vocabulary

▶ voice level
▶ appropriate

Continuum Connection

▶ Speak at an appropriate volume (p. 331)

Goal

Learn to monitor appropriate voice level.

Rationale

Voice volume needs to be taught explicitly so that children are able to independently determine the acceptable noise level for various settings, routines, and activities both inside and outside of the classroom.

Assess Learning

Observe children in a variety of learning activities. Notice if there is evidence of new learning based on the goal of this minilesson.

▶ Are children able to explain why voice level matters?
▶ Can they identify appropriate activities for each voice level?
▶ Are they able to use the appropriate level voice during independent reading time?
▶ Can they accurately evaluate whether they used the appropriate voice level?
▶ Do children imderstand the terms *voice level* and *appropriately*?

Minilesson

To help children think about the minilesson principle, engage them in talking about voice levels and constructing a reference chart. Here is an example.

▶ Talk about why a loud voice is sometimes appropriate and why a soft voice is better sometimes.

> One way to help each other do your best work in the classroom is to use an appropriate voice for the activity you are doing. For example, when you are outside for recess, would you use a loud voice or a soft voice?

> When you work in the classroom, how might your voice sound? Why?

▶ Record responses of someone being quiet.

> We can talk about the kind of voice to use by using a number. A 0 voice means that you are quiet; you are not saying anything.

▶ Write the numeral 0 on a sticky note and ask a child to place it under the picture on the chart that shows someone being quiet.

▶ Repeat the procedure for each voice level on the chart until the chart is made. Show that a 1 means whispering, a 2 means using a soft voice, and a 3 means using a loud voice.

Have a Try

Invite the children to talk about voice level.

▶ Call out a voice level number or activity name and have the children practice by saying hello using the appropriate voice level.

Summarize and Apply

Have the children practice the new instructional routine in an authentic learning situation.

▶ Review the voice chart.

> Look at our chart. What does it show you about which voice level to use?
>
> Now you are going to read books by yourself. Which voice level will you use?
>
> Your voice will be a level 0. It will be silent while you read by yourself.

▶ Some children will not be able to read silently yet. Instead, they will use a quiet whisper voice, or just move their lips.

▶ Make sure each child has one or more books to read during independent work time. Explain that they can read some books but other books may have words they can't read yet. They can look at the pictures and think about or tell the story or the information.

Share

Following independent work time, gather children in the meeting area to talk about their voice level while reading.

▶ Have children give a thumbs-up if they used a level 0 voice while they were reading.

> When you are inside or outside the classroom, think about whether you are using an appropriate voice for what you are doing.

Extend the Lesson (Optional)

After assessing children's understanding, you might decide to extend the learning.

▶ Review, practice, and evaluate voice levels before and after an activity.

▶ Add labels of activities to the chart, such as the following: for level 0: read to self; for level 1: read to partner; for level 2: read to partner; for level 3: play outside.

▶ Invite a few children to draw illustrations for the voice levels on the chart.

Reading Minilesson Principle

Move from one spot to another quickly and silently.

You Will Need

- chart paper and markers
- voice level chart [see page 73]

Academic Language / Important Vocabulary

- meeting area

Goal

Learn routines for classroom transitions.

Rationale

Setting clear expectations for transitions in the classroom increases time spent on learning.

Assess Learning

Observe children in a variety of learning situations. Notice if there is evidence of new learning based on the goal of this minilesson.

- Are children able to describe how to move during transitions?
- Can they identify the appropriate voice level for moving around the classroom?

Minilesson

To help children think about the minilesson principle, engage them in a demonstration and discussion of transition. Here is an example.

> You work in all different places in the classroom. Sometimes you sit at tables. Sometimes everyone comes to the meeting area. Why should you move quickly and silently when you move from one place to another?
>
> Why is it helpful to find and sit in your own spot?

- Invite three children to show how to go from the meeting area back to the tables quickly and silently.

  > We are going to watch _____, _____, and _____ walk from the meeting area back to the tables. Remember to walk quickly and silently, but do not run.

- Point out the voice chart.

  > Let's look at the voice chart. What voice level did they use when they moved from one area to another?

- Record a 0 on the chart.

  > What did you notice about the way they moved from one spot to another?

- Chart responses.

- Invite the three children to walk back to the meeting area.

  > Where did they put their hands and feet when they sat down in their spots?

- Chart responses.

Have a Try

Invite the children to apply the new thinking about moving from one spot to another.

> Now everyone will have a chance to practice moving about the classroom.

▶ Have children walk to their tables. Give a signal to come back to the meeting area.

▶ Ask children to use the chart to evaluate the transition.

Summarize and Apply

Have the children practice the new instructional routine in an authentic learning situation.

> What did you learn about moving from one spot to another? Look at the chart to remember what we talked about. Today, when you go to your place for reading time, walk quickly with a 0 voice. We will talk about how you did when we come back together.

> When it's time to come back to group meeting, put your materials away carefully and move quickly and silently.

Share

Following independent work time, gather children together in the meeting area to talk moving from one spot to another.

> Give a thumbs-up if you walked to your spot in the meeting area quickly and silently.

▶ Call on a few children to share.

> Raise your hand to share one thing you will remember to do the next time you come to the meeting area.

Extend the Lesson (Optional)

After assessing children's understanding, you might decide to extend the learning.

▶ Reinforce the routines by reviewing the chart immediately before instructing children to move to a new area in the classroom.

▶ Teach specific behaviors to support learning during whole-group instruction (for example, eye contact, body position).

▶ Teach children how to self-select spots on the rug efficiently and politely. Provide guidance at first by marking children's names on the floor with masking tape. After time, you can replace the names with letters or high-frequency words, assigning a child to each letter or word.

How to Move from One Spot to Another

Walk quickly, but do not run.

Use a 0 level voice.

Keep your hands and feet in your own space.

Section 1: Management

Reading Minilesson Principle
Listen carefully to each other.

You Will Need

- voice level chart (see page 73)
- chart paper and markers
- sticky notes

Academic Language / Important Vocabulary

- listen
- meeting area
- small group
- whole group

Continuum Connection

- Look at the speaker when being spoken to (p. 331)

- Speak at an appropriate volume (p. 331)

Goal

Learn expectations for listening during small- or whole-group meetings.

Rationale

When children listen to their peers during small- or whole-group instruction, they become effective communicators and collaborators.

Assess Learning

Observe children in a variety of learning situations. Notice if there is evidence of new learning based on the goal of this minilesson.

> Do the children understand why it is important to start working right away? Do they understand what it means to stay focused?

> Are they able to articulate a goal for doing their best work?

> Can they follow the expectations on the chart while working independently?

> Do they understand the terms *listen, meeting area, small group,* and *whole group?*

Minilesson

To help children think about the minilesson principle, engage them in discussing effective listening behaviors. Here is an example.

> Why is it important to listen carefully to one another when we meet together? When you listen to each other, you can do your best learning.

> Let's think about some ways you show you are listening when we read and talk about books. When someone is talking, what is everyone else doing?

> You should look at the speaker and raise your hand to talk.

> Record responses on a chart.

> What do you do when you turn and talk?

> Show the voice level chart from RML1.

> Which voice level should the person who is speaking use? You use a 2 voice in whole-group meeting.

> Which voice level do you use when someone else is talking? Use a 0 voice so you can think about what the person is saying.

Have a Try

Invite the children to talk with a partner about how to listen carefully.

> Turn and talk with your partner about something you will do the next time you listen to someone speak during group meeting.

Summarize and Apply

Summarize the learning and remind children to listen carefully to each other.

> What are some ways to show that you are listening carefully? Look at the chart to remember.

> During reading time today, find a page in your book that you think is interesting. Put a sticky note on it so that you can share it in group meeting.

Share

Following independent work time, gather children together in the meeting area to talk about how they listened carefully to each other.

▶ Invite a few children to share.

> A few people are going to share an interesting part of the book they read and tell why they chose it. Remember to show that you are listening.

▶ Invite the children to evaluate their sharing and listening using the chart.

Extend the Lesson (Optional)

After assessing children's understanding, you might decide to extend the learning.

▶ Over the next several days, review the chart How to Listen and Learn in Group Meeting each time the class gathers in the meeting area or meets in a small group. Continue to review the guidelines as needed.

▶ Reinforce behaviors by noticing specific ways children are following the expectations during whole-group instruction.

How to Listen and Learn in a Group Meeting

Think about what you hear.

I have a question.

Look at the speaker.

Raise your hand to talk.

Use a 2 voice.

Listen carefully.

Reading Minilesson Principle
Do your best work.

You Will Need

- four children prepared in advance to demonstrate the principle
- paper, pencils, and crayons
- chart paper and markers

Academic Language / Important Vocabulary

- focus

Goal

Learn ways to work well in the class.

Rationale

Teaching children explicitly to begin work promptly, work quietly, stay focused, and follow directions promotes independence. Setting the foundation early for independent work frees you to work effectively with children individually and in small groups.

Assess Learning

Observe children in a variety of learning activities. Notice if there is evidence of new learning based on the goal of this minilesson.

- ▶ Are they able to articulate a goal for doing their best work?
- ▶ Can they follow the expectations on the chart while working independently?
- ▶ Do they follow directions and work quietly?
- ▶ Do children understand the word *focus*?

Minilesson

To help children think about the minilesson principle, engage children in discussing how to do their best work. Here is an example.

> The work you do by yourself is important. Let's watch your classmates do their best work.

- ▶ Give directions to the four children you have prepared in advance to go to their tables and start drawing a picture. Have the rest of the class observe just long enough to see the four children get started promptly and focus on their work. Call the four children back to the meeting area.

> What did you notice about how they worked?

- ▶ Record children's responses on the chart paper.

> They got started right away, worked quietly, stayed focused, and followed directions. They put their materials away carefully and moved silently and quickly to our meeting area.

Have a Try

Invite the children to talk with a partner about what they can do to do their best learning.

- ▶ Read the chart aloud.

> Think about what you need to practice the most. Turn and talk to a partner about your goal for doing your best work. You can start by saying, "I am going to try to . . ."

- ▶ After they turn and talk, invite a few children to share with the whole group.

Summarize and Apply

Summarize the learning and remind children to think about doing their best work.

▶ Review the chart with the children.

> What did you learn today about how to do your best work? Look at the chart to remember.

> Today during independent work time, you can practice all the ways to do your best work.

Share

Following independent work time, gather children together in the meeting area to talk about how they did their best work.

> Give a thumbs-up if you began right away, worked quietly, stayed focused on your work, and followed directions.

▶ Invite a few children to share how they did their best work.

Extend the Lesson (Optional)

After assessing children's understanding, you might decide to extend the learning.

▶ Reinforce routines by frequently reviewing the chart Do Your Best Work.

▶ Provide accommodations for children who need support getting started or staying focused. For example, you might check in with them before or between small groups.

▶ Review the routines by having children model getting started quickly and staying focused for different activities.

Do your best work!
- Begin right away.
- Work quietly.
- Stay focused.
- Follow directions.

I did my best work!

Reading Minilesson Principle
Find ways to solve problems when you need help.

**Working Together
in the Classroom**

You Will Need

- chart paper and markers
- sticky notes

Academic Language / Important Vocabulary

- directions
- word wall
- classmate

Goal

Learn how to problem solve independently.

Rationale

When children learn how to collaborate and problem solve independently, they gain confidence and agency. It also allows you to work with small groups or individuals without interruption.

Assess Learning

Observe children in a variety of learning activities. Notice if there is evidence of new learning based on the goal of this minilesson.

- ▶ Are children able to try one or two ideas for problem solving independently?
- ▶ Are the ways children try to solve a problem appropriate?
- ▶ Do they understand the terms *directions, word wall,* and *classmate?*

Minilesson

To help children think about the minilesson principle, engage them in a discussion of how to problem solve independently. Here is an example.

> Sometimes when you are working, you may need help. When I am talking to another student or working with a group, I may not be available to help you right away.
>
> What are some things you can do to get help on your own?

▶ Record ideas on chart paper. If children have trouble generating ideas, help them think through different scenarios. For example, if they don't know how to spell a word, where could they look to find out? Lead them to think of resources in the room they can use and to understand that they can ask a classmate or, as a last resort, you.

> If you have done some of the work and are stuck, what could you do while you are waiting for help?

Have a Try

Invite the children to apply the new thinking with a partner.

- ▶ Invite a few children to act out the following scenarios:
  - You need to cut some paper, but you can't find the scissors.
  - You are not sure how to play a game.
  - You forgot how to write your name on your paper.
  - You are finished with your work and don't know what to do next.
- ▶ For each scenario, ask the children to turn and talk with a partner about how they could solve the problem on their own.

Summarize and Apply

Summarize the learning and remind children to think about how to solve problems.

> Look at the chart. What does it help you know how to do?

▶ Write the principle on the chart.

▶ For each scenario in Have a Try, ask one or two children to share what they talked about. Refer to the chart as appropriate.

> If you need help with your work, try to solve the problem yourself, ask a classmate, or do your best until the teacher is finished.

▶ Emphasize that they should try very hard to solve the problem before they ask others. Explain that if it is an emergency, such as someone is sick or hurt, they should tell the teacher immediately.

Share

Following independent work time, gather children together in the meeting area to talk about how they solved problems.

> Raise your hand if you needed help while you were working. How did you solve your problem?

Extend the Lesson (Optional)

After assessing children's understanding, you might decide to extend the learning.

▶ Revisit the chart prior to the beginning of any independent work.

▶ Add to the chart when a literacy center or work station is introduced.

Find ways to solve problems when you need help.

Reread the directions.

Use the word wall.

Ask a classmate in a soft voice.

Ask the teacher when she is not busy.

Reading Minilesson Principle
Take good care of classroom materials.

Working Together in the Classroom

You Will Need

- two children prepared in advance to demonstrate
- materials for activity in the meeting area
- chart paper and markers

Academic Language / Important Vocabulary

- materials
- observe

Goal

Learn to take care of and return materials and supplies independently.

Rationale

Teaching children how to take care of materials and return them to the same place promotes responsibility and independence and enables others to use materials when they need them.

Assess Learning

Observe children when they use classroom materials. Notice if there is evidence of new learning based on the goal of this minilesson.

- Do the children take good care of classroom materials?
- Are they able to get materials and return them to the appropriate place?
- Do they clean up quickly and quietly?

Minilesson

To help children think about the minilesson principle, engage them in a discussion of the different materials they use and where to find them. Here is an example.

> What are some of the materials you use to do your work in the classroom?
>
> Let's watch _____ and _____ get the materials they need for their work. Pay attention to what they do with the materials when they finish working.

- Provide a few minutes for the children to demonstrate getting and returning the supplies. Point out that the materials are labeled at the place they belong. Remind the children how to take good care of the materials.

  > What did you notice?
  >
  > How can your classmates take good care of the materials when they use them?

- Chart responses. If you have shelves and materials boxes labeled, show children how to match a materials box to its label on the shelf.

  > How should the classroom sound when you are cleaning up? At the end of a work time, return materials quickly and quietly.

Have a Try

Invite the children to practice taking care of classroom materials.

- Ask a few more children to model taking out different supplies and returning them. Have them explain how they can take care of the materials when they use them.

Summarize and Apply

Have the children practice the new routine in an authentic learning situation.

▶ Reread the chart.

It is important to get, care for, and return materials to the place where they belong so others can use them. Today when you are finished working, think about what you will do with the materials.

▶ During independent work time, monitor how children treat classroom materials, including books.

Share

Following independent work time, gather children in the meeting area to talk about how they returned materials.

Show a thumbs-up if you took care of the materials you used today.

Show a thumbs-up if you returned the materials to the place where they belong.

Did you return the materials quickly and quietly? Show a thumbs-up, thumbs-middle, or thumbs-down.

Extend the Lesson (Optional)

After assessing children's understanding, you might decide to extend the learning.

▶ Revisit the chart as needed.

▶ As a literacy center or work station is introduced, explain where various materials belong.

▶ Use interactive or shared writing to label bins that hold materials.

Take good care
of classroom materials.

* Get your materials.

* Use them carefully.

* Put materials back in the
  same place quickly and quietly.

Section 1: Management

Assessment

After you have taught the minilessons in this umbrella, observe children in a variety of classroom activities.

▶ What evidence do you have that they understand how to work well as a classroom community?

- Are children easily finding their spots in the meeting area?
- Are they actively listening when their teacher and peers are speaking?
- Do they move quickly and quietly from one place in the classroom to another?
- Do they start new work right away and stay focused?
- Do they follow directions?
- Do they work quietly?
- Are they using other resources for help besides the teacher?
- Are they taking good care of classroom materials and supplies?
- Are they returning materials and supplies and keeping the classroom clean and organized?
- Do they use vocabulary such as *voice level*, *materials*, and *meeting area*?

▶ What minilessons might you teach next to continue to build a respectful and responsible community of readers?

Use your observations to determine the next umbrella you will teach. You may also consult Minilessons Across the Year (p. 51) for guidance.

Minilessons in This Umbrella

RML1   Take good care of the books in the classroom library.

RML2   The classroom library is organized to find good books.

RML3   Choose books that you want to read.

RML4   Read quietly so everyone can enjoy reading.

RML5   Return your book to the same basket.

Before Teaching Umbrella 2 Minilessons

Before teaching this series of management minilessons, provide children with several opportunities to choose books from your classroom library. They will benefit from having opportunities to read quietly and explore books independently and with partners. One of the minilessons in this umbrella focuses on the importance of reading quietly during independent reading. (If children cannot yet read silently, they can read very softly or just move their lips.) Before teaching this minilesson, introduce children to the idea of appropriate voice levels inside and outside of the classroom (see pages 72–73 for a minilesson on developing a voice chart). Here are some suggestions for making your classroom library an inviting and organized space for children to select and explore books:

▸ Organize books into tubs or baskets in a way that allows children to see the front covers and provides easy access for browsing.

▸ Within each basket, display high-quality and interesting books that vary in size and genre and offer a range of difficulty.

▸ Label tubs and baskets with the topic, author, series, genre, or illustrator.

▸ If support is needed, put a colored dot on the basket label and a dot of the same color on the back of each book so children can easily return the books.

▸ Provide an empty basket in which children can place books if they are unsure where to return them.

▸ Take the children on a tour of the classroom library so they know it is a valued and beloved space in their classroom community.

Reading Minilesson Principle
Take good care of the books in the classroom library.

Using the Classroom Library for Independent Reading

You Will Need

- basket or tub of books from the classroom library
- chart paper and markers

Academic Language / Important Vocabulary

- classroom library
- pages

Goal

Take care of books in the classroom library.

Rationale

Teaching children to handle books with care promotes independence and a sense of responsibility in the classroom community.

Assess Learning

Observe children when they read books. Notice if there is evidence of new learning based on the goal of this minilesson.

- Do children hold a book with two hands and turn the pages carefully?
- Can they explain why it is important to handle books properly?
- Do they use the terms *classroom library* and *pages?*

Minilesson

To help children think about the minilesson principle, talk with them about how to care for books. Here is an example.

> What are some ways you take good care of the books from the classroom library?

- Record children's responses on the chart paper.

> I'm going to choose a book to read. Watch what I do when I hold and read my book.

- Model holding the book with two hands and turning the pages carefully.

> What did you see me do as I read my book?

> Why do you think it is important to hold books with two hands and turn the pages carefully?

Have a Try

Invite the children to practice taking good care of books with a partner.

- Pass out a book to each pair of children.

> Now you will work with a partner. First, one partner will hold the book with two hands and turn the pages carefully. Then, the other partner will have a turn.

- Give a signal to stop and put the book down.

> Give a thumbs-up if you and your partner held the book with two hands and turned the pages carefully.

Summarize and Apply

Summarize the learning and remind the children to think about how to take good care of books as they read.

> Today you learned some of the ways to take good care of the books in the classroom library.
>
> When you read your book today, be gentle and keep the book clean. Make sure you use two hands and turn the pages carefully. When we come back together, you can share how you took good care of your book while you were reading.

Share

Following independent work time, gather children in the meeting area to talk about how they took care of their books while they read.

▶ Have children bring their books as you come back together to share.

> Today we talked about ways you can take good care of the books in our classroom. Who would like to show how to hold a book carefully while you read?

▶ Choose a few children to demonstrate.

Extend the Lesson (Optional)

After assessing children's understanding, you might decide to extend the learning.

▶ Reinforce the behavior by noticing when children handle their books carefully during independent reading.

Taking Good Care of Books

- Be gentle.

- Keep the book clean.

- Hold the book with 2 hands.

- Turn the pages carefully.

Reading Minilesson Principle
The classroom library is organized to find good books.

Using the Classroom Library for Independent Reading

You Will Need

▶ several sets of books from the classroom library that can be grouped by author, illustrator, or topic (e.g., animal books, sports books, nature books)

▶ book baskets

▶ sticky notes

▶ chart paper and markers

Academic Language / Important Vocabulary

▶ topic

▶ author

▶ illustrator

▶ classroom library

Continuum Connection

▶ Connect text by obvious categories: e.g., author, character, topic, genre, illustrator (p. 28)

Goal

Understand that the classroom library is organized to help make good book choices.

Rationale

Children need to understand how the classroom library is organized so they can select books they want to read. When you involve children in the organization, they develop a sense of ownership and responsibility for maintaining the classroom library. They also learn how to sort and categorize books, which supports them in making connections among different texts.

Assess Learning

Observe children when they talk about the classroom library. Notice if there is evidence of new learning based on the goal of this minilesson.

▶ Can the children identify how books are alike?

▶ Can they articulate how books in the classroom library are organized? Do they understand that books are sometimes organized by topic, author, or illustrator?

▶ Do they understand the terms *topic, author, illustrator,* and *classroom library?*

Minilesson

To help children think about the minilesson principle, engage them in sorting books Here is an example.

▶ Select four or five books on two topics from your classroom library (for example, books about animals and books about sports). Spread these books out in front of the children.

> Take a look at these books from the classroom library.

▶ Read several titles aloud.

> How could we put them into these two baskets so that you know what kind of books are in the baskets?

▶ Place books in each basket according to the children's responses. You can temporarily label each basket with a sticky note so you and/or the children can make a permanent label for the basket at another time.

> One way to organize books is to put together books about the same thing, or topic. The topic is what a book is all about, like horses or volcanoes.

▶ Write the word *topic* on the chart paper. Write or draw examples of the topics of the books you sorted.

▶ Repeat the process with a group of books by the same author. Read aloud the titles and author's name.

▶ Place all the books by the same author in a basket and temporarily label the basket with the author's name. Write the word *author* on the chart.

You could also put together books that have the same illustrator. Write *illustrator* on the chart paper.

Have a Try

Invite the children to apply the new thinking about how the classroom library is organized.

▶ Hold up books that belong in each of the three baskets you created. As you hold up a book, ask children which basket it belongs in and why.

Summarize and Apply

Summarize the learning and remind children to think about how the classroom library is organized.

> Today you learned that the classroom library is organized to help you make good book choices.

> When you read today, choose books from the baskets that have books on the topics you like or books by authors and illustrators you enjoy.

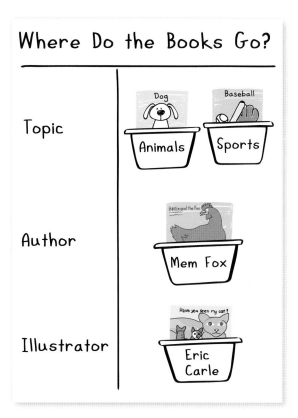

Share

Following independent work time, gather children in the meeting area to talk about how the classroom library is organized.

> Who would like to share the book you chose and where it came from?

▶ Add any new topics or ideas to the chart, such as series, characters, or poetry.

Extend the Lesson (Optional)

After assessing children's understanding, you might decide to extend the learning.

▶ When the children are ready, repeat this lesson with other categories.

▶ Take children on a tour of the classroom library to view baskets that you have already organized.

▶ Create a basket of favorite read-alouds and place books in it you have read to the class.

▶ **Drawing/Writing About Reading** Use interactive or shared writing to create labels for the baskets in the classroom library.

Reading Minilesson Principle
Choose books that you want to read.

Using the Classroom Library for Independent Reading

You Will Need

- four or five baskets of books from the classroom library
- chart paper and markers

Academic Language / Important Vocabulary

- front cover
- illustrations
- topics

Continuum Connection

- Articulate why they like a text (p. 28)

Goal

Learn how to choose a book for independent reading.

Rationale

As children learn different ways to choose books, they not only become more independent but also begin to develop their own interests and identities as readers.

Assess Learning

Observe children during independent reading time. Notice if there is evidence of new learning based on the goal of this minilesson.

- ▶ Do the children choose books by looking at the front cover and pictures?
- ▶ Can they explain what they like about the front cover and pictures?
- ▶ Do they use the terms *front cover, illustrations,* and *topics?*

Minilesson

To help children think about the minilesson principle, engage them in a discussion of how to choose books they want to read. Here is an example.

- ▶ Select three or four children to choose a book from the baskets. While they are selecting, ask the other children to think silently about some of the ways they choose books.
- ▶ Once the children have chosen their books, ask them to share how they made their choices.

   What were you thinking about when you chose your book? What made you want to read it?

- ▶ Record children's responses on chart paper. Ask the rest of the children to share their thinking.

   What are some other ways you choose books you want to read?

Have a Try

Invite the children to talk about choosing a book with a partner.

- ▶ Have children turn and talk to a partner about how they will choose a book to read.

   Look at the chart. Tell your partner how you might choose a book today for reading time.

Summarize and Apply

Remind the children to think about choosing books they want to read.

> Let's look at the chart. What are some ways you can choose a book to read?

> When you choose a book to read today, think about some of the ways you can choose a book you think you will enjoy.

Share

Following independent work time, gather children together in the meeting area to talk about the books they chose.

> Turn to your partner and tell why you chose your book.

> Give a thumbs-up if you enjoyed your book. Who would like to share the book and tell why you chose it?

Extend the Lesson (Optional)

After assessing your children's understanding, you might decide to extend the learning.

▶ Add to the chart (for example, books that have won awards, have favorite characters, or are funny) as children discover more ways to choose books.

▶ Build in opportunities during share time for children to tell about books they enjoy so other children might choose books based on classmates' recommendations.

▶ **Drawing/Writing About Reading** Introduce parts of *Reader's Notebook: Primary* (Fountas and Pinnell 2014) or have children set up pages in a plain notebook to start developing their reading identities and interests (for example, write and draw about things they like to read about, books they love, things they like to do). You may want to refer to Section Four: Writing About Reading for more ideas.

RML4
MGT.U2.RML4

Reading Minilesson Principle
Read quietly so everyone can enjoy reading.

Using the Classroom Library for Independent Reading

You Will Need

- a book for every child to read or look at
- voice level chart (see page 73)

Academic Language / Important Vocabulary

- independent reading
- classroom library

Goal

Learn to manage voice levels in different instructional contexts.

Rationale

Learning to speak at the appropriate volume in different instructional contexts is part of being a respectful member of the class. Teaching children to read quietly helps them learn to be respectful of their classmates, who will be able to read and think better in a quiet classroom. Children (reading at about level C or D and above) who can read completely silently should be encouraged to, but most beginning kindergarten children will not be able to and will need to be coached on how to read very quietly.

Assess Learning

Observe children during independent reading. Notice if there is evidence of new learning based on the goal of this minilesson.

- Do the children read silently or with a whisper voice during independent reading?
- Are they able to self-evaluate the voice level they used during independent reading?
- Do they understand the terms *independent reading* and *classroom library?*

Minilesson

To help children think about the minilesson principle, engage them in a short demonstration of reading quietly. Here is an example.

- Make sure every child has a book. Then, ask the class to start looking at the book or reading it silently (or in a whisper read if they are reading at about levels A–C or D) while seated in the meeting area. After a couple of minutes, signal for the children's attention.

    Were you enjoying reading your book? How did it sound in the classroom when everyone was reading?

    Look at the voice chart. Who can point to where independent reading is on this chart?

- Help children use the first picture to figure out that reading time should be at the quietest level, with the exception of whisper reading, which is between 0 and 1. You may choose to add a symbol of a book under the 0 to represent independent reading.

    Why do you think it is important to read silently or at a whisper when you are reading books by yourself?

Have a Try

Invite children to talk with a partner about appropriate voice levels.

> Choose a voice level on the chart. Turn and tell your partner what the level is and when it would be appropriate to use it.

Summarize and Apply

Summarize the learning and remind children to read quietly so everyone can enjoy reading.

> What kind of voice should you use when reading?

▶ Ask a child to point to the appropriate voice level on the chart.

> While you are reading today, remember to read silently or with a whisper voice.

Share

Following independent work time, gather children together in the meeting area to talk about their reading.

> Give a thumbs-up if you read quietly today.

▶ Ask one or two children to share how reading quietly helped them.

Extend the Lesson (Optional)

After assessing your children's understanding, you might decide to extend the learning over several days.

▶ Notice when children are reading silently or with a whisper voice and reinforce the behavior.

▶ Routinely ask children to self-assess their voice levels after reading independently.

▶ **Drawing/Writing About Reading** Use shared writing to add activities (for example, reading independently, talking with a partner, at recess) to the voice chart to reinforce appropriate voice levels.

RML5
MGT.U2.RML5

Reading Minilesson Principle
Return your book to the same basket.

Using the Classroom Library for Independent Reading

You Will Need

- baskets or tubs of books from the classroom library
- chart paper and markers
- three or four loose books that belong in the baskets

Academic Language / Important Vocabulary

- classroom library

Goal

Learn to put books back in the same basket.

Rationale

Teaching children to return materials to where they belong promotes responsibility and independence, allowing you more time to work effectively with individuals and small groups.

Assess Learning

Observe children during independent reading time. Notice if there is evidence of new learning based on the goal of this minilesson.

- Do children put their books back in the same place when they finished reading?

Minilesson

To help children think about the minilesson principle, provide a short demonstration. Here is an example.

- Invite two children to come up and each choose a book to read from the baskets you have selected from classroom library. Have the children sit in front of the class with their books.

  Did you notice the baskets your classmates took their books from?

  What will your classmates do with these books when they finish reading them?

- Invite the two children to put their books back in the baskets.

  What did you notice about where they put their books? How did they place the books in the basket? They put the books back in the same baskets that they took them from, face front and right side up. When you choose a book, make sure to notice where you got it from so you can put it back in the same place.

- If you have colored stickers on your books that match the labels on the baskets, explain how the stickers can help children find which basket each book belongs in. You may also want to introduce an empty basket labeled with a "?" for children to use when they don't know where a book belongs.

  What do you notice about every basket in the library?

  What can you do to make sure that the books are easy to see in the baskets?

- Make a chart of ideas for how best to return books to baskets, such as placing them right side up and with the covers face front.

Have a Try

Invite the children to practice returning a book.

▶ Hold up a book that belongs in one of the baskets used previously.

> Who can put this book in the right basket?
>
> How did you know where to put it?
>
> How did you put it in the basket?

▶ Repeat the process with several other books.

Summarize and Apply

Summarize the learning and remind children to return their books to the same basket.

> Today you learned to take a book from a basket and return it to the same place right side up and face front.

▶ Read the chart with the children.

> If you finish reading a book today, think about what to do with it when you are finished reading.
> Find the right place to put it back and place it the right way.

Share

Following independent work time, gather children in the meeting area to talk about returning their books.

> Give a thumbs-up if you finished a book today. What did you do with your book when you were finished reading?
>
> How did you put your book in the basket?

▶ Call on a few children to share how they knew where to put their books when they were finished reading.

Extend the Lesson (Optional)

After assessing children's understanding, you might decide to extend the learning.

▶ Notice when children put books back in the same place so you can reinforce the behavior.

▶ Build in time at the end of independent reading to evaluate the way children have taken and returned books.

Returning a Book

Put it back in the same basket.

Put it right side up.

Put it face front.

Hallie and the Fox

Mem Fox

Assessment

After you have taught the minilessons in this umbrella, observe your children as they choose books from the classroom library.

▶ What evidence do you have that they understand how to use and respect the classroom library?

- Do children handle books carefully, holding the books with two hands and gently turning pages?

- In what ways are they choosing books?

- Do they show respect for others by reading silently or in a whisper voice?

- What do you notice about how they return books to the baskets in the classroom library?

- Do they use academic language, such as *author, illustrator,* and *front cover?*

▶ What minilessons might you want to teach next to continue to build independence in reading?

Use your observations to determine the next umbrella you will teach. You may also consult Minilessons Across the Year (p. 51) for guidance.

Link to Writing

After teaching the minilessons in this umbrella, help children link the new learning to their own writing or drawing about reading:

▶ Consult the Writing About Reading minilessons in Section Four to think about how you might teach children to use a reader's notebook to assist them in making good book choices.

▶ Using interactive or shared writing, teach children how to write a book recommendation to share with their classmates.

Minilessons in This Umbrella

RML1	Read a book from the classroom library or your book box.
RML2	Listen to a book in the listening center.
RML3	Work on words in the word work center.
RML4	Write and draw in the writing center.
RML5	Read a book from your browsing box.
RML6	Read and illustrate a poem for your poetry notebook.
RML7	Read around the room with a pointer.
RML8	Read and put together a story, song, or poem in the pocket chart.
RML9	Read a book with a partner.
RML10	Look at your list to know what to do during reading time.

Before Teaching Umbrella 3 Minilessons

In these minilessons, teach children how to follow a work board and rotate through centers, though each minilesson can be easily modified if you prefer to have children work at their tables rather than at centers. Whether you have centers or not, introduce the literacy activities one at a time and make sure children understand the routines before introducing more. Plan on three to four weeks to get the centers presented here up and running on the work board.

Before teaching the minilessons in this umbrella, design classroom space to facilitate easy transitions and smooth movement between activity areas.

▶ Display and organize books in an inviting way in your classroom library. (See page 28.)

▶ Develop a writing center with organized, labeled supplies.

▶ Determine where you will store individual book boxes. Consider placing them in different parts of the classroom to avoid congestion when children use the boxes.

▶ Create a space for children to listen to audiobooks. Unless each child has reliable earbuds or headphones, select a space where children can listen to a device with a speaker without disturbing others.

Reading Minilesson Principle
Read a book from the classroom library or your book box.

Engaging in Classroom
Literacy Work

You Will Need

▸ two children prepared to
demonstrate reading from
individual book boxes [see page 64
for information on book boxes]

▸ independent reading icon

▸ work board [optional]

▸ individual book boxes/bags with
familiar books and books you know
children can read

▸ chart paper and markers

To download the following online
resources for this lesson, visit
resources.fountasandpinnell.com:

▸ independent reading icon

Academic Language /
Important Vocabulary

▸ book box or bag

▸ classroom library

▸ work board

▸ independent reading

Goal

Learn procedures for independent reading, including the use of the classroom library or individual book boxes.

Rationale

Children need to know where they can find books to read during independent reading time. The two main options are the classroom library and individual book boxes or clear, sealable bags. Umbrella 2: Using the Classroom Library for Independent Reading addresses the use of the library. But children need explicit teaching of the procedures for using individual book boxes or bags for independent reading. When you teach them how to manage their time and materials independently, they develop confidence and agency and you are free to work with other children.

Assess Learning

Observe children when they read books from their personal book boxes. Notice if there is evidence of new learning based on the goal of this minilesson.

▸ Do children quickly and quietly retrieve the book boxes and begin reading?

▸ Can children very quietly read several short books from front to back?

▸ Do they place books upright with the cover facing forward and return the boxes to where they found them?

▸ Do they know and use vocabulary related to independent reading?

Minilesson

To help children think about the minilesson principle, engage the children in a short demonstration of using a book box or bag for independent reading. Here is an example.

▸ Whether you are using a work board or list of activities, you can use an icon to indicate an activity. Show children the independent reading icon.

> When you see this picture, it means it is time for independent reading. Sometimes you will choose books to read from the classroom library and sometimes you will read from your book box [or a clear, sealable bag].

▸ Show children a book box. Point out where the book boxes (or bags) are kept in the classroom and how the books are placed in the box (upright and facing forward).

▸ Invite two children to show how they get their book boxes, read a page silently or in a very quiet whisper, and return the boxes.

> Let's watch _____ and _____ read from their book boxes.

▸ Ask questions to help children notice how the children got their book boxes and read. Then ask what they did when they finished reading.

▶ Summarize the responses on chart paper.

> It is important to choose four (or the number of books you think is feasible) books and read each one from the front to the back before you put them back in your book box (or bag).

Have a Try

Invite the children to apply the new thinking with a partner.

▶ Point to the independent reading icon on the work board or list.

> Turn and talk to a partner about what you are going to do with your book box when you see this picture.

Summarize and Apply

Have the children practice the new instructional routine in an authentic learning situation.

▶ Point to the independent reading icon on the work board or list.

> You learned that when you see this picture, it means it is time for independent reading. Today during independent reading, you will read books from your book box.

▶ Review the chart quickly. Invite children to get their book boxes and provide a short period for children to read.

▶ Call them back together before children lose focus, so they can feel successful at this task.

Share

Following independent work time, gather children together in the meeting area to talk about their reading.

▶ After reading, have children return the book boxes (or bags) and come to the meeting area. Invite children to evaluate what they did during independent reading, using the chart as a guide.

Extend the Lesson (Optional)

After assessing children's understanding, you might decide to extend the learning.

▶ Lengthen the period for reading each day until the children can sustain reading for longer periods of time.

▶ Teach children how to update their book boxes with new books. They return the books they have read or know well and select new ones from the classroom library.

▶ Once children understand the routine for independent reading, introduce another icon for the work board or list. As children become comfortable with the routines, vary the activities on the work board so that children are doing different things at different times.

Independent Reading

• Find your name.

• Carry your box to your spot.

• Read 4 books quietly.

• Put the book box away.

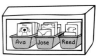

Section 1: Management

Reading Minilesson Principle
Listen to a book in the listening center.

Engaging in Classroom Literacy Work

You Will Need

- listening center icon
- listening device(s) (e.g., tablet, computer)
- headphones
- books
- two children prepared for the lesson
- chart paper and markers
- document camera (optional)

To download the following online resources for this lesson, visit **resources.fountasandpinnell.com:**

- listening center icon

Academic Language / Important Vocabulary

- listening center
- volume
- signal
- work board
- icon
- materials

Goal

Learn the work board icon and routines for the listening center.

Rationale

Listening to audiobooks allows children to engage with more difficult books than they can read on their own and provides a model of fluent reading. Teaching children explicitly how to use the equipment frees you to work effectively with other children in small groups.

Assess Learning

Observe children when they listen to books. Notice if there is evidence of new learning based on the goal of this minilesson.

- ▶ When sharing a book, how do they use the single copy while listening? Do they position the book fairly? Do they make sure everyone can see? Are they able to decide who will turn the pages?
- ▶ Do they know and use vocabulary related to the listening center?

Minilesson

To help children think about the minilesson principle, provide a short demonstration. Here is an example.

- ▶ Whether you are using a work board or list of activities, you can use an icon to indicate an activity. Show the listening center icon.

    When you see this picture on the work board under your name, you will be listening to books.

- ▶ Show the children where they will get books to listen to, whether it is a listening center or a place where the supplies are stored.

- ▶ Place the listening device in the middle of the meeting area and teach the children how to use it. If children have access to headphones or ear buds, demonstrate how to plug them in.

- ▶ Designate a specific volume level for children to use when listening to a book as a small group or set the volume yourself. You can use a little bright nail polish to mark the spot.

    When you are listening with a group, set the volume to level _____ (or use the volume that is set).

- ▶ Choose two children to model listening to a book. Demonstrate how to turn on the device and take what you need from the basket in the middle of the table.

    You need to hold your book with both hands and turn the pages carefully. Other times, you might need to share a book with a partner and decide who will turn the pages.

    _____ and _____ will show you how to listen to a book and turn the pages with a partner. Since there is only one book, how should partners hold it?

Let's listen to the first couple of pages of the story. Watch how your friends hold the book and turn the pages.

What did you notice your friends do as they listened to the book? How did you turn the pages?

Have a Try

Invite children to talk with a partner about what to do in the listening center.

> Turn and talk to a partner about what you should do when you use the listening center.

▶ Invite a few children to share with the whole group and record responses on chart paper and review the responses.

> You can check this chart if you need to remember what to do in the listening center.

Summarize and Apply

Have the children practice the new instructional routine in an authentic learning situation.

▶ Point to the listening center icon on the work board.

> Today you learned that when you see this picture, you are going to listen to a book. Notice that the listening center picture is under all the names. That means you are all going to practice listening to a book today.

▶ If possible, listen to a book for which you have multiple copies so each child can practice turning pages. Alternatively, share a single copy on a document camera with an assigned child to turn the pages. If you have more than one device, you can split the class in small groups and position them around the room.

Share

Following independent work time, gather children together in the meeting area to talk about listening to a book.

> Now that you have listened to a book, is there anything you think we should add to the directions for using the listening center?

Extend the Lesson (Optional)

After assessing children's understanding, you might decide to extend the learning.

▶ **Drawing/Writing About Reading** Teach children to respond by drawing or writing in a reader's notebook to the texts they listen to. You can connect this response to literary minilessons that relate to the audiobooks (see Section Two: Literary Analysis).

Listening Center

- Get what you need.

- Turn the page when it is time or when you hear a signal. —Beep

- Put the book and materials away.

Reading Minilesson Principle
Work on words in the word work center.

Engaging in Classroom Literacy Work

You Will Need

- word work center icon
- work board (optional)
- word work materials chart
- word work directions chart
- chart paper and markers
- magnetic letters

To download the following online resources for this lesson, visit **resources.fountasandpinnell.com:**

- word work center icon

Academic Language / Important Vocabulary

- icon
- word work
- directions
- materials

Goal

Learn to follow routines and handle supplies in the word work center.

Rationale

This minilesson establishes the basic routines for children to work independently in the word work center or at their seats so that only a brief introduction to the specific task will be required. Word work activities should reinforce the concepts learned during the whole-class phonics lesson.

Assess Learning

Observe children when they use the word work center. Notice if there is evidence of new learning based on the goal of this minilesson.

- Are they able to follow the directions independently during the word work activity?
- Do they handle their materials gently and return them to the appropriate place?
- Do children know and use vocabulary related to the word work center?

Minilesson

To help children think about the minilesson principle, a short demonstration that helps children understand the routines of the word work center. Here is an example.

- Whether you use a work board or list of activities, you can use an icon to indicate an activity. Show children the word work icon.

  The pictures on the work board are called icons. Icons are pictures that mean something. This is the icon for the word work center.

  What do you think you might do in the word work center?

- Show children the word work center with the materials placed there or where word work materials are kept in the classroom if they will need to get them.

  What do you notice about the materials in the word work center?

  The materials are organized and labeled so you can find and return them easily.

- Show children where the charts will be displayed.

  There will always be two charts posted in the word work center: one chart will show you the materials you need, and the other will tell you how to do the activity.

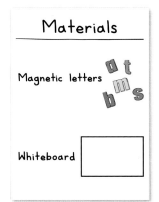

▶ Show the materials chart.

> What materials will you need for this activity?

▶ Read the directions for the children and demonstrate how to do the activity.

> What will you do when you are finished with your word work activity?

> Return the materials to the same place you found them.

Have a Try

Invite children to talk with a partner about what they will do in the word work center.

> Turn and talk with your partner about what you will do first in the word work center.

Summarize and Apply

Have the children practice the new instructional routine in an authentic learning situation.

> Today you learned what to do in the word work center. Always start by checking the materials chart.

▶ As you summarize the steps, record them on a chart.

> What will you do next?

> After you read the materials chart and take out the materials, you will read the directions chart and do the activity. What will you do when you have finished?

> Today everyone will have a chance to do the activity I showed you.

▶ Place the word work center icon across one row of the work board. Have children retrieve the materials and do the activity. Remind them to check the directions chart if they forget what to do.

Share

Following independent work time, gather children together in the meeting area to talk about their word work.

> Give a thumbs-up if you did the activity, handled the materials carefully, and put them back where you found them.

> What are some things you will remember to do when you go to the word work center?

Extend the Lesson (Optional)

After assessing children's understanding, you might decide to extend the learning.

▶ Continue to introduce new word work activities, such as lotto and bingo.

▶ Differentiate the activities based on the needs of the children.

Word Work Center

- Read the materials.

Materials
Magnetic letters

- Take out the materials.

- Read the directions.

Directions
• Make the word at

- Do the activity.

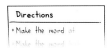

- Return the materials.

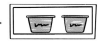

Reading Minilesson Principle
Write and draw in the writing center.

Engaging in Classroom Literacy Work

You Will Need

- writing center icon
- work board (optional)
- writing center materials
- directions for writing prompt
- chart paper and markers

To download the following online resources for this lesson, visit **resources.fountasandpinnell.com:**

- writing center icon

Academic Language / Important Vocabulary

- directions
- materials
- notes
- letters
- icon

Goal

Learn how to handle materials and follow routines in the writing center.

Rationale

Whether children work in a writing center or at their tables, they need to be taught explicitly how to choose materials, write, put materials away, and place their finished writing where it belongs. The writing center activity differs from the ongoing writing process work from the writer's workshop.

Assess Learning

Observe children when they write and draw during independent work time. Notice if there is evidence of new learning based on the goal of this minilesson.

- ▶ Do the children use the materials, such as markers and staplers, appropriately?
- ▶ Do they return the materials to the right place?
- ▶ Do they know and use vocabulary related to the writing center?

Minilesson

To help children think about the minilesson principle, engage them in a short demonstration of how to do a writing center activity. Here is an example.

- ▶ Whether you use a work board or list of activities, you can use an icon to indicate an activity. Show the writing center icon.

  When you see this icon, it means you will do writing and drawing from the writing center.

- ▶ Hold up some of the materials (for example, pencils, colored pencils, sticky notes, markers, paper, covers, correction tape, stapler, glue sticks, blank books) and point to the labels. If you plan to provide a list of the kinds of writing children can choose or a weekly writing prompt, show them where you will post the directions.

  What do you notice about the materials in the writing center?

  The materials are organized and labeled to help you find what you need. If you are making a book and want to add a page, what could you do?

- ▶ Have a child model how to get the materials, staple the new sheet (click–click), and return the stapler to its labeled spot. Emphasize how the hands are placed to use the stapler and demonstrate several times.

- ▶ Invite a child to model how to take the cap off and put the cap back on a marker.

  What did you notice about how _____ handled the marker? Listen for the clicking sound when you put the cap on markers and glue sticks so they don't dry up.

  What do you do when you are finished with your writing center work?

- ▶ Show children where to put their finished work in the basket.

Have a Try

Invite children to talk with a partner about what they will do in the writing center.

> Turn and talk with your partner about what you will do first in the writing center.

Summarize and Apply

Have the children practice the new instructional routine in an authentic learning situation.

▶ Create a chart as the children summarize their learning.

> What are some things you learned today about using the writing center?

> Now everyone will have a chance to do a writing center activity.

▶ Show and read the directions sheet for a short writing activity (for example, make a card for someone in your family) so that the whole class can work at the same time.

▶ Provide some writing materials on the children's tables.

> Some materials are on your tables, but if you need more, get what you need from the writing center. Remember to use the materials carefully and return them to where they belong when you are finished.

Writing Center

- Read the directions for writing.

Directions

- Get the materials you need.

- Take good care of materials. Click!

- Put your finished work in the basket.

Share

Following independent work time, gather children together in the meeting area to talk about their writing.

▶ After allowing the children time to write, gather everyone in the meeting area.

> Is there anything we need to add to the chart to help you remember what to do when you see the writing center icon?

Extend the Lesson [Optional]

After assessing children's understanding, you might decide to extend the learning.

▶ Provide for a variety of types of writing, for example, poster, response to interactive read-aloud, a book recommendation, poem, a recipe.

▶ Consider integrating social studies or science content into the writing center activities.

▶ Once children are comfortable with this routine, integrate one or two other familiar centers and have the whole class transition from one activity to the next. Eventually, you will vary the order of activities for each group.

Section 1: Management

Reading Minilesson Principle
Read a book from your browsing box.

Engaging in Classroom Literacy Work

You Will Need

- three children to demonstrate (prepare them ahead of time if necessary)
- browsing boxes icon
- work board
- browsing boxes with children's names listed or boxes of different colors (prepare ahead of time; see pages 64-65)
- chart paper and markers

To download the following online resources for this lesson, visit **resources.fountasandpinnell.com:**

- browsing boxes icon

Academic Language / Important Vocabulary

- browsing box
- classroom library
- icon
- work board

Goal

Learn to read books from browsing boxes during independent reading.

Rationale

Browsing boxes provide children with one option for reading books independently. Reading new books and rereading familiar books supports comprehension and fluency and builds stamina. Teaching children how to choose and return books to the browsing box promotes independence and allows you to work with small groups.

Assess Learning

Observe children when they read from a browsing box. Notice if there is evidence of new learning based on the goal of this minilesson.

- ▶ Are the children able to choose and read books from their browsing box?
- ▶ Do they read silently or in a whisper?
- ▶ Do they return the books to the correct browsing box, with the books upright and facing forward?
- ▶ Do they know and use vocabulary related to using a browsing box?

Minilesson

To help children think about the minilesson principle, provide a short demonstration using boxes with children's names listed. Here is an example.

- ▶ Whether you use a work board or list of activities, you can use an icon to indicate an activity. Show the icon for browsing boxes.

  This icon means your job is to choose four books from the browsing box. I will show you the browsing box that you will use. The box will have some books that you have already read and some new books that you might enjoy reading.

- ▶ Show where the browsing boxes with names (or specified colors) are in the classroom.

  _____, _____, and _____ are going to show you how they choose a book and read from their browsing boxes. Notice what they do.

- ▶ Invite three children to find their browsing boxes, choose four books, and start to read one of them. After a short time, have the readers put their books back in the browsing box and take their seats in the meeting area.

  What did you see your classmates do when they chose books?

  What voice level did they use when they were reading?

- ▶ Help children notice that they found their group's box, chose four books, and sat down to read.

- ▶ Glue the icon to the top of the chart and record responses.

  When it is time to read from browsing boxes, you will read four books.

Have a Try

Invite the children to apply the new thinking about browsing boxes with a partner.

> Turn and talk to a partner about how your classmates put their books back in the browsing boxes.

> You noticed that your classmates returned the books to the same box, upright, and facing front. That makes it easy for the next person to choose books from the browsing box.

Summarize and Apply

Have the children practice using a browsing box.

▶ Put the icon across the work board under each group. You might want to place browsing boxes around the room for this task to avoid congestion.

> For the rest of reading time today, choose books to read from your browsing box.

> Find your browsing box and choose four books to read quietly. If you finish your books, put them back and choose another book from your browsing box.

Share

Following independent work time, gather children together in the meeting area to talk about their reading.

▶ After they finish reading, have children return the books to the browsing boxes and come to the meeting area. Ask children to evaluate their behavior using the chart as a guide.

Extend the Lesson (Optional)

After assessing children's understanding, you might decide to extend the learning.

▶ Teach children to read books from browsing boxes to a partner.

▶ Revisit this lesson as new books are added to browsing boxes or as children transition from one browsing box to another.

▶ **Drawing/Writing About Reading** Children can use a reader's notebook to draw or write responses to books from the browsing boxes based on the literary analysis minilessons you teach.

Section 1: Management

Reading Minilesson Principle
Read and illustrate a poem for your poetry notebook.

Engaging in Classroom Literacy Work

You Will Need

- poetry notebook icon
- big book or chart of a familiar poem
- work board
- copies of the familiar poem in a small bin
- glue sticks and crayons
- chart paper and markers

To download the following online resources for this lesson, visit **resources.fountasandpinnell.com:**

- poetry notebook icon

Academic Language / Important Vocabulary

- work board
- poetry notebook
- poetry center
- poem
- illustration
- materials

Goal

Learn to read and respond to poetry independently.

Rationale

Poetry notebooks provide children with the opportunity to reread and respond to poems they have read in shared reading. Rereading and illustrating familiar poems supports comprehension, builds reading vocabulary, and promotes fluency.

Assess Learning

Observe children when they work with poetry notebooks. Notice if there is evidence of new learning based on the goal of this minilesson.

- Are the children able to follow the directions for how to use the poetry notebook?
- Do the children work well independently?
- Do they take turns and listen to a partner read?
- Do they know and use vocabulary related to using a poetry notebook?

Minilesson

To help children think about the minilesson principle, provide an inquiry-based lesson that you think will be meaningful to them. Here is an example.

- Whether you use a work board or list of activities, you can use an icon to indicate an activity. Show children the poetry icon.

   When you see this icon, you will work in your poetry notebook.

- Reread a familiar poem.

   We often read poems together like this one on our charts and in our big books. I am going to give you each a copy of a poem so you can glue it in your own poetry notebook.

- Show children where they will find the poetry notebooks and the materials for them.

- Demonstrate how to take a copy of the poem out of the bin, read it, glue it in the notebook, illustrate it, and read it silently or with a soft voice, and then read it softly to a partner.

   You will find small copies of the poems we have shared in this bin in the poetry center. Watch what I do when it is time to work on poetry.

   What did I do first?

- Make a chart titled Poetry Notebook.

   What did you notice about how I glued the poem in the notebook?

- Help children to notice that you used limited glue, glued the poem upright on the next page of the notebook, and put the cap back on the glue. Add to the chart.

▶ Read aloud the poem again.

In your poetry notebook, draw a picture of what the poem makes you think about. Poems make people think about different things, so your picture will be different from someone else's.

Turn and talk to a partner about what you might illustrate for this poem.

▶ Make a quick sketch for the poem and add to the chart.

After you finish drawing, read the poem to yourself and then read it to a partner.

Have a Try

Invite children to talk with a partner about what they will do in the poetry notebook center.

Turn and talk with your partner about what you would draw for the poem.

Summarize and Apply

Have the children practice using a poetry notebook.

▶ Review the chart for using poetry notebooks.

Now you are going to use your poetry notebook. Point to the poetry notebook icons across one row on the work board.

▶ Have each work board group retrieve the supplies they need and work at tables.

Follow the directions on the chart if you forget what to do.

Share

Following independent work time, gather children together in the meeting area to talk about their poetry notebooks.

▶ Have children clean up and gather in the meeting area with their poetry notebooks.

▶ Invite children to share their illustrations with a partner or small group.

▶ Revisit the chart and ask children to indicate with their thumbs (up, middle, or down) how each step went for them.

Extend the Lesson (Optional)

After assessing children's understanding, you might decide to extend the learning.

▶ In the poem, have children highlight words connected to phonics/word work principles.

▶ **Drawing/Writing About Reading** Use interactive writing to teach children how to compose a written response to a poem in their poetry notebooks.

Poetry Notebook

• Read the poem.

• Glue it in your notebook.

• Illustrate the poem.

• Read the poem to yourself.

• Read the poem to a partner.

Section 1: Management

RML7
MGT.U3.RML7

Reading Minilesson Principle
Read around the room with a pointer.

You Will Need

- read the room icon (see appendix)
- work board (optional)
- bins for long and short pointers
- charts to read
- voice level chart (optional; see page 73)
- chart paper and markers

To download the following online resources for this lesson, visit **resources.fountasandpinnell.com:**

- read the room icon

Academic Language / Important Vocabulary

- print
- pointer
- chart
- name chart
- alphabet chart

Goal

Learn how to read around the room with a pointer.

Rationale

When children learn how to reread shared texts with a pointer, early reading behaviors (such as voice-print match) are reinforced; children notice new things about the way print works; and children develop an increased awareness of the classroom print resources.

Assess Learning

Observe children when they read around the room. Notice if there is evidence of new learning based on the goal of this minilesson.

- ▶ Can children find parts of the room they can read?
- ▶ Do they use the pointers to point crisply under the words?
- ▶ Do children use the appropriate pointer for different types of charts?
- ▶ Do they know and use vocabulary related to reading around the room?

Minilesson

To help children think about the minilesson principle, provide a short demonstration of how to read around the room. Here is an example.

- ▶ Guide children to notice the different kinds of print around the room (for example, alphabet charts, poetry charts, interactive writing, word wall, labeled murals).

  Look at the walls in our classroom. What do you see on them?

  Watch me for a little bit.

- ▶ Take a pointer from the bin. Place the pointer under each word and read a variety of print, moving along the wall.

  What did you notice about what I did? What did my pointer do?

- ▶ Help children conclude that you pointed under the print and moved along the wall reading all the print. Also guide them to notice the level of the voice you used to read and how you returned the pointer to the bin.

- ▶ Title a chart Read Around the Room and record responses.

- ▶ Whether you use a work board or list of activities, you can use an icon to indicate an activity. Show the read around the room icon.

  When you use the work board to know what to work on, you will see an icon that looks like this.

  When you see this icon, use a pointer to read all the words around the room softly to your partner.

Have a Try

Invite children to talk about using pointers.

> Show children where the pointers are kept and explain when it is appropriate to use a long pointer and when to use a short pointer.

Summarize and Apply

Have the children practice the new instructional routine.

> Now everyone will have a chance to read around the room with a partner

▶ Hand one big and one small pointer to pairs of children, one pair at a time.

▶ Show each pair where to start reading so they can be spread out around the classroom.

> Choose which pointer you will use and take turns reading quietly. Then use walking feet and find something else to read with a pointer. Keep reading until you hear the signal to stop.

Share

Following independent work time, gather children together in the meeting area to talk about their reading.

▶ Signal children to stop. Ask them to return the pointers to the appropriate bins and gather in the meeting area.

> Give a thumbs-up if you and your partner followed the directions to read around the room.

> Turn and talk to your partner about one thing you will remember when you read around the room.

Extend the Lesson (Optional)

After assessing children's understanding, you might decide to extend the learning.

▶ Create a chart titled Things to Read Around the Room. Include alphabet charts, name charts, class routine charts, poems, murals, children's writing, and word walls.

▶ **Drawing/Writing About Reading** Have children carry a clipboard and record specific types of words as they read around the room (for example, write words that start with the first letter of your name).

Read Around the Room

- Get a pointer.

- Read the wall to your partner.

- Your partner reads the wall to you.

- Point under the words. Read in a soft voice.

- Put the pointer in the bin.

Section 1: Management

Reading Minilesson Principle
Read and put together a story, song, or poem in the pocket chart.

Engaging in Classroom Literacy Work

You Will Need

- enlarged version of a familiar poem or a chart
- pocket chart with the same familiar poem written on sentence strips
- pointers
- chart paper and markers
- work board (optional)
- enlarged poem and pocket chart sentence strips for each group
- pocket chart icon

To download the following online resources for this lesson, visit **resources.fountasandpinnell.com:**

- pocket chart icon

Academic Language / Important Vocabulary

- pocket chart
- sentence strips
- pointer

Goal

Learn how to use a pocket chart to create and reread stories, songs, and poems.

Rationale

When children rebuild the text of a familiar story, poem, or song, early literacy concepts are reinforced. Children learn how to search for and use different sources of information (meaning, syntax, and visual information) and have opportunities to self-monitor as they read.

Assess Learning

Observe children when they work with pocket charts. Notice if there is evidence of new learning based on the goal of this minilesson.

- ▶ Are children able to choose the correct sentence strips to rebuild the poem?
- ▶ Do the children check the original poem after placing sentence strips in the pocket chart?
- ▶ Do they know and use vocabulary related to using a pocket chart?

Minilesson

To help children think about the minilesson principle, provide a short demonstration of how to rebuild a text. Here is an example.

- ▶ Using a pointer, reread the enlarged poem together.
- ▶ Then show children the poem made with sentence strips in a pocket chart.

  Now, watch what I do.

- ▶ Read the poem in the pocket chart. Take the sentence strips out of the pocket chart and mix them up. Lay them out and model reading each sentence strip.
- ▶ Pick the first sentence strip of the poem. Place it in the first pocket of the pocket chart. Read aloud the sentence, checking it with the original poem.

  What did you notice that I did?

- ▶ Start a class chart titled Pocket Chart and show the icon.

  When you see the pocket chart icon, work with a partner. One of you will do what I just did, while your partner watches. Then you will switch.

  What do you think you should do once all the sentence strips are back in the pocket chart?

  How can you check that you placed them in the correct order?

- ▶ Add to the chart.
- ▶ Whether you use a work board or list of activities, you can use an icon to indicate an activity. Show the pocket chart icon.

  When you see this icon on the work board, you will know what to do.

Have a Try

Invite children to apply the new thinking about using a pocket chart.

▶ Have a pair of children model the process of how to read a pocket chart while the rest of the class watches and checks the actions against the chart.

Summarize and Apply

Have the children practice using a pocket chart.

▶ Put the pocket chart icon across the first row of the work board.

> You have learned how to use the pocket chart. Now you will practice mixing and fixing the sentence strips of a poem with a group.

▶ Spread the groups around the classroom with their own poems and sentence strips and review the directions on the chart Pocket Chart. If you have only one pocket chart, let groups lay poems out on a table.

> Each group will have its own poem and sentence strips. Take turns choosing the sentence strips to build the poem. You can read each sentence strip together.

Share

Following independent work time, gather children together in their groups to talk about using the pocket chart.

> Turn and talk with your group about what your group did well.

▶ Invite a few children to share.

> Now turn and talk about something that you would like to do better next time.

▶ Have a few children share.

Extend the Lesson (Optional)

After assessing children's understanding, you might decide to extend the learning.

▶ Revisit this lesson using different forms of writing (for example, stories composed during interactive writing, familiar songs). Include single cards so children can insert their own names into songs and poems.

▶ Incorporate pocket charts with other work board activities/centers once children are comfortable and independent with the routine.

Reading Minilesson Principle
Read a book with a partner.

Engaging in Classroom Literacy Work

You Will Need

- work board
- voice level chart (optional; see page 73)
- chart paper and markers
- partner reading icon

To download the following online resources for this lesson, visit **resources.fountasandpinnell.com:**

- partner reading icon

Academic Language / Important Vocabulary

- partner reading

Goal

Learn the routines for partner reading.

Rationale

Partner reading fosters good reading habits and cooperative learning. It adds to the overall enjoyment of reading and builds confidence and fluency in readers. Teaching the routines for partner reading enables children to work and problem solve independently.

Assess Learning

Observe the children reading with a partner. Notice if there is evidence of new learning based on the goal of this minilesson.

- How well do the children engage in the routines on the chart?
- Can they identify what they do well and what they need to work on?
- Do they know and use the term *partner reading?*

Minilesson

To help children think about the minilesson principle, provide a short demonstration for children to observe the process. Here is an example.

- Choose two children to model partner reading. Have them choose four books to share and sit with their books in the middle of the meeting area.

    How are _____ and _____ sitting?

    Sit next to each other, legs crisscrossed and arms elbow to elbow. Notice how they placed their books next to them.

- Have the two children ask each other who would like to read first.

    Where should _____ hold the book so her partner can see it well?

- Refer to the voice level chart if you have created one together.

    What voice level should she use to read her book?

    Use a level 1 quiet voice when you are reading to a partner.

- Have the partners model reading a few pages from one book.

    Turn and talk to a partner about something you noticed when the partners read.

- Ask a few children to share with the whole group. Make sure children notice that the listening partner followed along as the other partner read.

    What should the partners do now?

    Take turns reading until you and your partner have read four books together.

    Let's review what partners should do during partner reading.

- Record responses on a chart called Partner Reading. Glue the partner reading icon to the top of the chart.

- Whether you use a work board or list of activities, you can use an icon to indicate an activity.

  > Show the partner reading icon. You'll know it's time to read to a partner when you see this icon.

Have a Try

Invite children to talk with a partner about what they will do during partner reading.

> Turn and talk to your partner about what you will do first when you read with a partner.

Summarize and Apply

Have the children practice the new instructional routine in an authentic learning situation.

> Now everyone will have a chance to read to a partner.

- Review the chart. Send pairs of children to their browsing boxes to choose four books each and start partner reading.

Share

Following independent work time, gather children together in the meeting area to talk about their reading.

> As I read the chart, turn and show your partner with your thumb how you think you did with each part of partner reading.

> Now turn and talk with your partner about one or two things that you will do better the next time you partner read.

Extend the Lesson (Optional)

After assessing children's understanding, you might decide to extend the learning.

- Once children are familiar with the partner reading routines, teach new variations. For example, partners take turns reading each page of a book and talking about the story.

- Teach children different ways to talk about books with their partners. Make a chart with suggested language (for example, I'm wondering...; This part reminds me of...; I'm thinking...; I'm noticing...; I can't believe...; I think the character...).

Partner Reading

- Sit next to your partner.

- Hold the book so you can both see it.

- Read the book to your partner in a soft voice.

- Your partner reads the book to you.

Reading Minilesson Principle
Look at your list to know what to do during Reading time.

Engaging in Classroom Literacy Work

You Will Need

- work board or list with two or three icons under each group's name
- directions and materials at work centers
- chart paper titled *Work Board*
- markers

To download the following online resources for this lesson, visit **resources.fountasandpinnell.com:**

- work board icon

Academic Language / Important Vocabulary

- work board
- center

Goal

Learn to follow a work board to complete independent literacy activities.

Rationale

The work board allows children to manage their learning independently. Typically, children move from one activity to another without being signaled so they learn to self-regulate and self-assess when a task is complete. When children have learned the routines for several of the independent literacy activities, you can place more than a single icon on the work board or several tasks on a list for each group.

Assess Learning

Observe children when they work on their own. Notice if there is evidence of new learning based on the goal of this minilesson.

- ▶ Do children follow the order of activities on the work board?
- ▶ Do they follow directions and handle materials gently at each center?
- ▶ Are they able to work independently and assess if the task was completed?
- ▶ Do they use the terms *work board* and *center?*

Minilesson

To help children think about the minilesson principle, engage them in a discussion of the list of tasks or the work board. Here is an example.

- ▶ Display the work board. (If you use a different way of indicating what children should do during work time, amend this instruction accordingly.)

    What do you notice about the work board?

    The first thing to do when you use the work board is find your name.

- ▶ Record on the chart paper.

    The icons under your name show you what you will do during reading time.

- ▶ If children are new to rotating to centers, limit groups to two activities the first few times. Assign listening center to one group to avoid overlap. Have children identify each icon, quickly summarize the meaning, and locate the center or materials.

- ▶ Point to the first group's first icon.

    Where will these children go first?

- ▶ Repeat this question for each group.

    Once we start, you will go to the first center under your name, do your best work, and then clean up. How will you know that you are finished?

    What will you do next?

Have a Try

Invite the children to apply the new thinking and review the chart.

> Let's practice moving from center to center.
>
> Find your name on the work board and walk quietly to your first center. Turn and talk to a partner about what you will do.
>
> How will you know when you are finished?

▸ Ask one person from each group to share.

> What will you do when you are finished?

▸ Invite the class to answer chorally with "Clean up!"

> Now pretend you are finished. Think where you would go next. Quickly and quietly move to that center.

Summarize and Apply

Have the children practice the new instructional routine in an authentic learning situation.

> Today you learned how to use the work board to know what to do.
>
> Do the activities under your name on the work board. Go to each center to do your best work. When you finish, clean up and go to the next center on the list. When you hear the signal, clean up and come back to the meeting area quickly to share how things went.

Share

Following independent work time, gather children together in the meeting area to talk about their work centers.

▸ Help children solve problems that come up or that you noticed.

> What went well for you today?
>
> What would you do differently the next time you use the work board?

Extend the Lesson (Optional)

After assessing children's understanding, you might decide to extend the learning.

▸ As children become comfortable with centers, continue to add new ones.

▸ Once you start guided reading groups or other small-group teaching, explain to them how they will leave a center and return to it.

Section 1: Management

✗ **Assessment**

After you have taught the minilessons in this umbrella, observe the children as they work on independent literacy work activities.

▶ What evidence do you have that they understand how to work independently using the work board?

- Do children follow the work board and manage meaningful literacy tasks independently?

- Do particular children need a partner to support them until they can use a center independently?

- Do they use supplies appropriately and put them back where they belong?

- How are children self-assessing whether a task is complete? Do they stay focused at each center and move through centers at an appropriate pace?

- Do they use appropriate voice levels as they complete their work?

- How are they transitioning from one center to another?

- Do children use vocabulary such as *center, work board, materials,* and *directions* when they are working in the classroom?

▶ What minilessons might you teach to maintain and grow independent work habits?

- What activities might you add to the work board?

Use your observations to determine the next umbrella you will teach. You may also consult Minilessons Across the Year (p. 51) for guidance.

Section 2 | Literary Analysis

Literary analysis minilessons support children in a growing awareness of the elements of literature and the writer's and illustrator's craft. They help children learn how to think analytically about texts and to identify the characteristics of fiction and nonfiction genres. The books that you read during interactive read-aloud and shared reading can serve as mentor texts when applying the principles of literary analysis.

2 Literary Analysis

Fiction and Nonfiction

Nonfiction

Fiction

Minilessons in This Umbrella

RML1 The title of the book is on the front cover.

RML2 The author wrote the book. The illustrator created the pictures.

RML3 Think about the books you read and talk about your thinking with others.

RML4 Turn and talk to share your thinking with others.

RML5 When you read, mark places you want to talk about.

RML6 Read the book again to enjoy it and learn more.

Before Teaching Umbrella 1 Minilessons

Read and discuss books children will enjoy. Books with simple plots are wonderful choices for the first few weeks of school as you begin to teach children how to think and talk about texts with each other. Use the following texts from the *Fountas & Pinnell Classroom™ Interactive Read-Aloud Collection* text sets or use similar books.

The Alphabet

ABC I Like Me! by Nancy Carlson

A My Name Is Alice by Jane Bayer

On Market Street by Arnold Lobel

School

Miss Bindergarten Gets Ready for Kindergarten by Joseph Slate

Wemberly Worried by Kevin Henkes

I Love You All Day Long by Francesca Rusackas

Look Out Kindergarten, Here I Come! by Nancy Carlson

Nursery Rhymes

I'm a Little Teapot by Iza Trapani

Baa Baa Black Sheep by Iza Trapani

Guided Reading

One Dark Night by Pat McCann

As you read aloud and enjoy these texts together, help children

- notice the author and illustrator,
- think about the title of the book and predict what the book might be about, and
- think and talk about the book with each other.

The Alphabet

School

Nursery Rhymes

Guided Reading

Reading Minilesson Principle
The title of the book is on the front cover.

You Will Need

- two or three books with titles that give a clear idea of what the book is about, such as the following from Text Set: School:
  - *I Love You all Day Long* by Francesca Rusackas
  - *Miss Bindergarten Gets Ready for Kindergarten* by Joseph Slate
  - *Wemberly Worried* by Kevin Henkes
- chart paper and markers
- a book for each child

Academic Language / Important Vocabulary

- title
- front cover

Continuum Connection

- Notice a book's title and its author and illustrator on the cover and title page [p. 29]

Goal

Identify the title on the front cover of a book and use it to think about what the book might be about.

Rationale

Children begin constructing their understanding of a book when they read or hear the title. When you help them to think about the title before reading the book you support their comprehension. Thinking about titles will help children to select books independently.

Assess Learning

Observe children when they talk about the titles of books they have read or heard. Notice if there is evidence of new learning based on the goal of this minilesson.

- Are children able to identify the title of the books they read independently?
- What evidence do you have that children use the title to predict what the story might be about?
- Do the children use the terms *title* or *front cover* while discussing the books?

Minilesson

To help children think about the minilesson principle, choose familiar texts and examples to provide an inquiry-based lesson about book titles. Here is an example.

- Show the front cover of *I Love You All Day Long.*

  The title of this book is *I Love You All Day Long.* How do you know that is the title of the book?

  How does the title help you remember what the book is about?

- Show the front cover of *Miss Bindergarten Gets Ready for Kindergarten.* Point to the title and read aloud. Record the title on the chart paper.

  What does the title tell you about the book?

- Record the children's responses on the chart.

- Show the front cover of *Wemberly Worried.*

  What's the title of this book?

- Record the title on the chart.

  How does the title help you know what the story is going to be about?

  Before we read the book, you didn't know why Wemberly was worried, but you did know she was worried about something by reading the title.

Have a Try

Invite the children to apply the new thinking about book titles with a partner.

▶ Give a book to each child.

Point to the title of your book and tell your partner how you know it is the title.

What do you think your book will be about from looking at the title and front cover?

▶ Choose a few children to share with the class.

Summarize and Apply

Summarize the learning and remind children to think about the title of the book before they read.

▶ Review the chart with the children. After summarizing the learning, write the principle at the top.

Today you learned that the title of the book is on the front cover, and you can use it to help you think what the book will be about.

When you read today, notice the title on the front cover. Bring your book when we come back together.

The title of the book is on the front cover.

Title	What the Book Is About
	Mom loves Owen all day when he is at school.
	A teacher gets ready for school. A B C
Wemberly Worried by KEVIN HENKES	Wemberly is worried about going to school for the first time.

Share

Following independent work time, gather children together in the meeting area to talk about the title of the book.

Point to the title of the front cover of your book.

Turn and talk to a partner. Tell your partner the title and what the book is about.

Extend the Lesson (Optional)

After assessing your students' understanding, you might decide to extend the learning over several days.

▶ Continue to add titles to the chart during interactive read-aloud and shared reading. Ask children to think about the title before reading the story. Talk about the fact that sometimes you don't understand a title until the end of the story.

▶ When talking about the title on the front cover, also address the illustrations that the illustrator drew for the cover.

▶ **Drawing/Writing About Reading** Have children study several book covers to gather ideas for how to make covers for their own stories.

RML2
LA.U1.RML2

Reading Minilesson Principle
The author wrote the book. The illustrator created the pictures.

Thinking and Talking About Books

You Will Need

- four or five familiar texts, some with a single writer and illustrator and some with a different writer and illustrator, such as the following:
  - *I'm a Little Teapot* by Iza Trapani, from Text Set: Nursery Rhymes
  - *Baa Baa Black Sheep* by Iza Trapani, from Text Set: Nursery Rhymes
  - *ABC I Like Me!* by Nancy Carlson, from Text Set: The Alphabet
  - *Look Out Kindergarten, Here I Come!* by Nancy Carlson, from Text Set: School
  - *On Market Street* by Arnold Lobel, from Text Set: The Alphabet
  - *A My Name Is Alice* by Jane Bayer, from Text Set: The Alphabet
- highlighter tape (optional)
- chart paper and markers

Academic Language / Important Vocabulary

- front cover
- author
- illustrator

Continuum Connection

- Understand that an illustrator created the pictures in the book (p. 29)

Goal

Understand the literary terms *author* and *illustrator* and be able to identify who wrote and illustrated the book.

Rationale

When children are able to recognize their favorite authors and illustrators, they have a way to select books that they will want to read and will begin to recognize styles of writing and drawing that they like.

Assess Learning

Observe children when they talk about the author and illustrator of a new book. Notice if there is evidence of new learning based on the goal of this minilesson.

- ▶ Are children able to point to the author's and illustrator's names on front cover?
- ▶ Do they understand what the author and illustrator do?
- ▶ Can children use the terms *front cover*, *author*, and *illustrator*?

Minilesson

To help children think about the minilesson principle, provide an inquiry-based lesson about author and illustrator. Here is an example.

- ▶ Show the front covers of *Look Out Kindergarten, Here I Come!* and *ABC I Like Me!*

   What do you notice about both books?

- ▶ If children don't notice, point out that both books have the same name on the front covers.

   Why do you think her name is on the front cover of these books?

   She wrote the words and drew the pictures for these books. The person who writes the words of a book is the author.

- ▶ Write *author* on the chart paper and sketch a pencil and paper next to the word.

   The person who creates the pictures is called the illustrator.

- ▶ Write *illustrator* on chart and sketch a paint brush.

   Nancy Carlson is the author and the illustrator, so her name is on the front cover.

- ▶ Show the front cover of *A My Name Is Alice.*

   What do you notice on the front cover?

   There are two names. It says *by Jane Bayer, pictures by Steven Kellogg.* Who is the author?

   Who is the illustrator?

   How did you know that?

▶ Invite children to highlight the words *by* and *pictures by*, possibly with highlighter tape.

Have a Try

Invite the children to apply the new thinking about a book's author and illustrator with a partner.

▶ Show and read the front cover of *On Market Street*.

> Who are the author and illustrator of this book?

> Turn to a partner and tell what words help you know who the author and illustrator are.

Summarize and Apply

Summarize the learning and remind children to notice who wrote and illustrated the book they are reading.

> What did you learn today about the author and the illustrator?

▶ Write the principle at the top of the chart.

> Often the word *by* is used to tell you the author and the words *pictures by* or *illustrations by* are used to tell you who the illustrator is.

> When you read today, look for the author and illustrator of your book. Notice the words that tell who wrote the book and who created the pictures.

Share

Following independent work time, gather children together in the meeting area to talk about a book's author and illustrator.

> Turn to a partner and show the name of the author and illustrator. Point to the words that helped you know this.

Extend the Lesson (Optional)

After assessing children's understanding, you might decide to extend the learning over several days.

▶ Some books have information about the author and/or illustrator elsewhere in the book. Show children where the information can be found.

▶ Visit the website of a favorite author or illustrator to find out more information about the person behind the book.

▶ **Drawing/Writing About Reading** Introduce children to the Books I Read section of *Reader's Notebook: Primary* (Fountas and Pinnell 2014) or help them set up a page to record books they have read in a plain notebook. As you confer with children, add the title and author in the Books I Read section.

Section 2: Literary Analysis

RML 3

LA.U1.RML3

Reading Minilesson Principle
Think about the books you read and talk about your thinking with others.

Thinking and Talking About Books

You Will Need

- two or three familiar texts that the class enjoyed, such as the following:
  - *I Love You All Day Long* by Francesca Rusackas, from Text Set: School
  - *I'm a Little Teapot* by Iza Trapani, from Text Set: Nursery Rhymes
  - *On Market Street* by Arnold Lobel, from Text Set: The Alphabet
- chart paper and markers
- sticky notes

Academic Language / Important Vocabulary

- front cover
- illustrations

Continuum Connection

- Use evidence from the text to support statements about the text (p. 28)
- Articulate why they like a text (p. 28)

Goal

Express opinions about a text and use personal experience or evidence from the text to support opinions.

Rationale

Kindergarten children are learning that reading is thinking. As they share their thinking, they learn that others will agree or disagree. They develop their identities as readers as they articulate opinions, connect with books, and deepen their understanding and appreciation of texts.

Assess Learning

Observe children when they share their thinking about books. Notice if there is evidence of new learning based on the goal of this minilesson.

- ▶ Are the children able to identify an interesting part of a story and share it with a partner?
- ▶ Can the children explain why the part is interesting to them?
- ▶ Do they use the terms *front cover* and *illustrations*?

Minilesson

To help children think about the minilesson principle, engage them in a discussion of how to share their thinking about reading. Here is an example.

- ▶ Show the front cover of *I'm a Little Teapot*. Flip through the pages of the story to refresh children's memory of the story.

    In this book every page showed a different adventure with the teapot. What was an interesting part or adventure from this story?

- ▶ Call on one or two children to respond. Have them show the class the pages and tell what made the part of the story interesting.

- ▶ Show the front cover of *I Love You All Day Long*.

    Who would like to share an interesting part of this book?

    Why did you think this part was interesting?

- ▶ Ask the children to give a thumbs-up if they thought it was interesting, too.

    Who has a different part that was interesting? Show us that part in the book.

Have a Try

Invite the children to practice sharing their thinking about books they have read with a partner.

▶ Show the cover of *On Market Street*.

Think about the illustrations that went with each letter. Tell your partner which letter was interesting to you in this book and why. When you talk to your partner, sit and face your partner.

▶ Have two children demonstrate sitting comfortably facing each other, if necessary.

Summarize and Apply

Summarize the learning and remind children to share their thinking about books with others.

Today you learned that you can talk about books with other people. One thing you can share is an interesting part of a book.

As you read today, think about an interesting part of the book. Put a sticky note on the part so you can share it with the group.

Share

Following independent work time, gather children together in the meeting areas to talk about their thinking about books with others.

Turn to a partner and talk about an interesting part of the story.

Tell why it is interesting.

Extend the Lesson (Optional)

After assessing your children's understanding, you might decide to extend the learning over several days.

▶ Provide other minilessons that show children other ways to talk about books and continue to add to the chart about how to think and talk about books with friends. For example, share interesting characters, exciting parts, parts that made you angry, funny parts, and so forth.

▶ **Drawing/Writing About Reading** Encourage students to write and/or draw about interesting parts of the books they read in a reader's notebook.

Think about the books you read and talk about your thinking with others.

- Think about your book.
- Put a sticky note on an interesting part.
- Share your interesting part.

> I love this part because it made me think about my best friend!

Section 2: Literary Analysis

Reading Minilesson Principle
Turn and talk to share your thinking with others.

Thinking and Talking About Books

You Will Need

- one or two familiar texts that the children enjoy, such as the following:
  - *ABC I Like Me!* by Nancy Carlson, from Text Set: The Alphabet
  - *Wemberly Worried* by Kevin Henkes, from Text Set: School
- chart paper and markers

Academic Language / Important Vocabulary

- turn and talk

Continuum Connection

- Engage actively in conversational routines: e.g., turn and talk in pairs, triads (p. 331)

Goal

Develop guidelines for the engagement routine of turn and talk based on children's experiences with talking about texts.

Rationale

Turn and talk is a technique that provides all children an opportunity to articulate their thinking and engage in conversation with others. When you establish clear guidelines for the procedure you allow every child the opportunity to practice their thinking and speaking in a comfortable situation.

Assess Learning

Observe children when they talk about their thinking about books with a partner. Notice if there is evidence of new learning based on the goal of this minilesson.

- Do the children actively listen to one another when they turn and talk?
- Do children take turns, make eye contact, and use body language that show they are listening?
- Are they able to monitor voice level?
- Can children use the term *turn and talk*?

Minilesson

To help children think about the minilesson principle, choose familiar texts and examples to provide an inquiry-based lesson. Here is an example.

- Show the front cover of *ABC I Like Me!*

    Sometimes when you read a book, you turn and talk to a partner about your thinking. When you share your thinking with a partner, everyone gets to talk.

- Ask for a volunteer to talk with you about something interesting in the book.

    While we turn and talk, notice what we are doing with our bodies and voices.

    What did you notice about the way we turned and talked with each other?

- List children's responses on the chart paper to create guidelines for turn and talk.

Have a Try

Invite the children to apply the new thinking with a partner.

▶ Show the front cover of *Wemberly Worried*.

Turn and talk to your partner about what you found interesting in *Wemberly Worried*.

▶ Have them reflect by reviewing the guidelines and giving a thumbs-up or thumbs-down.

Summarize and Apply

Summarize the learning and remind children to think about what could share about their reading.

▶ Review the chart with the children.

Today you learned that you can turn and talk to share your thinking with others. You learned how to turn and talk, listen carefully, use a soft voice, and wait for your partner to finish.

When you read today, think about something you found interesting. You will share with a partner when we come back together. Be sure to bring your book to share.

Share

Following independent work time, gather children in the meeting area to share their thinking about a book.

Turn and talk to your partner about something you liked in the pictures, or illustrations, in your book.

How well did you follow the guidelines for turn and talk?

Extend the Lesson (Optional)

After assessing your students' understanding, you might decide to extend the learning over several days.

▶ Use turn and talk regularly during whole-class and small-group instruction (for example, in interactive read-aloud, shared reading, and guided reading).

▶ Continue to review guidelines as you use turn and talk. Ask children to self-assess regularly based on the guidelines.

Turn and talk to share your thinking with others.

 Turn to your partner.

 Look at your partner.

 Wait for your partner to finish talking.

 Use a soft voice.

 Listen to your partner's thinking.

 Stop talking and turn back when the teacher signals.

Section 2: Literary Analysis

RML5
LA.U1.RML5

Reading Minilesson Principle
When you read, mark places you want to talk about.

You Will Need

- *Baa Baa Black Sheep* by Iza Trapani, from Text Set: Nursery Rhymes, or another fiction book
- fiction books (one book for each pair of children)
- sticky notes

Academic Language / Important Vocabulary

- reread
- notice
- turn and talk

Continuum Connection

- Use evidence from the text to support statements about the text (p. 28)

Goal

Identify places in a book to talk about with others.

Rationale

When you teach children how to mark pages while reading, you are encouraging them to think about what they want to talk about with other readers. This prompts them to think more deeply about a text and prepares them for discussion.

Assess Learning

Observe children when they read and talk with others. Notice if there is evidence of new learning based on the goal of this minilesson.

- ▶ Are children able to identify and mark pages that they would like to talk about with a partner?
- ▶ Do children refer back to those pages when talking with a partner?
- ▶ Can children understand the terms *reread*, *notice*, and *turn and talk*?

Minilesson

To help children think about the minilesson principle, demonstrate how to mark pages to talk about. Here is an example.

- ▶ Show *Baa Baa Black Sheep*.

    As I reread this story I want you to think about what I am doing as a reader.

- ▶ Reread the book, stopping on the page where the sheep says no to the pig.

    I wonder why the sheep keeps saying no to everyone. I am going to put a sticky note on this page. I will leave the sticky note poking out a little so I can easily find the page later.

- ▶ Continue reading, stopping again on the page where the sheep says no to the horse. Add a sticky note.

    On this page I notice that the illustration shows how the horse is feeling. The horse looks annoyed. What did you notice about what I did while reading?

    What are some reasons why you might want to talk about a page in a book?

- ▶ List children's responses on the chart paper.

Have a Try

Invite the children to practice marking places in their book with a partner.

▶ Give each pair of children a book and a sticky note.

With your partner, look through the book and mark a place with a sticky note where you would want to share your thinking with others.

▶ Have children work in groups of four (two sets of partners) to share the pages they marked.

Summarize and Apply

Remind children to mark places in their book they want to talk about.

What did you learn about how you can share your thinking with others when you read?

▶ Write the principle at the top of the chart.

When you read today use a sticky note to mark the page that you would like to share with your partner. Bring your book when we come back together.

Share

Following independent work time, gather children in the meeting area to have them share the place they marked in their book.

Turn and talk to a partner about the page you marked in your book.

How did you decide which page to put your sticky note on?

▶ Refer children to the chart.

Extend the Lesson (Optional)

After assessing children's understanding, you might decide to extend the learning.

▶ Encourage children during guided reading or independent reading to mark pages in their books that they would like to share with a partner after reading.

▶ **Drawing/Writing About Reading** You might want to show children how to record their thinking about books in a reader's notebook. They can write about the page they marked with a sticky note. See Section Four: Writing About Reading for specific minilessons on using a reader's notebook.

When you read, mark places you want to talk about.

You can add a sticky note when...

- You wonder about something.
- You notice something interesting.
- You like the illustration.
- You like the words.
- You don't understand something.
- The story reminds you of something.

RML 6
LA.U1.RML6

Reading Minilesson Principle
Read the book again to enjoy it and learn more.

You Will Need

- a guided reading book at the text gradient of many of your children or use the Guided Reading book, *One Dark Night* by Pat McCann (level C)
- projector (optional)

Academic Language / Important Vocabulary

- illustration
- reread
- notice

Continuum Connection

- Gain new information from both pictures and print (p. 28)

Goal

Understand what it means to reread and why it can help to notice and learn more.

Rationale

When you explicitly teach children what rereading is, they can use *It* as a way to further enjoy and think about books and to notice and learn more as a reader.

Assess Learning

Your goal is to observe children when they read a book again for enjoyment. Notice if there is evidence of new learning based on the goal of this minilesson.

- Do children reread books independently?
- Are children able to talk more about a book after rereading?
- Do they understand the benefits of rereading?

Minilesson

To help children think about the minilesson principle, provide an inquiry-based lesson about rereading. Here is an example.

- Read aloud *One Dark Night* or another guided reading book. If possible, place the book on a projector so the illustrations are easier to see. Stop after reading page 6.

   The owl in the illustration makes this book seem spooky. I wonder if it is a Halloween story.

- Continue reading to the end of the book.

   That certainly surprised me. I didn't expect a birthday party! Watch what I do now.

- Start rereading the book and stop after reading after a few pages.

   What do you notice about what I'm doing?

   I read the book again. That's called rereading. When you reread something, you read it again.

- Keep reading and stop after page 10.

   I notice that the illustration shows the shadow of the boy. He looks a little scared.

- Continue reading and stop after page 14.

   I wonder what the boy might be thinking now. If I were the boy, I would be a little scared.

   What did you notice about the second time I read the book?

   The second time I read the book, I noticed things that I didn't notice the first time.

   How do you think rereading a book can help you?

- Record children's responses on the chart paper.

Have a Try

Invite the children to talk about rereading a book with a partner.

> Talk with your partner about something new you noticed when I reread *One Dark Night*.

Summarize and Apply

Summarize the learning and remind children to reread a book for enjoyment and to learn more.

> Today you learned that when you read a book again you can enjoy it and learn more from it.

▶ Write the principle at the top of the chart.

> You can choose a book that you have already read and read it again today. Notice if you learn anything new from reading the book again. Be ready to share when we come back together.

Share

Following independent work time, gather children in the meeting to talk about the book they reread for enjoyment and for more learning.

> Give a thumbs-up if you reread a book today.

> Who would like to share what you noticed the second time you read your book?

Extend the Lesson (Optional)

After assessing children's understanding, you might decide to extend the learning.

▶ **Drawing/Writing About Reading** You might want to show children how to record their thinking in a reader's notebook after rereading books. See Section Four: Writing About Reading for specific minilessons on using a reader's notebook.

Section 2: Literary Analysis

Assessment

After you have taught the minilessons in this umbrella, observe children as they talk and write about their reading across instructional contexts: interactive read-aloud, independent reading and literacy work, guided reading, shared reading, and book club. Use *The Literacy Continuum* (Fountas and Pinnell 2017) to observe children's reading and writing behaviors across instructional contexts.

▶ What evidence do you have of new understandings relating to thinking and talking about texts?

• Can children identify the title, author, and illustrator on the front cover of a book?

• Are children following the guidelines for turn and talk?

• In what ways are they sharing their thinking about books?

• Do they use academic language, such as *title, author, illustration, reread, notice,* and *turn and talk*?

▶ In what other ways, beyond the scope of this umbrella, are they thinking and talking about books?

Use your observations to determine the next umbrella you will teach. You may also consult Minilessons Across the Year (p. 51) for guidance.

Link to Writing

After teaching the minilessons in this umbrella, help children link the new learning to their own writing or drawing:

▶ If you are using *Reader's Notebook: Primary* (Fountas and Pinnell 2014), introduce the Books I Like to Read section. Children can record their favorite titles and authors and draw and write about an interesting part. If you are using a plain reader's notebook, help children set up a page to record books they have read. See Section Four: Writing About Reading for guidance in how to introduce and use a reader's notebook.

Minilessons in This Umbrella

RML1   Sometimes authors use patterns to tell their stories or give information.

RML2   Sometimes authors tell a story in the order it happened.

RML3   Sometimes authors repeat a part of a story and add something new until the end.

Before Teaching Umbrella 2 Minilessons

The minilessons in this umbrella focus on developing children's understanding of text structure and patterns. Prepare for teaching these minilessons by reading and discussing a variety of ABC books, counting books, cumulative tales, animal tales, and other books that have simple sequenced or chronological plots. Use the following books from the *Fountas & Pinnell Classroom™ Interactive Read-Aloud Collection* text sets, or use similarly patterned books from your classroom library.

Letters at Work: The Alphabet

   ABC I Like Me! by Nancy Carlson

   B Is for Bulldozer: A Construction ABC by June Sobel

Numbers at Work: Counting

   One Moose, Twenty Mice by Clare Beaton

   Fish Eyes: A Book You Can Count On by Lois Ehlert

Living and Working Together: Community

   Lola at the Library by Anna McQuinn

Exploring Animal Tales

   The Three Bears by Paul Galdone

   The Three Little Pigs by Patricia Siebert

Using Patterns: Cumulative Tales

   The Enormous Potato by Aubrey Davis

   Hattie and the Fox by Mem Fox

   Mr. Gumpy's Outing by John Burningham

As you read aloud and enjoy these texts together, help children:

- notice how the author organizes the book using alphabetical and numerical order,
- notice the text structure of cumulative tales (one thing/event added at a time), and
- identify when a writer tells a story in chronological (time) order.

The Alphabet

Counting

Community

Animal Tales

Cumulative Tales

RML1
LA.U2.RML1

Reading Minilesson Principle
Sometimes authors use patterns to tell their stories or give information.

You Will Need

- two or three familiar texts with clear patterns, such as these:
  - *ABC I Like Me!* by Nancy Carlson and *B Is for Bulldozer: A Construction ABC* by June Sobel, from Text Set: The Alphabet
  - *One Moose, Twenty Mice* by Clare Beaton and *Fish Eyes: A Book You Can Count On* by Lois Ehlert, from Text Set: Counting
- chart paper and markers
- basket of books that have alphabet or number patterns

Academic Language / Important Vocabulary

- author
- illustrator
- alphabet (ABC)
- numbers (123)
- order
- pattern

Continuum Connection

- Notice simple text organization: e.g., ABC, bigger to smaller, smaller to bigger (p. 30)

Goal

Notice simple text organization (e.g., ABCs, ascending and descending numbers).

Rationale

When you teach children to recognize different text structures and organizational patterns, you support their ability to make predictions. Knowing how a book works supports children's comprehension and level of engagement. It also helps them develop their ability to craft their own stories.

Assess Learning

Observe children when they talk about how books work. Notice if there is evidence of new learning based on the goal of this minilesson.

- Are the children able to recognize the pattern in a story?
- Can they anticipate what might come next based upon the pattern in the story?
- Do they use ABCs and patterns to describe what they have read?
- Do they use the terms *author, illustrator, order,* and *pattern?*

Minilesson

To help children think about the minilesson principle, engage them in looking for patterns of organization in books. Here is an example.

> In *ABC I Like Me!* you read about a pig and all the words she uses to describe herself. As I read some of the pages, notice the pattern the writer uses to tell the story.

- Read the pages from A through E.

  What pattern do you notice?

- Write responses on the chart.

  What letter do you think will be next? What makes you think that?

  Let's see if you're right.

- Reveal the next page.

  One Moose, Twenty Mice by Clare Beaton is also organized, or put together, in a special way—in fact, this book has two patterns!

- Read the parts about one moose, two crabs, and three ladybugs.

  What do you notice about the patterns the author uses in this book?

- Write responses on the chart.

Have a Try

Invite the children to apply the new thinking with a partner.

Listen to *Fish Eyes: A Book You Can Count On*, by Lois Ehlert. See if you notice a pattern.

▸ Read the first few pages.

Turn and talk with a partner about the pattern you noticed in this book.

▸ After they turn and talk, record their noticings on the chart.

Summarize and Apply

Summarize the learning and remind children to look for patterns as they read.

Today you learned that sometimes authors use a pattern, like the ABCs or number order, to tell a story.

▸ Review the chart and write the principle at the top.

▸ Show children the basket of books.

During independent reading time today, choose a book from this basket. Look for patterns in your book. When we come back together, we will talk about what you noticed.

Sometimes authors use patterns to tell their stories or give information.	
Title	Pattern
ABC I Like Me! by Nancy Carlson	A,B,C
One Moose, Twenty Mice	1, 2, 3 Repeating line
Fish Eyes A BOOK YOU CAN COUNT ON Lois Ehlert	1, 2, 3

Share

Following independent work time, gather children together in the meeting area to talk about their reading.

What are some other books you have read that use ABCs or numbers?

Did you find any other types of patterns?

Extend the Lesson (Optional)

After assessing children's understanding, you might decide to extend the learning.

▸ Continue to add to the chart as the children notice books organized in alphabetical or numerical order. Invite children to notice other patterns and add them to the chart as well.

▸ **Drawing/Writing About Reading** Invite children to make an ABC or numerical book.

Reading Minilesson Principle
Sometimes authors tell a story in the order it happened.

Noticing How Authors Tell Their Stories

You Will Need

- two or three familiar texts with clear time order, such as these:
  - *Lola at the Library* by Anna McQuinn, from Text Set: Community
  - *The Three Bears* by Paul Galdone and *The Three Little Pigs* by Patricia Siebert, from Text Set: Animal Tales
- chart paper and markers
- basket of books with simple chronological plots

Academic Language / Important Vocabulary

- order
- first
- next
- last

Continuum Connection

- Identify a fiction writer's use of time order or other established sequences such as numbers, time of day, days of the week, seasons (p. 28)

Goal

Identify when a writer tells a story in time order.

Rationale

Helping children understand how texts are structured and organized supports their reading comprehension and fluency. When readers know what to expect, they are able to make predictions without losing focus on the big ideas of the story. They also develop an understanding of possibilities for organizing their own stories.

Assess Learning

Observe children when they talk about how books work. Notice if there is evidence of new learning based on the goal of this minilesson.

- ▶ Are the children able to recognize when a story is told in chronological order?
- ▶ Do they use the words *order, first, next,* and *last?*

Minilesson

To help children think about the minilesson principle, engage them in noticing that sometimes authors tell their stories in the order they happen. Here is an example.

- ▶ Guide children to notice that authors sometimes tell a story in the order it happened.

    Let's look at *Lola at the Library* by Anna McQuinn. Lola loves to go to the library with her mom on Tuesdays.

- ▶ Turn to the first pages in the book.

    What does Lola do before she and Mommy go to the library?

- ▶ Write responses on chart paper. Show some of the pages from the middle of the book.

    Then Lola and Mommy get to the library. What do they do there?

- ▶ Write responses on chart paper. Show pages toward the end of the book.

    After Lola and Mommy go to the library, how do they end their day?

- ▶ Write responses on chart paper. Review the chart with the children.

    In what order does the author tell the story? The author told the story in the order that everything happened.

- ▶ Repeat a similar process for *The Three Bears* to help children notice that in this story, too, the author wrote what happened in order.

    Let's look at *The Three Bears* by Paul Galdone. In this story, the author writes about what happens when a little girl named Goldilocks goes into the three bears' house.

Have a Try

Invite the children to apply the new thinking with a partner.

> Think about the story *The Three Little Pigs* by Patricia Siebert. What happens first in this story? What happens next? What happens last? Turn and talk to a partner about how the author organized or told this story.

▶ After they turn and talk, invite a few pairs to share their responses, and record them on the chart paper.

Summarize and Apply

Summarize the learning and remind children to think about the order of the story as they read.

> Today you learned that sometimes authors tell a story in the order that it happened.

▶ Review the chart and write the principle at the top.

> During reading time today, if you are reading a story, notice if the writer tells the story in the order it happened.

Share

Following independent work time, gather children together in the meeting area to talk about their reading.

> What other books have you read in which the author tells a story in the order it happened?

▶ Choose a few children to share.

Extend the Lesson (Optional)

After assessing children's understanding, you might decide to extend the learning.

▶ Remind children that when they write their own stories, they can tell the stories in the order that they happened. They might tell several things that happened before the last thing.

▶ Use interactive writing to have children rewrite a familiar story that is told in chronological order.

▶ Provide opportunities for children to act out what happened first, next, and last in the stories they are reading.

▶ **Drawing/Writing About Reading** Use shared writing to model drawing/writing a story map to emphasize that some stories are told in chronological order.

Sometimes authors tell a story in the order it happened.

	First	Next	Last
Lola at the Library	Lola put the books and the card in her backpack.	Mom and Lola picked books.	Mom read to Lola.
The Three Bears	The bears went for a walk.	Goldilocks ate the porridge.	Goldilocks ran away.
The Three Little Pigs	The pig built a house.	The wolf blew down two houses.	The wolf ran away.

Reading Minilesson Principle

Sometimes authors repeat a part of a story and add something new until the end.

Noticing How Authors Tell Their Stories

You Will Need

▶ two or three familiar texts with clear patterns, such as these from Text Set: Cumulative Tales:

- *The Enormous Potato* by Aubrey Davis

- *Hattie and the Fox* by Mem Fox

- *Mr. Gumpy's Outing* by John Burningham

▶ chart paper and markers

▶ basket of books with cumulative structure

Academic Language / Important Vocabulary

▶ author

▶ illustrator

▶ events

Continuum Connection

▶ Notice when a book has repeating episodes or language patterns [p. 29]

Goal

Notice simple text organization in cumulative tales.

Rationale

Learning the structure of cumulative tales enables children to recognize this unique type of story. Understanding how cumulative tales build increases engagement, enjoyment, and comprehension. This understanding also supports children's ability to tell and write their own stories.

Assess Learning

Observe children when they talk about how books work. Notice if there is evidence of new learning based on the goal of this minilesson.

▶ Are the children able to recognize how characters, events, and parts are added one at a time in a cumulative story or tale?

▶ Are they able to find other examples of books that work the same way?

Minilesson

To help children think about the minilesson principle, engage them in noticing how the events in cumulative stories build to a climax. Here is an example.

▶ Show a few pages of *The Enormous Potato* by Aubrey Davis, starting when the farmer tries to pull up the potato.

> What keeps happening in this story? What pattern do you notice?

> A part of the story is repeated, and the author adds a new character each time. What makes the pattern stop?

▶ Write responses on chart paper. (Explain what a plus sign is if you use one to show how characters are added in the story.)

▶ Repeat the process with *Hattie and the Fox*, guiding children to notice how the story builds as another part of the fox is revealed each time. Start at the beginning, where Hattie sees a nose in the bushes.

> Let's look at *Hattie and the Fox*. What keeps happening in this story?

> What makes the pattern stop?

▶ Add responses to the chart.

> Sometimes authors repeat a part of a story and add something new each time.

Have a Try

Invite the children to apply the new thinking with a partner.

▶ Show a few pages of *Mr. Gumpy's Outing*.

Turn and talk with a partner about how this book is like *The Enormous Potato* and *Hattie and the Fox*.

▶ After the children turn and talk, choose a few pairs to share their responses. Ask them to explain what was added one at a time in *Mr. Gumpy's Outing*. Add their responses to the chart.

Summarize and Apply

Summarize the learning and remind the children to think about how the author tells the story as they read.

> You learned that sometimes authors repeat a part of a story and add something new until the end.

▶ Review the chart and write the minilesson principle at the top of the chart.

> Today you are going to read a story from this basket with a partner. In each story, the author repeats a part and adds something new until the end. Think about how the author tells the story. What does the author repeat? What is added each time? When we come back together, we will add what you noticed to the chart.

Share

Following independent work time, gather children together in the meeting area to talk about their reading.

> In the stories you read today, what part did the author repeat and what parts did the author add?

▶ Have the basket of books with examples accessible so children can show examples to support their thinking.

▶ Choose a few children to share.

Extend the Lesson (Optional)

After assessing children's understanding, you might decide to extend the learning.

▶ Invite children to dramatize a familiar cumulative tale as readers' theater, making use of the cumulative pattern to learn the parts.

▶ Encourage children to make puppets with paper craft sticks to use in acting out a cumulative tale.

▶ **Drawing/Writing About Reading** Use a combination of interactive writing and shared writing to rewrite a familiar cumulative tale as a mural, highlighting the parts/characters/events that are repeated and added.

Section 2: Literary Analysis

Assessment

After you have taught the minilessons in this umbrella, observe children as they talk and write about their reading across instructional contexts: interactive read-aloud, independent reading and literacy work, guided reading, shared reading, and book club. Use *The Literacy Continuum* (Fountas and Pinnell 2017) to observe children's reading and writing behaviors across instructional contexts.

▶ What evidence do you have of children's new understandings about the way different stories work?

- Can children identify when an author uses a pattern in the story (e.g., ABCs, numerical order)?

- Do children notice when a story is told in chronological (time) order?

- Have children continued to notice different books that follow a cumulative structure?

- Do they use vocabulary such as *first, next, last, author, illustrator,* and *order* to talk about how authors tell their stories?

▶ In what other ways, beyond the scope of this umbrella, are they talking about books?

- Do children notice how other books (e.g., nonfiction texts) are organized?

- Do they use patterns in books to help them predict what will come next?

Use your observations to determine the next umbrella you will teach. You may also consult Minilessons Across the Year (p. 51) for guidance.

Link to Writing

After teaching the minilessons in this umbrella, help children link the new learning to their own writing:

▶ Encourage children to think about writing their own books that follow a certain pattern (either an alphabet book or a counting book).

▶ Invite children to write or draw their own cumulative tales.

▶ Show children how to write their own stories in the order they happened. Begin by having children tell their stories orally in the order they happened. Suggest that children use words such as *first, next, then,* and *before,* but only as appropriate for a child. Use the texts from this umbrella as mentor texts.

Minilessons in This Umbrella

RML1　Authors have special ways of writing that you can notice when you study their books.

RML2　Illustrators have special ways of illustrating that you can notice when you study their books.

Before Teaching Umbrella 3 Minilessons

Author study supports children in knowing what to expect when beginning to read a text by a familiar author or illustrator. It helps children develop an understanding of the distinguishing characteristics of the author or illustrator and gives children the tools they need to find connections and make predictions. It also supports them in noticing and appreciating elements of the writer's/illustrator's craft—a foundation for thinking analytically about texts.

An author study has four broad steps, which are described in detail on page 39. Before beginning an author study, collect a set of mentor texts by the author. Then take children through the first two steps of the author study during interactive read-aloud by making sure that children think and talk about the meaning of each text before focusing on the author's or illustrator's work as a whole. Keep the primary focus on the enjoyment of the book. The following minilessons address the third step of an author study. Use the following books from the *Fountas & Pinnell Classroom™ Interactive Read-Aloud Collection* text sets or choose a similar set of books by a single author and illustrator:

Eric Carle: Exploring the Natural World

Have You Seen My Cat?

The Mixed-Up Chameleon

Does a Kangaroo Have a Mother, Too?

"Slowly, Slowly, Slowly," said the Sloth

From Head to Toe

Lois Ehlert: Exploring Found Objects

Feathers for Lunch　　　　　　*Market Day*

Mole's Hill　　　　　　　　　*Snowballs*

Top Cat

As you read aloud and enjoy these texts together, help children to:

* make language connections among texts,

* make illustration connections among texts,

* notice similar types of characters, and

* think about the topics that the author or illustrator chose.

Eric Carle

Lois Ehlert

Section 2: Literary Analysis

RML1
LA.U3.RML1

Reading Minilesson Principle
Authors have special ways of writing that you can notice when you study their books.

Studying Authors and Illustrators

You Will Need

- a set of familiar books by the same author, such as Eric Carle (see Minilesson and Have a Try)
- basket of books by a single author, such as Eric Carle, that children have read or heard (see Summarize and Apply)
- chart paper and markers

Academic Language / Important Vocabulary

- author
- similar
- alike

Continuum Connection

- Recognize that an author or illustrator may write or illustrate several books (p. 28)
- Recognize some authors by the topics they choose or the style of their illustrations (p. 31)

Goal

Recognize how books by the same author are similar.

Rationale

When you guide children to recognize the various features in texts by the same person, they begin to understand that writing a book is a process of decision making. And, once children get to know an author, they form a connection to the author, which increases engagement and sensitivity to author's craft.

Assess Learning

Observe children when they talk about books by the same author. Notice if there is evidence of new learning based on the goal of this minilesson.

- ▶ Do children notice ways books by the same author are alike?
- ▶ Are children able to talk about the characteristics of a familiar author's writing?
- ▶ Do children use the academic language *author* and comparatives, such as *similar* and *alike*?

Minilesson

To help children think about the minilesson principle, engage them in noticing how an author's style of writing is similar from one book to another. Here is an example.

- ▶ Show the covers of several books by Eric Carle.

    These books are all by Eric Carle.

- ▶ Read the titles and revisit a few pages to refresh children's memory.

    What do you remember about Eric Carle's books?

    Let's think about what we notice about Eric Carle's books. Look at the covers. What kinds of characters does Eric Carle write about?

    Now listen to his words.

- ▶ Read the first few pages of *Does a Kangaroo Have a Mother, Too?*, *"Slowly, Slowly, Slowly," said the Sloth*, and *Have You Seen My Cat?*

    What do you notice about the words? How are the words alike?

- ▶ Guide children to listen to the language, highlighting the repetition and rhyme.

- ▶ On chart paper, write Eric Carle's name and the word *Noticings*. Add a section for *always* and a section for *often*. Ask children what they noticed Eric Carle always did and what he did often or most of the time in his books. Record responses on the chart.

Have a Try

Invite the children to apply the new thinking about Eric Carle with a partner.

> As I read a few pages from the other books by Eric Carle, think about how Eric Carle writes his stories.

▶ Read a few pages from the *The Mixed-Up Chameleon* and/or *From Head to Toe*.

▶ Pause after each book to allow children to turn and talk what they notice: Do they notice some of the same things that they saw in the other books? What else do they notice? Ask volunteers to share their thinking and add to the noticings chart.

Summarize and Apply

Summarize the learning and remind children to notice authors' special ways of writing.

▶ Review the chart, emphasizing both the *always* category and the *often* category. Make sure children understand why the characteristics fit into each category.

> Today, some of you will read or look at a book from this basket. These books were also written by Eric Carle (or another author you may have used for this lesson). See if you notice some of the things we talked about. You might also notice something new. Bring the book when we meet so you can share.

Share

Following independent work time, gather children in the meeting area to talk about their reading.

> Did anyone read a book by Eric Carle today? Did you notice anything else about his writing that we should add to the chart?

Extend the Lesson (Optional)

After assessing children's understanding, you might decide to extend the learning.

▶ Encourage children to read more books by Eric Carle (or other favorite author), talk about the books, and make suggestions to add to the noticings chart.

▶ Many authors have a website, where you can find a picture of and some information about the author. Share this information with children so they learn to regard authors as real people.

▶ **Drawing/Writing About Reading** Create a class big book in the style of Eric Carle, using the language from a book with simple text such as *Have You Seen My Cat?* Have children compare the finished class big book to other books by Eric Carle.

Eric Carle

Noticings:

Always	Often
• He writes about animals and nature.	• He uses rhyming words. • He repeats words.

Section 2: Literary Analysis

Reading Minilesson Principle

Illustrators have special ways of illustrating that you can notice when you study their books.

Studying Authors and Illustrators

You Will Need

- three to five familiar books by the same illustrator, such as Lois Ehlert
- basket of books by the same illustrator, such as Lois Ehlert, with which children are familiar
- chart paper and markers

Academic Language / Important Vocabulary

- illustrator
- illustration
- label

Continuum Connection

- Recognize that an author or illustrator may write or illustrate several books (p. 30)

Goal

Recognize that an illustrator may illustrate several books.

Rationale

When you guide children to recognize the various features in illustrations by the same person, children begin to understand that illustrating a book is a process of decision making. And, once children get to know an illustrator, they form a connection to the illustrator, which increases engagement and sensitivity to illustrators' craft.

Assess Learning

Observe children when they talk about books illustrated by the same person. Notice if there is evidence of new learning based on the goal of this minilesson.

- Do children notice ways that illustrations by the same illustrator are alike?
- Are children able to talk about the characteristics of a familiar illustrator?
- Do children use the words *illustrator* and *label?*

Minilesson

To help children think about the minilesson principle, engage them in noticing how an illustrator's style is similar from one book to another. Here is an example.

- Have children sit in a circle. Show the covers and inside illustrations from several books by Lois Ehlert.

    These books are all by the same illustrator, Lois Ehlert. What do you notice about her illustrations? What helps you know that the illustrations in these books are by the same person?

- Guide children to notice features of the illustrations that are common in Ehlert's books, such as her use of shapes and all sorts of different objects for her illustrations.

- On chart paper, add Lois Ehlert's name to the top and the word *Noticings*. Add a section for *always* and a section for *often*. Ask children what they noticed Lois Ehlert always did and what she often did or did most of the time in her books. Record responses on the chart.

Have a Try

Invite the children to apply the new thinking to another book by Lois Ehlert.

▶ Hold up another book by Lois Ehlert, different from the ones you used earlier. Show some of the pages.

> What do you see in this book that is the same as something on the chart?

▶ Talk about how they can recognize a book by Lois Ehlert.

Summarize and Apply

Summarize the learning and remind children to notice the illustrations as they read.

> What are some things you noticed today about Lois Ehlert's illustrations?

▶ Review the chart, emphasizing both the *always* category and the *often* category. Make sure children understand why the characteristics fit into each category.

> Today, some of you will read or look at a book from the basket. The books are all illustrated by Lois Ehlert (or other illustrator used in the lesson). See if you notice any of the things we talked about. You also might notice something new. Bring the books when we meet so you can share.

Share

Following independent work time, gather children together in the meeting area to talk about their reading.

> If you read a book by Lois Ehlert, show the book and talk about the things you noticed about her illustrations.

Extend the Lesson (Optional)

After assessing children's understanding, you might decide to extend the learning.

▶ Continue to add to the noticings chart as you read more books by Lois Ehlert.

▶ Many illustrators have a website, where you can find a picture of and some information about the illustrator. Share this information with the children so that they learn to regard illustrators as real people.

▶ **Drawing/Writing About Reading** Have children create illustrations in the collage style of Lois Ehlert, and then compare their own illustrations to those in one or more books by Lois Ehlert.

Lois Ehlert

Noticings:

Always	Often
• She uses things like cloth, paper, and real toys in her illustrations.	• She uses photos to make her illustrations.
• She cuts or finds shapes and makes pictures with them.	• She adds labels around the illustrations.
• She makes illustrations about animals and nature.	

Assessment

After you have taught the minilessons in this umbrella, observe children as they talk and write about their reading across instructional contexts: interactive read-aloud, independent reading and literacy work, guided reading, shared reading, and book club. Use *The Literacy Continuum* (Fountas and Pinnell 2017) to observe children's reading and writing behaviors across instructional contexts.

▶ What evidence do you have of new understandings related to an author's or illustrator's craft?

- Can children identify the unique features of texts by authors and illustrators they have studied?

- Are children able to understand the noticings about the authors and illustrators?

- Do children talk with others about the similarities among books by the same author and/or illustrator?

- Do they understand academic language related to an author or illustrator study, such as *author, illustrator,* and *illustrations*?

▶ In what other ways, beyond the scope of this umbrella, are the children talking about author study?

- Do children begin to notice characteristics of other authors and illustrators who they become familiar with during independent reading?

Use your observations to determine the next umbrella you will teach. You may also want to consult Minilessons Across the Year (p. 51) for guidance.

Link to Writing

After teaching the minilessons in this umbrella, help children link the new learning to their own writing or drawing:

▶ After completing the steps in the author study process, have children make their own books using what they have learned about writing and illustrations. For example, they can use repeating words like Eric Carle or add labels to the illustrations and use collage like Lois Ehlert. Encourage them to compare their finished books to several texts by the original author or illustrator and talk about the similarities.

Minilessons in This Umbrella

Independent Reading

RML1   A book talk is a short talk about a book you want to recommend.

RML2   Tell the important information when you give a book talk about a story.

RML3   Tell something interesting you learned when you give a book talk about a nonfiction book.

RML4   Try to get your classmates interested in the book.

RML5   Speak clearly and show your excitement when you give a book talk.

RML6   Hold your book and your body so everyone can see.

RML7   Prepare for a book talk and practice it.

Before Teaching Umbrella 4 Minilessons

Before teaching this series of minilessons, build a collection of books organized by topic, author, genre, series, etc., and include in each category books that represent the variety of independent reading levels of the children in your class. (Note: You will not be organizing the library by level.) Establish a time for independent reading, when children self-select books that are just right for them to read and enjoy. The Section One: Management umbrellas, Using the Classroom Library (page 85–96) and Engaging in Classroom Literacy Work (page 97–118), provide support for building these routines. To prepare children to give book talks, build routines such as listening and talking about books together. Use the following books from the *Fountas & Pinnell Classroom™ Independent Reading Collection* or *Interactive Read-Aloud Collection*, or choose other books that children enjoy and can read.

Independent Reading Collection

Goodnight, Gorilla by Peggy Rathmann

Watch Your Step, Mr. Rabbit! by Richard Scarry

Run, Swim, Fly by Julie K. Lundgren

Noses by Melanie Mitchell

How to Ride a Giraffe by Alice Cary

A Moose Is Loose by Kana Riley

Family

Taking Care of Each Other: Family

Jonathan and His Mommy by Irene Smalls

As you model book talks using these books during the inquiry lessons, make sure to

- keep them short,

- include the title, author, and just a little information about the book,

- use an exciting lead that captures the children's interest, organize your thoughts before giving the book talk, and

- use eye contact, a confident, excited voice, and body language to engage the audience.

RML1
LA.U4.RML1

Reading Minilesson Principle
A book talk is a short talk about a book you want to recommend.

You Will Need

- a book that children have read, such as *Goodnight, Gorilla* by Peggy Rathmann, from the *Independent Reading Collection*
- chart paper and markers

Academic Language / Important Vocabulary

- book talk
- opinion
- recommendation

Continuum Connection

- Articulate why they like a text (p. 28)
- Express opinions about a text: e.g., interesting, funny, exciting (p. 29)

Goal

Understand that a book talk is a way to recommend books to classmates.

Rationale

Book talks are an opportunity for children to talk about a book they think their classmates will enjoy reading, providing the other children with an array of books they might choose to read. Giving a book talk requires a thoughtful analysis of the book to choose the parts that will entice other children to read it.

Assess Learning

Observe children when they talk about what they have learned about book talks. Notice if there is evidence of new learning based on the goal of this minilesson.

- Do children understand the rationale for a book talk?
- Are they able to choose a book to recommend?
- Do they understand the terms *book talk, opinion,* and *recommendation?*

Minilesson

To help children think about the minilesson principle, model a book talk for them. Here is an example.

- Choose an independent reading book from your classroom library, such as *Goodnight, Gorilla.*

  I am going to tell you about a book today. When I finish, I am going to ask you to talk about what you noticed about my book talk and about why someone gives a book talk.

  This book is called *Goodnight, Gorilla.* In this book, a zookeeper walks around the zoo saying goodnight to all the animals. The gorilla walks behind him and does something sneaky. The illustrations in this book are fun because they show you things that are happening that the zookeeper does not see.

- Show one.

  If you like books with great illustrations and sneaky characters, you will enjoy reading *Goodnight, Gorilla.*

Have a Try

Invite the children to about a book talk with a partner.

> Turn and talk to your partner about what you noticed about my book talk. What did I do? What kind of information did I tell you about the book? Do you think my book talk would make someone want to read this book? What makes you think so?

▸ After a few moments, ask two or three children to share their thinking. Then ask children why they think someone would give a book talk.

Summarize and Apply

Summarize the learning and remind children to think about the minilesson principle as they read.

> Today you learned that a book talk is a short talk about a book you want to recommend. In a book talk, you tell about a book you like, but you don't tell everything that happens in the book.

▸ Construct a chart to help children remember what a book talk is. Add the principle to the top of the chart.

> Today when you are reading, think about whether the book is one that you think your friends would enjoy and that you might decide to use for a book talk.

Share

Following independent work time, gather children together in the meeting area to talk about their reading.

> Today you thought about how to give a book talk—you learned how to recommend a book to your classmates. Who read a book that you would like to recommend to a classmate?

▸ Ask a few children to share the name of the book they would recommend. If there is time, partners can take a short beginning try at a book talk.

Extend the Lesson (Optional)

After assessing children's understanding, you might decide to extend the learning.

▸ Work with individual readers or a small group to choose books they would recommend to classmates. Talk about the elements of the book to include in a book talk. Have children give book talks to the small group or the class.

A book talk is a short talk about a book you want to recommend.

I like this book because it is funny. I think you will too.

Good Night, Gorilla

RML2
LA.U4.RML2

Reading Minilesson Principle
Tell the important information when you give a book talk about a story.

Giving a Book Talk

You Will Need

- a book that children can read, such as *Watch Your Step, Mr. Rabbit!* by Richard Scarry, from the *Independent Reading Collection*
- chart paper and markers

Academic Language / Important Vocabulary

- book talk
- opinion
- recommendation
- title
- author
- character

Continuum Connection

- Express opinions about a text: e.g., interesting, funny, exciting (p. 28)
- Explain and describe people, events, places, and things in a story (p. 331)

Goal

Understand the kind of information to tell when giving a book talk.

Rationale

When children identify information to include in a short book talk they synthesize the important information.

Assess Learning

Observe children when they give a book talk. Notice if there is evidence of new learning based on the goal of this minilesson.

- Do they include important information about the book when giving a book talk?
- Do they say why they like the book and try to get others interested in it?
- Do they understand the terms *book talk, opinion, recommendation, title, author,* and *character?*

Minilesson

To help children think about the minilesson principle, demonstrate the kind of information that should be included in a book talk. Here is an example.

> I like books that are funny. This book, called *Watch Your Step, Mr. Rabbit*, is funny. Mr. Rabbit is so busy reading the newspaper that he doesn't notice they are pouring new cement onto the road. Wait until you see what happens!

- Read aloud the page that says, "Now he is looking at his feet. His feet are stuck in the street."

> Mr. Rabbit's feet are stuck in the cement! I really like this book. I think you should read it to find out how they try to get Mr. Rabbit out of the cement and to find out if Mr. Rabbit learns his lesson to watch his step.
>
> What did you notice I included in this book talk that makes you want to read this book?

- Chart responses. If children mention something specific, extend to the bigger idea.

> What did you notice I told you about the end of the book? In a book talk you want to tell enough to get the reader interested, but not so much that you give away the whole story.

Have a Try

Invite the children to apply the new learning about book talks with a partner.

> Turn and talk to your partner about a book you know. It might be one that we have read together. Tell the title, the author's name if you know it, and a little bit about what happens in the book.

Summarize and Apply

Summarize the learning and remind children to think about the minilesson principle as they read.

> You learned that you tell the important information when you give a book talk about a story. You also learned that you don't give away too much information.

▶ Review the chart and add the principle to the top.

> Today think about what you would tell in a book talk about the book you are reading.

▶ During independent reading, sit with a few children to help them think through what they could say about their book in a book talk.

> Tell the important information when you give a book talk about a story.
>
> • The title — *Watch Your Step, Mr. Rabbit!*
>
> • The characters
>
> • Something important that happens
>
> • Something you like

Share

Following independent work time, gather children together in the meeting area to talk about, listen to, and discuss a book talk.

▶ Have a child you previously supported give a book talk.

> Think about two things as you listen. What does _____ share about the book? Would you want to read this book?

> What did you notice about _____'s book talk? What got you interested in reading this book?

Extend the Lesson (Optional)

After assessing children's understanding, you might decide to extend the learning.

▶ Work with individual readers or a small group to prepare a book talk.

▶ Have partners practice giving book talks to one another.

Reading Minilesson Principle

Tell something interesting you learned when you give a book talk about a nonfiction book.

Giving a Book Talk

You Will Need

- a book that children can read, such as *Run, Swim, Fly* by Julie K. Lundgren, from the *Independent Reading Collection*, with a page marked
- chart paper and markers
- sticky notes

Academic Language / Important Vocabulary

- book talk
- retell
- recommendation
- fiction
- nonfiction
- title
- author

Continuum Connection

- Report what is known or learned about in an informational text (p. 331)
- Express opinions and tell why (p. 331)

Goal

Share something you learned from a nonfiction book when you give a book talk.

Rationale

When children describe a nonfiction book they have the opportunity to tell what they learned from an informational text. The listeners learn about an array of books they might be interested in reading.

Assess Learning

Observe children when they give a book talk. Notice if there is evidence of new learning based on the goal of this minilesson.

- ❯ Do children include something interesting they learned?
- ❯ Can they identify why they like the book?
- ❯ Do they use vocabulary such as *fiction, nonfiction, title,* and *author* when they give a book talk?

Minilesson

To help children think about the minilesson principle, model a book talk for them. Here is an example.

- ❯ Choose a nonfiction independent reading book from your classroom library, such as *Run, Swim, Fly*. In advance, mark a page in the book with a sticky note to indicate something you learned from the book.

    I am going to give a book talk. When I finish my book talk, I'll ask you to talk about what you noticed.

    The title of this nonfiction book is *Run, Swim, Fly*. I learned about how different animals move.

- ❯ Refer to the page with the sticky note.

    For example, this page shows that some animals, like cheetahs, run. I liked this book because it taught me how animals move. It also has great photographs! So if you like animals, this is a book you will love.

Have a Try

Invite the children to talk about a book talk with a partner.

    Turn and talk to your partner about what you heard me include in my book talk to get you interested in reading this book.

- ❯ After they turn and talk, call on a few children to share their noticings. Chart responses.

Summarize and Apply

Summarize the learning and remind children to think about what their friends will find interesting.

> Today you learned to tell something interesting you learned when you give a book talk about a nonfiction book. You can mark the page that you want to share.

> Today during independent reading if you choose a nonfiction book, think about what you could say in a book talk.

▶ During independent reading, sit with a few children and support them as they think about what they might say in a book talk. Review the chart to remind children of the information to include in a book talk.

Share

Following independent reading time, gather children in the meeting area.

▶ Decide whether the children will practice a book talk with a partner, or if an individual child will give a book talk to the whole group. Or, ask a child you have previously supported to give a book talk.

> Listen to the book talk and think about two things: What does your friend share with you about the book, and would this be a book that you would want to read?

Extend the Lesson (Optional)

After assessing children's understanding, you might decide to extend the learning.

▶ Add new ideas to the chart as they come up.

▶ Work with individual readers or a small group to prepare a book talk for a nonfiction book.

▶ Have partners practice giving a book talk to one another using nonfiction books.

Tell something interesting you learned when you give a book talk about a nonfiction book.

• The title

• Something interesting you learned

• Why you like the book

RML4
LA.U4.RML4

Reading Minilesson Principle
Try to get your classmates interested in the book.

Giving a Book Talk

You Will Need

- books that children can read, such as the following:
  - *Noses* by Melanie Mitchell, from the *Independent Reading Collection*, with a page marked
  - *How to Ride a Giraffe* by Alice Cary, from the *Independent Reading Collection*
- chart paper and markers

Academic Language / Important Vocabulary

- book talk

Continuum Connection

- Express opinions about a text: e.g., interesting, funny, exciting (pp. 28, 30)
- Talk about a topic with enthusiasm (p. 331)

Goal

Share an interesting or funny part of a book to engage other readers.

Rationale

When you share something interesting or funny about a book, children learn ways to capture the attention of listeners in a variety of contexts.

Assess Learning

Observe children when they give a book talk. Notice if there is evidence of new learning based on the goal of this minilesson.

- Do they include ideas that make the book interesting to others?
- Are they including humor or different voice levels to engage listeners?

Minilesson

To help children think about the minilesson principle, demonstrate ways to make a book talk interesting. Here is an example.

- Choose a nonfiction independent reading book from your classroom library, such as *Noses*. In advance, mark a page in the book with a sticky note to indicate something engaging from the book.

  I am going to give a book talk. While I am giving my book talk, notice what I do to get you interested in the book. The title of this book is *Noses*. In this book, the author shows animals with all kinds of noses. Wait until you see some of these noses! Have you ever seen a horse's nose close up?

- Display the page with the sticky note.

  Look at that! If you are interested in learning about animal noses, you should read *Noses*. What did I do to get you interested in reading the book?

- Chart responses.

Have a Try

Invite the children to apply the new thinking with a partner.

- Do a book talk with a fiction book, such as *How to Ride a Giraffe*. Vary your voice level to add interest; for example, use a quieter voice for the sentence below that begins "The girl cannot really . . ."

  The title of this book is *How to Ride a Giraffe*. This fiction book tells you all you need to know to ride a giraffe. The girl cannot really ride a giraffe, but it is fun to read what she suggests. Each section of this book teaches you something you need to know about riding a giraffe. I want to read you my favorite part.

▶ Read the section titled How to Steer a Giraffe, emphasizing the line that reads "WARNING: Do not."

> Turn and talk to a partner about how I made my book talk interesting.

▶ Chart responses.

Summarize and Apply

Summarize the learning and remind children to think about how to make a book talk interesting.

> Today you thought about how to make your book talk interesting so that your classmates might want to read the book, too. If you say something interesting or funny about the book in your book talk, it will make other people want to read the book. Today when you read, think about how you might get your classmates interested in the book.

▶ During independent reading, support a few children in practicing a book talk.

Share

Following independent work time, gather children together in the meeting area to listen to a book talk.

> ▶ Invite a child you previously supported to give a book talk to the whole group.

> Listen as _____ shares a book talk with you. Think about what she says or does to get you interested in the book.

> ▶ Child gives book talk.

> What did you notice _____ did or said to get you interested in the book?

> ▶ If children mention something specific, extend to the bigger idea, and refer to or add to the chart.

> Who might be interested in reading this book?

Extend the Lesson (Optional)

After assessing children's understanding, you might decide to extend the learning.

> ▶ Add new ideas to make a book talk interesting or funny to the chart as they come up.

> ▶ Work with individual readers or a small group to prepare a book talk.

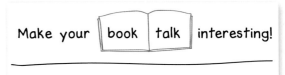

Make your book talk interesting!

- Sound excited!

- Ask a question.

- Show a picture.

- Tell your favorite part.

- Make your voice loud and soft.

RML5
LA.U4.RML5

Reading Minilesson Principle
Speak clearly and show your excitement when you give a book talk.

Giving a Book Talk

You Will Need

- *Jonathan and His Mommy* by Irene Smalls, from Text Set: Family
- chart paper and markers
- books that children can read or have heard read aloud

Academic Language / Important Vocabulary

- book talk
- volume
- pace

Continuum Connection

- Talk about a topic with enthusiasm (p. 331)
- Look at the audience (or other person) while speaking (p. 331)
- Speak at an appropriate rate to be understood (p. 331)

Goal

Speak with confidence and enthusiasm and use the appropriate rate and volume of speech.

Rationale

Children need to be taught to speak effectively to a group, and to capture the group's attention by using an appropriate pace and volume. This important skill will help children in book talks and in all of their academic experiences.

Assess Learning

Observe children when they give a book talk. Notice if there is evidence of new learning based on the goal of this minilesson.

- Do children speak with an appropriate volume?
- Are they using an appropriate pace?
- Do they show confidence and enthusiasm?
- Do they speak clearly and look at their classmates?
- Do they understand the terms book *talk, volume,* and *pace*?

Minilesson

To help children think about the minilesson principle, demonstrate effective communication skills when speaking to an audience. Here is an example.

- Choose a book from your classroom library, such as *Jonathan and His Mommy*.

  I am going to give a book talk. Listen carefully to my voice. When I am finished, I am going to ask you about how my voice sounded.

- Make sure to speak clearly, at a good pace, and with a little excitement as appropriate.

  The title of this book is *Jonathan and His Mommy*. In this book, the characters, Jonathan and his mommy, take a walk in the city. They walk in all different ways as they explore the city.

- Read aloud the page that begins, "After that we take itsy-bitsy baby steps."

  This is one of my favorite pages. I also like this book because the author uses fun words. Listen to this.

- Read aloud the next page showing excitement when saying, *"Hop-hop-hop (hip-hop, too, sometimes)."*

Have a Try

Invite the children to apply the new thinking with a partner.

> Turn and talk to your partner about how I made my voice sound.

▶ Have a few children share. Be sure to elicit thinking about volume, pace, and excitement. Chart responses. If they mention something specific, extend to the bigger idea.

Summarize and Apply

Summarize the learning to prepare children for giving a book talk.

> Today you learned to speak clearly and show your excitement when you give a book talk. This will help listeners think about and understand what you are saying.

▶ Review the chart and write the principle at the top.

▶ During independent reading, support a few children in practicing a book talk while the others read independently.

Share

Following independent work time, gather children together in the meeting area to talk about their reading.

▶ Invite a child you previously supported to give a book talk to the whole group.

> _____ is going to give a book talk. Listen and think about how her voice sounds.

▶ Refer or add to the chart as necessary.

Extend the Lesson (Optional)

After assessing children's understanding, you might decide to extend the learning.

▶ Add new ideas to the chart as they come up.

▶ Work with individual readers or a small group to prepare a book talk. Emphasize the use of appropriate volume, pace, and level of confidence.

▶ Have partners practice giving a book talk to one another.

Speak clearly and show your excitement when you give a book talk.

- Speak clearly.

- Don't speak too fast.

- Don't speak too slow.

- Look at people.

- Sound excited.

RML6
LA.U4.RML6

Reading Minilesson Principle
Hold your book and your body so everyone can see.

Giving a Book Talk

You Will Need

- a book that children can read, such as *A Moose Is Loose* by Kana Riley, from the *Independent Reading Collection*
- chart paper and markers

Academic Language / Important Vocabulary

- book talk
- recommend

Continuum Connection

- Look at the audience (or other person) while speaking (p. 331)

Goal

Understand how to use the book and body language in a book talk.

Rationale

It develops children's understanding of how to present information to others if they learn how to show the book they are talking about, where to focus their eyes, and what kind of body language to use. This helps children not only with book talks, but with presenting other information to classmates as well.

Assess Learning

Observe children when they give a book talk. Notice if there is evidence of new learning based on the goal of this minilesson.

- Do children sit or stand appropriately?
- Are they looking at the audience?
- Do they hold the book so everyone in the audience can see it?
- Do they use the terms *book talk* and *recommend?*

Minilesson

To help children think about the minilesson principle, demonstrate effective presentation skills when speaking to an audience. Here is an example.

- Choose an independent reading book from your classroom library, such *as A Moose Is Loose*, for a book talk. While speaking, demonstrate holding the book so that everyone can see illustrations that you show and holding your body so that there is no extra movement but enough movement so that you can make eye contact with the children.

  I would like to share another book talk with you. This time, notice how I hold the book, and what I do with my body. The title of this book is *A Moose Is Loose.* In this book, a girl named Maribelle keeps telling different family members that a moose is loose! The illustrations show the moose standing outside the window.

- Show the illustration, marked with a sticky note, moving it so that everyone can see, and continue with the book talk.

  Read this book to find out if the moose is real or not, and what Maribelle and her family do.

RML 6

LA.U4.RML6

Section 2: Literary Analysis

Have a Try

Invite the children to talk with a partner about what they observed about a book talk.

> Turn and talk to your partner about what you noticed about how I held the book and how I held and moved my body.

▶ Ask a few children to share. Chart responses.

Summarize and Apply

Summarize the learning to prepare children for giving a book talk.

> Today you learned how to hold your book and your body so everyone can see when you give a book talk.

▶ Review the chart and write the principle at the top.

> When you are reading independently today, if you have a book that you would like to recommend to your classmates, you can give a book talk. Think not only about the information to share, and how your voice will sound, but what your body will look like, too.

▶ During independent reading, support a few children in practicing a book talk.

Hold your book and your body so everyone can see.

- Look at the audience.

- Be sure the audience sees the book.

- Sit still.

Share

Following independent work time, gather the children in the meeting area to listen to a book talk.

> _____ is going to give a book talk. While you listen, focus on his eyes, how he sits (or stands), and how he holds the book.

> What did you notice about _____ 's book talk?

▶ Refer or add to the chart as necessary.

Extend the Lesson (Optional)

After assessing children's understanding, you might decide to extend the learning.

▶ Add new ideas to the chart as they come up.

▶ Work with individual readers or a small group to prepare a book talk using appropriate body language and eye contact.

▶ Have partners practice giving a book talk to one another.

Reading Minilesson Principle
Prepare for a book talk and practice it.

Giving a Book Talk

You Will Need

- charts from previous minilessons in this umbrella
- chart paper and markers

Academic Language / Important Vocabulary

- book talk
- prepare

Continuum Connection

- Have an audience in mind before starting to speak (p. 331)

Goal

Understand how to prepare for a book talk.

Rationale

Understanding what to do to prepare for a book talk supports children in thinking about the most important pieces to include in a book talk. It also supports them in learning how to prepare for other presentations to groups of children.

Assess Learning

Observe children when they give a book talk. Notice if there is evidence of new learning based on the goal of this minilesson.

- Are children willing to present a book talk to a small group? To a whole group?
- Do they show evidence of learning how to give a book talk that shows excitement?
- Do they understand the terms *book talk* and *prepare?*

Minilesson

To help children think about the minilesson principle, review what they have already learned about giving a book talk. Here is an example.

> We have talked about how to give a good book talk. What are some important things to remember?

- Refer to the charts from previous minilessons as appropriate.

> Now you will prepare a book talk, or get a book talk ready to share. What do you need to do to get ready for the book talk?

- Chart responses. The children may not mention the ideas in order, so ask prioritizing questions as needed: *What would you do first? Next? After that?*
- This will result in a chart that is created by the children, yet supported by you in its organization.

> About how long do you think the book talk should be? When you are planning how long the book talk should be, think about commercials on television. A book talk is like a commercial for a book!

Have a Try

Invite the children tell a partner the name of the book they will use for a book talk.

> Now that you understand what to do to prepare for a book talk, you will give a book talk. First, you need to choose a book. Turn to your partner and say the title of the book you will give a book talk about.

Summarize and Apply

Summarize the learning to prepare children for giving a book talk.

> Remember that you need to prepare for a book talk and practice it. You will now spend a few minutes preparing a book talk using one of the books in your independent reading box (or bag). Choose a book you have already read because that is what you do first.

▶ Have children work either individually or with a partner to prepare a book talk. From your observations over the past few days, choose an individual student that may need guidance or pull a small group of children together to plan one book talk together.

Share

Following independent work time, gather children together in the meeting area to practice book talks.

▶ Ask children to sit in groups of two, three, or four, and to practice giving a book talk with one another. When children finish practicing, ask a few children to share one thing they did well and one thing they will work on.

Extend the Lesson (Optional)

After assessing children's understanding, you might decide to extend the learning.

▶ Work with individual readers or a small group to prepare a book talk that includes all the necessary pieces.

▶ Have partners practice giving a book talk to one another.

▶ Create a calendar or a sign-up sheet for children to determine when they will give a book talk to their classmates.

Prepare for a book talk and practice it.

- Choose a book you read and liked.

- Think about the title.

- Mark a page to talk about.

- Tell why someone should read this book.

Assessment

After you have taught the minilessons in this umbrella, observe children as they talk and write about their reading across instructional contexts: interactive read-aloud, independent reading and literacy work, guided reading, shared reading, and book club. Use *The Literacy Continuum* (Fountas and Pinnell 2017) to observe children's reading and writing behaviors across instructional contexts.

> ❱ What evidence do you have of new understandings related to book talks?
>
>   • Do the children select books that are appropriate for book talks?
>
>   • Can they give a fiction book talk that includes the title of the book, the setting, the characters, and a little bit about what the characters do?
>
>   • Do they give a nonfiction book talk that includes the title of the book and a new, interesting idea that they learned?
>
>   • Are they able to describe what they liked about a book?
>
>   • Can they say something interesting to get friends to read it?
>
>   • While giving a book talk, do they look at the audience, hold the book appropriately, and sit in a way that allows listeners to focus?
>
>   • Do children speak clearly and show excitement while giving a book talk?
>
>   • Are children practicing and preparing before giving a book talk?
>
>   • Do they understand vocabulary related to book talks, such as *author, title, illustrator,* and *recommend*?
>
> ❱ In what other ways, beyond the scope of this umbrella, are children taking on the routine of giving book talks?
>
>   • Do children modify the way they give a book talk after becoming more comfortable with book talks?

Use your observations to determine the next umbrella you will teach. You may also consult Minilessons Across the Year (p. 51) for guidance.

Link to Writing

After teaching the minilessons in this umbrella, help children link the new learning to their own writing:

> ❱ Use interactive writing to develop book recommendations that can be shared within your classroom or shared with other kindergarten classrooms.

> ❱ Provide the opportunity to write a book recommendation as a choice at the writing center.

Minilessons in This Umbrella

RML1	Choose a book you would like to read and talk about.
RML2	Mark the pages you want to talk about.
RML3	Talk about your thinking in book club.
RML4	Learn how to have a good book club meeting.
RML5	Be sure everyone has a chance to talk during book club.
RML6	Talk about what went well and what you want to work on to get better.

Colors

Before Teaching Umbrella 5 Minilessons

The minilessons in this umbrella are designed to help you introduce and teach the procedures and routines to establish book clubs in your classroom. Book clubs are meetings with about four to six children of varying reading abilities, who come together to discuss a common text that they have chosen. The goal is for the children to share their thinking with each other and build a richer meaning than one reader could gain on his own. In a small book club, it will be easier for children to get to know one another's point of view and for everyone to have more opportunities to talk. In addition, the teacher can play a key role in scaffolding the children's responses (see pages 62–64 for more information on book clubs).

The minilessons in this umbrella use examples from the following text sets from the *Fountas & Pinnell Classroom™ Book Club Collection* and the *Interactive Read-Aloud Collection*, though you may choose others if you do not have access to these resources.

Book Club Collection: Friendship

Spring Is Here! by Will Hillenbrand

A Bedtime for Bear by Bonny Becker

All for a Dime! by Will Hillenbrand

My Friend Bear by Jez Alborough

Interactive Read-Aloud Collection: Noticing the Way the World Looks: Colors

What Color Is Nature? by Stephen R. Swinburne

Cat's Colors by Jane Cabrera

Section 2: Literary Analysis

Reading Minilesson Principle
Choose a book you would like to read and talk about.

Getting Started with Book Clubs

You Will Need

- prepare book talks for four books that children have not read or heard, such as these from the *Book Club Collection*: Friendship:
  - *Spring Is Here!* by Will Hillenbrand
  - *A Bedtime for Bear* by Bonny Becker
  - *All for a Dime!* by Will Hillenbrand
  - *My Friend Bear* by Jez Alborough
- chart paper and markers

Academic Language / Important Vocabulary

- author
- illustrator
- title

Continuum Connection

- Articulate why they like a text (p. 28)

Goal

Learn how to make a good book choice for book club meetings.

Rationale

Children are more engaged in book club when they choose the book for their discussion. Choice breeds engagement and motivation. When you teach children how to make good book choices, the book club meeting becomes more enjoyable and worthwhile for all participants.

Assess Learning

Observe children when they choose a book to read in book club. Notice if there is evidence of new learning based on the goal of this minilesson.

- Do children select the book they seem to want to talk the most about?
- How well can children problem solve when they have difficulty choosing a book?
- Are they able to articulate why they chose one book instead of another?
- Do they use vocabulary such as *author, illustrator,* and *title* when they talk about books?

Minilesson

To help children think about the minilesson principle, engage children in learning to choose a book for book club. Here is an example.

> In a book club, people get together to talk about a book they have all read. I am going to share four books with you. Think about which of these books you would like to read and talk about with friends in book club. If you choose a book that might be hard for you to read right now, I will talk with you later about how you can listen to it.

- Provide a short book talk for each of the selected books. Highlight what each book is about and talk about some of the features that will engage children in your class. Show a few illustrations or read a page or two to give children a sense of what the book is about. The goal of the book talk is to hook the children into wanting to read the books without giving away too much about any of the books.

Section 2: Literary Analysis

Have a Try

Invite the children to tell a partner what book they would like to read.

▶ Show all four book covers.

> Think about these four books. Which one do you want to choose for your book club and why?

▶ Ask a few children to share why they have chosen the book they think they want to read. Generalize their statements to make a chart to help them choose books for future book clubs.

Summarize and Apply

Summarize the learning and remind children to decide which book they want to read and talk about in book club.

> You need to choose one of the books I told you about for your book club meeting. If you are not sure, ask yourself the two questions on the chart.

▶ Review the chart and write the principle on the top. (Alternatively, give the children a slip of paper with four titles. Have them put a number 1, 2, and 3 to indicate their top three choices.)

▶ Record children's choices (or sort the slips) and make and post a list with the dates each book club will meet. (You might want to teach more of the minilessons in this umbrella before the children meet.)

Share

Following independent work time, gather children together in the meeting area to talk about choosing books for book club. Review the anchor chart.

> Turn and talk to your partner about which book you selected to read. Tell why you chose your book for book club.

Extend the Lesson (Optional)

After assessing children's understanding, you might decide to extend the learning.

▶ Observe the children's preferences for books and select books for future book clubs accordingly. If the children are using a reader's notebook, look to see the kinds of books they have read.

▶ Confer with children about their book interests to help them develop their preferences as readers.

Choose a book you would like to read and talk about.

Which book looks interesting?

Which book looks fun to read?

Cars

RML2

LA.U5.RML2

Reading Minilesson Principle
Mark the pages you want to talk about.

**Getting Started
with Book Clubs**

You Will Need

- a familiar book, such as *What Color Is Nature?* by Stephen R. Swinburne and *Cat's Colors* by Jane Cabrera, from Text Set: Colors, from the *Interactive Read-Aloud Collection*
- chart paper and markers
- sticky notes

Academic Language / Important Vocabulary

- author
- illustrator
- discussion
- book club

Continuum Connection

- Use evidence from the text to support statements about the text (p. 28)

Goal

Identify important information to discuss in preparation for book clubs.

Rationale

When you teach children to think about the pages they want to talk about, they learn the importance of preparing for a discussion and develop a way to refer to important ideas and information.

Assess Learning

Observe children when they prepare for book club. Notice if there is evidence of new learning based on the goal of this minilesson.

- Are children able to mark pages they want to discuss in their book club meeting?
- Do they use sticky notes appropriately?
- Do they understand the terms *author, illustrator, discussion,* and *book club*?

Minilesson

To help children think about the minilesson principle, model how to mark pages in a book to refer to later. Here is an example.

- Hold up *What Color Is Nature?*

  You had a lot of thinking to share when we read this book. As I show you the pages, think about which ones you might want to talk about. Quickly review the pages of the story.

- Invite a child to come up and locate a place in the book she wants to talk about.

  What are you thinking about this page? What could you do to remember the page that you want to talk about?

- Have the child place a sticky note on the page.

  A good way to remember the page is to put a sticky note on it. Put the sticky part down on the page and leave a little bit sticking over the edge of the page. That way, you can easily find it during book club.

Have a Try

Invite the children to continue talking about marking pages in a book.

▶ Hold up *Cat's Colors* by Jane Cabrera. Open to the green pages.

> How can you mark these pages to talk about?

▶ Help the child affix a sticky note.

> What is one thing you might want to talk about on these pages?

▶ Repeat the process with two or three other pages.

Summarize and Apply

Summarize the learning and remind children to mark places they want to talk about as they read.

> Today you learned that you can use a sticky note to mark the pages you want to talk about.

▶ Make a chart to illustrate the principle, and write the principle at the top.

> Today you are going to read the book that you chose for book club. Mark one or two pages you want to talk about when you meet with your group with a sticky note. I will put a pack of sticky notes in the middle of each table.

▶ Alternatively, give each child two sticky notes.

▶ Review the list of book club assignments and distribute the books.

Mark the pages you want to talk about.

Share

Following independent work time, gather children together in the meeting area to talk about their reading and review the chart.

> Give a thumbs-up if you marked some pages you want to talk about.

> If you aren't sure which pages to mark, what could you do?

Extend the Lesson (Optional)

After assessing children's understanding, you might decide to extend the learning.

▶ Encourage children to use sticky notes during independent reading to mark pages they want to talk about with a partner or talk about in group share.

▶ In interactive writing, demonstrate how children can draw or write a word on a sticky note to remind themselves of what they want to talk about on a page.

Reading Minilesson Principle
Talk about your thinking in book club.

Getting Started with Book Clubs

You Will Need

- four children you have prepared to model a book club discussion
- a book that children have heard or read and have multiple copies of, such as *My Friend Bear* by Jez Alborough, from Text Set: Friendship in the *Book Club Collection*
- chart paper and markers

Academic Language / Important Vocabulary

- author
- illustrator
- discussion
- book club

Continuum Connection

- Explain and describe people, events, places, and things in a story (p. 331)
- Express opinions and tell why (p. 331)

Goal

Learn how to identify important points to discuss during a book club meeting.

Rationale

Book clubs provide the opportunity for children to dig deeper into the author's intended meaning as they share their thinking with other members. When they benefit from each other's thinking, they develop a richer understanding than they would gain alone. In this minilesson, children will use familiar books to learn what a book club is and what kinds of thinking they can share in a book club.

Assess Learning

Observe children during a book club meeting. Notice if there is evidence of new learning based on the goal of this minilesson.

- ▶ Are children able to talk about a familiar book in some of the ways on the chart?
- ▶ Do they use the terms *author, illustrator, discussion,* and *book club?*

Minilesson

To help children think about the minilesson principle, provide a demonstration of a book club meeting. Here is an example.

> In book clubs, a group of children talk together about their thinking. _____, _____, _____, and _____ are going to talk about *My Friend Bear* by Jez Alborough. Notice what they do and be ready to talk about some of the things you hear.

▶ Seat the book club members in a small circle with you and have book club observers sit around them in an outside circle. Lead the four children to share their thinking about the story for about five minutes. Encourage them to take turns sharing their thinking and to show an illustration or page to support their comments.

> Think about some of the things your classmates talked about in their book club meeting. Let's make a list of the things they talked about.

▶ Invite children to share their noticings. When they share something specific to the book, extend it to the bigger idea.

▶ Record responses on a chart. Invite volunteers to add drawings to a few of the responses.

Summarize and Apply

Summarize the learning and remind children to talk about their thinking in book club.

> Today you learned that you talk about your thinking about books in a book club meeting. You noticed that you can say many different things about the book.

▶ Review the chart and write the principle at the top.

▶ Invite children to apply a few of the ideas you have listed on the chart to the last book you read to the whole class. Ask them to talk in pairs about two or three ideas on the chart.

Share

Following independent work time, continue talking with the children in the meeting area.

▶ After children have applied the ideas on the chart to a book, ask pairs to turn and talk to another pair about one of the things they talked about.

> You shared your thinking about many different things in this book. Is there anything that we should add to our list of things you might talk about during your book club meeting?

Extend the Lesson (Optional)

After assessing children's understanding, you might decide to extend the learning.

▶ Post the chart you made where children will meet for book club. Continue to add to the list as children share their thinking about books.

▶ Review the list of things to talk about before a book club meeting.

▶ **Drawing/Writing About Reading** Teach children how to draw and write about what they want to talk about during book club in a reader's notebook.

Talk about your thinking in book club.

- a character
- the problem in the story
- a favorite part
- an illustration
- a surprising part
- something you didn't understand

Section 2: Literary Analysis

Reading Minilesson Principle
Learn how to have a good book club meeting.

Getting Started with Book Clubs

You Will Need

- prepare one book club group to conduct a book club for the class
- chart paper and markers

Academic Language / Important Vocabulary

- respect
- author
- illustrator
- discussion
- book club

Continuum Connection

- Look at the speaker when being spoken to (p. 331)
- Take turns when speaking (p. 331)
- Speak at an appropriate volume to be heard, but not too loud (p. 331)

Goal

Identify the routines (e.g., showing the pages of a book) of book club and ways of showing respect during a discussion.

Rationale

Learning how to have a good book club means learning to show respect for others during a discussion, which is an important life skill. When you teach children to take turns, to make sure everyone is on the same page, and to make sure to look at the speaker during a book club meeting, you teach oral communication skills that they will transfer to other learning experiences throughout their lives.

Assess Learning

Observe children during a book club meeting. Notice if there is evidence of new learning based on the goal of this minilesson.

- Are children respectful of others during book club?
- Do they follow the suggestions on the chart?
- Do they understand vocabulary such as *respect, author, illustrator, discussion,* and *book club*?

Minilesson

To help children think about the minilesson principle, have a small group of children demonstrate routines for holding an effective book club meeting. Here is an example.

- Before teaching this minilesson, prepare a group of four children to demonstrate moving to book club and talking about a book respectfully. Set up a smaller circle of chairs. Conduct a short book club meeting with the group before asking them to model for the class.

  Today you are going to watch a few classmates move to their book club meeting to talk about the book they chose. Notice how the book club members show respect for one another, or treat each other kindly. Be ready to share your noticings.

- Have the small group move to the book club and discuss the book for a brief period (three to five minutes). You could use the fishbowl technique, where the class surrounds the small group to observe.

  What did you notice about how the members of the book club showed respect for each other's thinking?

- Create a chart as children respond. If necessary, ask questions to prompt their thinking, e.g., questions about their voice level, how they held their books, and whether they were prepared.

- Invite a few volunteers to add drawings to the chart.

Summarize and Apply

Summarize the learning and remind children to think about ways to have a good book club meeting.

▶ Review the chart.

> Why is it important to show respect for another's thinking during a book club?

> Today if you are part of a book club, keep these things in mind to work on so you can have a good book club meeting. The book club that meets today will share with the rest of the class how their discussion went when we come back together.

▶ Meet with a book club group while the other children are engaged in independent literacy work.

Share

Following independent work time, gather children together in the meeting area to talk about book clubs.

▶ Ask the children who participated in a book club to tell how they did. Encourage them to give an example of how they showed respect to their book club members.

> What did your group do to have a good book club discussion?

▶ Invite a few children to share.

Extend the Lesson (Optional)

After assessing children's understanding, you might decide to extend the learning.

▶ Review the list of behaviors before book clubs and help children self-evaluate their participation after book club.

▶ Remind children to show each other the same respect during other parts of the day, such as when they turn and talk with a partner or when they work in groups of three or four.

Ways to Have a Good Book Club

- Listen to the speaker.

- Take turns talking.

- Use a 0 voice when you walk to book club. **0**

- Use a 2 voice when you talk so everyone can hear. **2**

- Look at the speaker.

- Show the page you are talking about.

- Make sure you are on the same page as the speaker.

RML5
LA.U5.RML5

Reading Minilesson Principle
Be sure everyone has a chance to talk during book club.

Getting Started
with Book Clubs

You Will Need

- a book that children have read or heard, such as *All for a Dime!* by Will Hillenbrand, from Text Set: Friendship in the *Book Club Collection*
- four children you have prepared ahead to model a book club discussion
- chart paper and markers

Academic Language / Important Vocabulary

- author
- illustrator
- discussion
- book club

Continuum Connection

- Refrain from speaking over others (p. 331)
- Take turns when speaking (p. 331)

Goal

Understand the expectations of a discussion and learn facilitative language to invite others into the discussion.

Rationale

Children need to learn language that will invite others into a discussion. Learning how to enter and invite others into a conversation is an important life skill.

Assess Learning

Observe children during a book club meeting. Notice if there is evidence of new learning based on the goal of this minilesson.

- Are children able to generate a list of questions that encourage others to share?
- Do children ask questions to provide an opportunity for everyone to share?
- Do they use vocabulary such as *author, illustrator,* and *discussion* during book club meetings?

Minilesson

To help children think about the minilesson principle, engage them in noticing how to make sure all members of the book club have a chance to talk. Here is an example.

- Before teaching this minilesson, prepare a group of four children to demonstrate how everyone gets a chance to talk during book club. Teach the group how to invite everyone in the group into the conversation before asking them to model for the class.

  _____, _____, _____, and _____ are going to talk about *All for a Dime!* by Will Hillenbrand in a book club meeting. Notice how your classmates and I invite other people in the group to share an idea.

- Lead the discussion, while the rest of the class observes. Model facilitative talk (see the example chart on the next page).

  Think about what your friends and I said to encourage each other to talk about the book. Turn and talk to a partner about what you noticed.

  Let's make a chart of some of the questions you might ask your other book club members to make sure everyone gets a chance to share.

- Record responses on chart paper. Leave room at the top of the chart for the principle.

Summarize and Apply

Summarize the learning and remind children to be sure everyone has a chance to talk when they meet in their book clubs.

> What did you learn about talking with each other in book club today? Be sure everyone has a chance to talk during book club.

▶ Write the principle on the top of the chart.

> When you meet in book club, notice if everyone has a chance to talk. You can invite others to share by using the questions from the chart.

▶ Reread the chart.

▶ Meet with one or two book club groups to lead and facilitate the discussion and model how to invite others into the discussion while the other children are engaged in independent literacy work.

Share

Following independent work time, gather children together in the meeting area to talk about book clubs.

▶ Ask two or three children who participated in a book club to share their experience with the class. Invite them to share how they made sure everyone had a chance to share their thinking. Add any new ideas to the chart.

Extend the Lesson (Optional)

After assessing children's understanding, you might decide to extend the learning.

▶ Post the chart with questions and encourage children to ask these questions during other reading time activities, such as partner reading.

▶ Record children having a discussion about a book. Watch the video as a group to notice the questions that children asked to invite others to participate.

Be sure everyone has a chance to talk during book club.

- What are you thinking?

- What did you notice?

- What surprised you?

- Who can add to that idea?

- What do you think about the illustrations?

RML 6
LA.U5.RML6

Reading Minilesson Principle
Talk about what went well and what you want to work on to get better.

Getting Started with Book Clubs

You Will Need

- charts from RML1 to RML5
- chart paper and markers
- groups prepared to discuss a book in book clubs

Academic Language / Important Vocabulary

- discussion
- checklist
- book club

Continuum Connection

- Take turns when speaking (p. 331)
- Express and reflect on their own feelings and recognize that others' feelings might be different (p. 331)

Goal

Develop guidelines to self-assess the book club meeting.

Rationale

It is important for children to learn how to reflect on their behaviors and self-assess areas of strength and areas for improvement. Children's sense of ownership and level of engagement in book club meetings increase when they are a part of developing the guidelines for the discussion. If you have children who are not comfortable sharing their thinking, provide other opportunities for these children to self-evaluate their participation as a book club member.

Assess Learning

Observe children during a book club meeting. Notice if there is evidence of new learning based on the goal of this minilesson.

- ▶ Are children able to identify the qualities of a good book club discussion?
- ▶ Can they use the list effectively to self-assess a book club discussion?
- ▶ Do they use the terms *discussion, checklist,* and *book club?*

Minilesson

To help children think about the minilesson principle, review and summarize the learning that has happened in previous minilessons. Here is an example.

- ▶ Review the charts you have created together in this umbrella.

  We made some charts together to help you have good book club meetings. Let's make a list to help you remember what to do before, during, and after your book club meeting.

- ▶ Create the list on chart paper as children respond and draw a thumbs-up and thumbs-down next to each item.

  What do you need to do before you come to book club? If everyone thought about the story and marked a page in the book to talk about, which thumb would you circle? If only a few people were prepared, or no one was prepared to talk about the book, then you would circle the thumbs-down. That means you are still working on those things.

  You are still working on ways to have a good book discussion. What do you think you need to work on?

  What do you think you should do when you finish your book club meeting?

Have a Try

Invite children to talk with a partner about what to do in a book club meeting.

> Turn and talk to a partner about some of the important things to remember to do in your book club meeting.

▶ Add to the list according to children's responses.

Summarize and Apply

Summarize the learning and remind children to think about the list when they meet for book club.

> Today you learned how to talk about what went well and what you want to work on to get better in book club. After your book club discussion this week, you are going to use this list to talk about what went well and what you need to work on as a group.

▶ Continue to meet with a book club during independent literacy work. After their discussion, guide the group to self-assess.

Share

Following independent work time, gather children together in the meeting area to talk about their book club meeting.

▶ Invite the book clubs that you met with to share their self-assessment and explain why they chose the thumbs-up or thumbs-down for each of the questions on the list.

Extend the Lesson (Optional)

After assessing children's understanding, you might decide to extend the learning.

▶ If children have difficulty self-assessing, conduct a fishbowl discussion and have the children on the inside and outside of the circle assess the discussion using the list. Talk about differences in opinions that might arise.

▶ Have children read the book club list before each book club meeting and ask them to evaluate using the list at the end of each book club meeting.

Talk about what went well and what you want to work on to get better.

Before
Did you move quietly and get ready to start quickly? 👍 👎

Did everyone mark a page to talk about? 👍 👎

During
Did everyone show respect for people's thinking? 👍 👎

Did everyone get a turn to share their thinking? 👍 👎

After
Did everyone take off the sticky notes and put away the books? 👍 👎

Section 2: Literary Analysis

Assessment

After teaching the minilessons in this umbrella, observe children as they talk and write about their reading before, during, and after book club. Use *The Literacy Continuum* (Fountas and Pinnell 2017) to observe children's reading and writing behaviors across instructional contexts.

▶ What evidence do you have of new understandings related to ways for children to talk and write about their reading before, during, and after book club?

- Do children understand how to select books to read and talk about?

- Are children transitioning quietly from one activity and getting ready to start the book club promptly?

- Are children having meaningful conversations about books?

- In the book club, does the child who is speaking show the page that he wants to talk about and make sure the others are on the same page?

- Are children using body language to show respect to the speaker by turning toward and looking at the speaker?

- Do children use facilitative language to invite others to share their ideas and are they taking turns?

- Do they mark pages with sticky notes to remember what they want to talk about during book club?

- Are they able to self-assess their participation after book club?

- Do they use vocabulary related to book clubs, such as *author, title, illustrator, discussion,* and *respect*?

▶ In what other ways, beyond the scope of this umbrella, are the children talking about books and book clubs?

- Are the children showing respect to others while listening in other content area discussions?

- During independent reading, is there evidence that children are using sticky notes to indicate something they would like to discuss?

Use your observations to determine the next umbrella you will teach. You may also consult Minilessons Across the Year (p. 51) for guidance.

Link to Writing

After teaching the minilessons in this umbrella, help children link the new learning to their own writing:

▶ Encourage children to get ideas from the book discussions. For example, if someone talks about another way the book could end during book club, children could write an alternative ending for the story. If they discuss the writer/illustrator's craft, they could write about what the writer or illustrator did.

Minilessons in This Umbrella

RML1   Fiction books are alike in some ways.

RML2   The definition of a fiction story is what is always true about a story.

RML3   Nonfiction books are alike in some ways.

RML4   The definition of nonfiction is what is always true about nonfiction.

RML5   The author tells about things that are made-up in fiction books.

RML6   The author tells about things that are real in nonfiction books.

RML7   Writers tell stories that have characters, a problem, and a solution.

RML8   Writers tells true facts in nonfiction books.

RML9   Think about whether a book is fiction or nonfiction when you read.

Before Teaching Umbrella 6 Minilessons

Genre study supports children in knowing what to expect when reading a text. There are six broad steps in a genre study (see page 37). For this genre study, select books that are clear examples of both fiction and nonfiction, preferably fiction and nonfiction books on the same topic so children can learn to distinguish them by comparing and contrasting. At the end of the genre study, children can use what they have learned to revise the definitions of fiction and nonfiction. Use the following texts from *The Fountas & Pinnell Classroom™ Interactive Read-Aloud Collection* text sets or other books that are clear examples of fiction or nonfiction.

Taking Care of Each Other: Family
Elizabeti's Doll by Stephanie Stuve-Bodeen

The Place Called Home
Houses and Homes by Ann Morris
Two Homes by Claire Masurel

Exploring Fiction and Nonfiction
Hats, Hats, Hats by Ann Morris
All Pigs Are Beautiful by Dick King-Smith
Piggies by Audrey Wood
Caps for Sale by Esphyr Slobodkina
Chickens Aren't the Only Ones by Ruth Heller

The Importance of Friendship
Jessica by Kevin Henkes
A Visitor for Bear by Bonny Becker

The Importance of Kindness
Jamaica's Find by Juanita Havill

Sharing the Earth: Animals
Elephants Swim by Linda Capus Riley
Actual Size by Steve Jenkins

As you read aloud and enjoy these texts together, help children

- think and talk about the meaning of each text, and
- notice what is similar in fiction and in nonfiction texts.

Family

Home

Fiction and Nonfiction

Friendship

Kindness

Animals

Reading Minilesson Principle
Fiction books are alike in some ways.

Studying Fiction
and Nonfiction

You Will Need

- baskets of familiar fiction books
- chart paper and markers

Academic Language / Important Vocabulary

- fiction
- characters
- alike
- problem
- solved

Continuum Connection

- Make connections (e.g., content, topic, theme) across fiction texts that are read aloud (p. 28)
- Understand that there are different types of books and that you can notice different things about them (p. 28)
- Understand that fiction stories are imagined (p. 28)

Goal

Notice and understand the characteristics of fiction as a genre.

Rationale

When children develop understandings about a genre through inquiry, noticing the recurring patterns, structures, and features of that particular genre, they form a deeper understanding of the text. They also develop their comprehensions skills as they are able to anticipate the characteristics as they read.

Assess Learning

Observe children when they talk about fiction stories they have read. Notice if there is evidence of new learning based on the goal of this minilesson.

- Do children notice ways that fiction stories are alike?
- Are children able to talk about characteristics of fiction?
- Do children use *fiction, characters, alike, problem,* and *solved* to talk about fiction stories?

Minilesson

To help children think about the minilesson principle, engage children in an inquiry-based lesson to determine what is always or often true about fiction. Here is an example.

- Choose several fiction books you have read with the class. Include realistic fiction and animal fantasy. Show a few pages from each book to remind children of the stories.

  Think for a moment about one way all these stories are the same.

  How are all these stories alike?

- Help children decide whether the characteristic is always or often a part of fiction stories, explaining what those words mean if necessary. Record responses on chart paper.

Have a Try

Invite children to apply the new thinking about fiction stories with a partner or in a small group.

- To deepen the conversation, consider providing one or more of the following prompts for children to turn and talk about in pairs or small groups:

  What do you notice about the characters in all these stories? Are they real?

  What do you notice about where all the stories take place?

  Did the story really happen?

  What is the problem in each story?

  What happens to the problem in each story?

Summarize and Apply

Summarize the learning and remind the children to think about the items on the chart as they read.

> Let's look at the things you noticed today about how fiction stories are alike in some ways.

▶ Review the chart, emphasizing both the *always* category and the *often* category. Make sure children understand why the characteristics fit into each category.

▶ Provide a few baskets of books for children to read or look at.

> Today, choose a fiction story to read and see if you notice any of these things in your book. Bring the book when we meet so you can share what you find.

Share

Following independent work time, gather children together in the meeting area to talk about their reading in groups of three.

> Show the fiction story you read and say if you noticed some of the things on the chart.

▶ As needed, read through the chart to prompt the conversation.

> Did you notice other ways that fiction stories are alike? Share what you noticed so we can add it to the chart.

Extend the Lesson (Optional)

After assessing children's understanding, you might decide to extend the learning.

▶ Continue to add to the noticings chart as you read more fiction stories. Teach a minilesson for any new noticings. (See also the minilessons in this umbrella.)

Fiction

Noticings:

Always	Often
• The story has made-up characters.	• The characters are animals that act like people.
• The place where the story happens can be made-up or real.	
• The story never really happened.	
• The story has a problem.	
• The problem gets solved.	

Reading Minilesson Principle
The definition of a fiction story is what is always true about a story.

Studying Fiction and Nonfiction

You Will Need

- Fiction Noticings chart from RML1
- a basket of familiar fiction books
- chart paper and markers

Academic Language / Important Vocabulary

- fiction
- characters
- definition

Continuum Connection

- understand that fiction stories are imagined (p. 28)

Goal

Create a working definition of the fiction genre.

Rationale

The inquiry process allows children to construct their own understandings about the genre, based on what they know at the time, so they will be able to identify books in the genre as they encounter them independently. They can use their genre understandings to anticipate as they read a text and develop greater understanding.

Assess Learning

Observe children when they talk about fiction stories they have read. Notice if there is evidence of new learning based on the goal of this minilesson.

- Are children able to describe characteristics of fiction stories?
- Do they understand the working definition of the fiction genre?
- Can they classify a book that they read independently as fiction, using the definition?
- Do children use the academic words *character*, *fiction*, and *definition*?

Minilesson

To help children think about the minilesson principle, choose familiar texts and examples to help them construct a working definition of fiction. Here is an example.

- Review the noticings chart from the previous minilesson with the class.

  We can use the noticings chart to write what all fiction stories are like. Let's write a definition of what fiction stories are like. Our definition will tell what is true about all fiction stories.

- Write *Fiction stories are* on chart paper as you say them.

  We can start with *Fiction stories are*. Think about how you could finish this sentence.

- Combine children's ideas to compose a simple definition as a whole class. Write the definition at the top of the chart paper.

Have a Try

Invite children to apply the new thinking about fiction stories with a partner.

▶ Have partners turn and talk to one another about a fiction story they have read, explaining how they knew the story was made-up.

Summarize and Apply

Summarize the learning and remind children to think about whether their book fits their definition of fiction stories.

> Today we wrote a definition of fiction stories. Our definition is what is always true about a story.

> Choose a book from the fiction basket when you read today, and think about the way you described fiction stories. Can we describe all of the books in the fiction basket this way?

▶ Reread the definition from the chart paper.

> Bring your book when we meet so you can share.

Share

Following independent work time, gather children together in the meeting area to talk about their reading.

▶ Review the definition and prompt the conversation as needed.

> Show the fiction story you read today. Does your book fit our sentence about fiction stories? How do you know?

▶ Invite a couple of children to share how they know their book is fiction.

Extend the Lesson (Optional)

After assessing children's understanding, you might decide to extend the learning.

▶ When you read a fiction book in interactive read-aloud or shared reading, talk with the children about how they know the book is fiction.

▶ **Drawing/Writing About Reading** If children are keeping a reader's notebook, they can draw or write about fiction books that they read.

Fiction

Fiction stories are stories that the author made up.

Reading Minilesson Principle
Nonfiction books are alike in some ways.

Studying Fiction and Nonfiction

You Will Need

- a basket of familiar nonfiction books
- chart paper and markers

Academic Language / Important Vocabulary

- nonfiction
- topic
- alike
- illustrations
- photographs

Continuum Connection

- Understand that there are different types of books and that you can notice different things about them (p. 30)
- Understand when a book is nonfiction (true information) (p. 30)

Goal

Notice and understand the characteristics of nonfiction as a genre.

Rationale

When children develop understandings about a genre through inquiry, noticing the recurring patterns, structures, and features of that particular genre, they form a deeper understanding of the text and genre. They also develop their comprehension skills as they are able to anticipate the characteristics as they read.

Assess Learning

Observe children when they talk about nonfiction books. Notice if there is evidence of new learning based on the goal of this minilesson.

- Do children notice ways that nonfiction books are alike?
- Are children able to talk about characteristics of nonfiction?
- Do they use vocabulary, such as *nonfiction, topic,* and *alike,* to talk about nonfiction books?

Minilesson

To help children think about the minilesson principle, engage them in an inquiry-based lesson to determine what is always or often true about nonfiction. Here is an example.

- Remind children of several nonfiction books that they have heard or read by showing the covers and reading the titles. Then show several examples of the types of illustrations used in each book.

    Turn and talk to a partner about the ways these books are the same.

- After time for discussion, ask several children to share their thinking. Help them decide whether the characteristic is *always* or *often* a part of the books. Record responses on chart paper. Consider one or more of the following prompts to encourage deeper discussion:

    What do you notice about what types of things all these authors write about? The topic is what the author writes about.

    What do you notice about what the author tries to teach you in all the books?

    Think about the pictures (illustrations or photographs). How do they help you learn about the topics in all the books?

    Is there anything else you notice?

Have a Try

Invite children to talk with a partner about a nonfiction book.

> Turn to a partner and tell about a nonfiction book you know. What was it about?

Summarize and Apply

Summarize the learning and remind children to think about the items on the chart as they read.

▶ Review the chart, emphasizing both the *always* category and the *often* category. Make sure children understand why the characteristics fit into each category.

> Tell some ways the nonfiction books are alike.

▶ Put out a basket of nonfiction books.

> Today, choose a nonfiction book to look at or read and notice how your book is like the books we talked about. Bring the book when we meet so you can share what you find.

Share

Following independent work time, gather children together in the meeting area to talk about their reading.

▶ As needed, read through the noticings chart to prompt the conversation.

> Turn and talk to a partner about anything you noticed that was like the nonfiction books we talked about earlier.

▶ After a few minutes, ask for children's attention.

> Did anyone notice other ways that nonfiction books are alike? Share what you noticed so we can add it to the chart.

Extend the Lesson (Optional)

After assessing children's understanding, you might decide to extend the learning.

▶ Continue to add to the noticings chart as you read more nonfiction books. Teach a minilesson for any new noticings. (See also the minilessons in this umbrella.)

Nonfiction

Noticings:

Always	Often
• This book is about real things.	• The illustrator gives more information in the pictures.
• The author teaches you facts and information about a topic.	• The author uses diagrams and labels to give information.

Section 2: Literary Analysis

RML4
LA.U6.RML4

Reading Minilesson Principle
The definition of nonfiction is what is always true about nonfiction.

Studying Fiction and Nonfiction

You Will Need

- Nonfiction Noticings chart (see RML3)
- a basket of familiar nonfiction books
- chart paper and markers

Academic Language / Important Vocabulary

- nonfiction
- topic

Continuum Connection

- Understand when a book is nonfiction (true information) (p. 30)

Goal

Create a working definition of the nonfiction genre.

Rationale

When you work with children to define a genre, you help them to think about the most important characteristics of that genre based on their knowledge at that time. The inquiry process allows them to construct their own understandings about the genre so they will be able to identify books in the genre as they encounter them independently.

Assess Learning

Observe children when they talk about nonfiction books they have read. Notice if there is evidence of new learning based on the goal of this minilesson.

- Are children able to describe characteristics of nonfiction books?
- Do they understand the working definition of the nonfiction genre?
- Can they classify a book that they read independently as nonfiction, using the description?
- Do children use the academic words *nonfiction* and *topic?*

Minilesson

To help children think about the minilesson principle, choose familiar texts and examples to help them construct a working definition of nonfiction. Here is an example.

- Review the Nonfiction Noticings chart from the previous minilesson with the class.

  Our noticings chart for nonfiction is a good place to start your thinking about a definition for nonfiction books. Our definition will be true for all nonfiction books. Look at the chart and think about how we can tell about nonfiction books.

  What are some of the things nonfiction books always have?

  What are nonfiction books about?

  Authors of nonfiction books usually write about one thing, such as fish or the rain forest. Those things are called topics. The author gives information about the topic of the book. You can tell what nonfiction books are like by thinking about what you know about nonfiction books.

- Write *Nonfiction books have* on chart paper as you say them.

  We can start with *Nonfiction books have.* Think about how you could finish this sentence.

- Combine children's ideas to compose a definition as a whole class. Write the definition on the chart paper.

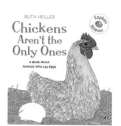

Have a Try

Invite children to apply the new thinking about nonfiction books with a partner.

> Think about a nonfiction book you know. What was it about? What was the topic? Turn and tell your partner.

Summarize and Apply

Summarize the learning and remind the children to think about the minilesson principle as they read.

> Today we wrote a definition of nonfiction books. Our definition is what is always true about nonfiction.

▶ Reread the definition from the chart paper.

> Choose a book from the nonfiction basket when you read today, and notice if what we wrote about nonfiction books works with the book you chose. Bring the book when we meet so you can share.

Share

Following independent work time, gather children together in the meeting area to talk about their reading.

> Hold up the nonfiction book you read today. Is what we wrote on the chart true about your book? How do you know? Turn and talk to a partner about that.

▶ Ask several children to share. Prompt the conversation as needed.

Extend the Lesson (Optional)

After assessing children's understanding, you might decide to extend the learning.

▶ When you read a fiction book in interactive read-aloud or shared reading, talk with the children about how they know the book is nonfiction.

▶ **Drawing/Writing About Reading** If children are keeping a reader's notebook, they can draw or write about nonfiction books that they read.

Reading Minilesson Principle

The author tells about things that are made-up in fiction books.

Studying Fiction
and Nonfiction

You Will Need

- three or four familiar books that can be easily identified as fiction, such as these:
  - *Caps for Sale* by Esphyr Slobodkina and *Piggies* by Audrey Wood, from Text Set: Fiction and Nonfiction
  - *Elizabeti's Doll* by Stephanie Stuve-Bodeen, from Text Set: Family
- chart paper and markers

Academic Language / Important Vocabulary

- fiction
- author
- character

Continuum Connection

- Understand that fiction stories are imagined (p. 28)

Goal

Understand that fiction books are imagined by the author.

Rationale

When children are able to understand that fiction authors tell made-up stories about characters, animals, places, and things, they are better able to distinguish between fiction and nonfiction books.

Assess Learning

Observe children when they talk about books they have read. Notice if there is evidence of new learning based on the goal of this minilesson.

- Are children able to identify whether a book is fiction?
- Can children describe the characters, places, and things imagined by the author?
- Do they use the academic words *fiction*, *author*, and *character*?

Minilesson

To help children think about the minilesson principle, choose familiar texts and examples that will help children understand that authors tell about things that are made-up in fiction stories. Here is an example.

> Listen again to part of *Caps for Sale* and think about the characters and what is happening.

- Read pages 23–28.

  > How do you know this is a story that the author made up?

- On chart paper, draw a picture of an author's face with thought bubbles for people, places, animals, and things. Add children's suggestions to the picture.

  > What part of *Caps for Sale* could not really happen? The monkeys would not really be in a tree copying what the man does, so you know the author made up the story.

  > Here is another fiction book, *Elizabeti's Doll*. Sometimes, authors make up stories about things that could happen in real life. They could happen, but they didn't. What things did the author make up in this book?

- Add a few of children's ideas to the chart.

Have a Try

Invite the children to apply the new thinking about fiction books with a partner.

> Here is another fiction book, *Piggies*. Listen as I read a few pages, and think about why this book is fiction.

▶ Read a few pages.

> Turn and talk to a partner about why this book is fiction. Talk about what parts could not really happen.

▶ After a few minutes of discussion, invite two or three children to share their thinking.

Summarize and Apply

Summarize the learning and remind children to notice if they are reading a fiction book.

> Today you learned that the author tells about things that are made-up in fiction books.

▶ Add the minilesson principle to the top of the chart and then read it aloud.

> When you read today, think about whether the author tells about things that are made-up. Bring the book when we come back together so you can share.

Share

Following independent work time, gather children together in the meeting area to talk about their reading.

> Turn and talk to a partner about the book you read. Talk about if the book is fiction and how you can tell.

Extend the Lesson (Optional)

After assessing children's understanding, you might decide to extend the learning.

▶ Use interactive writing to start a list of familiar fiction books.

▶ Provide simple props and have children work in groups to make up a story using the props so they can think about how an author uses imagination to write stories.

▶ **Drawing/Writing About Reading** Have children draw and/or write about a familiar fiction book. Children can draw the characters and something that happened in the story that is made-up.

The author tells about things that are made-up in fiction books.

People
Animals
Places
Things
Fiction Author

Reading Minilesson Principle
The author tells about things that are real in nonfiction books.

Studying Fiction and Nonfiction

You Will Need

- three or four familiar books that are clearly nonfiction, such as these from Text Set: Fiction and Nonfiction:
  - *Hats, Hats, Hats* by Ann Morris
  - *All Pigs Are Beautiful* by Dick King-Smith
  - *Chickens Aren't the Only Ones* by Ruth Heller
- chart paper and markers

Academic Language / Important Vocabulary

- nonfiction
- author
- topic

Continuum Connection

- Understand when a book is nonfiction (true information) (p. 30)

Goal

Understand that nonfiction authors tell about real people, animals, places, and things.

Rationale

When children understand that nonfiction authors tell about people, places, animals, and things that are real, they are better able to distinguish between fiction and nonfiction books.

Assess Learning

Observe children when they talk about nonfiction books. Notice if there is evidence of new learning based on the goal of this minilesson.

- ▶ Do children understand that the people, places, animals, or things are real in a nonfiction book?
- ▶ Do they use the academic words *nonfiction, author,* and *topic?*

Minilesson

To help children think about the minilesson principle, choose familiar texts and examples that will help children understand that authors tell about things that are real in nonfiction books. Here is an example.

- ▶ Before the lesson, draw a sketch of an author with thought bubbles for people, places, animals, and things.

    Think about what real people, places, or things you notice as I read part of *Hats, Hats, Hats.*

- ▶ Read several pages.

    What did you notice?

- ▶ Add a few children's suggestions to the thought bubbles.

    The author tells about real people around the world and the hats they wear.

- ▶ Show the cover of *All Pigs Are Beautiful.*

    The topic is what the writer writes about. As I read a few pages, notice the real information about the topic.

- ▶ Read pages 11–14.

    What real things do you notice that the author tells about? How do you know these things are real?

- ▶ Draw sketches of the ideas in the thought bubbles on the chart.

Have a Try

Invite the children to to talk about something real in a nonfiction book.

> Look at these pages from *Chickens Aren't the Only Ones*. Notice what things the author tells about that are real.
>
> Turn and talk to a partner about one thing the author tells about that is real.

▶ After time for discussion, ask a few volunteers to share. Draw a sketch of their ideas in the thought bubbles on the chart.

Summarize and Apply

Summarize the learning and remind children to notice that in nonfiction books the author tells about real things.

▶ Use the chart to help the children review what they have learned about nonfiction books. Add the minilesson principle to the top of the chart, and then read it aloud.

> When you read today, notice whether your book is fiction or nonfiction. Bring the book to group meeting so you can share.

Share

Following independent work time, gather children together in the meeting area to talk about their reading.

> Give a thumbs-up if you read a nonfiction book today. How did you know it was nonfiction?

▶ Ask two or three children to share their thinking.

Extend the Lesson (Optional)

After assessing children's understanding, you might decide to extend the learning.

▶ During interactive read-aloud or shared reading, ask children to tell how they know that a book is nonfiction.

▶ Explore topics that are of interest to the children by searching for facts, photos, and videos online.

▶ **Drawing/Writing About Reading** If children are using a reader's notebook, have them record an interesting fact from a nonfiction book the class has read.

The author tells about things that are real in nonfiction books.

People · Animals · Places · Things

Reading Minilesson Principle

Writers tell stories that have characters, a problem, and a solution.

Studying Fiction and Nonfiction

You Will Need

- three or four familiar books that can be easily identified as fiction, such as the following:
  - *Caps for Sale* by Esphyr Slobodkina, from Text Set: Fiction and Nonfiction
  - *A Visitor for Bear* by Bonny Becker and *Jessica* by Kevin Henkes, from Text Set: Friendship
- chart paper and markers

Academic Language / Important Vocabulary

- fiction
- author
- character
- story

Continuum Connection

- Understand that fiction stories are imagined [p.28]

Goal

Understand that writers tell stories in fiction books.

Rationale

When children understand that fiction books have made-up characters that take part in a series of events and sometimes have problems, they are better able to recognize fiction books and know what to expect from them.

Assess Learning

Observe children when they talk about books they have read. Notice if there is evidence of new learning based on the goal of this minilesson.

- Can children identify the characters and the important events in a fiction story?
- Do they use *fiction*, *author*, *character*, and *story* when they talk about stories?

Minilesson

To help children think about the minilesson principle, choose familiar texts and examples to help them notice elements that are common to fiction stories. Here is an example.

- Use a familiar book to help children identify common elements of fiction stories: characters, problem, and solution.

  Here is a fiction book you know, *Caps for Sale.* Think about the story that the author tells. Who is the book about?

  What problem does the peddler have?

  How does the peddler's problem get solved? Record responses on a chart.

- Repeat the process with *A Visitor for Bear* by Bonny Becker to emphasize the common elements of a story.

Have a Try

Invite the children to talk with a partner about the characters, problem, and solution in a story.

▶ Show the cover of *Jessica*.

Let's see if another fiction book you know has the same parts as *Caps for Sale* and *A Visitor for Bear*. Here is *Jessica* by Kevin Henkes. Does this story have characters, a problem, and a solution? Turn to a partner and talk about that.

Summarize and Apply

Summarize the learning and remind the children to look for characters, their problems, and the solutions when they read.

What do you know about the stories that authors tell in fiction books?

▶ Review the chart and write the principle at the top.

If you read a fiction book today, look to see if it has characters, a problem, and a solution in the story. Bring the book to group meeting so you can share.

Share

Following independent work time, gather children together in the meeting area to talk about their reading.

▶ Refer to the chart as you ask children to share their thinking about their reading.

Turn and talk to a partner about who the characters are in your book.

▶ Repeat with problem and solution, as time allows.

Extend the Lesson (Optional)

After assessing children's understanding, you might decide to extend the learning.

▶ Refer to the minilessons in Section Two: Literary Analysis that support children's understanding of character, problem, and solution.

▶ Have children gather in small groups to talk about the stories authors tell in books they enjoy.

▶ **Drawing/Writing About Reading** Have children draw and/or write about a fiction story that they enjoyed. Have them think about the characters and the events from the story before they begin writing.

Writers tell stories that have characters, a problem, and a solution.

Reading Minilesson Principle
Writers tell true facts in nonfiction books.

Studying Fiction and Nonfiction

You Will Need

- three or four familiar books that are clearly nonfiction, such as these:
  - *Houses and Homes* by Ann Morris, from Text Set: Home
  - *Chickens Aren't the Only Ones* by Ruth Heller and *All Pigs Are Beautiful* by Dick King-Smith, from Text Set: Fiction and Nonfiction
- prepared chart and markers
- basket of nonfiction books

Academic Language / Important Vocabulary

- nonfiction
- author
- facts

Continuum Connection

- Understand when a book is nonfiction (true information) (p. 30)

Goal

Understand that nonfiction writers provide facts about a topic.

Rationale

When children understand that nonfiction writers provide facts about a topic, they are better able to distinguish between fiction and nonfiction books and are prepared to think about the new knowledge they will encounter.

Assess Learning

Observe children when they talk about nonfiction books. Notice if there is evidence of new learning based on the goal of this minilesson.

- Can children explain that a book is nonfiction because it tells facts?
- Can children retell some of the facts from a nonfiction book?
- Do they use *nonfiction*, *author*, and *facts* when they talk about nonfiction?

Minilesson

To help children think about the minilesson principle, choose familiar texts and examples and provide an inquiry-based lesson for them to generalize that nonfiction writers provide true information. Here is an example.

- Before the lesson, draw a picture of a reader on chart paper. (See next page.)
- Show the cover of *Houses and Homes*. Read a few pages and show illustrations.

  What facts or true information does the writer of this nonfiction book tell you?

- Add a sketch of a house and children's ideas about the book to the chart.

  This author writes about true facts in this nonfiction book.

- Read pages from *Chickens Aren't the Only Ones* that give information, such as the two-page spread that shows the snake and some other animals that lay eggs.

  What true facts does the author tell you?

- Add a few drawings and words to the chart to show children's ideas.

Have a Try

Invite the children to talk with a partner about a fact in *All Pigs Are Beautiful*.

▶ Read a few pages from *All Pigs Are Beautiful*.

Turn and talk to a partner about a fact that the author tells you about pigs.

▶ After time for discussion, invite a few children to share with the group. Add a sketch and a few words to the chart based on children's noticings.

Summarize and Apply

Summarize the learning and remind children to notice true facts in a nonfiction book.

▶ Use the chart to help the children review what they have learned about nonfiction books. Add the minilesson principle to the top of the chart, and then read it aloud.

Do you think all writers tell true facts in nonfiction books? When you read today, choose a nonfiction book from the basket and notice if there are true facts in the book. Bring the book to group meeting so you can share.

Share

Following independent work time, gather children together in the meeting area to talk about their reading.

Turn and talk to a partner about a true fact that you learned in the nonfiction book you read today.

Extend the Lesson (Optional)

After assessing children's understanding, you might decide to extend the learning.

▶ Use interactive writing to create lists of facts from books read during interactive read-aloud or shared reading. Post the list in the classroom to provide new ideas for children to read and write about.

▶ **Drawing/Writing About Reading** Have children draw and/or write about facts they liked learning from a nonfiction book in a reader's notebook.

RML 9

LA.U6.RML9

Reading Minilesson Principle
Think about whether a book is fiction or nonfiction when you read.

Studying Fiction
and Nonfiction

You Will Need

- three or four familiar books that are clearly fiction or nonfiction, such as these:
  - *Jamaica's Find* by Juanita Havill, from Text Set: Kindness
  - *Elephants Swim* by Linda Capus Riley and *Actual Size* by Steve Jenkins, from Text Set: Animals
  - *Two Homes* by Claire Masurel, from Text Set: Home
- chart paper and markers

Academic Language / Important Vocabulary

- fiction
- nonfiction
- author
- character
- topic
- facts

Continuum Connection

- Understand that fiction stories are imagined (p. 28)
- Understand when a book is nonfiction (true information) (p. 30)

Goal

Notice and understand when a book is fiction or nonfiction.

Rationale

When you teach children to distinguish between fiction and nonfiction books, they are better able to do the kind of thinking they need to do to understand the text.

Assess Learning

Observe children when they talk about books they have read. Notice if there is evidence of new learning based on the goal of this minilesson.

- ▶ Are children able to identify a book as fiction or nonfiction?
- ▶ Can they provide clear explanations about how they know?
- ▶ Do they use *fiction, nonfiction, author, character, topic,* and *facts* when they talk about fiction and nonfiction books?

Minilesson

To help children think about the minilesson principle, choose familiar texts and examples to provide an inquiry-based lesson about noticing whether a book is fiction or nonfiction. Here is an example.

- ▶ On chart paper, create two sections, one labeled *fiction* and the other *nonfiction*. Show the cover of a fiction book, such as *Jamaica's Find*.

  Listen to a few pages of this book. Think about whether this book tells a made-up story and is fiction, or if it tells true facts and is nonfiction.

- ▶ Read aloud a few pages.

  Do you think this book is fiction or nonfiction? What makes you think that?

- ▶ Add the title of this book to the fiction part of the chart.
- ▶ Show the cover of a nonfiction book, such as *Elephant's Swim*. Read a few pages.

  Do you think this book is fiction or nonfiction? What makes you think that?

- ▶ Add the title of this book to the nonfiction side.

Have a Try

Invite the children to work with a partner to decide if a book is fiction or nonfiction and why.

▶ Show a fiction and a nonfiction book, such as *Two Homes* and *Actual Size*.

> After I read a few pages of each book, turn and talk to a partner about whether the book is fiction or nonfiction and why.

▶ After a brief time, ask two or three children to share and explain their thinking.

Summarize and Apply

Summarize the learning and remind children to think about whether a book is fiction or nonfiction when they read.

▶ Use the chart to help the children review how they categorized the books. Add the minilesson principle to the top of the chart, and then read it aloud.

> How can you tell if a book is fiction or nonfiction?

> Why is it a good idea to think about whether the book you are reading is fiction or nonfiction?

> When you read today, think about whether the book you are reading is fiction or nonfiction. Bring the book to group meeting so you can share.

Share

Following independent work time, gather children together in the meeting area to talk about their reading.

> Turn and talk to your partner about whether the book you read today is fiction or nonfiction. Tell how you know.

Extend the Lesson (Optional)

After assessing children's understanding, you might decide to extend the learning.

▶ Have children use what they have learned about fiction and nonfiction books to help you sort books in the classroom library.

▶ **Drawing/Writing About Reading** When children write in a reader's notebook, have them write whether the book is fiction or nonfiction. This information can also be added to a class reading log.

Think about whether a book is fiction or nonfiction when you read.

Fiction | Nonfiction

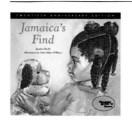

Section 2: Literary Analysis

Assessment

After you have taught the minilessons in this umbrella, observe children as they talk and write about their reading across instructional contexts: interactive read-aloud, independent reading and literacy work, guided reading, shared reading, and book club. Use *The Literacy Continuum* (Fountas and Pinnell 2017) to observe children's reading and writing behaviors across instructional contexts.

▶ What evidence do you have of new understandings related to the characteristics of fiction and nonfiction?

- Can children determine the characteristics of fiction and nonfiction books?
- Do children understand the difference between fiction and nonfiction?
- Are children able to identify whether a book is fiction or nonfiction?
- Can children discuss the made-up things in fiction stories?
- Can they discuss the real things in nonfiction books?
- Are children able to identify the facts they learn from nonfiction books?
- Do they use academic language, such as *fiction, nonfiction, character, problem, solution,* and *fact*?

▶ In what other ways, beyond the scope of this umbrella, are the children talking about genre?

- Are children talking about whether a character seems real or not real?
- Are children noticing that some fiction stories could happen in real life while others could not?
- Do they notice that some nonfiction books use drawn or painted illustrations to provide more information?

Use your observations to determine the next umbrella you will teach. You may also consult Minilessons Across the Year (p. 51) for guidance.

Read and Revise

After completing the steps in the genre study process, help children to read and revise their definition of the genre based on their new understandings.

▶ **Fiction**

- **Before:** Fiction books are stories the author made up.
- **After:** Fiction stories are stories that didn't really happen. The author made up what to write about the characters, places, and things.

▶ **Nonfiction**

- **Before:** Nonfiction books have true information about topics.
- **After:** Nonfiction books have true facts about a topic. They are about real people, animals, places, or things.

Minilessons in This Umbrella

Animal Tales

RML1	Animal tales are alike in some ways.
RML2	The definition of an animal tale is what is always true about it.
RML3	Animal characters act like people in animal tales.
RML4	Animal tales have good characters and bad characters.
RML5	Good things happen to the good characters. Bad things happen to the bad characters.
RML6	The number three is often important in animal tales.
RML7	Words are repeated over and over in some animal tales.

Before Teaching Umbrella 7 Minilessons

When children study a genre, they learn what to expect when beginning to read a text and develop important comprehension skills. They develop an understanding of the distinguishing characteristics of a genre and develop the tools they need to navigate a variety of texts. There are six broad steps in a genre study. Before you teach this umbrella, you may want to read pages pages 36–38, which detail the steps in the genre study process, including the fact that children must have read multiple animal tales before beginning a genre study of them.

For this genre study, it is important to select books that are clear examples of animal tales. Animal tales are a specific type of folktale in which animals talk and act like human beings. Be sure that children enjoy the story and think and talk about its meaning in their first experience with the book. After several books they will be able to notice and generalize the characteristic of the genre. Use the following books from the *Fountas & Pinnell Classroom™ Interactive Read-Aloud Collection* text sets or use animal tales that you have on hand.

Studying Animal Tales

The Three Bears by Paul Galdone

The Little Red Hen by Paul Galdone

The Three Little Pigs by Patricia Seibert

The Three Billy Goats Gruff by Peter Asbjørnsen

As you read aloud and enjoy these texts together, help children to:

• make connections among texts,

• notice similar types of characters,

• notice language patterns (e.g., repeating phrases or words), and

• notice common story outcomes.

Section 2: Literary Analysis

RML1

LA.U7.RML1

Reading Minilesson Principle
Animal tales are alike in some ways.

Studying Animal Tales

You Will Need

- chart paper and markers
- a basket of animal tales that children have heard or read

Academic Language / Important Vocabulary

- animal tales
- characters

Continuum Connection

- Connect texts by obvious categories: e.g., author, character, topic, genre, illustrator (p. 28)
- Notice and understand the characteristics of some specific fiction genres: e.g., realistic fiction, folktale, animal fantasy (p. 28)

Goal

Notice and understand the characteristics of animal tales as a genre.

Rationale

When children develop understandings about a genre through inquiry, they notice the recurring patterns, structures, and features of that particular genre and can develop their understanding of a text.

Assess Learning

Observe children when they talk about animal tales. Notice if there is evidence of new learning based on the goal of this minilesson.

- Do children notice ways that animal tales are alike?
- Are they able to talk about characteristics of animal tales?
- Do children use *characters* and *animal tales*?

Minilesson

To help children think about the minilesson principle, engage children in an inquiry-based lesson to determine what is always or often true about animal tales. Here is an example.

- Review three to five animal tales you have read with children. Show the covers to remind children of the stories, and offer a very brief summary of each book.

  Think about one way all of these animal tales are alike. Turn and talk about your idea.

- After a short time for discussion, ask children to share their thinking. As children share, help them decide whether the characteristic is always or often a part of animal tales. Record responses on chart paper.

- If children need assistance noticing different characteristics, consider offering the following prompts:

  - *What do you notice about the characters in animal tales?*
  - *What do you notice about the ways the animals act?*
  - *What do you notice that happens to the good characters at the end of these stories? The bad characters?*
  - *Think about the titles. In what ways are they alike?*
  - *What do you notice about the ways the characters solve their problems in these stories?*
  - *Do you notice anything about the language?*

Have a Try

Invite children to apply the new thinking about animal tales with a partner.

> Choose one of the things from the *Always* list on the chart. Turn and talk to your partner about how you have seen this in the books we have read.

Summarize and Apply

Summarize the learning and remind children to notice how animal tales are alike.

> Today you noticed that all animal tales are alike in some ways.

▶ Review the chart, emphasizing which characteristics are *always* present and which characteristics are *often* present.

> If you read an animal tale from the basket today, see if you notice any other ways that animal tales are alike and you can share when we come back together.

Share

Following independent work time, gather children together in the meeting area to talk about their reading.

> Did anyone read an animal tale today? If you did, give a thumbs-up if you noticed some of the things on the noticings chart.

▶ As needed, read through the noticings chart to prompt the conversation.

> Did you notice other ways that animal tales are alike? Share what you noticed so we can add it to the chart.

Extend the Lesson (Optional)

After assessing children's understanding, you might decide to extend the learning.

▶ Continue to add to the noticings chart as you read aloud and study animal tales.

▶ Teach specific minilessons on each characteristic that your children notice. (Refer to the other minilessons in this umbrella.)

▶ Plan for animal tale book clubs in which children select animal tales to read and discuss in groups (see the minilessons on book clubs in Section Two: Literary Analysis).

Animal Tales

Noticings:

Always	Often
• All or most of the characters are animals.	• The number three is important.
• The animals act like people.	• The characters use cleverness and tricks to solve problems.
• Good things happen to the good characters.	• Some of the words and sentences repeat.
• Bad things happen to the bad characters.	

Section 2: Literary Analysis

RML2
LA.U7.RML2

Reading Minilesson Principle
The definition of an animal tale is what is always true about it.

Studying Animal Tales

You Will Need

- chart paper and markers
- a basket of animal tales that children have heard or read

Academic Language / Important Vocabulary

- animal tales
- characters
- definition

Continuum Connection

- Notice and understand the characteristics of some specific fiction genres: e.g., realistic fiction, folktale, animal fantasy (p. 28)

- Understand when a story could happen in real life (realistic fiction) and when it could not happen in real life (folktales, animal fantasy) (p. 28)

Goal

Create a working definition of the animal tales genre.

Rationale

When you work with children to define a genre, you help them to think about the most important characteristics of that genre based on their knowledge at that time. The inquiry process allows them to construct their own understandings about the genre so they will be able to identify books in the genre as they encounter them independently.

Assess Learning

Observe children when they talk about animal tales. Notice if there is evidence of new learning based on the goal of this minilesson.

- Are children able to describe characteristics of animal tales?
- Do they understand the working definition of the animal tales genre?
- Can they categorize books they read independently, noticing whether the story is an animal tale?
- Do children understand the words *character(s)*, *animal tales*, and *definition*?

Minilesson

To help children think about the minilesson principle, choose familiar texts and examples to help them construct a working definition of animal tales. Here is an example.

- Review the chart with the class.

  > We can use the noticings chart to write a definition of animal tales. A definition of an animal tale is what is always true about an animal tale. Look at the noticings chart and think about how to describe animal tales. What are some of the things you know about animal tales that are always true? Using that information for the definition of animal tales is a good idea.

  > Let's try to tell what animal tales are in just a few sentences. We can start with *Animal tales are . . .* Turn and talk about how we can finish this sentence.

- Ask a few volunteers to share their thinking. Combine children's ideas to compose a definition as a whole class. Write the definition on the chart paper.

Summarize and Apply

Summarize the learning and remind children to think about what animal tales are like as they read.

> Today we wrote a definition to describe what is always true about animal tales.

▶ Reread the definition from the chart paper.

> If you read an animal tale from the basket today, think about the ways we described animal tales. Can the book you read be described like that? If you read an animal tale, bring the book when we meet so you can share.

Share

Following independent work time, gather children together in the meeting area to talk about their reading.

> Put your thumb up if you read an animal tale today. Who would like to share your animal tale with the group? Tell how it fits our definition.

▶ Review the definition and prompt the conversation as needed.

Extend the Lesson (Optional)

After assessing children's understanding, you might decide to extend the learning.

▶ Teach specific minilessons on each characteristic the children notice. (Refer to the other minilessons in this umbrella.)

▶ Ask the librarian to give book talks for animal tales that you have not read yet with the class. Choose a couple of the books to use in interactive read-aloud. Then talk about how they fit the noticings and the definition.

▶ Revisit the definition as children gain more knowledge about the genre. Revise the definition based on new understandings.

Animal Tales

Animal tales are made-up stories with animal characters that act like people.

Good things happen to the good characters and bad things happen to the bad characters.

Reading Minilesson Principle
Animal characters act like people in animal tales.

Studying Animal Tales

You Will Need

- a chart with the title of each book you'll discuss and a sketch of each main character
- markers
- three or four familiar animal tales, such as these from Text Set: Animal Tales:
  - *The Three Little Pigs* by Patricia Seibert
  - *The Three Bears* by Paul Galdone
  - *The Little Red Hen* by Paul Galdone
- a basket of animal tales that children have heard or read

Academic Language / Important Vocabulary

- animal tales
- characters

Continuum Connection

- Understand that animals in stories sometimes act like people (animal fantasy) (p. 29)

Goal

Notice that animal characters that act like people are a distinguishing characteristic of animal tales.

Rationale

When you teach children that animal tales have animal characters that act like people, children are better able to classify stories as animal tales, so they can predict what will happen next in the story and make connections between the actions of the characters and things real people say and do.

Assess Learning

Observe children when they talk about animal tales. Notice if there is evidence of new learning based on the goal of this minilesson.

- Are children able to identify the animal characters in the story?
- Can children describe how the animal characters act like people?
- Do children use the academic words *animal tales* and *character(s)*?

Minilesson

To help children think about the minilesson principle, provide familiar texts and examples to engage children in noticing how the animal characters act like people. Here is an example.

- Show *The Three Little Pigs*.

    We read this animal tale together. Think about what the animal characters do that is like what people would do.

- Review pages if necessary, such as the page that begins "After each pig had built."

    What do the animal characters do? The pigs build homes and they play together, and the wolf and the pigs talk just like people.

- Add a speech bubble for the pig to the chart.

    Now think about what the animal characters in *The Three Bears* do that is like what people do.

    What do you notice about the animal characters? The bears have bowls of porridge and sit in chairs to read. That is just like what people do.

- Add a speech bubble for the bear to the chart.

    Are there any other ways that the bears act like people?

Have a Try

Invite the children to talk with a partner about how the characters in *The Little Red Hen* act like people.

> Here is another animal tale that we read, *The Little Red Hen*. Think about what the animal characters do that is like what people do.

▶ Read the page that says "Who will eat this cake" and continue reading on the next two pages.

> Turn and talk about what you noticed about the characters and how they act like people.

▶ After time for discussion, ask volunteers to share. Add a speech bubble for the hen to the chart.

Summarize and Apply

Summarize the learning and remind children to notice how the animal characters act as they read.

> Today you talked about how animal characters act like people in animal tales. How does our chart show this?

▶ Write the minilesson principle on the top of the chart.

> When you read today, choose an animal tale from the basket. As you read, think about how the animal acts like a person. Bring the book when we meet so you can share.

Share

Following independent work time, gather children together in the meeting area to talk about their reading.

> Who would like to share the animal tale you read today? How did the animal characters act like people?

Extend the Lesson (Optional)

After assessing children's understanding, you might decide to extend the learning.

▶ As you read other animal tales with children, add the characters to the chart.

▶ Encourage dramatic play involving the characters from familiar animal tales.

▶ **Drawing/Writing About Reading** Use interactive writing to recreate an animal tale. Have children draw and/or write about animal characters that are acting like people.

Section 2: Literary Analysis

Reading Minilesson Principle
Animal tales have good characters and bad characters.

Studying Animal Tales

You Will Need

- chart with one column labeled *Good* and one labeled *Bad*; add the title of each book you will use
- markers
- three or four familiar animal tales, such as these from Text Set: Animal Tales:
  - *The Three Bears* by Paul Galdone
  - *The Three Little Pigs* by Patricia Seibert
  - *The Little Red Hen* by Paul Galdone
- a basket of animal tales that children have heard or read

Academic Language / Important Vocabulary

- animal tales
- characters

Continuum Connection

- Notice recurring themes or motifs in traditional literature and fantasy: e.g., talking animals, magic, good and bad characters (p. 28)
- Understand that the same types of characters may appear over and over again in traditional literature: e.g., sly, brave, silly, wise, greedy (p. 29)

Goal

Notice and identify good and bad characters as a recurring motif in animal tales.

Rationale

When you teach children that animal tales have good and bad characters, children are better able to classify a story as an animal tale and to think about the characters and their actions to make predictions and connections.

Assess Learning

Observe children when they talk about animal tales. Notice if there is evidence of new learning based on the goal of this minilesson.

- Do children know which characters act in a good way and which characters act in a bad way?
- Can children support their opinions based on evidence from the text as they categorize the good and bad characters?
- Do children understand the words *character(s)* and *animal tales*?

Minilesson

To help children think about the minilesson principle, provide familiar texts and examples to engage children in talking about how there are good characters and bad characters in animal tales. Here is an example.

- Show *The Three Bears* and read pages 9–12.

  Listen as I read, and think about who are the good and bad characters. Who is good and who is bad? Why do you think that?

- Add characters to the chart. Be sure children understand that Goldilocks acts in a way that is wrong, or bad, because she goes into the bears' house without permission. The three bears are good because they don't do anything wrong.

  Now think about the good and bad animal characters in *The Three Little Pigs*.

- Read the page that begins "Soon enough, the wolf. . . ," and continue on the next two pages.

  Turn and talk about the good and bad characters and what you notice about them.

- After time for discussion, ask volunteers to share their thinking. Add characters to the chart.

Have a Try

Invite the children to talk with a partner about good characters and bad characters.

> Here is another animal tale we have read, *The Little Red Hen*. Listen as I read, and think about the good and bad characters.

▶ Begin reading on the page that says, "She raked" and read the next three pages.

▶ After time for discussion, ask children to share what characters should be added to the chart and why they are good or bad.

Summarize and Apply

Summarize the learning and remind children to think about the minilesson principle as they read.

> Today you talked about how animal tales have good characters and bad characters. Where are the good characters on our chart? Where are the bad characters?

▶ Record the principle on the chart.

> When you read today, choose an animal tale from the basket. As you read, think about which characters act in a good way and which characters act in a bad way. Bring the book when we meet so you can share.

Share

Following independent work time, gather children together in the meeting area to talk about their reading in group of three.

> Show the book you read and talk about the animal characters. Talk about the things the characters do in the story that help you know if they are acting in a good way or in a bad way.

Extend the Lesson (Optional)

After assessing children's understanding, you might decide to extend the learning.

▶ As you read additional animal tales, add other good and bad characters to the chart.

▶ Encourage dramatic play involving the animal characters from the tales children are familiar with.

Animal tales have good characters and bad characters.

Good	Bad
Bear	Goldilocks
Pig	Wolf
Hen	Cat

RML 5
LA.U7.RML5

Reading Minilesson Principle
Good things happen to the good characters. Bad things happen to the bad characters.

Studying Animal Tales

You Will Need

- a chart with one column labeled *Good* and one labeled *Bad*
- markers
- three or four familiar animal tales, such as these from Text Set: Animal Tales:
  - *The Three Billy Goats Gruff* by Peter Asbjørnsen
  - *The Three Little Pigs* by Patricia Seibert
  - *The Little Red Hen* by Paul Galdone
- a basket of animal tales that children have heard or read

Academic Language / Important Vocabulary

- animal tales
- characters

Continuum Connection

- Notice story outcomes typical of traditional literature: e.g., cleverness overcomes physical strength, good defeats evil (p. 28)

Goal

Understand the story outcomes typical of animal tales.

Rationale

When you teach children that good characters are usually rewarded and bad characters are usually punished in animal tales, children are better able to classify a story as an animal tale and to know what to expect when reading this genre.

Assess Learning

Observe children when they talk about animal tales. Notice if there is evidence of new learning based on the goal of this minilesson.

- Are children able to identify the good and bad characters in the story?
- Can they articulate what happens to the good and bad characters at the end?
- Do children understand the words *character(s)* and *animal tales*?

Minilesson

To help children think about the minilesson principle, choose familiar texts and examples and provide an inquiry-based lesson to help children learn what happens to good and bad characters in animal tales. Here is an example.

- Show the cover of *The Three Billy Goats Gruff*.

  Who are the good characters and who are the bad characters in this story? Listen to the end of the story. Notice what happens to the good characters and the bad characters.

- Begin reading on the page where the troll tells the goat, "Now I am . . ." and read through the end of the book.

  What happens to the good and bad characters at the end?

- Add a sketch of the goats and the troll to the chart in the correct columns.

  Listen to the end of *The Three Little Pigs* and think about what happens to the characters.

- Begin reading on the page that says "After resting" and continue reading to the end.

  What happens to the pigs and the wolf at the end?

- Add a sketch of the pigs and the wolf to the chart in the correct columns.

  What do you notice about what happens to the good and the bad characters at the end of an animal tale?

Have a Try

Invite the children to talk with a partner about what happens to the good characters and bad characters in *The Little Red Hen*.

> Think about what happens to the characters in *The Little Red Hen*. Turn and talk about who the good and bad characters are in this story and what happens to them at the end.

▶ After time for discussion, ask volunteers to share their thinking. Add to the chart.

Summarize and Apply

Summarize the learning and remind children to think about the minilesson principle as they read.

> We have been talking about how good things happen to the good characters and bad things happen to the bad characters.

▶ Write the principle in two parts on the chart.

> When you read today, choose an animal tale from the basket. As you read, think about what happens to the characters. Bring the book when we meet so you can share.

Good things happen to the good characters.   Bad things happen to the bad characters.

Good   Bad

Share

Following independent work time, gather children together in the meeting area to talk about their reading in groups of three.

> Talk about the animal tale you read today and about what happened to the good and bad characters at the end.

Extend the Lesson (Optional)

After assessing children's understanding, you might decide to extend the learning.

▶ As you continue reading other animal tales, have children think about what happens to the good and bad characters in the end and add to the class chart.

▶ Play a game called *What Would You Do Differently*? Create game cards by adding the names and pictures of different characters from familiar animal tales to each card. Have children play in groups by choosing a card from the pile and talking about or acting out how that character could change so that the story would end in a different way.

RML6
LA.U7.RML6

Reading Minilesson Principle
The number three is often important in animal tales.

Studying Animal Tales

You Will Need

- three or four familiar animal tales, such as these from Text Set: Animal Tales:
  - *The Three Bears* by Paul Galdone
  - *The Three Little Pigs* by Patricia Seibert
  - *The Three Billy Goats Gruff* by Peter Asbjørnsen
- chart paper and markers
- a basket of animal tales that children have heard or read

Academic Language / Important Vocabulary

- animal tales
- characters

Continuum Connection

- Notice recurring themes or motifs in traditional literature and fantasy: e.g., talking animals, magic, good and bad characters (p. 28)

Goal

Understand that the number three is often a recurring motif in animal tales.

Rationale

When you teach children that the number three is often important in animal tales, children are better able to identify animal tales and know what to expect when reading them.

Assess Learning

Observe children when they talk about animal tales. Notice if there is evidence of new learning based on the goal of this minilesson.

- Can children talk about the occurrences of the number three in a variety of animal tales?
- Are children able to identify the number three in an animal tale that they read independently?
- Do children correctly use the words *characters* and *animal tales*?

Minilesson

To help children think about the minilesson principle, choose familiar texts and examples and provide an inquiry-based lesson about the number three in animal tales. Here is an example.

- Show pages 4–9 of *The Three Bears*.

  As you look at a few pages in *The Three Bears*, think about what number seems important in this book.

- On chart paper, write a large numeral 3 in the middle. Based on children's noticings, add sketches of examples to the chart. Then read the chart to the class, asking children to join in.

  There are three bears, three bowls, three chairs, and three beds.

- Repeat the process with *The Three Little Pigs*.

  What number seems important in this book? How can you tell?

Have a Try

Invite the children to talk with a partner about the number three in *The Three Billy Goats Gruff*.

▶ Review the pages of *The Three Billy Goats Gruff* that introduce the three billy goats.

> Turn and talk to your partner about what number seems important in this story.

▶ After time for discussion, have volunteers share their thinking and add to the chart.

> Did you notice anything about the titles of the stories we looked at today?

Summarize and Apply

Summarize the learning and remind children to notice if the number three is important as they read.

> What number is often important in animal tales?

▶ Write the principle on the chart.

> When you read today, choose an animal tale from the basket. As you read, notice whether the number three is important in the story. Bring the book when we meet so you can share.

Share

Following independent work time, gather children together in the meeting area to talk about their reading.

> Did anyone find the number three in an animal tale today? It might be three characters, three things, or something that happens three times.

Extend the Lesson (Optional)

After assessing children's understanding, you might decide to extend the learning.

▶ As you read other animal tales with the children, add to the chart.

▶ Provide a variety of items in sets of three. Have children work in groups to create an oral animal tale using the items.

▶ **Drawing/Writing About Reading** Use shared writing to create an animal tale that uses the number three.

The number three is often important in animal tales.

Reading Minilesson Principle
Words are repeated over and over in some animal tales.

Studying Animal Tales

You Will Need

▸ three or four familiar animal tales, such as these from Text Set: Animal Tales:
  • *The Three Bears* by Paul Galdone
  • *The Three Little Pigs* by Patricia Seibert
  • *The Little Red Hen* by Paul Galdone
▸ chart paper and markers
▸ a basket of animal tales that children have heard or read

Academic Language / Important Vocabulary

▸ animal tales
▸ characters
▸ repeat

Continuum Connection

▸ Notice when a book has repeating episodes or language patterns (p. 29)

Goal

Understand that animal tales often have words that are repeated.

Rationale

When you teach children that animal tales often have words that are repeated, children are better able to identify animal tales and know what to expect when reading them.

Assess Learning

Observe children when they talk about animal tales. Notice if there is evidence of new learning based on the goal of this minilesson.

▸ Are children able to identify repeating words in animal tales?

▸ Do children understand the words *animal tales*, *characters*, and *repeat*?

Minilesson

To help children think about the minilesson principle, choose familiar texts and examples to engage them in a discussion about repeated language in animal tales. Here is an example.

▸ Read pages 6–7 and pages 15–17 of *The Three Bears*.

> Listen as I read part of *The Three Bears* and think about the words that the author uses over and over. What did you notice?

▸ Add a sketch and a few of children's noticings about repetition to the chart.

▸ Begin reading *The Three Little Pigs* on the page that says, "Soon enough," and read through the next four pages (the wolf's and pigs' refrains).

> Listen carefully to the words as I read. What do you notice about the words in this animal tale?

▸ Add children's noticings to the chart.

> Knowing that the wolf and pig repeat the same words helps you know what will come next.

Have a Try

Invite the children to talk with a partner about repeated words in *The Little Red Hen*.

> Listen to part of *The Little Red Hen* and think about the words that the writer repeats.

▶ Begin reading on the page that says "Who will plant this wheat" and read several more pages.

> Turn and talk to your partner about what you noticed about the words that the author repeats.

▶ After time for conversation, ask volunteers to share and add to the class chart.

Summarize and Apply

Summarize the learning and remind children to notice repeating words when they read.

▶ Review the repeated language on the chart.

> What did you notice about the words in all of the animal tales today?

▶ Write the principle on the chart.

> When you read today, choose an animal tale from the basket. As you read, think about whether the story has repeating words. Bring your book when we meet so you can share.

Share

Gather children together in the meeting area to talk about their reading.

▶ Invite children to share some repeated language they found. Ask the other children to join in on the repeated words.

Extend the Lesson (Optional)

After assessing children's understanding, you might decide to extend the learning.

▶ Encourage children to join in when you read an animal tale that has repeating words. Challenge them to read the words the way the character would say them.

▶ Talk about why the author uses the repeating words in an animal tale.

▶ **Drawing/Writing About Reading** Use shared writing to make up a chant that uses repeating words and the characters from a favorite animal tale.

Assessment

After you have taught the minilessons in this umbrella, observe children as they talk and write about their reading across instructional contexts: interactive read-aloud, independent reading and literacy work, guided reading, shared reading, and book club. Use *The Literacy Continuum* (Fountas and Pinnell 2017) to observe children's reading and writing behaviors across instructional contexts.

▶ What evidence do you have of new understandings related to the characteristics of animal tales?

- Can children talk about ways that animal tales are alike?
- Do they recognize that the animal characters act like people?
- Are they able to identify the good and bad characters and discuss characteristics of each?
- Do they understand ways that the good characters are rewarded and the bad characters are punished?
- Do they notice the significance of the number three in some animal tales?
- Are they able to identify repeated words in some animal tales?
- Do they use the academic terms *animal tales* and *characters* correctly?

▶ In what other ways, beyond the scope of this umbrella, are the children talking about genre?

- Can children compare and contrast animal tales by the same and/or different authors?
- Are they able to organize books into sets based on genre?

Use your observations to determine the next umbrella you will teach. You may also consult Minilessons Across the Year (p. 51) for guidance.

Read and Revise

After completing the steps in the genre study process, help children to read and revise their definition of the genre based on their new understandings.

▶ **Animal Tales**

- **Before:** Animal tales are made-up stories with animal characters that act like people. Good things happen to the good characters, and bad things happen to the bad characters. Everyone learns a lesson in the end.
- **After:** Animal tales are made-up stories with animal characters that act like people. The animals are not real. Good things happen to the good characters, and bad things happen to the bad characters. Everyone learns a lesson in the end. The number three is often important.

Minilessons in This Umbrella

RML1   The author gives a message in a story.

RML2   The author gives a message in a nonfiction book.

RML3   Some authors give the same message.

Before Teaching Umbrella 8 Minilessons

Read and discuss books with simple plots in which the author's message can be easily inferred. Select the following books from the *Fountas & Pinnell Classroom™ Interactive Read-Aloud Collection* text sets or choose books with a clear author's message from your own library.

The Importance of Kindness

Say Hello by Jack and Michael Foreman

Celebrating Differences

Leo the Late Bloomer by Robert Kraus

It's Okay to Be Different by Todd Parr

The Story of Ferdinand by Munro Leaf

The Cow that Went OINK by Bernard Most

Understanding Feelings

Mouse Was Mad by Linda Urban

Exploring Nonfiction

Shoes Shoes Shoes by Ann Morris

How to Hide a Butterfly & Other Insects by Ruth Heller

Building a House by Byron Barton

As you read aloud and enjoy these texts together, help children

- think about the events in the story and talk about the author's message when applicable,
- talk about what a nonfiction author wants readers to know, and
- connect books that have a similar message.

Kindness

Differences

Feelings

Nonfiction

RML1

LA.U8.RML1

Reading Minilesson Principle
The author gives a message in a story.

Thinking About the Author's Message

You Will Need

- two or three stories by different authors with different messages, such as these:
  - *Say Hello* by Jack and Michael Foreman, from Text Set: Kindness
  - *The Cow that Went OINK* by Bernard Most, from Text Set: Differences
  - *Mouse Was Mad* by Linda Urban, from Text Set: Feelings
- chart paper and markers
- a basket of books that have been read before

Academic Language / Important Vocabulary

- author
- message
- story

Continuum Connection

- Infer simple messages in a work of fiction (p. 28)

Goal

Infer simple messages in a work of fiction.

Rationale

When you teach children to think about the simple message in a book, you support them in thinking about the deeper meaning that lies below the surface characters and events.

Assess Learning

Observe children when they talk about the author's message in stories they have read. Notice if there is evidence of new learning based on the goal of this minilesson.

- ▶ Are children able to identify the author's message in a story?
- ▶ Can children talk with their partner about the messages they notice?
- ▶ Can they use academic language, such as *author, message,* and *story*?

Minilesson

To help children think about the minilesson principle, choose familiar texts and examples to help them discover that an author gives a message in a fiction story. Here is an example.

- ▶ Show the book *Say Hello*.

  What happens to the dog in the beginning of this story? What happens to the little boy? The dog didn't want the boy to feel lonely anymore. He didn't want the boy to stand and watch; he wanted the boy to be included.

  What do you think Jack and Michael Foreman want you to learn from this story? What is the authors' message?

- ▶ Record responses on chart.

  Now let's think about *The Cow That Went OINK* by Bernard Most.

- ▶ Record title.

  Who remembers what happens in this story?

- ▶ Read aloud page that states, "And the other animals laughed at her, too."

  What did the cow and pig do in this story?

- ▶ Show and read the last page.

  What do you think is the author's message in this story? What is the author trying to tell you?

- ▶ Record responses on the chart.

Have a Try

Invite the children to talk with a partner about the message in *Mouse Was Mad*.

> Now think about *Mouse Was Mad* by Linda Urban. Talk with your partner about all the ways Mouse tried to deal with being angry in this story. What finally worked for Mouse?
>
> Talk with your partner about the message in the story.

▶ Record responses.

Summarize and Apply

Summarize the learning and remind children to think about the author's message as they read.

> Today you learned that the author gives a message in a story, or that the author wants you to learn something from reading the story.

▶ Review the chart and record the principle at the top.

▶ Provide a basket of books you have previously read aloud to the children. Have them choose a book to read and think about the message of the story.

> Bring your book when we come back together. Think about the message you will share.

Share

Following independent work time, gather children together in the meeting area to talk about their reading.

> Tell your partner the author's message in one of the stories you read today.

Extend the Lesson (Optional)

After assessing the children's understanding, you might decide to extend the learning.

▶ Discuss the author's message of interactive read-aloud or shared reading books. Let children know that sometimes a story will mean something different to different people and that's okay.

▶ **Drawing/Writing About Reading** Use interactive writing to have children add more author's messages to the chart as they encounter more stories in interactive read-aloud.

The author gives a message in a story.

Say Hello — It's important to include everyone.

The Cow That Went OINK — It's OK to be different.

MOUSE WAS MAD — When you are mad, calm yourself.

Reading Minilesson Principle
The author gives a message in a nonfiction book.

Thinking About the Author's Message

You Will Need

- three or four simple informational texts with a clear message, such as these books from Text Set: Nonfiction:
  - *Shoes Shoes Shoes* by Ann Morris
  - *How to Hide a Butterfly & Other Insects* by Ruth Heller
  - *Building a House* by Byron Barton
- chart paper and markers

Academic Language / Important Vocabulary

- nonfiction
- author
- message

Continuum Connection

- Infer the significance of nonfiction content to their own lives (p. 31)

Goal

Infer the author's message in a nonfiction text.

Rationale

When you teach children to think about the message in a nonfiction book, you support them in making connections between details and therefore in thinking about the deeper meaning of the informational text.

Assess Learning

Observe children when they talk about the message in nonfiction books they have read. Notice if there is evidence of new learning based on the goal of this minilesson.

- Are children able to identify the author's message in a nonfiction book?
- Can children talk with a partner about the messages they notice?
- Do children understand that a book can have more than one message?
- Can they use academic language, such as *nonfiction, author,* and *message*?

Minilesson

To help children think about the minilesson principle, choose familiar texts and examples to help them discover that in addition to facts an author gives a message in a nonfiction book. Here is an example.

- Show the cover of *Shoes Shoes Shoes* and read the title.

  We read this book. What is it about?

  The author shows all different kinds of shoes. Why do you think Ann Morris did that? What does she want you to learn?

- Record responses on chart. Accept different responses, emphasizing that a book can have more than one message.

- Show *How to Hide a Butterfly & Other Insects* and read the title.

  What does the author, Ruth Heller, tell you about in this book?

  The author shows you how different insects hide in nature. Why do you think the author did that? What was her message?

- Record responses on chart.

Have a Try

Invite the children to talk with a partner about the message in *Building a House*.

▶ Show *Building a House*.

Think about what the author told you in this book.

Turn and talk with your partner about what you think the author's message is, or what big idea the author wants you to learn.

▶ Ask a few pairs to share, and record their responses.

Summarize and Apply

Summarize the learning and remind children to think about the author's message as they read a nonfiction book.

Today you learned that the author gives a message in a nonfiction book. The author's message is something that the author wants you to think about beside all the facts the author gives.

▶ Write the principle at the top of the chart.

Today, read a nonfiction book and think about the author's message. Be ready to share when we come together.

Share

Following independent work time, gather children together in the meeting area to share authors' messages.

Turn and talk to your partner about the author's message in the nonfiction book you read today.

Extend the Lesson (Optional)

After assessing children's understanding, you might decide to extend the learning.

▶ Encourage children to think and talk about the author's message when discussing nonfiction books in small groups or during interactive reading.

▶ **Drawing/Writing About Reading** Use interactive or shared writing to have children add more authors' messages to the chart as they encounter more nonfiction books in interactive read-aloud.

The author gives a message in a nonfiction book.

People all over the world wear clothes (like shoes) to protect themselves.

All animals have behaviors that help them survive.

To build a house, people need to do lots of different things. They need to work together.

Section 2: Literary Analysis

Thinking About the Author's Message

You Will Need

- three or four stories by different authors with the same message, such as these:
  - *It's Okay to Be Different* by Todd Parr, *Leo the Late Bloomer* by Robert Kraus, and *The Story of Ferdinand* by Munro Leaf, from Text Set: Differences
  - *Mouse Was Mad* by Linda Urban, from Text Set: Feelings
- chart paper and markers

Academic Language / Important Vocabulary

- message
- story
- author

Continuum Connection

- Infer simple messages in a work of fiction (p. 28)

Goal

Notice the same message across multiple works of fiction.

Rationale

Teaching children to notice the same message across stories helps them make both personal and intertextual connections.

Assess Learning

Observe children when they talk about the author's message in different stories they have read. Notice if there is evidence of new learning based on the goal of this minilesson.

- ▶ Are children able to identify the message in different stories?
- ▶ Do they notice when two or more stories have the same message?
- ▶ Can they use academic language, such as *message*, *story*, and *author*?

Minilesson

To help children think about the minilesson principle, choose familiar texts and examples and provide an inquiry-based lesson about author's messages across texts. Here is an example.

> Listen to this part of It's *Okay to Be Different*.

- ▶ Read the last page.

  > What is the author's message in this story? What does the author, Todd Parr, want you to learn or think about?

- ▶ Record responses on the chart and then hold up another book.

  > Think about *Leo the Late Bloomer*. What happens to Leo in this story? What do you think the author, Robert Kraus, wants you to learn or think about? What is the message?

- ▶ Record responses and then hold up a third book.

  > Now think about the message in *The Story of Ferdinand*. Was Ferdinand the same as the other bulls? Listen to the end. "And for all I know he is sitting there still, under his favorite cork tree, smelling the flowers just quietly. He is very happy." What is the message of this story by Munro Leaf?

- ▶ Record responses on the chart.

Have a Try

Invite the children to talk with a partner about the messages in the three books just discussed.

▶ Review the chart with the children.

> What do you notice about the author's message in of all three books? Turn and talk to a partner about that.

▶ Invite two or three children to share what they talked about.

> Sometimes different authors write books that have the same or almost the same message.

Summarize and Apply

Summarize the learning and remind children to think about the author's message as they read different stories.

> Today you noticed that some authors give the same message.

▶ Write the principle at the top of the chart.

> When you read today, think about the author's message in your story. Be ready to share. When we come back together, we will see if some of you have read some books that have the same message.

Share

Following independent work time, gather children together in the meeting area to talk about the author's message.

> Who wants to share the message of the story you read? Did anyone else read a story with the same message?

Extend the Lesson (Optional)

After assessing the children's understanding, you might decide to extend the learning.

▶ Extend exploration of common messages by having children group stories together in baskets by author's message.

▶ Discuss similar author's messages during interactive read-aloud.

▶ **Drawing/Writing About Reading** Use interactive writing to write about how two stories have the same message.

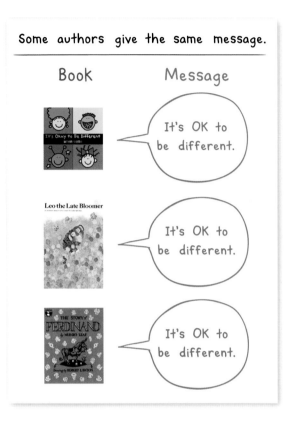

Assessment

After you have taught the minilessons in this umbrella, observe children as they talk and write about their reading across instructional contexts: interactive read-aloud, independent reading and literacy work, guided reading, shared reading, and book club. Use *The Literacy Continuum* (Fountas and Pinnell 2017) to observe children's reading and writing behaviors across instructional contexts.

▶ What evidence do you have of new understandings related to an author's message?

- Can children identify the message of a story and of a nonfiction book?
- Are children able to make connections about message across different stories?
- Do they use academic language, such as *author, story, nonfiction,* and *message,* correctly?

▶ In what other ways, beyond the scope of this umbrella, are they talking about books?

- Do children notice common messages in different stories written by the same author?
- Are they noticing other things that books have in common, such as characters, author or illustrator, or genre?

Use your observations to determine the next umbrella you will teach. You may also consult Minilessons Across the Year (p. 51) for guidance.

Link to Writing

After teaching the minilessons in this umbrella, help children link the new learning to their own writing or drawing about reading:

▶ When children write their own stories, encourage them to think about why the story they are writing is important to them. What do they want their reader to learn from the story they are writing?

Minilessons in This Umbrella

RML1   Nonfiction writers tell information about a topic.

RML2   The authors of nonfiction books know and care about their topics.

RML3   Sometimes nonfiction writers tell information in the order it happens.

RML4   Sometimes the author of a nonfiction book tells about many different kinds of people and places.

RML5   An author has a reason for writing a nonfiction book.

RML6   Think what you know about a topic before you read.

RML7   Think what you learned about a topic after you read.

Before Teaching Umbrella 9 Minilessons

Most minilessons assume that the children are familiar with the books used as examples: either they have read them or heard them read aloud. That is the case for four out of the five minilessons in this umbrella. However, RML6 is different. For this lesson to be effective, children must not have any familiarity with the books. Use the following texts from the *Fountas & Pinnell Classroom™ Interactive Read-Aloud* or *Independent Reading Collections*, or choose nonfiction books that you have on hand.

Exploring Nonfiction

Building a House by Byron Barton

Shoes Shoes Shoes by Ann Morris

I Love Our Earth by Bill Martin Jr. and Michael Sampson

How to Hide a Butterfly & Other Insects by Ruth Heller

Sharing the Earth: Animals

Elephants Swim by Linda Capus Riley

Exploring Fiction and Nonfiction

Chickens Aren't the Only Ones by Ruth Heller

Hats Hats Hats by Ann Morris

All Pigs Are Beautiful by Dick King-Smith

Independent Reading Collection

I Make Clay Pots by Leslie Johnson

Milk to Ice Cream by Lisa M. Herrington

Big Cats, Little Cats by Bernette Ford

Eggs, Eggs, Eggs by Aamir Bermiss

What Can Fly? by D. H. Figueredo

As you read aloud and enjoy these texts together, help children

- understand that a nonfiction book is about a single topic,

- notice how nonfiction writers sometimes organize information,

- understand that writers know and care about their topics,

- recognize that nonfiction books may be about different people and places, and

- think about what they already know and what they have learned about a topic.

Nonfiction

Animals

Fiction and Nonfiction

Independent Reading Collection

RML1
LA.U9.RML1

Reading Minilesson Principle
Nonfiction writers tell information about a topic.

Learning About Nonfiction Books

You Will Need

- three or four simple expository texts about one topic, such as sthe following:
  - *Shoes Shoes Shoes* by Ann Morris, from Text Set: Nonfiction
  - *Elephants Swim* by Linda Capus Riley from Text Set: Animals
  - *How to Hide a Butterfly & Other Insects* by Ruth Heller, from Text Set: Nonfiction
- chart paper and markers

Academic Language / Important Vocabulary

- nonfiction
- author
- information
- fact
- organize
- topic

Continuum Connection

- Understand that a writer is presenting facts about a single topic (p. 30)

Goal

Understand that the facts in a nonfiction book are all related. The book is about a single topic.

Rationale

When you teach children that some nonfiction writers write about a single topic, you help them understand that all the information in a nonfiction book is related in some way.

Assess Learning

Observe children when they talk about nonfiction books. Notice if there is evidence of new learning based on the goal of this minilesson.

- ▶ Do children notice that everything in a nonfiction book goes together?
- ▶ Do children understand and use the words *nonfiction, author, information, fact, organize,* and *topic?*

Minilesson

To help children think about the minilesson principle, choose familiar texts and examples to provide an inquiry-based lesson on nonfiction books. Here is an example.

- ▶ Show some pages from *Shoes Shoes Shoes.*

  What does the author tell you about on these pages?

- ▶ Make a list on chart paper.

  All of these words tell about different kinds of shoes.

  The author tells about a lot of different kinds of shoes, so shoes is the topic, or the one thing the whole book is about.

- ▶ Show some pages from *Elephants Swim.*

  What does the author tell about on these pages?

- ▶ Make a list on chart paper.

  The author tells about how all these animals swim.

  Animals That Can Swim is the topic because it is the one thing the whole book is about. The author tells about how all these animals swim.

Have a Try

Invite the children to talk with a partner about the topic of a nonfiction book.

> Look at these pages from *How to Hide a Butterfly*. Turn and talk to your partner about the one thing this whole book is about.

▶ Ask a few pairs to share their thinking.

Summarize and Apply

Summarize the learning and remind children when they read a nonfiction book to notice what their nonfiction book is all about.

▶ Review the chart, using these questions for each book.

> What is everything on the list about? So, what is one thing the book is about?

> Each book is about one thing.

▶ Write the principle at the top of the chart.

> If you read a nonfiction book today, notice the one thing the whole book is about. Bring the book to share the topic when we come back together.

Share

Following independent work time, gather children together in the meeting area to talk about nonfiction books.

> Give a thumbs-up if you read a nonfiction book today. What one topic did the author write about?

▶ Invite a few children to share.

Extend the Lesson (Optional)

After assessing children's understanding, you might decide to extend the learning.

▶ **Drawing/Writing About Reading** As you read other nonfiction books, use shared or interactive writing to make lists of the information in the books and talk about how all the information goes together.

Nonfiction writers tell information about a topic.

Shoes	Animals That Can Swim
work shoes	elephants
play shoes	hippos
snow shoes	walruses
rain shoes	

Reading Minilesson Principle
The authors of nonfiction books know and care about their topics.

Learning About Nonfiction Books

You Will Need

- three or four familiar nonfiction books, such as the following:
  - *Building a House* by Byron Barton, from Text Set: Nonfiction
  - *I Love Our Earth* by Bill Martin Jr. and Michael Sampson from Text Set: Nonfiction
  - *All Pigs Are Beautiful* by Dick King-Smith, from Text Set: Fiction and Nonfiction
- chart paper and markers
- baskets of nonfiction books

Academic Language / Important Vocabulary

- author
- writer
- nonfiction
- information
- facts
- learn
- topic

Continuum Connection

- Infer the writer's attitude toward a topic (how the writer "feels") (p. 30)

Goal

Understand that nonfiction books include information and facts about a topic the author knows about and cares about.

Rationale

When you teach children that authors know and care about the topics they write about in nonfiction books, you help them understand why an author chooses to write a particular book. Children also learn that authors have feelings for the things they write about, which might inspire children to write about topics they care about.

Assess Learning

Observe children when they talk about nonfiction books they have read. Notice if there is evidence of new learning based on the goal of this minilesson.

- Do the children understand that nonfiction authors write about topics they know and care about?
- Do the children understand that the author needs to know or learn about the topic to write about it?
- Do they use academic language, such as *author, nonfiction,* and *topic* correctly?

Minilesson

To help children think about the minilesson principle, choose familiar texts and examples to help children understand that authors know and care about their topics. Here is an example.

> Let's think about *Building a House* by Byron Barton. What did Byron Barton have to know before he wrote this book?

- Write responses on chart paper.

  > How might an author know information about a topic she wants to write about?

- Help children understand that sometimes people know a lot about something but other times they do research to find out information.

  > How do you think Byron Barton feels about the topic? Tell what makes you think that.

- Hold up *I Love Our Earth* by Bill Martin Jr. and Michael Sampson. Ask questions similar to those asked about *Building a House*. Record responses on the chart.

  > The title *I Love Our Earth* is a clue that the authors care about their topic.

Have a Try

Invite the children to talk with a partner about what the author knows and cares about.

> Now let's think about the book *All Pigs Are Beautiful*. How can you tell the author knows and cares about pigs? Turn and talk to your partner about that.

Summarize and Apply

Summarize the learning and remind children to think about the minilesson principle as they read.

▶ Review the chart.

> What can you say about authors and their topics?

▶ Write the principle on the chart. Then point out several nonfiction baskets.

> Today, choose a nonfiction book from the baskets. When you read a nonfiction book today, think about what topic the author knows about and how you know he cares about the topic.

Share

Following independent work time, gather children together in the meeting area to talk about nonfiction books.

> Think about the nonfiction book you read today. Turn and tell your partner the topic the author wrote about. Tell why you think the author cares about that topic.

▶ Choose a few children to share with the whole group.

Extend the Lesson (Optional)

After assessing children's understanding, you might decide to extend the learning.

▶ Visit the website of an author who writes nonfiction, such as one of the authors in this lesson. Look to see if there are clues about why the author chose to write about a particular topic.

▶ After reading a nonfiction book, ask children to talk about how they think the author might have learned about the topic.

▶ As a resource for independent writing and book choice, use shared writing to make an ongoing list of topics children know about and topics they would like to learn about.

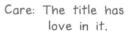

The authors of nonfiction books know and care about their topics.

Know: How to build a house

Care: He wrote and illustrated a whole book about building houses.

Know: What the earth is like

Care: The title has <u>love</u> in it.

Know: What pigs are like

Care: The title has <u>beautiful</u> in it.

RML3
LA.U9.RML3

Sometimes nonfiction writers tell information in the order it happens.

Learning About Nonfiction Books

You Will Need

- three simple expository texts that are organized chronologically, such as these *Independent Reading* books:
  - *I Make Clay Pots* by Leslie Johnson
  - *Milk to Ice Cream* by Lisa M. Herrington
- chart paper and markers

Academic Language / Important Vocabulary

- nonfiction
- order
- information
- author

Continuum Connection

- Notice when a writer is telling information in order (a sequence) [p. 30]

Goal

Notice that some nonfiction writers organize information in the order that it happens.

Rationale

When children understand that some nonfiction books are organized chronologically, they can understand how the information fits together.

Assess Learning

Observe children when they talk about nonfiction books. Notice if there is evidence of new learning based on the goal of this minilesson.

- ▶ Do children notice when the author of a nonfiction book tells about something in the order that it happens?
- ▶ Are children able to identify what happens first, next, and last in a chronological nonfiction book?
- ▶ Do children use the words *nonfiction*, *order*, *information*, and *author*?

Minilesson

To help children think about the minilesson principle, choose the texts and examples that you think will be most meaningful to them and provide an inquiry-based lesson to help them notice how authors organize information in order. Here is an example.

- ▶ Read aloud *I Make Clay Pots*. As you read, guide children to notice the chronological sequence of the book.

    What does the girl do first? What does she do next? What does she do last?

    The author of this book tells a lot of interesting information about how to make clay pots. How do you think she decided what information to write first, what to write next, and what to write last?

    The author tells the steps to make a clay pot in the order that they happen.

- ▶ Record steps on chart paper.

Have a Try

Invite the children to talk with a partner about the order of information in a nonfiction book.

▶ Read aloud pages 9–25 of *Milk to Ice Cream*.

> Turn and talk to your partner about what you notice about how the author tells the information in the book.

> Invite a few pairs to share their thinking.

Summarize and Apply

Summarize the learning and remind children to notice the order of information as they read a nonfiction book.

> Look at the chart. What can you say about how some nonfiction writers tell information?

▶ Write the principle at the top of the chart.

> If you read a nonfiction book today, think about whether the author is telling about something in the order it happens. If so, be ready to share when we come back together.

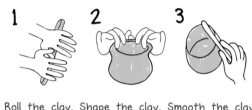

Sometimes nonfiction writers tell information in the order it happens.

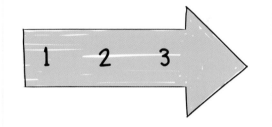

Roll the clay. Shape the clay. Smooth the clay.

Share

Following independent work time, gather children together in the meeting area to talk about nonfiction books.

> Give a thumbs-up if you read a nonfiction book that tells about something in the order it happens. What happens first, next, and last in your book?

Extend the Lesson (Optional)

After assessing children's understanding, you might decide to extend the learning.

▶ Use interactive or shared writing to create a nonfiction text that is organized chronologically.

▶ **Drawing/Writing About Reading** Use interactive or shared writing to create a timeline of the events in a familiar chronological nonfiction book.

Reading Minilesson Principle
Sometimes the author of a nonfiction book tells about many different kinds of people and places.

Learning About Nonfiction Books

You Will Need

- three or four familiar nonfiction books such as the following:
  - *Shoes Shoes Shoes* by Ann Morris, from Text Set: Nonfiction
  - *I Love Our Earth* by Bill Martin Jr. and Michael Sampson, from Text Set: Nonfiction
  - *Hats Hats Hats* by Ann Morris, from Text Set: Fiction and Nonfiction
- chart paper and markers
- several baskets of nonfiction books

Academic Language / Important Vocabulary

- author
- illustrator
- facts
- photographs
- places
- people
- topics

Continuum Connection

- Recognize and understand that nonfiction texts may be about different kinds of people and different places where they live (p. 30)

Goal

Recognize and understand that authors of nonfiction texts can tell about different kinds of people and places.

Rationale

Children often learn about unfamiliar topics when they read nonfiction books. Thinking and talking about different people and places around the world helps to build background knowledge and expands understanding about a variety of topics.

Assess Learning

Observe children when they talk about nonfiction books they have read. Notice if there is evidence of new learning based on the goal of this minilesson.

- Can the children explain that nonfiction writers tell about different people and places?
- Do the children use vocabulary such as *people, places,* and *topics* to discuss nonfiction?

Minilesson

To help children think about the minilesson principle, choose familiar nonfiction texts and examples to help children notice what they can learn. Here is an example.

- Show children the front cover and show several pages of *Shoes Shoes Shoes.*

  Talk about the differences in the people Ann Morris writes about. What do you notice about what they are wearing?

  What do you notice about the places?

- Record responses on chart paper.
- Show some of the pages in *I Love Our Earth* and read them.

  Think about the pictures and words. What do you notice about the people and places in this book?

- Write responses on the chart.

Have a Try

Invite the children to talk with a partner about the people and places in a nonfiction book.

▶ Show some pages from *Hats Hats Hats*.

Turn and talk to your partner about what you notice about the people and places in this book.

▶ After the children turn and talk, choose a few pairs to share their answers. Record the ideas on the chart.

Summarize and Apply

Summarize the learning and remind children to notice the different people and places in nonfiction books.

What did you learn today about the topics authors write about in nonfiction books? Take a look at the chart.

▶ Write the principle on the chart. Then show several baskets of nonfiction books.

Choose a nonfiction book to read today. When you read, think about if the writer tells about different people and places.

Share

Following independent work time, gather children together in the meeting area to talk about their reading.

Today you learned that writers tell about many different kinds of people and places. What are some other people or places you have read about?

▶ Choose a few children to share.

Extend the Lesson (Optional)

After assessing children's understanding, you might decide to extend the learning.

▶ Use interactive writing to write about the different people and places children learned about in *I Love Our Earth* or *Shoes Shoes Shoes*.

▶ **Drawing/Writing About Reading** Invite children to draw pictures and write in a reader's notebook about the things they learned about different people or places from reading a nonfiction book.

Reading Minilesson Principle
An author has a reason for writing a nonfiction book.

Learning About Nonfiction Books

You Will Need

- three or four familiar nonfiction books, such as the following books from Text Set: Nonfiction:
  - *Building a House* by Byron Barton
  - *Shoes Shoes Shoes* by Ann Morris
  - *I Love Our Earth* by Bill Martin Jr. and Michael Sampson
- chart paper and markers
- baskets of nonfiction books

Academic Language / Important Vocabulary

- author
- illustrator
- facts
- information

Continuum Connection

- Understand that a writer has a purpose in writing about a topic (p. 30)

Goal

Understand that a writer has a purpose in writing about a topic.

Rationale

When you teach children to think about the author's purpose, they learn to focus on the deeper meaning of the text and think about what the author is trying to teach the reader.

Assess Learning

Observe children when they talk about nonfiction books they have read. Notice if there is evidence of new learning based on the goal of this minilesson.

- ▶ Do the children understand that authors have a reason for writing nonfiction books?
- ▶ Can they talk about an author's reason (or a purpose) for writing about a topic?
- ▶ Do they use the words *facts* and *information* to describe what they learned?

Minilesson

To help children think about the minilesson principle, choose familiar texts and examples to show that authors have a purpose in writing nonfiction books. Here is an example.

- ▶ Show the children the front cover of *Building a House* by Byron Barton and read the title.

  Why would Byron Barton—or anyone else—write a book about how to build a house?

- ▶ Write responses on chart paper.

- ▶ Show pages from *Shoes Shoes Shoes* that illustrate different types of shoes.

  Why would Ann Morris write a book about shoes?

- ▶ Write responses on chart paper.

Have a Try

Invite the children to talk with a partner about the reason an author wrote a book.

> I'm going to read you the first few pages of *I Love Our Earth* by Bill Martin Jr. and Michael Sampson.

▶ Read the first few pages and show children pages from the beginning, middle, and end of the book.

> Turn and talk with your partner about why you think the authors wrote this book.

▶ After they turn and talk, record their comments on chart paper.

Summarize and Apply

Summarize the learning and remind the children to think about the author's purpose as they read.

> What did you learn today about why an author decides to write a nonfiction book?

> Even though the reasons might be different, an author has a reason for writing a nonfiction book.

▶ Write the principle on the chart. Then point out some of the nonfiction baskets.

> Today, I'd like you to choose a nonfiction book to read. Be sure to think about why the author wrote the book. Bring the book when we come back after independent work time.

Share

Following independent work time, gather children together in the meeting area to talk about nonfiction books.

> Give a thumbs-up if you thought about why the author wrote the book you read.

> Turn and talk to your partner about that book. Tell your partner why you think the author wrote the book.

▶ Choose a couple of children to share with the whole class.

Extend the Lesson (Optional)

After assessing children's understanding, you might decide to extend the learning.

▶ During interactive read-aloud and shared reading, stop to think with the children about an author's reason for writing a book. Sometimes the book will have that information on the back cover or on a page inside.

RML6
LA.U9.RML6

Think what you know about a topic before you read.

Learning About Nonfiction Books

You Will Need

- three or four simple expository texts that children have not previously read, such as these *Independent Reading* books:
  - *Big Cats, Little Cats* by Bernette Ford
  - *Eggs, Eggs, Eggs* by Aamir Bermiss
  - *What Can Fly?* by D. H. Figueredo

Academic Language / Important Vocabulary

- nonfiction
- topic
- fact
- information
- author

Continuum Connection

- Use background knowledge to understand texts that are read aloud (p. 30)

Goal

Think about what you know about a topic before you read a nonfiction book.

Rationale

When children recall what they know about a topic before they read a nonfiction book, they are better prepared to acquire new knowledge. They can make connections to what they know and gain a deeper understanding of the book's content.

Assess Learning

Observe children when they talk about nonfiction books. Notice if there is evidence of new learning based on the goal of this minilesson.

- Can children identify the topic of a nonfiction book before reading it?
- Can children talk about what they already know about the topic before reading?
- Do they use vocabulary such as *nonfiction, topic, fact, information,* and *author* when talking about what they know before they read?

Minilesson

To help children think about the minilesson principle, choose texts and examples that the children have not read or heard before to demonstrate the principle. Here is an example.

- Display a nonfiction book that children are not familiar with, such as *Big Cats, Little Cats*. Read the title.

  What do you see on the cover? What do you already know about big cats?

  Tell what you know about little cats, like the one on the cover.

- Record responses on the chart.

  You know a lot about big cats and little cats already. You can learn even more about them if you read this book.

- Show a second book, such as *Eggs, Eggs, Eggs*. Read the title.

  What does the title say this this book is about? The topic of this book is eggs. What do you know about eggs?

  What are the names of some animals that lay eggs? Why do animals lay eggs?

- Record responses on chart.

  You know a lot of things about eggs already. When you think about what you know about a topic before you read a nonfiction book, you get ready for the new facts and information that you will learn from the book.

Have a Try

Invite the children to apply the new thinking with a partner.

▶ Show a third book, such as *What Can Fly?* Read the title.

> What do you think this book is about? Turn and talk to your partner about what you already know about this topic. Talk about different things that can fly, where you might see these things, and what else you know about things that can fly.

▶ Invite a few pairs to share their thinking; record their responses on the chart

Summarize and Apply

Summarize the learning and remind children to think about what they know before they read.

> What can you do before you read a nonfiction book?

> When you think about what you already know before you read, it is easier for you to learn new information.

▶ Write the principle at the top of the chart.

> Today, you are going to read a nonfiction book during partner reading. Before you read, share what you know about the topic with your partner.

Share

Following independent reading time, gather children together in the meeting area and turn and talk to a partner about their reading.

> What did your partner say she knew about the topic before reading? How did thinking about what you already know help you when you were reading? How?

Extend the Lesson (Optional)

After assessing children's understanding, you might decide to extend the learning.

▶ Continue to encourage children to think and/or talk about their prior knowledge of the topic before reading or listening to any new nonfiction book.

▶ **Drawing/Writing About Reading** Use shared or interactive writing to create a list of prior knowledge about a topic of a book you are sharing with the whole class. After reading, add something new.

Think what you know about a topic before you read.

Big Cats, Little Cats
by Nanette Ford

· Big cats: lions, tigers, leopards, cheetahs

· Little cats: pet cats

· Lions roar.

· Little cats meow and purr.

Eggs, Eggs, Eggs

· Chickens lay eggs.

· Baby chickens come out of those eggs.

· People eat eggs.

What Can Fly?
by D. R. Figueredo

· Birds fly.

· Planes fly.

· Insects fly.

RML7
LA.U9.RML7

Reading Minilesson Principle
Think what you learned about a topic after you read.

Learning About Nonfiction Books

You Will Need

- three or four familiar simple expository texts, such as these from Text Set: Nonfiction:
  - *Building a House* by Byron Barton
  - *Shoes Shoes Shoes* by Ann Morris
  - *How to Hide a Butterfly & Other Insects* by Ruth Heller
- chart paper and markers

Academic Language / Important Vocabulary

- nonfiction
- topic
- fact
- information

Continuum Connection

- Gain new information from both pictures and print (p. 30)

Goal

Think about newly acquired knowledge after reading nonfiction.

Rationale

When you teach children to think about what they learned about a topic after they read a nonfiction book, they begin to develop self-awareness about their reading and they are more likely to remember the newly acquired knowledge. Thinking about new information may also generate questions that children will want to find answers to.

Assess Learning

Observe children when they talk about nonfiction books. Notice if there is evidence of new learning based on the goal of this minilesson.

- Can children identify the topic of a nonfiction book?
- Do children talk about what they learned about the topic after reading the book?
- When they talk, do they use vocabulary such as *nonfiction, topic, fact,* and *information*?

Minilesson

To help children think about the minilesson principle, choose the texts and examples that you think will be most meaningful to them and provide an inquiry-based lesson. Here is an example.

- Show *Building a House.*

   You learned a lot from reading this book about building houses. What did you learn about building a house that you didn't already know?

- Record responses on the chart.

   You learned some new facts about how houses are built.

- Show *Shoes Shoes Shoes.*

   Think about what you learned from this book that you didn't already know.

- Record responses on the chart.

   You learned some interesting new information about shoes from this book.

Have a Try

Invite the children to talk with a partner about what they learned from reading a nonfiction book.

▶ Show *How to Hide a Butterfly & Other Insects*.

Turn and talk to your partner about what you learned from this book.

▶ Invite a few pairs to share, and record their responses on the chart.

Summarize and Apply

Summarize the learning and remind children to think about what they learned after they read.

What did we talk about doing after you read?

▶ Write the principle at the top of the chart.

Today, choose a nonfiction book to read. Think about the new facts and information you learned about the topic. Be ready to share what you learned when we come back together.

Think what you learned about a topic after you read.

- The people who make the floor are called carpenters.

- The person who puts in wires is called an electrician.

- There are special shoes for climbing up ice.

- There are special shoes for riding a horse.

- Butterflies and other insects can hide by making themselves look like other things that are around them.

Share

Following independent work time, gather children together in the meeting area to talk about their reading.

Turn and talk about what you learned about the topic of the nonfiction book you read today.

Extend the Lesson (Optional)

After assessing children's understanding, you might decide to extend the learning.

▶ Before reading a nonfiction book, discuss and record what children already know about the topic. After reading, discuss and record what they learned about the topic. Encourage children to compare what they knew before with what they know after reading (e.g., did they learn that something they thought was true is actually not true).

▶ **Drawing/Writing About Reading** After reading nonfiction books during interactive read-aloud, use interactive or shared writing to create a list of facts the children learned about the book's topic. Alternatively, have children write or draw about what they learned in a reader's notebook.

Assessment

After you have taught the minilessons in this umbrella, observe your children as they talk and write about their reading across instructional contexts: interactive read-aloud, independent reading and literacy work, guided reading, shared reading, and book club. Use *Literacy Continuum* (Fountas and Pinnell 2017) to observe children's reading and writing behaviors across instructional contexts.

▶ What evidence do you have of new understandings related to nonfiction books?

- Can children identify an author's purpose or reason for writing a nonfiction book?

- Are children expressing an understanding that writers need to know about or become an expert about a topic to write about it?

- Can children share new information learned from illustrations and photographs?

- Are children expressing new learning about different people and places they read about in nonfiction?

- Can children identify the topic of a nonfiction book?

- Do they notice when an author tells information in time order?

- Do they use academic language, such as *nonfiction, topic, fact, information,* and *author*?

▶ In what other ways, beyond the scope of this umbrella, are children reading, discussing, and learning from nonfiction books?

- Do children notice the photographs or illustrations in nonfiction books?

- Do they notice the parts of a nonfiction book, such as the table of contents or sidebars?

Use your observations to determine the next umbrella you will teach. You may also consult Minilessons Across the Year (p. 51) for guidance.

Link to Writing

After teaching the minilessons in this umbrella, help children link the new learning to their own writing or drawing about reading:

▶ Through interactive writing, have children write about topics they know about. Encourage them to add simple photographs or illustrations to help readers understand the topic.

▶ When children are writing, ask them to write about real topics they know a lot about or care a lot about.

Minilessons in This Umbrella

RML1	Some nonfiction books have illustrations and some have photographs.
RML2	The illustrations and photographs show information about a topic.
RML3	Authors and illustrators label illustrations and photographs to give more information.

Before Teaching Umbrella 10 Minilessons

Read and discuss simple expository texts about familiar topics that have illustrations and/or photographs (some of which have labels). Use the following texts from the *Fountas & Pinnell Classroom™ Interactive Read-Aloud* and *Shared Reading Collections*, or choose texts that have similar characteristics.

Nonfiction

Exploring Nonfiction

A Fruit Is a Suitcase for Seeds by Jean Richards

Shoes Shoes Shoes by Ann Morris

I Love Our Earth by Bill Martin Jr. and Michael Sampson

How to Hide a Butterfly & Other insects by Ruth Heller

Exploring Fiction and Nonfiction

All Pigs Are Beautiful by Dick King-Smith

Fiction and Nonfiction

Sharing the Earth: Animals

Actual Size by Steve Jenkins

Animals

Shared Reading Collection

Fly Away by Alina Kirk

A Rainbow of Fruit by Brooke Matthews

As you read aloud and enjoy these texts together, help children

- discuss the illustrations and photographs,
- talk about information that is conveyed through the illustrations and photographs, and
- notice labels on the illustrations and photographs.

Shared Reading Collection

Section 2: Literary Analysis

RML1
LA.U10.RML1

Reading Minilesson Principle
Some nonfiction books have illustrations and some have photographs.

Learning Information from Illustrations/Graphics

You Will Need

- two nonfiction books with illustrations, such as these from Text Set: Fiction and Nonfiction:
  - *All Pigs Are Beautiful* by Dick King-Smith
  - *A Fruit Is a Suitcase for Seeds* by Jean Richards
- two nonfiction books with photographs, such as these from Text Set: Nonfiction:
  - *Shoes Shoes Shoes* by Ann Morris
  - *I Love Our Earth* by Bill Martin Jr. and Michael Sampson
- chart paper and markers

Academic Language / Important Vocabulary

- nonfiction
- illustration
- photograph

Continuum Connection

- Gain new understanding from illustrations (p. 30)
- Understand that an illustrator created the pictures in the book (p. 31)

Goal

Understand that nonfiction can have both illustrations and photographs.

Rationale

When you teach children that nonfiction books can have both illustrations drawn by an illustrator and photographs, they begin to think about the information that can be gained from these images. They also learn not to assume that a book with illustrations is necessarily a fiction book. Technically, the term *illustrations* includes photographs. This distinction should be made with the children.

Assess Learning

Observe children when they talk about nonfiction books. Notice if there is evidence of new learning based on the goal of this minilesson.

- Can they explain how they know whether an image is a picture an illustrator drew or a picture taken by a photographer?
- Do they use vocabulary such as *nonfiction*, *illustration*, and *photograph*?

Minilesson

To help children think about the minilesson principle, choose familiar texts and examples and discuss photographs and illustrations. Here is an example.

- Show some pages in *A Fruit Is a Suitcase for Seeds*.

  How do you think the pictures in this book were made?

  Who remembers what we call a picture in a book that someone painted or drew? This picture is an illustration because a person, called an illustrator, drew or painted it. Some nonfiction books have pictures that an illustrator drew or painted.

- Write *Illustrations* on the chart and place the book on that side of the easel/chart.
- Show some pages in *Shoes Shoes Shoes*.

  How do you think this picture was made?

  This picture is of a real boy holding real shoes. Somebody took this picture with a camera. What do we call a picture that you take with a camera?

  This is a photograph because it shows real things that someone took a picture of with a camera. Some nonfiction books have photographs.

- Write *Photographs* on the chart and place the book on this side of the easel/chart.

Have a Try

Invite the children to work with a partner to compare the pictures in two nonfiction books.

- Show some pages of *All Pigs Are Beautiful* and of *I Love Our Earth*.

  Turn and talk to your partner about what you notice about the pictures in these two books. Which book is it like? How do you know?

- Ask two children to place the books on the correct side of the easel/chart.

  Do you agree with where the books are?

Summarize and Apply

Summarize the learning and remind children to notice the illustrations and photographs as they read.

  Look at our chart. What does it show about nonfiction books?

- Write the principle at the top of the chart.

  Today, choose a nonfiction book to read during independent work time. As you're reading, notice whether the book has illustrations, photographs, or both. Be ready to share when we come back together.

Share

Following independent work time, gather children together in the meeting area to talk about the pictures in nonfiction books.

  Turn and talk to your partner about whether the nonfiction book you read had illustrations or photographs and how you were able to tell.

Extend the Lesson (Optional)

After assessing children's understanding, you might decide to extend the learning.

- During interactive read-aloud or shared reading, take time to have children study the photographs or illustrations. Ask what they can learn from them.

- **Drawing/Writing About Reading** Show children a photograph or a created illustration from a nonfiction book and have them write or draw a response to it in a reader's notebook (for example, What did you learn from this photograph? What does it make you think about?).

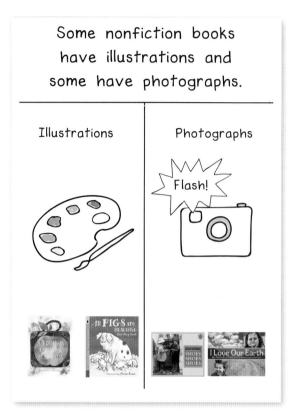

Some nonfiction books have illustrations and some have photographs.

Illustrations | Photographs

Flash!

Reading Minilesson Principle

The illustrations and photographs show information about a topic.

Learning Information from Illustrations/Graphics

You Will Need

- three or four familiar nonfiction books, such as the following:
  - *Shoes Shoes Shoes* by Ann Morris, from Text Set: Nonfiction
  - *How to Hide a Butterfly* by Ruth Heller, from Text Set: Nonfiction
  - *Actual Size* by Steve Jenkins, from Text Set: Animals
- chart paper and markers
- a nonfiction book for each pair of children
- sticky notes

Academic Language / Important Vocabulary

- illustrator
- illustration
- picture
- photograph
- information

Continuum Connection

- Gain new understanding from illustrations (p. 31)

Goal

Notice and search for information in simple graphics in a nonfiction book.

Rationale

Nonfiction books have special features that add meaning and provide information about the topic. Teaching children to use these features (illustrations and photographs) will expand their knowledge about the topic as well as the genre of nonfiction.

Assess Learning

Observe children when they talk about nonfiction books. Notice if there is evidence of new learning based on the goal of this minilesson.

- Do children notice and search for information in simple graphics?
- Can children tell what they learned from illustrations and photographs?
- Do they use the words *illustrator, illustration, picture, photograph,* and *information* to talk about nonfiction books?

Minilesson

To help children think about the minilesson principle, choose familiar texts and examples to demonstrate that illustrations and photographs convey information. Here is an example.

- Show and read aloud pages 26–27 of *Shoes Shoes Shoes*.

  You can learn some information about shoes from the words I just read. But, what do you learn about shoes from these photographs?

- Show and read the pages about the moth from *How to Hide a Butterfly & Other Insects*.

  Let's look at *How to Hide a Butterfly & Other Insects* by Ruth Heller. How do these illustrations help you learn about the moth?

- Show and read the pages about the giant squid from *Actual Size*.

  Now we'll look at *Actual Size* by Steve Jenkins. What information do you learn from this illustration? Is there something that you can learn from the picture that is not in the words?

Have a Try

Invite the children to talk with a partner about what they can learn from an illustration or photograph.

▶ Give a nonfiction book to each pair of children.

With your partner, turn to a page with an illustration or photograph. Talk about what you learn from the illustration or photograph.

▶ After the children turn and talk, choose a few pairs to share their responses.

Summarize and Apply

Summarize the learning and remind children to look at the illustrations and photographs as they read.

What did you learn today about photographs and illustrations in nonfiction books? Let's make a chart to help us remember to look at the illustrations and photographs to learn more about a topic.

▶ Make a chart and write the principle to the top.

If you read a nonfiction book today, put a sticky note on a page where you learned information about the topic from the illustrations or photographs.

The illustrations and photographs show information about a topic.

Share

Following independent work time, gather children together in the meeting area to talk about nonfiction books.

Who has an illustration or photograph to share? What did you learn from it?

▶ Choose a few children to share.

Extend the Lesson (Optional)

After assessing children's understanding, you might decide to extend the learning.

▶ Ask children to write and illustrate a class book on a nonfiction topic they are familiar with. Encourage them to begin by discussing what to include in the illustrations.

▶ **Drawing/Writing About Reading** Ask children to draw pictures and write in a reader's notebook about a topic that they read about today.

Reading Minilesson Principle

Authors and illustrators label illustrations and photographs to give more information.

Learning Information from Illustrations/Graphics

You Will Need

- three or four nonfiction books with labeled illustrations, such as these:
  - *A Fruit Is a Suitcase for Seeds*, by Jean Richards from Text Set: Nonfiction
  - *Fly Away* by Alina Kirk and *A Rainbow of Fruit* by Brooke Matthews, from *Shared Reading Collection*
- chart paper and markers
- sticky notes

Academic Language / Important Vocabulary

- label
- illustration
- photograph
- nonfiction
- topic
- author

Continuum Connection

- Notice and search for information in simple graphics: e.g., drawing with label (p. 31)

Goal

Understand that the labels on illustrations and photographs in nonfiction books offer more information.

Rationale

When children understand that labels on illustrations and photographs give more information, they know to look for labels when reading a nonfiction book. They are able to gain information from the labels, enhancing their understanding of the illustrations and photographs and of the book's content.

Assess Learning

Observe children when they talk about nonfiction books. Notice if there is evidence of new learning based on the goal of this minilesson.

- Do children notice labels in nonfiction books?
- Can children explain the purpose of the labels?
- Do they understand the terms *label, illustration, photograph, nonfiction, topic,* and *author*?

Minilesson

To help children think about the minilesson principle, choose familiar texts and examples to show how labels add information to photographs and illustrations. Here is an example.

- Open *A Fruit Is a Suitcase for Seeds* to page 11.

  What do you notice about the illustration on this page?

- If nobody comments on the labels, ask guiding questions, such as these:

  Point to the word *cherry*. Why do you think the word *cherry* is here? This book has labels that tell you what the different fruits are called.

- Turn to the next page. Have a child point to a label on the page. Point to and read aloud each label.

- Read page 2 of *Fly Away*. Point to the photograph and the label of the bird.

  What do you notice about this photograph?

  What does the label tell you about the photograph?

  Why did the author put the label here?

- Read a few more pages. On each page, ask a child to point to the label.

  This book has labels that tell you what the different flying animals and machines are called. They give more information about the topic of the book.

Have a Try

Invite the children to talk with a partner about the photographs in *A Rainbow of Fruit*.

❯ Display pages 10–11 of *A Rainbow of Fruit*.

> Turn and talk to your partner about the photographs on these pages. Are there any labels? What do they say? How do the labels help you better understand the book?

Summarize and Apply

Summarize the learning and remind children to pay attention to labels when they read nonfiction.

> What did you notice today about the labels in nonfiction books?

> Labels give you more information about the topic of the book. Let's make a chart so you will remember that.

> Choose a nonfiction book to read today. Look carefully to see if there are any labels. If you find any, make sure to read them because they will give more information.

Share

Following independent work time, gather children together in the meeting area to talk about labels in nonfiction books.

> Give a thumbs-up if you read a nonfiction book that has labels on the illustrations or photographs.

❯ Invite children to share examples of labels in their books.

Extend the Lesson (Optional)

After assessing children's understanding, you might decide to extend the learning.

❯ Direct children to draw their own illustrations with labels. For example, they might draw pictures of their families and label the different family members. Understanding labels could also be incorporated into lessons in various subject areas.

❯ **Drawing/Writing About Reading** Use interactive or independent writing to have children create labels for different objects or areas in the classroom (e.g., stapler, bookshelf, classroom library).

Section 2: Literary Analysis

Assessment

After you have taught the minilessons in this umbrella, observe children as they talk and write about their reading across instructional contexts: interactive read-aloud, independent reading and literacy work, guided reading, shared reading, and book club. Use *The Literacy Continuum* (Fountas and Pinnell 2017) to observe children's reading and writing behaviors across instructional contexts.

▶ What evidence do you have of new understandings related to learning information from graphics and illustrations?

- Can children identify whether a nonfiction book has drawn or painted illustrations or photographs?

- Are children talking about what they are learning from illustrations and photographs in nonfiction books?

- Do children notice labels in nonfiction books and understand their purpose?

- Can they understand and use academic language, such as *illustrations, photographs, author, label, topic,* and *nonfiction* when talking about nonfiction books?

▶ In what other ways, beyond the scope of this umbrella, are they thinking and talking about nonfiction books?

- Do they notice text features (e.g., a table of contents, index, or sidebar)?

- Do they notice the different ways that nonfiction books are organized?

Use your observations to determine the next umbrella you will teach. You may also consult Minilessons Across the Year (p. 51) for guidance.

Link to Writing

After teaching the minilessons in this umbrella, help children link the new learning to their own writing:

▶ Help children create their own nonfiction books about familiar topics that interest them (e.g., animals, sports, vehicles). Let children decide whether they want to use drawings or photographs to illustrate their books, and help them find or create relevant images. They can take photographs, cut out photographs from magazines, or download pictures from approved online sources. Remind them to use images that help the reader learn more information about the topic. Encourage children to add labels to their drawings or photographs.

Minilessons in This Umbrella

RML1 A table of contents lists the smaller topics in a nonfiction book.

RML2 Authors and illustrators use sidebars to tell more about a topic.

RML3 Read all parts of a page in a nonfiction book.

Before Teaching Umbrella 11 Minilessons

Read and discuss high-quality nonfiction books that have nonfiction text features, such as a table of contents and sidebars.

Use the following texts from the *Fountas & Pinnell Classroom™ Independent Reading Collection* or *Shared Reading Collection*, or choose books that have similar characteristics. Choose simple, familiar factual texts with topics that engage children and reinforce and expand their knowledge of self and the world.

Independent Reading Collection

> *Whales* by Ryan Nagelhout
>
> *I See a Chipmunk* by Alex Appleby

Shared Reading Collection

> *In the Arctic* by Tess Fletcher
>
> *Playing Basketball* by Louis Petrone
>
> *Spin, Spin, Spin* by Alina Kirk
>
> *The Log* by Joseph Petronaci
>
> *Animal Masks* by Jennifer Blizin Gillis

As you read aloud and enjoy these texts together, help children

- think and talk about the books with one another,

- notice and briefly discuss the table of contents and sidebars, and

- demonstrate reading all parts of the page to gain new information about the topic.

Independent Reading

Shared Reading Collection

Section 2: Literary Analysis

RML1
LA.U11.RML1

Reading Minilesson Principle
A table of contents lists the smaller topics in a nonfiction book.

Using Text Features to Gain Information

You Will Need

- two or three nonfiction books that have a table of contents, such as these *Independent Reading* books:
  - *Whales* by Ryan Nagelhout
  - *I See a Chipmunk* by Alex Appleby
- chart paper and markers
- document camera (optional)

Academic Language / Important Vocabulary

- table of contents
- nonfiction
- writer
- section
- topic

Continuum Connection

- Understand the purpose of some organizational tools: e.g., title, table of contents (p. 31)

Goal

Understand what a table of contents is and does.

Rationale

Typically, a nonfiction book has several sections, and each has a topic that is related to the larger topic. When you teach children that some nonfiction writers use a table of contents as an organizational tool, you support children in understanding one way to navigate nonfiction texts. Looking at a table of contents helps readers think about what they know about the bigger topic and the smaller topics before reading the book. It also has helps them locate specific information in the book.

Assess Learning

Observe children when they talk about nonfiction books. Notice if there is evidence of new learning based on the goal of this minilesson.

- Can children describe how a table of contents is a helpful tool?
- Do they use the table of contents to get an overview of what the book will be about?
- Can they use the table to contents to find certain information that interests them?
- Do they understand the terms *table of contents, nonfiction, writer, section,* and *topic?*

Minilesson

To help children think about the minilesson principle, choose texts and examples to demonstrate what a table of contents is. Here is an example.

- Show the table of contents of *Whales*. (If you have a document camera, you can project the pages.)

  The topic of this book is whales. This page is called the contents page, or the table of contents. Let's take a close look at it to find out what we can learn from it.

- Read the table of contents to the children.

  What are some of the things you will learn about whales?

- Show the table of contents, pointing to the page numbers.

  What are these numbers for?

  Tell how you could use the page numbers from the table of contents.

- Read a topic from the table of contents and its page number. Then go to that page. Repeat to build the concept that the table of contents shows the information in the order it appears in the book.

Have a Try

Invite the children to talk with a partner about a table of contents.

▶ Show the table of contents for *I See a Chipmunk* and read it aloud.

> Turn and talk to your partner about what you will learn about the topic from this table of contents.

Summarize and Apply

Summarize the learning and remind children to look for a table of contents in nonfiction books.

> Today we talked about the table of contents. What did you learn about it?

▶ Record children's responses on a chart and then summarize the learning by writing the principle at the top.

> If you are reading a nonfiction book today, notice if there is a table of contents. If there is, think about how it can help you. Be ready to share when we come back together.

Share

Following independent work time, gather children together in the meeting area to talk about tables of contents.

> Give a thumbs-up if your nonfiction book has a table of contents. What did it tell you?

▶ Ask one or two children to share. (Use a document camera, if possible, so everyone can see what different tables of contents look like.)

Extend the Lesson (Optional)

After assessing children's understanding, you might decide to extend the learning.

▶ During shared reading or interactive read-aloud, use the table of contents to help children think about what they know or what they want to learn about the topic.

▶ **Drawing/Writing About Reading** If children are writing nonfiction books, they might want to add a table of contents.

A table of contents lists the smaller topics in a nonfiction book.

- Shows the information in the book.
- Shows the order of information in the book.
- Tells the page number.

Table of Contents

Types of Whales . . 3

What Whales Eat . . 10

Big Whales 14

Little Whales 20

Section 2: Literary Analysis

RML 2
LA.U11.RML2

Reading Minilesson Principle

Authors and illustrators use sidebars to tell more about a topic.

Using Text Features to Gain Information

You Will Need

- three or four nonfiction books that have sidebars, such as these *Shared Reading* books:
  - *In the Arctic* by Tess Fletcher
  - *Playing Basketball* by Louis Petrone
- chart paper and markers
- basket of nonfiction texts

Academic Language / Important Vocabulary

- sidebar
- nonfiction
- writer
- topic

Continuum Connection

- Understand the purpose of some organizational tools: e.g., title, table of contents (p. 31)

Goal

Notice and use sidebars to gain more information about the topic.

Rationale

When you teach children that some nonfiction books have sidebars, they learn that the author gives information in different ways in a nonfiction book. They need to read all the information on a page. Sidebars can be read before or after reading the page.

Assess Learning

Observe children when they talk about nonfiction books. Notice if there is evidence of new learning based on the goal of this minilesson.

- Do the children notice if a nonfiction text has sidebars?
- Can they describe how sidebars are helpful?
- Do they read sidebars to gain more information about the topic?
- Do they understand the terms *sidebar, nonfiction, writer,* and *topic?*

Minilesson

To help children think about the minilesson principle, choose the texts and examples that you think will help them understand the purpose of sidebars. Here is an example.

> Take a look at this book called *In the Arctic*.

- Show pages 2–5.

> What do you notice about how the writer shows you information?

> The boxes on the side are called sidebars. They give extra information about the topic of the book.

- Read the regular text on a page and then read the sidebar so that children can talk about how the sidebar adds information about the topic. Explain that you can read the sidebar before or after reading the page.

Have a Try

Invite the children to talk with a partner about information in sidebars.

> I'm going to show and read you a few pages from *Playing Basketball.* Then you will talk to your partner about the information the writer wrote in the sidebars.

� Read aloud pages 4–9. After children turn and talk, invite a few to share their findings.

Summarize and Apply

Summarize the learning and remind children to look for sidebars as they read.

> Let's make a chart that shows how authors and illustrators use sidebars. What did you learn about sidebars?

▸ Summarize the learning by writing the principle at the top.

> Today you can read a nonfiction book from the basket. Notice if there are any sidebars and what extra information you learn about the topic. Be ready to share when we come together.

Authors and illustrators use sidebars to tell more about a topic.

Information

More Information

Share

Following independent work time, gather children together in the meeting area to talk about nonfiction books.

> Give a thumbs-up if you read a book with sidebars today. What did you learn?

▸ Ask one or two children to share. (Place the book on a document camera, if possible, so everyone can see.)

Extend the Lesson (Optional)

After assessing children's understanding, you might decide to extend the learning.

▸ When you read an interactive read-aloud or shared reading book that has sidebars, be aware that children will need coaching on how to approach a page that has a sidebar.

Section 2: Literary Analysis

RML 3
LA.U11.RML3

Reading Minilesson Principle
Read all parts of a page in a nonfiction book.

Using Text Features to Gain Information

You Will Need

- three or four nonfiction books with various text features, such as these *Shared Reading* books:
  - *Spin, Spin, Spin* by Alina Kirk
  - *The Log* by Joseph Petronaci
  - *Animal Masks* by Jennifer Blizin Gillis
- chart paper and markers
- basket of nonfiction texts
- document camera (optional)

Academic Language / Important Vocabulary

- sidebar
- label
- nonfiction
- writer

Continuum Connection

- Gain new information from both pictures and print (p. 30)

Goal

Understand and read all parts of a page in nonfiction to gain information.

Rationale

When you teach children to read all parts of the page in a nonfiction text, you support them in maximizing the learning from a nonfiction text. They can read the extra information before or after they read the page.

Assess Learning

Observe children when they talk about nonfiction books. Notice if there is evidence of new learning based on the goal of this minilesson.

- ▶ Do the children read all parts of the page in a nonfiction book?
- ▶ Can they describe what they learned from reading all parts of the page?
- ▶ Do they understand and use the terms *sidebar, label, nonfiction,* and *writer*?

Minilesson

To help children think about the minilesson principle, choose familiar texts and examples to demonstrate reading all the features (for example, sidebar, label) on a nonfiction book page. Here is an example.

> Listen while I read part of the book *Spin, Spin, Spin*.

- ▶ Read pages 4–7 aloud, reading all the text features and pointing to them as you read.

  > What did you notice about how I read these pages?

- ▶ Guide children to notice that you read both the body text and the labels on the photographs.

  > What did you notice about how I read the parts of the pages? What are the parts of the page called?

  > Now I will read part of *The Log*. Then you will turn and talk to your partner about what you noticed I did as a reader.

- ▶ Read aloud pages 2–5. Invite a few children to share what they noticed.

Have a Try

Invite the children to notice the sidebars in a book.

▸ Show pages 4 and 5 to the children.

▸ Have a few children come up to point to parts of the page where you should read. Then read aloud pages 4–5.

> Did I read everything on the pages?

Summarize and Apply

Summarize the learning and remind children to read all parts of a page as they read.

> Let's make a chart to help you remember to read all the parts of a page in a nonfiction book.

▸ Summarize the learning by writing the principle at the top.

> If you read a nonfiction book today, be sure to read all the parts of the page. You can choose a book from this basket of books. Be ready to share when we meet after independent work time.

Share

Following independent work time, have children sit in pairs in the meeting area to talk about nonfiction books.

> Choose a page you read to share with your partner. Show your partner everything you needed to read so you could learn about the topic.

▸ If available, use a document camera to share one child's book with the whole group.

Extend the Lesson (Optional)

After assessing children's understanding, you might decide to extend the learning.

▸ During shared reading or interactive read-aloud, point out when you read information from a sidebar, label, or other nonfiction text feature.

▸ **Drawing/Writing About Reading** If children write a nonfiction book, encourage them to include a sidebar.

Assessment

After you have taught the minilessons in this umbrella, observe children as they talk and write about their reading across instructional contexts: interactive read-aloud, independent reading and literacy work, guided reading, shared reading, and book club. Use *The Literacy Continuum* (Fountas and Pinnell 2017) to observe children's reading and writing behaviors across instructional contexts.

▶ What evidence do you have of new understandings related to nonfiction text features?

- Do children notice and understand how to use the table of contents to find information?

- Do they understand the value of sidebars and read them without prompting?

- Do they read all the parts of a page in a nonfiction book?

- Can they describe what they learned from all parts of the page?

- Do children understand and use academic language, such as *table of contents, sidebar, label,* and *nonfiction?*

▶ In what other ways, beyond the scope of this umbrella, are they talking about nonfiction books?

- Do children notice how a nonfiction book is organized?

- Do they talk about the topic of a nonfiction book?

Use your observations to determine the next umbrella you will teach. You may also consult Minilessons Across the Year (p. 51) for guidance.

Link to Writing

After teaching the minilessons in this umbrella, help children link the new learning to their own writing:

▶ Help children incorporate the text features they studied into their own informational writing. Encourage children to think about how they can provide more information for the reader using sidebars. Remind children that they can support the reader in finding information in their book by including a table of contents or an index.

Minilessons in This Umbrella

RML1   The pictures and the words show where a story happens.

RML2   Stories happen in different places.

Before Teaching Umbrella 12 Minilessons

Read and discuss high-quality fiction picture books set in a variety of places. Point out the setting, or where the book takes place, as you read and enjoy each book together. Use the following books from the *Fountas & Pinnell Classroom™ Interactive Read-Aloud Collection* text sets or other high-quality picture books with illustrations that clearly show the setting.

Learning to Be Yourself

Three Hens and a Peacock by Lester Laminack

Celebrating Differences

Big Al by Andrew Clements

Living and Working Together: Community

Lola at the Library by Anna McQuinn

My Steps by Sally Derby

Taking Care of Each Other: Family

Elizabeti's Doll by Stephanie Stuve-Bodeen

Grace Lin: Exploring Family and Culture

Dim Sum for Everyone! by Grace Lin

As you read aloud and enjoy these texts together, help children

- think about where the story takes place, and
- make personal connections to the settings in the stories.

Be Yourself

Differences

Community

Family

Grace Lin

Section 2: Literary Analysis

Reading Minilesson Principle
The pictures and the words show where a story happens.

Thinking About Where Stories Happen

You Will Need

- three or four books that children have read or heard, such as these:
  - *Big Al* by Andrew Clements, from Text Set: Differences
  - *Lola at the Library* by Anna McQuinn, from Text Set: Community
  - *Three Hens and a Peacock* by Lester Laminack from Text Set: Be Yourself
- chart paper and markers
- sticky notes

Academic Language / Important Vocabulary

- title

Continuum Connection

- Recall important details about setting after a story is read [p. 28]

Goal

Use information from the pictures and words to understand where a story happens.

Rationale

When children think about where a story takes place, they understand the characters and the plot at a deeper level. When they notice details in the pictures and words, they learn how to analyze the writer's and illustrator's craft. It is not necessary for children to use the word *setting*, but they are learning the concept.

Assess Learning

Observe children when they talk about where stories they have read take place. Notice if there is evidence of new learning based on the goal of this minilesson.

- ▶ Do children notice and describe where the story takes place?
- ▶ Can they explain how they know where the story takes place?
- ▶ Do they know and use the word *title*?

Minilesson

To help children think about the minilesson principle, choose familiar texts that have examples of different settings to provide an inquiry-based lesson. Here is an example.

- ▶ Show the cover of *Big Al*.

  Listen to the first sentence in *Big Al*. "In the wide blue sea there was a very friendly fish named Big Al." Where is Big Al? Where does this story happen?

- ▶ Record responses.

  How did you know that?

- ▶ Show the cover of *Lola at the Library*.

  Think about *Lola at the Library*. How can you tell where this story happens?

- ▶ Record responses.

  Give a thumbs-up if you have been to a library. How does the picture show you Lola is at the library?

Have a Try

Invite the children to talk with a partner about where a story takes place.

> Now think about *Three Hens and a Peacock*.

> ▸ Show the book and read the first page.

> Think about how you know where the story happens. Turn and talk to your partner about that.

> ▸ After children turn and talk, ask a few of them to share with the whole group. Record responses.

Summarize and Apply

Summarize the learning and remind the children to think about where the story happens as they read.

> How can you tell where a story happens?

> ▸ Record the principle at the top of the chart.

> If you read a story today during independent work time, think about where the story happens. Put a sticky note on a picture or near some words that tell where it takes place. Bring your book when we come back together.

Share

Following independent work time, have children sit with a partner in the meeting area to talk about their reading.

> Talk to your partner about where your story happens. Show the words and pictures that helped you know where the story takes place.

Extend the Lesson (Optional)

After assessing children's understanding, you might decide to extend the learning.

> ▸ During interactive read-aloud, shared reading, and guided reading, provide opportunities for children to notice and discuss the setting. Continue to add to the chart as you encounter new settings.

> ▸ Create a mural of a setting from a book. Use interactive writing to create labels of specific things that identify the setting (e.g., a tractor on a farm).

> ▸ **Drawing/Writing About Reading** Encourage children to draw and label the setting of stories from their independent reading in a reader's notebook.

The pictures and the words show where a story happens.

	Pictures	Words
		the wide blue sea
		the library
		Tucker's Farm

Section 2: Literary Analysis

Thinking About Where Stories Happen

You Will Need

- three or four texts with a diversity of settings, such as the following:
  - *Three Hens and a Peacock* by Lester Laminack, from Text Set: Be Yourself
  - *My Steps* by Sally Derby, from Text Set: Community
  - *Elizabeti's Doll* by Stephanie Stuve-Bodeen, from Text Set: Family
  - *Dim Sum for Everyone!* by Grace Lin, from Text Set: Grace Lin
- chart paper and markers
- sticky notes

Academic Language / Important Vocabulary

- title
- dedication page
- title page

Continuum Connection

- Recognize and understand that texts may have settings related to different places and people (p. 28)

Goal

Recognize and understand that stories happen in a variety of places and that a single story can have more than one setting.

Rationale

When kindergarteners are able to notice that books take place in a variety of settings, they expand their background knowledge and develop a foundation for thinking about the impact of the setting on the plot and the characters.

Assess Learning

Observe children when they talk about where stories they have read take place. Notice if there is evidence of new learning based on the goal of this minilesson.

- ▶ Can children identify where a story takes place and tell how they know?
- ▶ Do they notice that different stories can happen in different places?
- ▶ Do they notice when a single story has different settings?

Minilesson

To help children think about the minilesson principle, choose familiar texts with examples of different settings to provide an inquiry-based lesson. Here is an example.

▶ Show the book *Three Hens and a Peacock*.

> Look at the dedication and title pages. Where does this story take place? How do you know?

▶ Record responses on chart paper. Show the book *My Steps*.

> Listen to this part of *My Steps*: "Whenever it's a pretty day I play on my steps while cars and buses swoosh down the street and people walk by on the sidewalk."
>
> Where does this story happen? How do you know?

▶ Record responses.

> Does *My Steps* happen in the same place as *Three Hens and a Peacock*?

▶ Show several pages from *Elizabeti's Doll* that show different locations.

> Think about where Elizabeti is in this story. Where does this story happen?

▶ Record responses.

> Elizabeti is sometimes outside, sometimes on the road to the village, and sometimes inside, like when she is in the cooking hut. She is always in the part of the world called Africa.

Have a Try

Invite the children to talk with a partner about where *Dim Sum for Everyone!* takes place.

▶ Read this part of *Dim Sum for Everyone!*: "Everyone eats a little bit of everything."

Look at this picture. Turn and talk to your partner about where this story happens and how you know.

▶ After they turn and talk, ask a few partners to share their thinking. Record responses on the chart paper.

Summarize and Apply

Summarize the learning and remind the children to think about where stories take place as they read.

▶ Review the chart with the children.

What did you learn about where stories happen? Write the principle on the chart. You also noticed that one story can happen in more than one place,

When you are reading today, think about where the story takes place and how you know. Bring your book when we come back together so that you can share where your story happens.

▶ As children are reading, ask several individuals where their story takes place and how they know. Write the location on a sticky note and put it on the child's book cover.

Share

Following independent work time, gather children together in the meeting area to talk about their reading.

▶ Have the children with sticky notes put them on the chart paper. As they do, ask them to tell the class where the story happens and how they know.

Extend the Lesson (Optional)

After assessing children's understanding, you might decide to extend the learning.

▶ During interactive read-aloud and guided reading, invite children to talk about where the story takes place. Encourage the children to tell you which details in the illustrations and which words in the story show where the story takes place.

▶ Some children will notice that there are books that take place in similar places (two stories that take place in a school, for example) and that take place in more than one place. When they do, take time to discuss these different aspects of setting.

Assessment

After you have taught the minilessons in this umbrella, observe the children as they talk and write about their reading across instructional contexts: interactive read-aloud, independent reading and literacy work, guided reading, shared reading, and book club. Use *The Literacy Continuum* (Fountas and Pinnell 2017) to observe children's reading and writing behaviors across instructional contexts.

▶ What evidence do you have of new understandings related to setting?

- Can children identify the place where a story happens?

- Can they find evidence in the text to identify the place where the story takes place?

- Do they recognize that books can take place in several different places at different points in time?

- Do children know and use the word *title* to talk about a story?

▶ In what other ways, beyond the scope of this umbrella, are they talking about stories?

- Are they noticing that although stories have different settings they sometimes have similar themes or plot lines?

- Do children notice that details in the illustrations show not only setting but other information?

Use your observations to determine the next umbrella you will teach. You may also consult Minilessons Across the Year (p. 51) for guidance.

Link to Writing

After teaching the minilessons in this umbrella, help children link the new learning to their own writing or drawing about reading:

▶ During writers' workshop encourage children to include details about the setting in their stories. Demonstrate how to put details in illustrations to show where the story is happening. Notice and celebrate when children incorporate elements of setting in their drawing and writing.

Minilessons in This Umbrella

RML1   A story has a problem that gets solved.

RML2   Sometimes a character has a problem that is like a problem you have had.

RML3   Stories usually end when the problem is solved.

RML4   Think about how the story will end.

RML5   Talk about the problem and how it is solved when you tell about a story.

Before Teaching Umbrella 13 Minilessons

Read and discuss books that have simple plots with clear problems and solutions. As with most minilessons, the children should have heard or read the stories before they are used to teach a concept. However, for RML4, which is about predicting how a story will end, choose stories that the children have not heard or read. Use the following texts from the *Fountas & Pinnell Classroom™ Interactive Read-Aloud Collection* text sets or choose books with clear problem and solution from your own classroom or school library.

Eric Carle: Exploring the Natural World

   Have You Seen My Cat? by Eric Carle

The Importance of Friendship

   Big Al and Shrimpy by Andrew Clements

Taking Care of Each Other: Family

   Don't You Feel Well, Sam? by Amy Hest

   Elizabeti's Doll by Stephanie Stuve-Bodeen

The Importance of Kindness

   Say Hello by Jack and Michael Foreman

Celebrating Differences

   Leo the Late Bloomer by Robert Kraus

   Big Al by Andrew Clements

As you read aloud and enjoy these texts together, help children

- notice the problem and how it is solved,

- think about times they have had a problem like the character,

- predict how the story will end, and

- notice that the story usually ends shortly after the problem is solved.

Eric Carle

Friendship

Family

Kindness

Differences

Section 2: Literary Analysis

Reading Minilesson Principle
A story has a problem that gets solved.

Understanding How Stories Work

You Will Need

- two or three books with a simple plot (a clear problem and solution), such as the following:
  - *Have You Seen My Cat?* by Eric Carle, from Text Set: Eric Carle
  - *Don't You Feel Well, Sam?* by Amy Hest, from Text Set: Family
  - *Big Al and Shrimpy* by Andrew Clements, from Text Set: Friendship
- chart paper and markers

Academic Language / Important Vocabulary

- character
- problem
- solve
- solution

Continuum Connection

- Follow the events in simple narratives (p. 28)
- Notice and understand a simple plot with a problem and a solution (p. 28)

Goal

Notice and understand a simple plot with a problem and a solution.

Rationale

When children understand that simple narratives often have a problem and a solution, they are better able to understand how stories work. When they understand the structure of a story, they are able to anticipate outcomes and follow the important events.

Assess Learning

Observe children when they talk about stories they have read or heard. Notice if there is evidence of new learning based on the goal of this minilesson.

- ▶ Are children able to identify both the problem and the solution in simple stories?
- ▶ Do children use the words *character, problem, solve,* and *solution*?

Minilesson

To help children think about the minilesson principle, choose familiar texts and examples of problems and solutions to provide an inquiry-based lesson. Here is an example.

- ▶ Show *Have You Seen My Cat?* by Eric Carle.

  What was the boy's problem in this story? What did he need to do?

- ▶ Record responses on chart paper.

  What happened at the end? The boy solved his problem by looking all over for his cat until he found her.

- ▶ Show *Don't You Feel Well, Sam?*

  What problem did Sam have in this story?

- ▶ Record responses.

  How do you know he didn't want to take his medicine?

  How was Sam's problem solved?

- ▶ Record responses.

  Sometimes other people help the character solve a problem, like Sam's mother did in this story. So what did you notice about every story?

  In each story, the character had a problem, and the story was about how the problem was solved.

Have a Try

Invite the children to talk about the problem in *Big Al and Shrimpy* with a partner.

> What is the problem in *Big Al and Shrimpy*? How do the characters solve it? Turn and talk to your partner about the problem and the solution.

▶ Ask partners to share after they turn and talk. Record responses.

Summarize and Apply

Summarize the learning and remind children to notice the problem and how it is solved as they read.

▶ Review the chart with the children.

> A story has a problem that gets solved. The story is about how the character solves the problem.

▶ Write the principle on the chart.

> When you read today, notice if a character has a problem and how it gets solved. If you read a story and the character has a problem, bring your book when we come back together.

A story has a problem that gets solved.

Title	Problem	How it was solved.
Have you seen my cat? Eric Carle	A boy lost his cat.	The boy found his cat.
Don't You Feel Well, Sam?	Sam is sick and doesn't want to take his medicine. Hck, hck!	Sam took his medicine. COUG SYRU
BIG AL	Big Al is stuck down deep.	Shrimpy and the other fish helped Big Al get free.

Share

Following independent work time, gather children together in the meeting area to talk about their reading.

▶ Survey the children to find out how many children read a story with a problem. If several children raise their hand, ask partners to turn and talk. Alternatively, share examples as a whole group.

Extend the Lesson (Optional)

After assessing children's understanding, you might decide to extend the learning.

▶ Talk about problems and solutions in the stories read during interactive read-aloud and shared reading.

▶ Provide opportunities for children to act out (possibly with puppets) the problem in stories with simple plots.

▶ **Drawing/Writing About Reading** Use interactive writing to demonstrate how to draw and write about the problem in familiar stories. Support children in using a reader's notebook to draw and write about the problem in stories they are reading or listening to independently.

Section 2: Literary Analysis

Reading Minilesson Principle

Sometimes a character has a problem that is like a problem you have had.

Understanding How Stories Work

You Will Need

- two or three books with simple plots (a clear problem and solution), such as the following:
  - *Elizabeti's Doll* by Stephanie Stuve-Bodeen, from Text Set: Family
  - *Say Hello* by Jack and Michael Foreman, from Text Set: Kindness
  - *Don't You Feel Well, Sam?* by Amy Hest, from Text Set: Family
- chart paper and markers
- sticky notes

Academic Language / Important Vocabulary

- character
- problem

Continuum Connection

- Relate texts to their own lives (p. 28)
- Use background knowledge to understand settings, problems, and characters (p. 28)

Goal

Relate texts to one's own life and use background knowledge to understand problems.

Rationale

When children connect personally to the problem in a story, they build a deeper understanding of a character's feelings and motivations, which strengthens their understanding of the plot. When they make personal connections to a text, they empathize with characters and become more invested in the stories they read.

Assess Learning

Observe children when they talk about problems in stories. Notice if there is evidence of new learning based on the goal of this minilesson.

- ▶ Are children able to relate to problems in the stories they read or hear?
- ▶ Do children use the words *character* and *problem*?

Minilesson

To help children think about the minilesson principle, choose familiar texts and examples of problems to provide an inquiry-based lesson. Here is an example.

> Let's think about the problem in *Elizabeti's Doll*. What happened when Elizabeti ran outside to get Eva? What was Elizabeti's problem?

▶ Record responses on the chart.

> If you have ever lost something special to you, put your thumb up. Many of you have had a problem like Elizabeti's, so you can understand her problem and you know how she felt.
>
> Now think about the story, *Say Hello*.

▶ Read and show the page that says "Why am I the lonely one?"

> What is the boy's problem in this story? Record responses.
>
> Think about a time you had the same problem as the boy. Some of you can understand the character's problem because you had a problem like his.
>
> Now think about Sam's problem in *Don't You Feel Well, Sam?*

▶ Read and show the part of the story that begins with "Open wide, Sam!" and ends with "Sam put the blanket on his head."

> What was Sam's problem?

▶ Record children's responses on the chart.

Have a Try

Invite the children to talk with a partner about a problem they have had.

▶ Ask children to turn and talk about a time when they had the same problem as any of these characters.

▶ After a few minutes, ask children to share.

   Who has ever had the same problem as Elizabeti?

▶ Write each name on a sticky note and have the children place their own note next to Elizabeti on the chart. Repeat for the other characters on the chart.

Summarize and Apply

Summarize the learning and remind children to think about the minilesson principle as they read.

   Look at the chart we made. What did you learn about the problem in a story?

   When you think about your problem, it helps you understand the character's problem better.

▶ Write the principle at the top of the chart.

   If you read a story today, think about if you ever had the same problem as the character in your story.

Share

Following independent work time, gather children together in the meeting area to talk about their reading.

   Give a thumbs-up if you read a story today that made you think about a problem you had.

▶ Invite a few children to share an example with the group.

Extend the Lesson (Optional)

After assessing children's understanding, you might decide to extend the learning.

▶ Have children act out a problem they had to solve that was like a problem in a story. Encourage them to show emotion as they share their stories and to express how they felt.

▶ **Drawing/Writing About Reading** Use interactive writing to create a class list of objects children have lost, like Elizabeti in *Elizabeti's Doll*, or write about a class problem that relates to a story.

Section 2: Literary Analysis

Reading Minilesson Principle
Stories usually end when the problem is solved.

You Will Need

- two or three books with simple plots (a clear problem and solution) such as the following:
  - *Have You Seen My Cat?* by Eric Carle, from Text Set: Eric Carle
  - *Big Al and Shrimpy* by Andrew Clements, from Text Set: Friendship
  - *Elizabeti's Doll* by Stephanie Stuve-Bodeen, from Text Set: Family
- chart paper and markers

Academic Language / Important Vocabulary

- character
- problem
- ending

Continuum Connection

- Follow the events in simple narratives (p. 28)
- Notice and understand a simple plot with a problem and solution (p. 28)

Goal

Understand that the story usually ends soon after the character solves the problem.

Rationale

This lesson provides a foundation for understanding the structure of stories. When children notice that stories usually end when the problem is resolved, it supports their ability to predict and comprehend stories with simple plots.

Assess Learning

Observe children when they talk about how stories end. Notice if there is evidence of new learning based on the goal of this minilesson.

- ▶ Do children understand that stories usually end after the problem is solved?
- ▶ Do they use the academic language *character*, *problem*, and *ending*?

Minilesson

To help children think about the principle, choose familiar texts with examples of problems and solutions to provide an inquiry-based lesson. Here is an example.

- ▶ Review the pages of *Have You Seen My Cat?* as you talk.

  Think about *Have You Seen My Cat?* by Eric Carle. The boy's cat was missing, and he solved the problem by looking and looking until he found his cat. What happened after the boy solved his problem?

- ▶ Under the headings "The character has a problem" and "The character solves the problem," make quick sketches on chart paper to represent the problem and the solution. Prompt children to notice that the story ends soon after the problem is solved and that most of the story was about how the boy solved his problem.

  Think about *Big Al and Shrimpy*.

- ▶ Read the end of the book, beginning with "There was a big party that night."

  Why was everyone having a party?

  Shrimpy had solved the problem. What happened in the story after the party?

- ▶ Record responses on the chart.

Have a Try

Invite the children to talk with a partner about what happened after Elizabeti's problem was solved.

> Think about the problem in *Elizabeti's Doll* and how it was solved. Elizabeti lost her rock baby, and then she found it. Her problem was solved. Turn and talk to your partner about what happened after the problem was solved.

▶ After children turn and talk about what happened, invite them to share their thinking. Record responses.

Summarize and Apply

Summarize the learning and remind children to think about the minilesson principle as they read.

▶ Review the chart.

> What did you learn about stories today? Turn and talk to your partner about what you learned.

▶ After they have had a chance to talk, invite a few people to share with the whole group.

> You learned that stories usually end when the problem is solved.

▶ Write the principle on the top of the chart.

> If you read a story today, notice if your story ends when the problem is solved. Bring your book when we meet after independent work time.

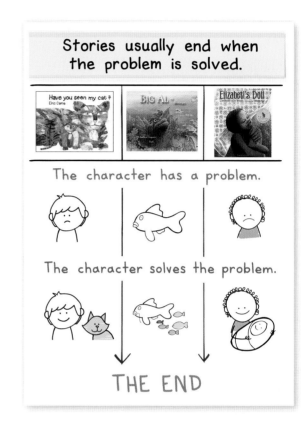

Stories usually end when the problem is solved.

The character has a problem.

The character solves the problem.

THE END

Share

Following independent work time, gather children together in the meeting area to talk about how stories end.

> Give a thumbs-up if you read a story that had a problem today. Now give a thumbs-up if your story ended soon after the problem was solved.

Extend the Lesson (Optional)

After assessing children's understanding, you might decide to extend the learning.

▶ Reinforce understandings about story structure during interactive read-aloud and shared reading.

▶ **Drawing/Writing About Reading** Use interactive writing to make a large story map for a familiar book. Include the problem at the beginning of the map and the solution at the end.

Section 2: Literary Analysis

Reading Minilesson Principle
Think about how the story will end.

Understanding How Stories Work

You Will Need

- two or three unfamiliar fiction books that lend themselves to making authentic predictions, such as the following from Text Set: Differences:
  - *Leo the Late Bloomer* by Robert Kraus
  - *Big Al* by Andrew Clements
- chart paper and markers

Academic Language / Important Vocabulary

- character
- problem
- solution

Continuum Connection

- Predict story outcomes (p. 28)

Goal

Predict story outcomes.

Rationale

To make a logical prediction for the outcome of a story, children must synthesize what they know already with new story information. When children develop their prediction skills, and use evidence from the text to support their thinking, they are encouraged to engage with and think critically about the text.

Assess Learning

Observe children when they make predictions about story outcomes. Notice if there is evidence of new learning based on the goal of this minilesson.

- Do children think about and predict how a story might end?
- Are children able to use text evidence and/or background knowledge to make logical predictions?

Minilesson

To help children think about the minilesson principle, choose unfamiliar texts and examples to provide an inquiry-based lesson about predicting story outcomes. Here is an example.

- Show the cover of an unfamiliar fiction book that lends itself to making authentic predictions about the story's outcome, such as *Leo the Late Bloomer*.

  This is a new story called *Leo the Late Bloomer*. A *late bloomer* is someone who learns things a little later than others, like Leo the tiger.

- Read pages 1–2 and show the illustrations on pages 2–3.

  What are all of the other animals doing that Leo is not doing?

  What is Leo's problem?

- On chart paper, use children's suggestions to write Leo's problem. Then, read through page 9.

  Why does Leo look so sad?

  Based on what you know so far, what do you think will happen to Leo by the end of the story?

- As children offer suggestions, write the things that could happen to Leo. Encourage children to support their ideas with what they know about the story or with personal experiences.

  Let's find out what actually happens to Leo.

- Read to the end of the book.

  How did the story end, or what was the solution for Leo?

- Write the solution on chart paper. Reinforce that it does not matter if predictions were right or wrong.

Have a Try

Invite the children to talk with a partner to make a prediction.

▶ Show the cover of another new book that lends itself to authentic predictions, such as *Big Al*.

> Here is another new book called *Big Al*. As you listen to the story, think about how it might end.

▶ Read pages 1–6.

> Turn and talk about Al's problem and how you think the story might end.

▶ After time for discussion, ask volunteers to share. Encourage children to support predictions with text evidence or background knowledge. Read the rest of the story and have children turn and talk about how it ends.

Summarize and Apply

Summarize the learning and remind children to think about how a story might end as they read or listen to a new book.

> Today you learned to think about how a story might end while you are reading or listening.

> If you read a story today, think about how the story might end. Bring the book when we come back together to meet so you can share.

Share

Following independent work time, gather children together in the meeting area to talk about predictions they made when reading a new book.

> If you read a book for the first time today, did you think about how the story might end? Tell us about it.

Extend the Lesson (Optional)

After assessing children's understanding, you might decide to extend the learning.

▶ During interactive read-aloud and shared reading, ask children to predict story outcomes.

Think about how the story will end.

Problem
Leo could not do the things that his friends could do.

What Could Happen
Leo's parents could help him do things.
Leo's friends could teach him.
He could learn to write, draw, eat, and talk like his friends.

Solution
Leo learned to read.
He learned to write.
He learned to draw.
He learned to eat neatly.
He learned to talk when he was ready.

Leo the Late Bloomer

Section 2: Literary Analysis

RML5
LA.U13.RML5

Talk about the problem and how it is solved when you tell about a story.

Understanding How Stories Work

You Will Need

- two or three books with simple plots (a clear problem and solution), such as the following:
  - *Have You Seen My Cat?* by Eric Carle, from Text Set: Eric Carle
  - *Big Al and Shrimpy* by Andrew Clements, from Text Set: Friendship
  - *Elizabeti's Doll* by Stephanie Stuve-Bodeen, from Text Set: Family
- chart paper and markers (or refer to the chart from RML3)
- the principle written on a sentence strip.

Academic Language / Important Vocabulary

- character
- problem
- solution
- ending

Continuum Connection

- Include the problem and its resolution in telling what happened in a text (p. 28)

Goal

Include the problem and the solution when telling what happened in a story.

Rationale

When children articulate the story problem and describe the solution, they focus on the important ideas of the story and demonstrate understanding of the story. Before teaching this minilesson, be sure that children have a good understanding of problem and solution.

Assess Learning

Observe children when they talk about stories. Notice if there is evidence of new learning based on the goal of this minilesson.

- ▶ Do children describe the problem and solution when they tell about or act out a story?
- ▶ Do they use the academic language *character, problem, solution,* and *ending*?

Minilesson

To help children think about the minilesson principle, choose familiar texts and examples of problems and solutions to provide an inquiry-based lesson. Here is an example.

- ▶ If you taught RML3, review the chart you made with the class. If not, create a similar chart by asking children to describe the problem and solution in *Have You Seen My Cat?* and *Big Al and Shrimpy*.

  Who can tell about the story, *Have You Seen My Cat?* You can use the chart to help you remember the story.

- ▶ After a child tells about the story, comment on what you noticed.

  I noticed that _____ told the problem and solution when telling about *Have You Seen My Cat?* That helped me understand what the story was mostly about.

- ▶ Repeat the process with *Big Al and Shrimpy*.

  Who would like to tell what happened in this story? Why is it important to tell how Shrimpy saved Big Al?

Have a Try

Invite the children to tell about the story *Elizabeti's Doll*.

▷ Hold up the book *Elizabeti's Doll*.

Remember how Elizabeti lost Eva? That was Elizabeti's problem. Think about how her problem got solved. Who would like to tell what this story is about? Be sure to include the problem and how the character solved it.

▷ If you have a chart from RML3, a child can use it to tell the story.

Summarize and Apply

Summarize the learning and remind the children to think about the minilesson principle as they read.

What did you learn today about how to tell about a story?

You learned that it's important to tell the problem and how it is solved because that's what the story is mostly about.

If you read a story today, think about how to tell the important parts of the story. Bring your book when we meet.

Share

Following independent work time, have children sit with a partner to tell about the story they read.

Turn and talk to your partner about the story you read. Be sure to tell about the problem and how the character solved it.

Extend the Lesson (Optional)

After assessing children's understanding, you might decide to extend the learning.

▷ Provide the opportunity for children to retell or act out the plot of familiar books using simple paper puppets.

▷ When you hold a conference with a child, ask him or her to tell about a story. Make sure the child includes the problem and the solution.

Talk about the problem and how it is solved when you tell about a story.

The character has a problem.

The character solves the problem.

THE END

Assessment

After you have taught the minilessons in this umbrella, observe children as they talk and write about their reading across instructional contexts: interactive read-aloud, independent reading and literacy work, guided reading, shared reading, and book club. Use *The Literacy Continuum* (Fountas and Pinnell 2017) to observe children's reading and writing behaviors across instructional contexts.

▶ What evidence do you have of new understandings related to elements of plot?

- Can children identify the problems in stories and discuss how characters solve them?

- Are children able to relate to some of the problems in stories?

- Do they include the problem and solution when they talk about books?

- Are children able to predict story outcomes?

- Are they using academic language such as *character, problem,* and *ending*?

▶ In what other ways, beyond the scope of this umbrella, are they talking about stories?

- Do you see evidence of children checking that they understand the plot of the story? Do they ask questions if meaning is lost?

- Do they talk about the characters in a story?

Use your observations to determine the next umbrella you will teach. You may also consult Minilessons Across the Year (p. 51) for guidance.

Link to Writing

After teaching the minilessons in this umbrella, help children link the new learning to their own writing.

▶ Provide opportunities for children to tell their own stories about problems they have had. Help them to articulate the problem and how they solved it.

▶ Use shared writing to write about a class problem and how it was solved. Invite children to illustrate the written piece to show the problem and solution.

Minilessons in This Umbrella

RML1   Stories have important characters.

RML2   Sometimes the animals act like people in stories.

RML3   The words and pictures help you understand how a character feels.

RML4   Sometimes you feel like a character in a book.

Before Teaching Umbrella 14 Minilessons

Read and discuss books that have simple plots with one or two important characters whose feelings can be easily inferred from the pictures and words. Use the following books from the *Fountas & Pinnell Classroom™ Interactive Read-Aloud Collection* text sets, or choose other books that have one or two important characters.

Learning and Playing Together: School

Look Out Kindergarten, Here I Come! by Nancy Carlson

The Importance of Friendship

A Visitor for Bear by Bonny Becker

I Love You All Day Long by Francesca Rusackas

Yo! Yes? by Chris Raschka

Big Al and Shrimpy by Andrew Clements

As you read aloud and enjoy these texts together, help children

- notice and name important characters,
- notice when animals act like people,
- think about how the characters feel throughout the story, and
- think about a time they felt the way the characters feel.

School

Friendship

Section 2: Literary Analysis

Reading Minilesson Principle
Stories have important characters.

Understanding Characters in Stories

You Will Need

- three or four books that have strong main characters, such as the following:
  - *A Visitor for Bear* by Bonny Becker, from Text Set: Friendship
  - *Big Al and Shrimpy* by Andrew Clements, from Text Set: Friendship
  - *I Love You All Day Long* by Francesca Rusackas, from Text Set: School
- chart paper and markers

Academic Language / Important Vocabulary

- important character
- story

Continuum Connection

- Notice and remember characters in simple narratives (p. 29)

Goal

Identify the important characters in simple fictional narratives.

Rationale

Characters are an essential element of fiction texts. Children need to be able to identify and think about the important characters in a story so that they can appreciate the meaning of the text and are able to discuss it with others. The important characters children identify and think about are the animals or people the story is mostly about.

Assess Learning

Observe children when they talk about the characters in stories they have heard or read. Notice if there is evidence of new learning based on the goal of this minilesson.

- ▶ Are children able to identify the important characters in books?
- ▶ Are they able to distinguish the most important characters from less important characters?
- ▶ Do the children use the terms *story* and *important character*?

Minilesson

To help children think about the minilesson principle, choose familiar texts and examples to use in an inquiry-based lesson. Here is an example.

- ▶ Show the front cover of *A Visitor for Bear*.

  A character in a story can be an animal or a person. In *A Visitor for Bear*, which characters is the story mostly about?

- ▶ Write the characters' names on chart paper, along with a quick sketch of Bear and Mouse.

  Bear and Mouse are the most important characters. Why are these characters important?

- ▶ Read the first two pages of *I Love You All Day Long*.

  Who are the most important characters in this story?

  How can you tell Owen and his mommy are the most important characters in this story?

- ▶ Again, write the characters' names, along with a quick sketch of Owen and his mommy. Show pages 10 and 11.

  Notice there are other characters in the story, but the story is mostly about Owen and his mommy.

Have a Try

Invite the children to talk about the important characters in *Big Al and Shrimpy*.

- Show the front cover and the first few pages of *Big Al and Shrimpy*.

    Turn and talk to your partner about who the most important characters are in this book.

- After children have shared their thinking with their partner, ask a few children to share.

    How did you know Big Al and Shrimpy were the important characters in the story?

- Record the characters' names and draw sketches on the chart.

Summarize and Apply

Summarize the learning and remind the children to think about the important characters in a story while they read.

- Review the chart with the children.

    What does the chart show?

    Today you learned that stories have important characters.

- Write the principle on the chart.

    If you read a story today, think about which characters the story is mostly about. Be ready to share who the characters are. Remember that sometimes only one character is important.

Share

Following independent work time, gather children together in the meeting area to talk about the characters in their reading.

Who were the important characters from the story you read today?

Why did you think that these were the important characters?

Extend the Lesson (Optional)

After assessing children's understanding, you might decide to extend the learning.

- Encourage dramatic play involving important characters from books you have read to the class.

- During interactive read-aloud and shared reading, discuss how some characters are animals and some books have the names of the important characters in the titles.

- **Drawing/Writing About Reading** Have children draw and label the important characters from familiar books.

RML2
LA.U14.RML2

Reading Minilesson Principle
Sometimes the animals act like people in stories.

Understanding Characters in Stories

You Will Need

- three or four familiar books that have animal characters, such as the following:
  - *Look Out Kindergarten, Here I Come!* by Nancy Carlson, from Text Set: School
  - *I Love You All Day Long* by Francesca Rusackas, from Text Set: School
  - *A Visitor for Bear* by Bonny Becker, from Text Set: Friendship
- chart paper and markers

Academic Language / Important Vocabulary

- important character

Continuum Connection

- Understand that animals in stories sometimes act like people (p. 28)
- Recall important details about characters after a story is read (p. 28)

Goal

Understand that animal characters in stories can sometimes act like people.

Rationale

Children begin to explore the genre of animal fantasy as they consider how animals sometimes act like people in stories. Noticing similarities of the actions of animal characters and human characters helps children begin to make authentic personal connections to the characters in animal fantasies.

Assess Learning

Observe children when they talk about characters in stories they have heard or read. Notice if there is evidence of new learning based on the goal of this minilesson.

- ▶ Are children able to find examples of animals that act like people?
- ▶ Can children explain the similarity of how the animal acts and how people act?
- ▶ Do children use the term *important character*?

Minilesson

To help children think about the minilesson principle, choose familiar texts and examples to use in an inquiry-based lesson about animal characters. Here is an example.

- ▶ Show and read page 3 from *Look Out Kindergarten, Here I Come!*

  Look at what the mouse does to get ready for school. What do you notice about what the mouse does?

  How does he act like a person?

- ▶ Write and draw children's responses on chart paper.

- ▶ Show and read pages 2–3 from *I Love You All Day Long*.

  How does Owen feel and act like a person in this part of the story?

  Can a pig really talk and go to school? In this story, Owen acts just like people do.

- ▶ Write and draw children's responses on the chart.

Have a Try

Invite the children to talk to a partner about animal characters that act like people in *A Visitor for Bear*.

▶ Read page 2 of *A Visitor for Bear*.

Turn and talk to a partner about how Bear and Mouse act like people.

▶ Ask several children to share their thinking and write and draw their responses on the chart.

Summarize and Apply

Summarize the learning and remind children to think about how animals in stories can act like people.

What does the chart tell you about the animal characters in stories? Today you learned that sometimes the animal characters in stories act like people.

▶ Write the principle at the top of the chart.

If you read a story today, notice if the important character is an animal. Think about how the animal character acts like a person.

Share

Following independent work time, gather children together in groups of three in the meeting area to talk about animal characters.

Talk about a part of your book where an animal character acts like a person.

Extend the Lesson (Optional)

After assessing children's understanding, you might decide to extend the learning.

▶ Help children think about how stories would be different if the characters were people or other animals.

▶ Encourage discussions about why the author chose to make the characters animals instead of people.

▶ **Drawing/Writing About Reading** Use interactive writing to draw an animal character from a familiar book and write a sentence telling how the animal behaves like a person.

Sometimes the animals act like people in stories.

Book	Animal Characters	How Animal Character Acts Like a Person
Look Out Kindergarten, Here I Come!	Henry	He gets ready for kindergarten. He wears clothes and sneakers. He brushes his teeth. He washes behind his ears.
I Love You All Day Long	Owen	He feels nervous. He talks. He plays with a toy. He eats breakfast on a plate.
A Visitor for Bear	Bear and Mouse	They laugh and talk. They drink tea. They become friends.

RML3
LA.U14.RML3

Reading Minilesson Principle
The words and pictures help you understand how a character feels.

Understanding Characters in Stories

You Will Need

- three or four familiar texts with memorable characters, such as the following:
  - *Big Al and Shrimpy* by Andew Clements, from Text Set: Friendship
  - *A Visitor for Bear* by Bonny Becker, from Text Set: Friendship
  - *Yo! Yes?* by Chris Raschka, from Text Set: Friendship
- chart paper and markers
- sticky notes

Academic Language / Important Vocabulary

- characters
- illustrations
- illustrator
- writer

Continuum Connection

- Infer characters' intentions, feelings, and motivations using text and pictures (p. 29)

Goal

Infer or identify a character's feelings by using the words and pictures.

Rationale

Children naturally empathize and connect with the characters in stories. When you help them to think about how the character is feeling and how they know, children will begin to understand how pictures and words can work together to communicate ideas. Understanding the character's feelings also will help children to understand the story's plot.

Assess Learning

Observe children when they talk about characters in stories they have heard or read. Notice if there is evidence of new learning based on the goal of this minilesson.

- Are the children able to identify the words and pictures that help them understand how the characters feel?
- Are children beginning to make inferences of characters' feelings from the words and pictures?
- Do the children use vocabulary such as *characters, illustrations, illustrator,* and *writer*?

Minilesson

To help children think about the minilesson principle, choose familiar texts and examples to use in an inquiry-based lesson about characters' feelings. Here is an example.

- Read and show the page in *Big Al and Shrimpy* where Shrimpy falls into the Big Deep ("Oh no! Hellllp!").

  Tell how you think Shrimpy feels on this page.

  What makes you think that?

- Write and draw children's responses on the chart paper.
- Read and show the pages in *A Visitor for Bear* where Bear roars, "Be gone!"

  Bear roared, "Be gone!" to the mouse. How do you think Bear is feeling?

  How do the pictures help you understand how Bear feels?

- Write and draw children's responses on the chart.

Have a Try

Invite the children to talk about the characters' feelings with a partner.

▶ Show and read pages 13–14 from *Yo! Yes?*

Turn to your partner and talk about how the characters feel.

How does the author/illustrator help you understand how the characters feel?

▶ Record their noticings on the chart.

Summarize and Apply

Summarize the learning and remind children to think about how words and pictures can help them understand how a character feels.

Look at the chart. How did you know how those characters were feeling?

Today you learned that the words and pictures in a story help you understand how a character feels.

▶ Write the principle at the top of the chart.

If you read a story today, notice how the words and pictures help you understand how a character feels. Mark a spot in the story with a sticky note to share with the class when we gather in the meeting area after independent work time.

Share

Following independent work time, gather children together in pairs in the meeting area to talk about the characters in their reading.

Turn and talk to your partner about how a character feels in your book. Show your partner the words or pictures that helped you understand the character's feelings.

Extend the Lesson (Optional)

After assessing children's understanding, you might decide to extend the learning over several days.

▶ During interactive read-aloud and shared reading, ask children to talk about how characters are feeling.

▶ **Drawing/Writing About Reading** Encourage children to draw and/or write in a reader's notebook to show a character's feelings from a book they have read.

The words and pictures help you understand how a character feels.

Book	Character	How Character Feels
Big Al	Shrimpy	Scared
A Visitor for Bear	Bear	Mad
Yo! Yes?	Boy in the green shirt	Lonely Sad

Section 2: Literary Analysis

RML4
LA.U14.RML4

Reading Minilesson Principle
Sometimes you feel like a character in a book.

Understanding Characters in Stories

You Will Need

- three or four books that show characters' feelings, such as the following:
  - *Yo! Yes?* by Chris Raschka, from Text Set: Friendship
  - *Look Out Kindergarten, Here I Come!* by Nancy Carlson, from Text Set: School
  - *Big Al and Shrimpy* by Andrew Clements, from Text Set: Friendship
- chart paper and markers
- sticky notes

Academic Language / Important Vocabulary

- character

Continuum Connection

- Learn from vicarious experiences with characters in stories (p. 29)

Goal

Relate texts to their own lives and use their own experiences to understand a character's feelings.

Rationale

When you help children relate their own experiences to those of characters in books, children will develop a deeper understanding of the characters' feelings. In doing this, you will help them to develop empathy for others. This empathy will contribute to a stronger comprehension of the text.

Assess Learning

Observe children when they talk about characters in stories they have read. Notice if there is evidence of new learning based on the goal of this minilesson.

- Can children identify how a character is feeling?
- Are children able to tell about something that made them feel the way a character felt in a story? Or about a time they felt that way?
- Do children use the term *character*?

Minilesson

To help children think about the minilesson principle, choose familiar texts and examples to use in an inquiry-based lesson. Here is an example.

- Show pages 13–14 of *Yo! Yes?* ("Why? No fun.")

  How does the boy in the green shirt feel?

  Turn and talk to a partner about a time when you felt like that.

- Record children's responses on the chart paper.

- Show page 5 of *Look Out Kindergarten, Here I Come!*

  How does Henry feel about going to school?

  Turn and talk to a partner about something you are excited about in school.

- Record children's responses on the chart paper.

- Ask several volunteers to tell when they felt the same way as the characters just discussed. Write each volunteer's name on a sticky note and place each note on the chart next to the corresponding feeling.

Have a Try

Invite the children to talk about Big Al's feelings with a partner.

▶ Show pages 21–22 of *Big Al and Shrimpy* ("Halfway down in the Big Deep").

How does Big Al feel?

Have you ever felt scared like Big Al? What did you think about?

Turn and talk to a partner about a time you felt scared and needed help like Big Al.

▶ Record children's responses on the chart.

Summarize and Apply

Summarize the learning and remind children to think about how they can feel like a character in a book.

Today you learned you can notice how characters feel and you can think about how you might have felt the same way once.

▶ Write the principle at the top of the chart.

If you read a story today, notice how the characters feel. If you find a place that makes you think about a time you felt like the character, mark it with a sticky note to share with the class.

Share

Following independent work time, gather children together in groups of three in the meeting area to talk about the characters in their reading.

Turn and talk to the others in your group about how a character in your book feels.

Talk about how you might have felt the same.

Extend the Lesson (Optional)

After assessing children's understanding, you might decide to extend the learning.

▶ Continue to add titles, characters, and feelings to the chart so children see the range of emotions that characters experience.

▶ Provide opportunities during interactive read-aloud for children to turn and talk about times they experienced the same feelings as the characters in the story.

▶ **Drawing/Writing About Reading** Encourage children to write or draw in a reader's notebook about a time they felt like a character in a story.

Assessment

After you have taught the minilessons in this umbrella, observe children as they talk and write about their reading across instructional contexts: interactive read-aloud, independent reading and literacy work, guided reading, shared reading, and book club. Use *The Literacy Continuum* (Fountas and Pinnell 2017) to observe children's reading and writing behaviors across instructional contexts.

▶ What evidence do you have of new understandings related to characters?

- Can children identify the most important characters in a story?
- Can children identify when animal characters are acting like people?
- Are children using the pictures and words in a story to understand the way the characters feel?
- Are children making connections between their own feelings and the feelings of characters in a story?
- Do they know and use academic words, such as *character, illustration, illustrator,* and *writer* when they talk about stories?

▶ In what other ways, beyond the scope of this umbrella, are the children talking about characters?

- Have they begun to express opinions about characters?
- Do they talk about characters' motivations?
- Can they identify character traits?
- Do they notice problems that characters face?

Use your observations to determine the next umbrella you will teach. You may also consult Minilessons Across the Year (p. 51) for guidance.

Link to Writing

After teaching the minilessons in this umbrella, help children link the new learning to their own writing or drawing:

▶ Help children talk about the characters in their stories and how the characters feel. Have them draw facial expressions that show emotion and label their pictures with feeling words (e.g., *happy, sad, mad*).

Reader's Notebook

When this umbrella is complete, provide copies of the minilesson principles (see resources.fountasandpinnell.com) for children to glue into a reader's notebook (in the Minilessons section if using *Reader's Notebook: Primary* [Fountas and Pinnell 2014]), where they can reference the information as needed.

Minilessons in This Umbrella

RML1   Characters in a story can be different or alike.

RML2   Notice what the characters say and what they do.

RML3   Think about why a character says or does something.

RML4   Think about whether you would like to be friends with a character.

RML5   Think about whether you would act like the character.

Before Teaching Umbrella 15 Minilessons

Read and discuss books that have well-defined characters with strong character traits. Use the following books from the *Fountas & Pinnell Classroom™ Interactive Read-Aloud Collection* text sets or choose books that have characters with strong character traits from your own library.

Exploring Animal Tales

The Little Red Hen by Paul Galdone

The Three Bears by Paul Galdone

The Importance of Friendship

A Visitor for Bear by Bonny Becker

I'm the Best by Lucy Cousins

Yo! Yes? by Chris Raschka

The Importance of Kindness

Jamaica's Find by Juanita Havill

The Teddy Bear by David McPhail

As you read aloud and enjoy these books together, help children

- discuss character traits,
- consider whether they like a character,
- talk about how a character's choices make them feel,
- think about why characters behave the way they do, and
- consider what they would do in a character's situation.

Animal Tales

Friendship

Kindness

Section 2: Literary Analysis

Reading Minilesson Principle
Characters in a story can be different or alike.

You Will Need

- two or three familiar texts with characters that have clear character traits, such as the following:
  - *A Visitor for Bear* by Bonny Becker, from Text Set: Friendship
  - *The Three Bears* by Paul Galdone from Text Set: Animal Tales
  - *The Little Red Hen* by Paul Galdone, from Text Set: Animal Tales
- chart paper and markers

Academic Language / Important Vocabulary

- character

Continuum Connection

- Recall important details about characters after a story is read (p. 29)
- Infer a character's traits from story events (p. 29)

Goal

Infer character traits.

Rationale

Through comparison, children can articulate different character traits. When children think about character traits, it helps them make predictions about a character's choices and reactions.

Assess Learning

Observe children when they talk about the characters in books they have read or heard. Notice if there is evidence of new learning based on the goal of this minilesson.

- How do the children talk about the characters in books they have read or heard? Is there evidence that they can identify specific character traits?
- Are they able to compare and contrast characters in a book?
- Do they use the word *character* correctly?

Minilesson

To help children think about the minilesson principle, choose familiar texts to engage children in comparing and contrasting the characters. Here is an example.

> Think about the two characters, Bear and the mouse, in *A Visitor for Bear*.

- Read pages 9–10 ("I told you to leave!").

  > Think about the words and the pictures. How are Bear and the mouse different from each other? What makes you think that?

- Record contrasting descriptions for the characters.

  > How are Bear and the mouse alike? What do they both want?

- Record responses.
- Read the first paragraph on page 12 of *The Three Bears*.

  > Now listen to this part about Goldilocks.

- Read the last two lines on page 12.

  > How are Goldilocks and the three bears different from each other?

  > Think about the whole story. How are they alike?

- Record responses on the chart.

Have a Try

Invite the children to talk about the characters from *The Little Red Hen* with a partner.

> Now think about *The Little Red Hen*.

▶ Show pages 2–7.

> Look! The cat, dog, and mouse are sleeping all day.

▶ Show page 8 and read, "So the little red hen had to do all the housework."

> Turn and talk with your partner about how the little red hen is different from the other characters in this story. Is there any way that they are all alike?

▶ Record responses.

Summarize and Apply

Summarize the learning and remind children.

▶ Review the chart with the children.

> What did you learn about characters in a story?

> When you think about how characters are different or alike, it helps you understand the characters better.

> If you read a story today, think about how the characters are different from one another and how they are alike. Bring your book to share in group meeting.

Share

Following independent work time, gather children together in the meeting area to talk about characters in their books.

> Turn and talk to your partner about the characters in your book. How are the characters different from each other and how are they alike?

Extend the Lesson (Optional)

After assessing children's understanding, you might decide to extend the learning.

▶ Continue to discuss characters from other stories during interactive read-aloud.

▶ Create a mural comparing different characters from a familiar story.

▶ **Drawing/Writing About Reading** Encourage children to draw characters from their independent reading and label their characteristics in the same way you did on the class chart.

Different and Alike

A Visitor for Bear

    big
mean
bossy
needs a friend

    small
happy
friendly
needs a friend

The Three Bears

    rude
selfish
likes porridge

    kind
trusting
likes porridge

The Little Red Hen

    fair
helpful
likes cake

lazy
not helpful
likes cake

Section 2: Literary Analysis

RML2
LA.U15.RML2

Reading Minilesson Principle
Notice what the characters say and what they do.

You Will Need

- two to three familiar texts with characters that have clear character traits, such as the following:

  - *I'm the Best*
    by Lucy Cousins,
    from Text Set: Friendship

  - *A Visitor for Bear*
    by Bonny Becker,
    from Text Set: Friendship

  - *The Little Red Hen*
    by Paul Galdone,
    from Text Set: Animal Tales

  - *The Teddy Bear*
    by David McPhail,
    from Text Set: Kindness

- chart paper and markers

Academic Language / Important Vocabulary

- character

Continuum Connection

- Infer a character's traits from story events (p. 29)

Goal

Notice characters and their behavior (e.g., funny, bad, silly, nice, friendly).

Rationale

When you teach children to notice the characters' actions and words, you give them a reason to think about the text in a deeper way and help them develop the ability to think critically.

Assess Learning

Observe children when they talk about the characters in books they have read or heard. Notice if there is evidence of new learning based on the goal of this minilesson.

▶ Can children tell what they learned about a character from noticing what he or she says or does?

▶ Do they use academic language, such as *character?*

Minilesson

To help children think about the minilesson principle, choose familiar texts and examples to provide an inquiry-based lesson. Here is an example.

> Listen to what Dog says in *I'm the Best*.

▶ Read the first four pages of the book.

> What did Dog say? What does that make you think about Dog?

▶ Encourage a variety of responses (e.g., Dog brags a lot; Dog is mean). Write what Dog says and what it means on the chart paper.

▶ Read the ending of *The Little Red Hen*.

> Tell what the little red hen is like. What makes you think that about her? Does anyone think something different?

▶ Invite children to express different opinions (e.g., some children might think she is acting fairly since the other characters didn't do any of the work, but others might think she is being selfish and should share with her friends.)

> You can learn about characters in stories by noticing what they say and what they do.

Have a Try

Invite the children to talk about the boy with a partner.

> Listen to this part of *The Teddy Bear*.

▷ Read page 25.

> Turn and talk to a partner about the boy. What is he like? What did he say or do to make you think that?

▷ Invite children to share their thinking.

Summarize and Apply

Summarize the learning and remind children to think about the characters as they read.

> Today you learned that if you notice what characters say and what they do, you can learn something about the characters. For example, you might think what a character says or does is nice, mean, unfriendly, or kind. Let's make a chart so you will remember what you learned today.

▷ Make a chart to remind children of today's lesson. Record the principle at the top.

> If you read a story today, think about what the character says or does. What does that make you think about that character? Be ready to share when we come back together.

Notice what the characters say and what they do.

	What Character Says or Does	What It Means
I'm the Best	Dog says, "I'm the best!"	Dog brags a lot. Dog is mean.
The Little Red Hen	The little red hen does not share the cake.	She is fair. She is selfish.
The Teddy Bear	The boy gives the bear to the man.	He is very nice.

Share

Following independent work time, gather children together in the meeting area to talk about what they learned about the characters in the books they read.

> Who would like to share something about a character? Tell something you learned about a character by noticing what the character says and does in the story.

Extend the Lesson (Optional)

After assessing children's understanding, you might decide to extend the learning.

▷ Demonstrate for children how to share their thinking about what characters say and do during partner reading.

▷ **Drawing/Writing About Reading** Use shared or interactive writing to write letters to characters about their actions and words. For example, you might write a letter to Dog telling him that he seems like he is being mean to his friends when he says, "I am the best."

Reading Minilesson Principle
Think about why a character says or does something.

Getting to Know the Characters in Stories

You Will Need

▸ two to three familiar texts with characters that have clear character traits, such as the following:

- *I'm the Best* by Lucy Cousins, from Text Set: Friendship

- *The Little Red Hen* by Paul Galdone, from Text Set: Animal Tales

- *Jamaica's Find* by Juanita Havill, from Text Set: Kindness

▸ chart paper and markers

Academic Language / Important Vocabulary

▸ character

Continuum Connection

▸ Infer characters' intentions, feelings, and motivations using text and pictures (p. 29)

Goal

Infer characters' feelings and motivations.

Rationale

When children think about a character's motivation, they develop a deeper understanding of what the character is like. Often, a character's motivation influences the direction of the story's plot.

Assess Learning

Observe children when they talk about the characters in books they have read or heard. Notice if there is evidence of new learning based on the goal of this minilesson.

▸ Are children able to infer character motivation by thinking about what the character says or does?

▸ Do they use academic language, such as *character?*

Minilesson

To help children think about the minilesson principle, choose familiar texts and examples to provide an inquiry-based lesson on characters' intentions. Here is an example.

> Think about this part of *I'm the Best.*

▸ Read page 26, where Dog says he is sorry to the animals.

> Why do think the dog said he was sorry?

▸ Record responses on the chart paper.

> What might have happened if Dog didn't tell his friends he was sorry?

> Listen to what the little red hen says and does at the very end of *The Little Red Hen.*

▸ Read pages 34–36.

> Why do you think the little red hen ate all the cake herself?

▸ Record responses on the chart.

> What does that make you think about the little red hen?

Have a Try

Invite the children to talk about Jamaica with a partner.

> Think about *Jamaica's Find*.

▶ Read this line from page 23: "Mother, I want to take the dog back to the park," Jamaica said.

> Turn and talk to a partner about why you think Jamaica decided to turn the stuffed dog into the lost and found.

▶ Ask two or three children to share what they learned about Jamaica from thinking about why she put the stuffed dog in the lost and found.

Summarize and Apply

Summarize the learning and remind children to think about what the characters do as they read.

> Today you learned to think about why a character says or does something. When you do that, you learn something about the character.

▶ Write the principle on the chart.

> If you read a story today, think about what characters say and do and why you think they are saying or doing that. Be ready to share your thinking.

Share

Following independent work time, gather children together in the meeting area to talk about their reading in groups of three.

> Turn and talk to your group about what the character in the story you read says or does and why you think the character says or does that.

Extend the Lesson (Optional)

After assessing children's understanding, you might decide to extend the learning.

▶ During interactive read-aloud, support children in thinking about why characters say or do certain things.

▶ **Drawing/Writing About Reading** Use interactive or shared writing to continue to add to the chart about character motivation.

Think about why a character says or does something.

I'm the Best	Dog said he was sorry.	He felt sorry. He was mean to his friends.
The Little Red Hen	The little red hen does not share the cake.	Her friends did not help her. She was mad at her friends.
Jamaica's Find	Jamaica took the dog to the park.	The dog was not hers. She felt bad.

RML4
LA.U15.RML4

Reading Minilesson Principle
Think about whether you would like to be friends with a character.

You Will Need

- two or three familiar texts with two or three characters that have clear character traits, such as the following:
  - *The Little Red Hen* by Paul Galdone, from Text Set: Animal Tales
  - *The Three Bears* by Paul Galdone, from Text Set: Animal Tales
  - *Jamaica's Find* by Juanita Havill, from Text Set: Kindness
- chart paper and markers
- sticky notes

Academic Language / Important Vocabulary

- character
- opinion

Continuum Connection

- Express opinions about characters and their behavior: e.g., funny, bad, silly, nice, friendly (p. 29)
- Give reasons (either text-based or from personal experience) to support thinking (p. 28)

Goal

Think deeply about characters.

Rationale

When you teach children to consider whether they would like to be friends with a character, you help them learn how to think about what the characters are like. Deciding whether to be friends with a character is a way that children can learn to express an opinion about a character.

Assess Learning

Your goal is to listen when children talk about characters in the books they have read or heard. Notice if there is evidence of new learning based on the goal of this minilesson.

- ▶ Are the children able to explain why they would or would not want to be friends with a character?
- ▶ Do children provide evidence from the book to support their thinking?
- ▶ Do they know and understand the words *character* and *opinion?*

Minilesson

To help children think about the minilesson principle, choose familiar texts and examples to provide an inquiry-based lesson about story characters. Here is an example.

> Think about the characters in *The Little Red Hen*. Would you like to be friends with the little red hen? Put your thumb up if you would like to be friends, or put your thumb down if you would not like to be friends.

- ▶ Choose several children to share their thinking, asking them what in the book makes them think the way they do. Accept all responses. Some children might want to be friends with the little red hen because she did all the work to make the cake, while others might not want to be friends because she did not share in the end.

> Turn and talk about the dog, the cat, or the mouse in this book. Tell your partner if you would like to be friends with that character or if you would not. Tell your reason.

- ▶ Invite a few children to share their thinking with the whole class.
- ▶ Show *The Three Bears* by Paul Galdone.

> Now think about Goldilocks in *The Three Bears*. Would you like to be her friend? What makes you think that?

Have a Try

Invite the children to talk about Jamaica with a partner.

> In *Jamaica's Find*, Jamaica first takes home the stuffed dog. Later, she returns it to the lost and found. Turn and talk to your partner about if you would like to be friends with Jamaica or not. Tell why you think that.

▶ Construct a chart about *Jamaica's Find* with a place for the children to respond. Give each child a sticky note. Read the question and ask children to come to the chart and place their sticky note next to either *Yes* or *No*. Ask children to share their reasons. Notice if children have similar or different opinions.

Summarize and Apply

Summarize the learning and remind children to think about the characters as they read.

> Today you thought about whether you would like to be friends with the characters in some of the books we have read. You talked about how sometimes you like the way characters act in books and sometimes you don't.

> If you read a story today, think about whether you would like to be friends with one of the characters. Bring the story to share when we come back together.

Share

Following independent work time, gather children together in the meeting area to talk about their reading.

▶ Share in groups of two or three depending on how many children brought examples.

> Turn and talk to a partner (or your group) about whether you would like to be friends with one of the characters in the story you read. Be sure to tell what makes you think that.

Extend the Lesson (Optional)

After assessing children's understanding, you might decide to extend the learning.

▶ During interactive read-aloud, encourage children to think about whether they would like to be friends with the characters in the story. Have children articulate why they like or dislike the way characters act.

▶ **Drawing/Writing About Reading** Have children keep a running list of characters they would like to be friends with in a reader's notebook.

Would you like to be friends with the character?

Book

Character — Jamaica

Yes

No

Reading Minilesson Principle
Think about whether you would act like the character.

Getting to Know the Characters in Stories

You Will Need

- two to three familiar texts with characters that have situations in which children could imagine themselves, such as the following:
  - *Yo! Yes?* by Chris Raschka, from Text Set: Friendship
  - *Jamaica's Find* by Juanita Havill and *The Teddy Bear* by David McPhail, from Text Set: Kindness
- basket of fiction books

Academic Language / Important Vocabulary

- character

Continuum Connection

- Express opinions about characters and their behavior: e.g., funny, bad, silly, nice, friendly [p. 29]
- Learn from vicarious experiences with characters in stories [p. 29]

Goal

Express whether one would behave like a character in a story.

Rationale

When children evaluate whether they would respond to a situation by acting in the same way as the character, they make a personal connection to the character and gain a deeper understanding of a character's feelings and motivations. Comparing their own actions to the character's actions is a way of expressing an opinion about a character.

Assess Learning

Your goal is to listen when children talk about characters in the books they have read or heard. Notice if there is evidence of new learning based on the goal of this minilesson.

- Can children put themselves in the place of a character in a story and decide how they would act?
- Are children able to apply the principle to their independent reading?
- In what ways do you notice that they agree or disagree with characters' behaviors and actions?
- Do they use academic language, such as *character*?

Minilesson

To help children think about the minilesson principle, choose familiar texts and examples to engage children in a discussion about characters in stories. Here is an example.

- Read and show the pages from *Yo! Yes?* by Chris Raschka that let you know that the character with the green sweater has no friends.

  Turn and talk to a partner about would you do if you were this character (point to the character with the red circle on his shirt) and found out the other boy does not have friends.

  Raise your hand if you would do the same thing as this character. Did anyone decide you would do something different? What makes you think that?

- Mark the chart with a check mark to represent each child's response.
- Read page 27 in *The Teddy Bear*.

  Would you have given the teddy bear back to the man? Thumbs up if you would have given the bear to the man. Thumbs down if you would not have given the bear to the man. Turn and talk to a partner about why.

- Again, mark the chart to show children's responses.

Have a Try

Invite the children to talk about Jamaica with a partner.

> Think about *Jamaica's Find*. Jamaica decided to return the stuffed dog to the lost and found. Turn and talk to a partner about what you would do if you found the stuffed dog. Would anyone like to share with the group?

Summarize and Apply

Summarize the learning and remind children to think about the characters as they read.

> You learned that when you read, you can think about whether you would act like the character in a story. It helps you understand the story better when you think about what you would do if you were the character.

▶ Write the principle at the top of the chart.

> Read a fiction book today. Think about whether you would act like a character in your book. Be ready to share when we come back together after independent work time.

Think about whether you would act like the character.

	Character	Same?	Different?
Yo! Yes? — Chris Raschka		卌 ‖ 卌 ‖ 卌 ‖	卌 ‖ Why?
The Teddy Bear — David McPhail		卌 ‖ 卌 ‖ ‖	卌 ‖ 卌 ‖ Why?
Jamaica's Find		卌 ‖ 卌 ‖ 卌 ‖ ‖	卌 ‖ Why?

Share

Following independent work time, gather children together in the meeting area to talk about their reading.

▶ Ask for volunteers to share what they would do if they were the character in the story they read.

▶ If children have trouble coming up with examples, ask them to share one important thing a character in the book did. Invite the class to share if they would do that same thing.

Extend the Lesson (Optional)

After assessing children's understanding, you might decide to extend the learning.

▶ Provide opportunities for children to act out the stories and show what they would do in the same situation.

▶ **Drawing/Writing About Reading** Use interactive or shared writing to write an alternative ending or part to a story.

Assessment

After you have taught the minilessons in this umbrella, observe your children as they talk and write about their reading across instructional contexts: interactive read-aloud, independent reading and literacy work, guided reading, shared reading, and book club. Use *The Literacy Continuum* (Fountas and Pinnell 2017) to observe your children's reading and writing behaviors across instructional contexts.

▶ What evidence do you have that children are thinking about characters in the stories they read?

- Are children using academic language, like the term *character*?
- In what ways are children comparing and contrasting characters?
- Do children talk about why characters say and do certain things?
- Can they use information in the book to explain why they think a certain way about a character?
- Can children explain why would choose to behave the same way as the character or in a different way?
- Do they use the academic word *character* correctly?

▶ In what other ways, beyond the scope of this umbrella, are they talking about characters?

- Are children noticing details in the illustrations that show how a character is feeling
- Do they carry their opinions of characters with them when the characters are in a new story?
- Do they notice when a character has changed by the end of a story?

Use your observations to determine the next umbrella you will teach. You may also consult Minilessons Across the Year (p. 51) for guidance.

Link to Writing

After teaching the minilessons in this umbrella, help children link the new learning to their own writing.

▶ Kindergarten children begin writing about their own lives and things that have happened to them. Encourage them to think about the people in their lives. Invite them to compare and contrast different people they know.

▶ Teach children how to add details to their drawings, including speech bubbles that show what a character is like.

Minilessons in This Umbrella

RML1 Characters change from the beginning to the end of a story.

RML2 A character can learn a lesson in a story.

Before Teaching Umbrella 16 Minilessons

Use the following books from the *Fountas & Pinnell Classroom™ Interactive Read-Aloud Collection* text sets, or choose books from your own classroom or school library in which the characters change in an obvious way or learn a lesson.

Celebrating Differences

Big Al by Andrew Clements

Understanding Feelings

Mouse Was Mad by Linda Urban

Learning to Be Yourself

Harold Finds a Voice by Courtney Dicmas

Ruby the Copycat by Peggy Rathmann

Three Hens and a Peacock by Lester Laminack

As you read aloud and enjoy these texts together, help children

- think about how a character grows or changes by the end of a story,
- notice how a character deals with a problem and learns from the experience, and
- make connections between characters' experiences and their own lives.

Differences

Feelings

Be Yourself

Section 2: Literary Analysis

Reading Minilesson Principle
Characters change from the beginning to the end of a story.

Understanding
Character Change

You Will Need

- two or three familiar books that have characters that change in some way by the end of the story, such as these:
  - *Big Al* by Andrew Clements, from Text Set: Differences
  - *Harold Finds a Voice* by Courtney Dicmas, from Text Set: Be Yourself
  - *Mouse Was Mad* by Linda Urban, from Text Set: Feelings
- chart paper and markers

Academic Language / Important Vocabulary

- character

Continuum Connection

- Notice when a character changes or learns a lesson (p. 29)

Goal

Notice how and why a character changes from the beginning to the end of a story.

Rationale

As children encounter more complex texts, you will need to help them think about character development to fully understand the story. When you teach them to notice how and why characters change, you help them understand the connection between the characters and the events that happen in the story.

Assess Learning

Observe your children when they talk about characters in books they have heard or read. Notice if there is evidence of new learning based on the goal of this minilesson.

- Are children able to talk to a partner about how and why a character changes from the beginning to the end of the story?
- Do they use the term *character*?

Minilesson

To help children think about the minilesson principle, choose familiar texts and examples to use in an inquiry-based lesson on character change. Here is an example.

- First, show the front cover of *Mouse Was Mad*. Then, show the endpapers at the beginning of the book. Finally, show the endpapers at the end of the book.

  What do you notice that's different about Mouse at the beginning of the story and Mouse at the end?

  Why do you think he changed?

- Record children's responses on the chart paper. Add a quick sketch of Mouse.

- Read page 8 of *Harold Finds a Voice*. If necessary, help children understand that the word *tired* can mean "bored, or not interested."

  How did Harold feel at the beginning of the story?

  Why do you think he felt like this?

- Read the last page of the story.

  How did Harold feel at the end of the book?

  What caused his feelings to change?

- Record the children's responses on the chart with a sketch.

Have a Try

Invite the children to talk to a partner about whether Big Al changed.

▶ Read page 5 of *Big Al* and page 24.

Turn and talk to a partner about how Big Al changed from the beginning of the story to the end and what happened to cause him to change.

▶ Record the children's responses on the chart.

Summarize and Apply

Summarize the learning and remind children to think about how a character changed.

▶ Read what you wrote about Mouse on the chart.

What did you learn about Mouse in *Mouse was Mad*?

▶ Repeat for Harold and Big Al. Prompt children to notice that they learned that sometimes characters change from the beginning to the end of a story. Write the principle on the chart.

When reading today, think about the characters. Notice if a character changes and think about why the character changed. If you find an example, bring it with you to our group meeting.

Share

Following independent work time, gather children in the meeting area to talk about a character who changed from the beginning to the end of the story.

Turn and talk to a partner about a character who changed from the beginning to the end of the story you read.

Extend the Lesson (Optional)

After assessing your children's understanding, you might decide to extend the learning.

▶ Repeat the minilesson using other familiar stories as examples.

▶ During interactive read-aloud, help children notice how and why characters change.

▶ Invite children to role-play how characters change across a book. Assign partners a character. Have one child portray the character at the beginning of the book and the other portray the character at the end of the book.

▶ **Drawing/Writing About Reading** Use interactive writing to write about how characters change in the story.

Characters change from the beginning to the end of a story.

 Mouse was mad.

 Mouse is happy.

 Harold was bored.

 Harold is happy.

 Big Al was lonely.

 Big Al is happy.

Section 2: Literary Analysis

RML 2

LA.U16.RML2

Reading Minilesson Principle
A character can learn a lesson in a story.

Understanding Character Change

You Will Need

- two or three familiar books that have characters that learn a lesson, such as the following:
  - *Ruby the Copycat* by Peggy Rathmann, from Text Set: Be Yourself
  - *Three Hens and a Peacock* by Lester Laminack, from Text Set: Be Yourself
  - *Mouse Was Mad* by Linda Urban, from Text Set: Feelings
- chart paper and markers
- sticky notes

Academic Language / Important Vocabulary

- character
- lesson

Continuum Connection

- Notice when a character changes or learns a lesson (p. 29)
- Learn from vicarious experiences with characters in stories (p. 29)
- Understand that the "lesson" in fantasy or traditional literature can be applied to their own lives (p. 28)

Goal

Notice when a character learns a lesson in a story and apply this lesson to one's own life.

Rationale

You will support children's inferential thinking as they identify a lesson learned by a character. Children deepen their understanding of a story when they identify a lesson learned by a character and connect the character's learning to their own lives.

Assess Learning

Observe your children when they talk about characters in books they have heard or read. Notice if there is evidence of new learning based on the goal of this minilesson.

- ▶ Are children able to infer the lessons that characters learned?
- ▶ Can they apply the lessons that characters learned to their own lives?
- ▶ Do they use the terms *character* and *lesson*?

Minilesson

To help children think about the minilesson principle, choose familiar texts and examples to use in an inquiry-based lesson. Here is an example.

- ▶ Show the front cover of *Ruby the Copycat.*

  What was Ruby like at the beginning of this story?

- ▶ Read the part of the story that begins "Miss Hart turned on the tape player and said."

  What lesson did Ruby learn?

- ▶ Write children's responses on chart paper.

  How can this lesson help you in your own life?

- ▶ Ask two or three children to share. Record the children's responses on sticky notes and have those children attach the sticky notes to the chart.

- ▶ Read page 24 of *Three Hens and a Peacock*, when the peacock tried to get into the henhouse. Then read page 30, when one of the hens admits that the peacock's job is harder than it looks.

  What did the peacock and the hens learn in this story?

- ▶ Write responses on the chart.

  How can this lesson help you, too?

- ▶ Record on sticky notes as before.

Have a Try

Invite the children to talk with a partner about the lesson Mouse learned.

▶ Show *Mouse Was Mad*. Read the last sentence on page 24 and then all of page 25.

Turn and talk to a partner about what you think Mouse learned.

How can you use the lesson Mouse learned in your own life?

▶ Record several children's responses on sticky notes and attach to the chart.

Summarize and Apply

Summarize the learning and remind children to think about the lesson a character learned.

What did you learn today about characters in stories?

You learned that characters often learn a lesson in a story. You also learned that sometimes you can learn a lesson from a story.

▶ Write the principle at the top of the chart.

When you read today, notice if a character learns a lesson. If you find a book that has a character who learns a lesson, bring it to group meeting.

Share

Following independent work time, gather children together in groups of three or four in the meeting area to talk about a lesson a character learned.

What lesson did your character learn?

How can you use this lesson in your life?

Extend the Lesson (Optional)

After assessing your children's understanding, you might decide to extend the learning.

▶ Provide or have children make puppets so they can act out stories in which characters learn a lesson.

▶ **Drawing/Writing About Reading** Encourage children to write and/or draw about the lessons the characters learned in the stories they have read in a reader's notebook. If your children have *Reader's Notebook: Primary* (Fountas and Pinnell 2014), suggest that they write in the Books I Read section.

A character can learn a lesson in a story.

Ruby learned to be herself.

Diego: I will be myself.

Andrew: I can sing a song I made up.

The peacock and the hens learned that everyone has a job to do.

Makayla: I will clean my room.

Colton: I will do the dishes.

Noah: I will help my mom.

Mouse learned that being still can calm you down.

Gabe: If I stay still, I'm not mad.

Lilly: Staying still makes me happy.

Assessment

After you have taught the minilessons in this umbrella, observe children as they talk and write about their reading across instructional contexts: interactive read-aloud, independent reading and literacy work, guided reading, shared reading, and book club. Use *The Literacy Continuum* (Fountas and Pinnell 2017) to observe children's reading and writing behaviors across instructional contexts.

> ▶ What evidence do you have of new understandings related to character development?
>
> > • Do children notice when characters change?
> >
> > • Are they able to identify the reason or events that led to the change?
> >
> > • Do they make connections between the characters' experience and their own lives?
> >
> > • Are they able to infer if a character learned a lesson and articulate what the lesson is?
> >
> > • In what ways are they connecting to the lessons learned through books?
> >
> > • Do they use the terms *character* and *lesson* when they talk about character change?
>
> ▶ In what other ways, beyond the scope of this umbrella, are children talking about characters?
>
> > • Do children talk about characters' motivations or intentions?
> >
> > • Have they begun to notice that sometimes other characters influence another character's decisions and actions?

Use your observations to determine the next umbrella you will teach. You may also consult Minilessons Across the Year (p. 51) for guidance.

Link to Writing

After teaching the minilessons in this umbrella, help children link the new learning to their own writing or drawing.

> ▶ In writers' workshop, encourage children to write about a time in their lives when they learned a lesson or changed in some way.

Minilessons in This Umbrella

RML1 Use the pictures to read a story.

RML2 Each time you tell the story from a picture book, add more information.

RML3 The important things that happen in a story are always the same.

Before Teaching Umbrella 17 Minilessons

This umbrella is designed to support early readers in telling stories by using picture cues and familiarity with the stories—an early form of "reading" a book. Before teaching this umbrella, immerse children in stories with simple plots. Use books with words and strong picture support and wordless picture books. Use the following books from the *Fountas & Pinnell Classroom™ Interactive Read-Aloud Collection* text sets, or use wordless books or books with strong picture support that you have in your classroom.

Exploring Pictures: Wordless Books

> *Float* by Daniel Miyares
>
> *The Girl and the Bicycle* by Mark Pett

Learning and Playing Together: School

> *Look Out Kindergarten, Here I Come!* by Nancy Carlson

Taking Care of Each Other: Family

> *Don't You Feel Well, Sam?* by Amy Hest
>
> *Elizabeti's Doll* by Stephanie Stuve-Bodeen
>
> *Jonathan and His Mommy* by Irene Smalls

As you read and enjoy these texts together, help children

- notice details in the illustrations, such as the facial expressions of the characters or details in the setting,

- notice what the characters are doing in the story and imagine what they might be thinking or saying, and

- discuss the idea that people interpret illustrations differently.

Wordless Books

School

Family

Section 2: Literary Analysis

RML1

LA.U17.RML1

Reading Minilesson Principle
Use the pictures to read a story.

Using Pictures in a Book to Tell the Story

You Will Need

- two or three familiar wordless books and picture books with highly supportive pictures, such as these:

  - *Look Out Kindergarten, Here I Come!* by Nancy Carlson, from Text Set: School

  - *Jonathan and His Mommy* by Irene Smalls, from Text Set: Family

  - *The Girl and the Bicycle* by Mark Pett and *Float* by Daniel Miyares, from Text Set: Wordless Books

- projector (optional)

- chart paper and markers

- basket of familiar picture books, including some wordless books

Academic Language / Important Vocabulary

- author

- illustrator

- illustration

- picture book

- wordless book

Continuum Connection

- Tell the important events of a story using the pictures (after hearing the text read several times) (p. 29)

- Tell stories in response to pictures (p. 29)

Goal

Tell the important events in a story using the pictures.

Rationale

When children use the pictures to tell a story, they begin to internalize narrative structure. When children use illustrations to tell a story, they learn more about the act of reading, use the language of the story, and improve their understanding of the story.

Assess Learning

Observe children when they use pictures to read a story. Notice if there is evidence of new learning based on the goal of this minilesson.

- ▶ Do children take time to look carefully at the pictures?

- ▶ Are they able to tell a story that matches the illustrations?

- ▶ Do they understand the terms *author, illustrator, illustration, picture book,* and *wordless book?*

Minilesson

To help children think about the minilesson principle, choose familiar wordless texts to demonstrate how to tell a story from the pictures. Here is an example.

- ▶ Show *Look Out Kindergarten, Here I Come!* Take time to show the illustration on the first page before speaking. Hold up (or project) the illustration while you speak.

  > Watch and listen to what I do. Henry's mom said, "Wake up Henry!"

- ▶ Show the picture on the next page.

  > Henry jumped out of bed!

- ▶ Display the next two pages.

  > Henry brushed his teeth and washed his ears. He got dressed and tied his shoes. What did I do to tell the story?

  > What information from the pictures did I use to tell the story?

- ▶ Display the first two pages of *Jonathan and His Mommy.*

  > Jonathan and his mom were going for a walk.

- ▶ Display the next two pages.

  > They walked with their arms out and smiled at the kids who were drawing in the street.

▶ Display the next two pages.

> They lifted their knees and took big, giant steps! What did I do to tell this story?

> What information in the pictures did I use?

> Did you notice that I looked carefully at the pictures and thought about what was happening?

Have a Try

Invite the children to talk to a partner about *Float*.

▶ Show the first few pages of *Float*.

> Turn and talk to a partner about what is happening in this part of the story.

> Then your partner will have a turn to tell you.

▶ Invite a few children to share their stories with the whole class.

Summarize and Apply

Summarize the learning and remind children to look carefully at the pictures in a book.

> What did you learn about using the pictures in a book to tell the story?

▶ Work with children to make a chart to remind them how to use the pictures to read a story.

> Today you and a partner will choose a book from this basket of books. Some of the books have words and some don't. If you read a book that has words, use both the pictures and the words to tell the story. Take turns telling parts of the story.

Share

Following independent work time, gather children in the meeting area to talk about how they told their stories.

> What did you do to tell the story?

Extend the Lesson (Optional)

After assessing children's understanding, you might want to extend the learning.

▶ Display an illustration from a wordless picture book. Use shared and/or interactive writing to record what children say is happening in the illustration.

▶ Put together a basket of props, such as miniature toys or stuffed animals, along with a copy of the picture books children have read and encourage them to retell the story using some of the props.

How to Use the Pictures to Tell the Story

Look carefully at the pictures.

Think about what is happening in the picture.

Tell the story!

The first little pig...

Using Pictures in a Book to Tell the Story

You Will Need

- two or three familiar picture books, some wordless, such as the following:
  - *Look Out Kindergarten, Here I Come!* by Nancy Carlson, from Text Set: School
  - *The Girl and the Bicycle* by Mark Pett, from Text Set: Wordless Books
  - *Float* by Daniel Miyares, from Text Set: Wordless Books
- projector (optional)
- chart paper and markers

Academic Language / Important Vocabulary

- details
- illustrations
- characters
- wordless book
- picture book

Continuum Connection

- Tell the important events of a story using the pictures (after hearing the text read several times) (p. 29)
- Tell stories in response to pictures (p. 29)

Goal

Notice details in illustrations to add more information to the story when retelling it.

Rationale

It is important for children to understand that they can continue to add details to their storytelling as they become more familiar with a book. When you teach children to reread and add details to the story, you support their oral language development, enhance use of vocabulary, and deepen understanding of the book.

Assess Learning

Observe children when they tell a story. Notice if there is evidence of new learning based on the goal of this minilesson.

- ▷ Do children add more details to their stories?
- ▷ Do they understand the terms *details, illustrations, characters, wordless book,* and *picture book?*

Minilesson

To help children think about the minilesson principle, choose familiar picture books and wordless picture books to demonstrate how to tell a story from the pictures. Here is an example.

- ▷ Show the first two pages of *Look Out Kindergarten, Here I Come!*

  Listen to my story: Henry's mom lifts up his covers and tells Henry to get up because it is his first day of kindergarten. Henry looks over at his mom and smiles and then gets out of bed.

  Now listen how I tell the story this time: Henry's mom said, "Wake up. It's the first day of kindergarten!" Henry, a mouse wearing pajamas, jumped out of bed and shouted, "Yay, it's time to go to school!" What was different?

- ▷ Guide children to notice the details you added: what the characters said and what Henry looked like. Write responses on chart paper.
- ▷ Show (or project) the second two-page spread of *The Girl and the Bicycle.*

  Listen to my story: The brother and sister are holding hands and walking on the sidewalk. The boy drops his ice cream cone.

  Now listen for the details I add: The brother and sister are walking past a toy store that has a green bike in the window. The girl is so excited that she runs fast and her brother drops his ice cream cone. He is very sad.

  What was different?

▶ Guide children to notice the details you added: more about where the characters are and how they feel. Write responses on chart paper.

Have a Try

Invite the children to talk about *Float* with a partner.

▶ Display the first two pages of *Float*.

> Look at the pictures. Take turns with your partner to tell the story that the pictures show. Then, do it again. Add some details when you tell the story again.

▶ Invite a few children to share their stories and talk about what they added.

Summarize and Apply

Summarize the learning and remind the children to think about adding more information when telling a story.

> Look at the chart. What information can you add when you tell a story?

> Choose two pages from a book that you know. Sit with a partner and tell that part of the story. Look at the chart to remember to add details when you tell the story.

Share

Following independent work time, gather children together in the meeting area to talk about telling stories.

> Who would like to share how they used information from the pictures to add details when they tell a story?

Extend the Lesson (Optional)

After assessing children's understanding, you might decide to extend the learning.

▶ Invite children to record themselves telling the story in a wordless picture book. After the first recording, ask them to revisit the chart from this lesson and retell the story with more details. Record the new version of the story. Have them listen to both stories and compare the two recordings.

▶ When children are writing their own stories, encourage them to add details to their illustrations, the way illustrators do in picture books.

Add More Details

Tell what the characters are saying.

Tell more about what the characters are doing.

Tell what the characters look like.

Tell more about where the characters are.

Tell what the characters are feeling.

Section 2: Literary Analysis

RML3

Reading Minilesson Principle
The important things that happen in a story are always the same.

Using Pictures in a Book to Tell the Story

You Will Need

- two or three familiar picture books, such as the following:
  - *Elizabeti's Doll* by Stephanie Stuve-Bodeen and *Don't You Feel Well, Sam?* by Amy Hest, from Text Set: Family
  - *Look Out, Kindergarten, Here I Come!* by Nancy Carlson, from Text Set: School
- projector (optional)
- chart paper and markers
- basket of familiar picture books, including wordless books

Academic Language / Important Vocabulary

- authors
- illustrators
- characters
- dialogue

Continuum Connection

- Understand that illustrations can have different meanings for different people (p. 29)

Goal

Understand that pictures in a story can be interpreted differently by people but the basic events are always the same.

Rationale

When you teach children that people can have different interpretations of illustrations, you teach them that each person brings his own perspective to a situation. You want to help children understand that each person's interpretation can vary, but the events remain consistent.

Assess Learning

Observe children when they talk about the illustrations in a story. Notice if there is evidence of new learning based on the goal of this minilesson.

- Are children able to understand that different people can think differently about pictures but that the events of the story remain the same?
- Do they use the terms *authors, illustrators, characters,* and *dialogue?*

Minilesson

To help children think about the minilesson principle, choose familiar picture books to provide an inquiry-based lesson. Here is an example.

- Show or project the first two pages of *Elizabeti's Doll.*

  Look carefully at these two pages and think about what this picture shows you.

  What do you think Elizabeti and her mom are doing and thinking on this page?

  Some of you think that Elizabeti is thinking one thing, and some of you think she is thinking something else. The author doesn't tell. But, we all agree that Elizabeti and her mother love the baby.

- Show or project the first two pages of *Don't You Feel Well, Sam?*

  What do you think is happening here?

  We might have different ways to describe this picture, but we all agree that it is a cold night, and the bears are inside their house.

Have a Try

Invite the children to talk with a partner about *Look Out Kindergarten, Here I Come!*

▶ Show the page in *Look Out Kindergarten, Here I Come!* where Henry looks in the classroom and says, "I want to go home!"

> Turn and talk to a partner about what is happening.

> Does someone have a different idea of what is happening?

Summarize and Apply

Summarize the learning and remind children to think about how the important things that happen in a story are always the same.

> Today you learned that important events in a story are always the same, even if people think differently about them. Let's make a chart together to remember this.

> You and a partner are going to read a book from this basket. You will take turns telling the story.

> Notice that sometimes the pictures will mean something different to each of you but the important things that happen are always the same.

The important things that happen in a story are always the same.

The boy sees the dog. He is afraid of dogs.

The boy sees the dog. He wants to pet the dog.

Share

Following independent work time, gather children together in the meeting area to talk about their reading.

> Was there a picture that you and your partner thought differently about?

> Show the picture and tell what you and your partner thought about it.

Extend the Lesson (Optional)

After assessing children's understanding, you might decide to extend the learning.

▶ Encourage children to share their thinking about illustrations during interactive read-aloud. Notice when children interpret the pictures differently.

▶ **Drawing/Writing About Reading** Use interactive writing to create thought bubbles for characters from an illustration in a book. Write different thought bubbles for the same picture to emphasize that different people can interpret the pictures and what people might be thinking in different ways, but that doesn't change what happens in a story.

Assessment

After you have taught the minilessons in this umbrella, observe your children as they talk and write about their reading across instructional contexts: interactive read-aloud, shared reading, guided reading, and independent reading. Use *The Literacy Continuum* (Fountas and Pinnell 2017) to observe your children's reading and writing behaviors across instructional contexts.

▶ What evidence do you have of new understandings related to using the pictures to tell stories?

- Are children able to tell what is happening in the pictures?
- Are they able to explain what the characters are doing in the story?
- Can they tell what the characters in the story might be thinking or saying?
- Is there evidence that they understand that pictures can mean different things to different people?
- Do they understand that the important events and basic message on each page remains consistent?
- Do they use the words *illustration, illustrator, character,* and *detail* correctly?

▶ In what other ways, beyond the scope of this umbrella, are children discussing the pictures to help them enjoy and understand books?

- Do children notice sound and movement in the pictures?
- Do children notice consistency in how the illustrator draws the characters and the backgrounds?

Use your observations to determine the next umbrella you will teach. You may also consult Minilessons Across the Year (p. 51) for guidance.

Link to Writing

After teaching the minilessons in this umbrella, help children link the new learning to their own writing.

▶ When children illustrate their own stories, encourage them to add details to the illustrations (e.g., where the story happens, what the characters are wearing, what the characters are feeling).

▶ Ask partners to read their own stories to each other and ask questions so details can be added to the pictures.

Minilessons in This Umbrella

RML1 The illustrator shows information in the pictures that the author does not tell in the words.

RML2 The illustrator shows sound and movement in pictures to help you understand the story.

RML3 The illustrator puts details in the background to help you understand the story.

RML4 The illustrator draws the characters so they look the same on every page.

RML5 The illustrator draws the background the same way through the book.

Before Teaching Umbrella 18 Minilessons

Read and discuss fiction picture books that have strong illustrative support. Use the following books from *the Fountas & Pinnell Classroom™ Interactive Read-Aloud Collection* text sets or choose other books with detailed illustrations.

Learning and Playing Together: School
Miss Bindergarten Gets Ready for Kindergarten by Joseph Slate

Taking Care of Each Other: Family
Jonathan and His Mommy by Irene Smalls
Do Like Kyla by Angela Johnson

The Place Called Home
Two Homes by Claire Masurel

Having Fun with Language
Creak! Said the Bed by Phyllis Root

Learning to Be Yourself
Harold Finds a Voice by Courtney Dicmas
The Pig in the Pond by Martin Waddell

Grace Lin: Exploring Family and Culture
Dim Sum for Everyone! by Grace Lin
Kite Flying by Grace Lin

Noticing the Way the World Looks: Colors
Dog's Colorful Day by Emma Dodd

As you read aloud and enjoy these texts together, help children

- think and talk about the books with one another,
- notice how the illustrations support an understanding of the story, and
- notice how illustrators draw characters and backgrounds consistently within a book.

School

Family

Home

Fun with Language

Be Yourself

Grace Lin

Colors

Section 2: Literary Analysis

Reading Minilesson Principle

The illustrator shows information in the pictures that the author does not tell in the words.

Looking Closely at Illustrations

You Will Need

- three or four fiction books with detailed illustrations, such as these:
  - *Miss Bindergarten Gets Ready for Kindergarten* by Joseph Slate, from Text Set: School
  - *Two Homes* by Claire Masurel, from Text Set: Home
  - *Harold Finds a Voice* by Courtney Dicmas, from Text Set: Be Yourself
- chart paper and markers

Academic Language / Important Vocabulary

- illustrator
- illustration
- author

Continuum Connection

- Gain new information from both pictures and print (p. 28)
- Understand that an illustrator created the pictures in the book (p. 29)

Goal

Gain new information from the illustrations in fiction texts.

Rationale

When you encourage children to notice details in the illustrations, they develop an understanding of the illustrator's craft and how the words and pictures in fiction books together communicate the meaning.

Assess Learning

Observe children when they talk about illustrations in books they have read. Notice if there is evidence of new learning based on the goal of this minilesson.

- Do children notice details in illustrations that are not described in the text?
- Do children use the academic words *illustration, illustrator,* and *author?*

Minilesson

To help children think about the minilesson principle, choose familiar texts and examples to show how the print and illustrations work together. Here is an example.

- Read pages of *Miss Bindergarten Gets Ready for Kindergarten* on which the pictures add more information to the story, such as pages 3, 7, and 11. Do not show the illustrations.

  I am going to read a few pages of *Miss Bindergarten Gets Ready for Kindergarten.* What does the author tell you?

- Write responses on the chart.

  Now I will read these pages to you again.

- Reread the same pages, pausing to show the illustrations.

  What does the illustrator show you?

- Make a quick sketch on the chart.

  What does the illustrator show you that the author doesn't tell you?

- Repeat the procedure for pages 4–7 and 10–11 of *Two Homes.*

  What does the author tell you about the boy's two homes?

  What does the illustrator show you about the boy's two homes?

Have a Try

Invite the children to talk about the illustrations in *Harold Finds a Voice* with a partner.

▶ Show the cover of *Harold Finds a Voice*. Read from the page that says "Harold was a gifted bird" through the next three pages without showing the pictures.

Turn and talk to your partner about what the author tells you.

▶ Write responses on chart. Reread and show the illustrations.

Turn and talk to your partner about what the illustrator shows you that the author doesn't tell you.

▶ Make a quick sketch on the chart.

Summarize and Apply

Summarize the learning and remind the children to look carefully at the pictures when they read.

Look at the chart. What does it show you?

Today you learned that illustrators show information in the pictures that the author does not tell in the words.

If you read a picture book today, notice how the illustrator adds information to the story. Be ready to share your example when we meet after independent work time.

Share

Following independent work time, gather children together in the meeting area to talk about their reading.

▶ Choose a few children to share with the class.

Who would like to share details from an illustration that shows something that the author does not tell you in the words?

Extend the Lesson (Optional)

After assessing children's understanding, you might decide to extend the learning.

▶ During interactive read-aloud, encourage children to look carefully at the illustrations in a book to find out more information about the story.

▶ **Drawing/Writing About Reading** Remind children to add detail in the illustrations they make to go with their stories.

Illustrators Show More

	Author Says	Illustrator Shows
Miss Bindergarten Gets Ready for Kindergarten	"Ian Lowe says I won't go."	
Two Homes	"Sometimes I'm with Daddy."	
Harold finds a voice	"Harold was a gifted bird."	"Ring! Ring! Ring!"

RML2
LA.U18.RML2

Reading Minilesson Principle
The illustrator shows sound and movement in pictures to help you understand the story.

Looking Closely at Illustrations

You Will Need

- three or four fiction books with illustrations that show sound or motion, such as these:
  - *Dog's Colorful Day* by Emma Dodd, from Text Set: Colors
  - *The Pig in the Pond* by Martin Waddell, from Text Set: Be Yourself
  - *Kite Flying* by Grace Lin, from Text Set: Grace Lin
- chart paper and markers

Academic Language / Important Vocabulary

- illustrator
- illustration
- movement
- sound

Continuum Connection

- Gain new information from both pictures and print (p. 28)
- Understand that an illustrator created the pictures in the book (p. 29)

Goal

Notice how an illustrator creates the illusion of sound and motion in illustrations.

Rationale

When you teach children to notice the ways illustrators use the illusion of sound and motion in a story through illustrations, they can learn about illustrator's craft and apply their understanding to their own stories.

Assess Learning

Observe children when they talk about illustrations in books they have heard or read. Notice if there is evidence of new learning based on the goal of this minilesson.

- Do children notice depictions of motion or sound in illustrations?
- Do they understand the words *illustration, illustrator, sound,* and *movement*?

Minilesson

To help children think about the minilesson principle, choose familiar texts and examples to provide an inquiry-based lesson. Here is an example.

- Show the cover of *Dog's Colorful Day* and read page 2.

  Let's take a look at a few illustrations in this book. What do you notice about Dog?

- If children have difficulty noticing the movement, ask questions such as these: *What do you notice about the tail? The illustrator drew lines next to the dog's tail to show the tail moving.*

- Read page 16 and ask what children notice about the ball.

  How can you tell it is moving?

  Do you think it made a sound?

- Add a sketch to the chart paper.

- Read pages 14–15 of *The Pig in the Pond*.

  What do you notice about the ducks' mouths? Why do you think the ducks' mouths are open? The illustrator made the ducks' mouths open to show that they are saying "Quack, quack, quack, quack!"

- Add a sketch to the chart.

Have a Try

Invite the children to talk about the book *Kite Flying*.

> Let's look again at *Kite Flying*. As I show you the pictures, put your thumb up when you see a picture that shows that the wind is blowing. Tell me how the illustrator shows that the wind is blowing. What looks like it is moving?

▶ Add a sketch to the chart.

Summarize and Apply

Summarize the learning and remind the children to look carefully at the illustrations as they read.

> Look at the chart. What do some illustrators show in their pictures?

> When you read today, look for an example of movement or sound in the pictures. Bring the example to share when we come back together.

Share

Following independent work time, gather children together in the meeting area to talk about their reading.

> Who found an example of an illustrator who shows movement or sound in the pictures?

▶ Choose a few children to share with the class. If no one found an example, share another example of movement and/or sound from a picture book.

Extend the Lesson (Optional)

After assessing children's understanding, you might decide to extend the learning.

▶ Have children look for examples of movement within illustrations from other books.

▶ Perform various movements (for example, jumping jacks, running in place, or clapping hands) and direct children to draw a picture depicting each movement.

▶ **Drawing/Writing About Reading** Have children use movement in a drawing that goes with a story they have written.

Looking Closely at Illustrations

You Will Need

- three or four fiction books with interesting background details in the illustrations, such as these:
  - *Jonathan and His Mommy* by Irene Smalls and *Do Like Kyla* by Angela Johnson, from Text Set: Family
  - *Creak! Said the Bed* by Phyllis Root, from Text Set: Fun with Language
- chart paper and markers

Academic Language / Important Vocabulary

- illustration
- illustrator
- background

Continuum Connection

- Gain new information from both pictures and print (p. 28)
- Understand that an illustrator created the pictures in the book (p. 29)
- Notice that the background details in pictures often reveal characters' feelings or traits (p. 29)

Goal

Notice the details the illustrator puts in the background to communicate meaning.

Rationale

When you teach children to notice the details the illustrator includes in the background, children are able to use the information to understand the story.

Assess Learning

Observe children when they talk about illustrations in books they have read. Notice if there is evidence of new learning based on the goal of this minilesson.

- ▶ Can children notice and talk about details in the background of illustrations?
- ▶ Do they understand the words *background, illustrator,* and *illustration*?

Minilesson

To help children think about the minilesson principle, choose familiar texts and examples to provide an inquiry-based lesson. Here is an example.

- ▶ In *Do Like Kyla*, read and show the two-page spread where the girls are crunching through the snow.

  There are Kyla and her sister. Look carefully at the part of the picture around the girls. What can you tell about where they live by looking at the background?

  The illustrator put details in the background to help you learn more about the story.

- ▶ Write children's responses on the chart paper.
- ▶ Show the two-page spread from *Creak! Said the Bed* that shows the house in the thunderstorm.

  Look at this whole picture. What can you learn about the storm from this picture?

  The people are sleeping inside the house. What does that tell you about them?

  How does the dog feel about thunderstorms?

- ▶ Add children's responses to the chart.

  You learned a lot from looking at the background of the pictures.

Have a Try

Invite the children to talk about *Jonathan and His Mommy* with a partner.

▶ Show a few pages from *Jonathan and His Mommy*. Point out the characters and then focus children's attention on the background.

Turn to your partner and tell what you see in the background. What do you learn from the background details about where the characters are or what they are like?

Summarize and Apply

Summarize the learning and remind the children to look carefully at the background of the pictures when they look at a book.

What did you learn today about the details that illustrators put in the background to help you understand the story?

▶ Review the chart and write the principle at the top.

If you read a story today, look carefully at the backgrounds. Be ready to share what you noticed when we come back together.

Share

Following independent work time, gather children together in the meeting area to talk about their reading.

▶ Invite a few children to share.

Who would like to share what they noticed in the backgrounds of the illustrations in a book they read?

Extend the Lesson (Optional)

After assessing children's understanding, you might decide to extend the learning.

▶ During interactive read-aloud or shared reading, have children look for details that the illustrator drew in the background to help them understand the story.

▶ **Drawing/Writing About Reading** Encourage children to include sounds in the illustrations that accompany their writing.

The illustrator puts details in the background to help you understand the story.

They live where it is cold.

The yards are big.

The thunderstorm is loud.

The people are good sleepers.

The dog is scared.

Reading Minilesson Principle
The illustrator draws the characters so they look the same on every page.

Looking Closely at Illustrations

You Will Need

- three or four illustrated fiction books with human characters, such as these:
  - *Jonathan and His Mommy* by Irene Smalls, from Text Set: Family
  - *Do Like Kyla* by Angela Johnson, from Text Set: Family
  - *Two Homes* by Claire Masurel, from Text Set: Home
- chart paper and markers

Academic Language / Important Vocabulary

- illustration
- illustrator
- character

Continuum Connection

- understand that an illustrator created the pictures in the book (p. 29)

Goal

Notice the consistent way illustrators draw characters so they are recognizable throughout the book.

Rationale

When you teach children to notice that illustrators draw characters consistently throughout the book, they are able to keep track of the various characters while reading and better understand the story. They are also better prepared to draw characters consistently in their own writing pieces.

Assess Learning

Observe children when they talk about illustrations in books they have read. Notice if there is evidence of new learning based on the goal of this minilesson.

- Are children able to describe what a character looks like?
- Can children identify the same character on multiple pages?
- Do children use the words *character, illustration*, and *illustrator*?

Minilesson

To help children think about the minilesson principle, choose familiar texts and examples to provide an inquiry-based lesson. Here is an example.

- Show the cover of *Jonathan and His Mommy*. Point to Jonathan.

  This is Jonathan. What do you notice about him?

- Open to a page that shows Jonathan and at least one other character.

  Where is Jonathan on this page? How do you know that this character is Jonathan?

- Turn to another page and point to a character that is not Jonathan.

  Is this Jonathan? How do you know it's not Jonathan? How does the illustrator make it easy for you to find Jonathan on each page?

- Show *Do Like Kyla*. Open to a page that clearly shows both Kyla and her sister. Ask children what they notice about each character. Then show some other pages on which the two girls are pictured.

  How can you tell which character is Kyla and which character is her sister on each page?

  The illustrator drew each character the same way on each page. Even though the characters do different things on different pages, you can still recognize the character.

- Make sketches on the chart paper to illustrate the principle.

Have a Try

Invite the children to talk about *Two Homes* with a partner.

▶ Show the cover of *Two Homes*.

Turn and talk to your partner about what you notice about Alex.

▶ Turn to the page that shows Alex on a rocking chair at Daddy's house.

Turn and talk to your partner about which character is Alex, and how you know it's Alex, even though he is doing different things on different pages.

▶ Add a sketch to the chart.

Summarize and Apply

Summarize the learning and remind children to notice how a character looks the same in a book.

Today you looked at how the illustrator draws the characters so they look like the same person on every page. This makes it easier for you to know which character is which and understand the story.

▶ Write the principle at the top of the chart.

If you read a fiction book today, choose one character and try to find the character on every page. Be ready to share your example when we come back together.

The illustrator draws the characters so they look the same on every page.

Jonathan   Mommy   Mommy   Jonathan

Kyla's sister   Kyla   Kyla's sister   Kyla

Alex   Alex

Share

Following independent work time, gather children together in the meeting area to talk about their reading.

Who would like to share a story you read? Show us the same character on several pages. How were you able to find the character on each page?

Extend the Lesson (Optional)

After assessing children's understanding, you might decide to extend the learning.

▶ When children write and illustrate their own picture books, remind them of the importance of drawing characters consistently throughout the book.

▶ **Drawing/Writing About Reading** After reading a book during interactive read-aloud, have children choose their favorite character and draw the character in several different situations or settings from the story. Remind them of the importance of drawing characters consistently.

RML5
LA.U18.RML5

Reading Minilesson Principle
The illustrator draws the background the same way through the book.

Looking Closely at Illustrations

You Will Need

- three or four fiction books with consistent background details in the illustrations, such as these:
  - *Creak! Said the Bed* by Phyllis Root, from Text Set: Fun with Language
  - *Kite Flying* and *Dim Sum for Everyone!* by Grace Lin, from Text Set: Grace Lin

Academic Language / Important Vocabulary

- background
- detail
- illustration
- illustrator

Continuum Connection

- Understand that an illustrator created the pictures in the book (p. 29)

Goal

Notice the consistent way the illustrator draws the background of the story.

Rationale

When you teach children to notice that illustrators draw backgrounds consistently throughout the book, they are better able to notice the details in the setting and recognize it throughout the book to better understand the story events. They are also better prepared to draw backgrounds consistently in their own writing pieces.

Assess Learning

Observe children talking about illustrations in books they have read. Notice if there is evidence of new learning based on the goal of this minilesson.

- Can children describe details in the backgrounds of illustrations?
- Do children notice when background details stay the same in the book?
- Do they use the words *detail*, *background*, *illustration*, and *illustrator*?

Minilesson

To help children think about the minilesson principle, choose familiar texts and examples to show how illustrators draw backgrounds consistently. Here is an example.

- Open *Creak! Said the Bed* to pages 1–2.

  What do you see in Momma and Poppa's room? What does their room look like?

- Show several more pages.

  Is this Momma and Poppa's room? How can you tell?

  How does the illustrator make it easy for you to tell that the room on this page is Momma and Poppa's room?

  The illustrator drew the room the same way on every page so you know that the whole story takes place in Momma and Poppa's room.

- Make sketches on the chart to show that illustrators draw the background the same in a book.

- Open to pages 3–4 of *Kite Flying*.

  Let's look at the background in this illustration. What do you notice about the room the characters are in?

- Turn to pages 7–8.

  Are they in the same room or a different room now? How can you tell? What do you notice about the backgrounds on both these sets of pages?

  The illustrator drew the background the same way so you know that the characters are in the same room as before.

Have a Try

Invite the children to talk about *Dim Sum for Everyone!* with a partner.

▶ Open to the dedication page in *Dim Sum for Everyone!* Point to the background (the seating area of the restaurant).

Turn and talk to your partner about what you notice about the background. What kind of place is this?

▶ Turn to page 4 and point out the table in the top right corner.

Turn and talk to your partner about if you think this is the same place or a different place. Tell what makes you think that.

Summarize and Apply

Summarize the learning and remind the children to notice how the backgrounds are the same in a book.

What did you notice about how the illustrator draws the background on every page in the book?

▶ Write the principle at the top of the chart.

If you read a fiction book today, look closely at details in the background of the illustrations. See if you can find the same details on different pages in the book.

The illustrator draws the background the same way through the book.

Share

Following independent work time, gather children together in the meeting area to talk about their reading.

Who found an example of a book with background details that stay the same throughout the book?

▶ Invite a few children to share.

Extend the Lesson (Optional)

After assessing children's understanding, you might decide to extend the learning.

▶ Remind children to draw the background consistently in their illustrations for personal narratives.

▶ **Drawing/Writing About Reading** After reading a fiction book during interactive read-aloud, have children draw a series of events from the book. Remind them of the importance of drawing background details consistently.

Section 2: Literary Analysis

Assessment

After you have taught the minilessons in this umbrella, observe children as they talk and write about their reading across instructional contexts: interactive read-aloud, independent reading and literacy work, guided reading, shared reading, and book club. Use *The Literacy Continuum* (Fountas and Pinnell 2017) to observe children's reading and writing behaviors across instructional contexts.

▶ What evidence do you have of new understandings related to illustrations?

- Do children notice and talk about details in the illustrations that are not described in the text?

- Do children notice the illusion of movement and sound in illustrations?

- Do children notice and describe background details in illustrations?

- Do children recognize that illustrators draw characters and backgrounds consistently throughout a book?

- Do they use the words *background, detail, character, illustration,* and *illustrator* when they talk about illustrations?

▶ In what other ways, beyond the scope of this umbrella, are children talking about illustrations?

- Are children noticing and talking about images in nonfiction books?

- Are they noticing that some books use illustrations only to tell a story (wordless picture books)?

Use your observations to determine the next umbrella you will teach. You may also consult Minilessons Across the Year (p. 51) for guidance.

Link to Writing

After teaching the minilessons in this umbrella, help children link the new learning to their own writing.

▶ Help children incorporate the illustration strategies they have learned into their own writing. Support children in thinking about how they can show more in their illustrations to elaborate on the details provided in the text. Encourage children to think about where they can indicate sound or movement within the illustration.

Section 3 | Strategies and Skills

The strategies and skills minilessons are designed to bring a few important strategic actions to temporary, conscious attention so that students can apply them in their independent reading. By the time students participate in these minilessons, they should have engaged these strategic actions successfully in shared or guided reading as they build in-the-head literacy processing systems. These lessons reinforce the effective reading behaviors.

3 Strategies and Skills

Shared Reading

Minilessons in This Umbrella

RML1   Look at the picture and think what would make sense.

RML2   Read the sentence again and think what would sound right.

RML3   Read the sentence again and get your mouth ready for the first sound.

RML4   Look for a part you know.

RML5   Read the words you know quickly.

Before Teaching Umbrella 1 Minilessons

Read and discuss shared reading texts that offer enlarged print (big books) so the children can participate in the reading. Use the selected texts from the *Fountas & Pinnell Classroom™ Shared Reading Collection* listed below, or choose similar texts from your own library, to support the concepts developed in this umbrella.

Shared Reading Collection

On the Go by Abbey Grace Moore

Mondo by Quentin Ripple

Not Quite Right by Helen Lorraine

Wiggles: Poems to Make You Wiggle Your Fingers and Toes

Pitter Patter by Miriam David

As you read aloud and enjoy these texts together, help children

- discuss what the book is about,
- follow and understand the ideas in the book,
- demonstrate control of early reading behaviors, such as left-to-right directionality, return sweep, and word-by-word matching, and
- recognize high-frequency words.

Section 3: Strategies and Skills

RML1
SAS.U1.RML1

Reading Minilesson Principle
Look at the picture and think what would make sense.

Searching for and Using Meaning, Language, and Visual Information

You Will Need

▸ an enlarged text, such as *On the Go* by Abbey Grace Moore, from *Shared Reading Collection*

▸ sticky notes

▸ chart paper and markers

▸ document camera (optional)

Academic Language / Important Vocabulary

▸ makes sense

▸ illustration

Continuum Connection

▸ With teacher support, use features of print in enlarged texts to search for and use visual information: e.g., letters, words, "first" and "last" word, period (p. 116)

▸ Make connections between the body of the text and illustrations (p. 117)

Goal

Use illustrations (meaning) to solve words while reading a text.

Rationale

When you teach children to search for and use information from the illustrations to help them read a word they do not know, they learn how to problem solve as they construct meaning from print. Children need to know that pictures are just one source of meaning information they can use while reading. Ultimately, they should search for and use meaning, language, and print in an integrated way to achieve fluent reading.

Assess Learning

Observe children when they read. Notice if there is evidence of new learning based on the goal of this minilesson.

▸ When children come to a word they don't know, do they search for and use information to solve an unknown word?

▸ Do they use the terms *makes sense* and *illustration* correctly?

Minilesson

To help children think about the minilesson principle, choose familiar texts and examples to demonstrate how to search for and use meaning to solve words. Alternatively, you could use a text they have not seen before and place a few sticky notes prior to the first reading. Here is an example.

▸ Use *On the Go* by Abbey Grace Moore or another enlarged text. With a sticky note, cover the word *down* in the sentence "Kangaroos hop up and down" on page 10. Read up to the sticky note and pause.

> What could this word be? Why do you think so?

> There is a photograph of kangaroos hopping, and it makes sense that they would hop up and down. How can I check? What letter do you expect to see at the beginning of *down*?

▸ Take off the sticky note and confirm that the word is *down*.

▸ Cover the word *horse* on page 12 and repeat the process, making sure that the children know to use the picture to search for meaning when they come to a word they don't know.

Have a Try

Invite the children to think about solving a word with a partner.

▶ Cover the word *worm* on page 14. Read the page up to the covered word and show the illustration to the children.

Turn and talk to your partner about what the word could be and how you could learn what it is

▶ After they turn and talk, ask a few pairs to share what they think the word is and why they think so. Then reveal the word and show them how to confirm their prediction.

Summarize and Apply

Summarize the learning and remind children to look at the picture and think what would make sense when they come to a tricky word.

What is something you can do when you are reading and you come to a word you don't know? Let's make a chart to remind you to look at the picture and think what would make sense with the illustration and the meaning of the story.

When you are reading today, if there is a word you are not sure of, use the illustration and think about what word would make sense. Then, look at the word again to check whether you are right.

Share

Following independent work time, gather children together in the meeting area to talk about solving words.

▶ Invite a couple of children to share.

Give a thumbs-up if you used the picture to help you read a tricky word today.

▶ Hold up the children's book so everyone can see the illustration. (If possible, project the pages.)

Did anyone solve a word in a different way?

Extend the Lesson (Optional)

After assessing children's understanding, you might decide to extend the learning.

▶ Continue to support this behavior in shared reading, guided reading, or reading conferences. From *Prompting Guide, Part 1* (Fountas and Pinnell 2012), use language such as this: *Can the picture help you think about this part of the story? Try that again and think of what would make sense.* Follow with reinforcing language, such as this: *That makes sense in this part of the story.*

RML2
SAS.U1.RML2

Reading Minilesson Principle
Read the sentence again and think what would sound right.

Searching for and Using Meaning, Language, and Visual Information

You Will Need

- an enlarged text, such as *Mondo* by Quentin Ripple, from *Shared Reading Collection*
- sticky notes
- chart paper and markers
- document camera (optional)

Academic Language / Important Vocabulary

- sounds right
- writer

Continuum Connection

- Use language syntax and repeating language patterns to anticipate the text: e.g., next word, next phrase, or sentences (p. 116)

Goal

Search for and use information from language structure.

Rationale

When children are aware that they can use the language they know to anticipate what the print will say, they learn the power of the feet-forward aspect of language structure. Rereading the sentence helps them focus on the predictability of the language structure. Children need to know that the language is only one source of information to use when reading but a very important one. Ultimately, they should search for and use meaning, language, and print in an integrated way to achieve fluent reading.

Assess Learning

Observe children when they read. Notice if there is evidence of new learning based on the goal of this minilesson.

- Do children solve unfamiliar words by reading the sentence again and thinking what would sound right?
- Do they use the terms *sounds right* and *writer* correctly?

Minilesson

To help children think about the minilesson principle, choose familiar texts and examples to demonstrate how to reread and search for and use language structure to solve unfamiliar words. Alternatively, use a text the children have not seen before and place a few sticky notes prior to the first reading. Here is an example.

- Use *Mondo* by Quentin Ripple or another enlarged text. With a sticky note, cover the word *mess* in the sentence "Tabby saw the mess" on page 4. Read only up to the unknown word. Stop and reread the sentence again.

    What word would sound right in this sentence?

- Try each suggestion in the sentence and ask children if it sounds right.

    Do you think the covered-up word could be *mess*? What makes you think that?

- Reveal the word. Run your finger left to right under the word as you read it. Then reread the whole sentence to confirm the word makes sense, sounds right, and looks right.

Have a Try

Invite the children to think about solving a word with a partner.

▶ Cover the word *laundry* in the sentence "Mondo played with the laundry" on page 8. Read the sentence up to the word *laundry* and stop.

> Turn and talk to your partner about what word would sound right in this sentence.

▶ After they turn and talk, ask what word they think is under the sticky note. Reread the sentence with the word children suggest and ask whether it makes sense and sounds right. Uncover the word to confirm it looks right.

Summarize and Apply

Summarize the learning and remind children what they can do when they come to a word they don't know.

> What is something you can do when you come to a word you know? Let's make a chart to remind you to read the sentence again and think what would sound right.

▶ Use children's suggestions or use the chart shown as a model.

> When you are reading today, if there is a word you don't know, remember to read the sentence again and think what would sound right. Then look at the word again and check to see if it looks right, too.

Share

Following independent work time, gather children together in the meeting area to talk about solving words.

▶ Invite a couple of children to share. Use a document camera to project the pages from the children's books or write a sentence on chart paper.

> Who thought about what would sound right to help read a new word? Did anyone solve a word in a different way?

Extend the Lesson (Optional)

After assessing children's understanding, you might decide to extend the learning.

▶ Continue to support this behavior during guided reading or reading conferences. From *Prompting Guide, Part 1* (Fountas and Pinnell 2012), use prompts, such as these: *Can the picture help you think about this part of the story? Read from the beginning and try it again.* Follow up with reinforcing language, such as this: *You made it sound right.*

Section 3: Strategies and Skills

RML3
SAS.U1.RML3

Reading Minilesson Principle
Read the sentence again and get your mouth ready for the first sound.

Searching for and Using Meaning, Language, and Visual Information

You Will Need

- enlarged text, such as *Not Quite Right* by Helen Lorraine, from *Shared Reading Collection*
- sticky notes
- chart paper and markers
- document camera (optional)

Academic Language / Important Vocabulary

- make sense
- predict
- sound
- letter
- word

Continuum Connection

- Begin to notice and connect features and parts of words: e.g., phonograms, first letter, word endings (p. 116)

Goal

Use visual information (first letter) and meaning to predict a word.

Rationale

When you teach children to search for and use visual information (first letter) and meaning to read a word, you support them in initiating problem-solving actions as readers. Children need to know that this is just one way to solve words that they do not know. Ultimately, they need to search for and use meaning, language, and print in an integrated way to achieve fluent reading.

Assess Learning

Observe children when they predict a word. Notice if there is evidence of new learning based on the goal of this minilesson.

- Do children reread the sentence, make the first sound of the unknown word, and think about what would make sense?
- Do they use the terms *make sense, predict, sound, letter,* and *word* correctly?

Minilesson

To help children think about the minilesson principle, choose familiar texts and examples. Alternatively, use a text the children have not seen before and place a few sticky notes prior to the first reading. Here is an example.

- Use *Not Quite Right* by Helen Lorraine or choose another shared reading book (enlarged text). With sticky notes, cover the words *windows* and *doors*, on pages 2 and 3, except for the first letter in each word. Begin reading the pages, pointing under each word and stopping before the word *windows*.

    "Carly's mom made a playhouse for her. It had little [*pause*]." I am going to read the sentence again and get my mouth ready for the first sound of the word. "It had little" /w/. Look at the picture. There's the playhouse. What does it have that starts with /w/?

    Window begins with /w/.

- Reveal the word.

    "It had little *windows* and a big /d/." What could this word be? Why do you think so?

- Reveal the word.

    "It had little windows and a big door." When you get to a word you don't know, you can read the sentence again, think about the first sound of the word, and check the picture to help you read the word.

- Cover the word *table*, except for the *t*, on pages 4 and 5 and repeat the process.

Have a Try

Invite the children to think about solving a word.

▶ Use a sticky note to cover the word *toys*, except for the first letter, on pages 8 and 9. Read aloud,

> "So Carly got some [*pause*]."

Think about what the word could be. Look at the first letter and get your mouth ready for the first sound. "So Carly got some" /t/. Turn and talk to your partner about what that word might be.

▶ After they turn and talk, ask a few children to share what they think the word is and why they think so. Reveal the word and read the sentence with the children.

> Does that look right and make sense with the story? Does it sound right?

Summarize and Apply

Summarize the learning and remind children to get their mouths ready for the first sound and think what would make sense when they come to a word they don't know.

> Today you learned that when you come to a word you don't know, you can read the sentence again and get your mouth ready for the first sound. What can we put on a chart to help you remember?

▶ Use children's suggestions or use the chart shown as a model.

> When you are reading today, if you come to a word you don't know, read the sentence again, get your mouth ready to make the first sound of the word, and think about what word makes sense and sounds right, too.

Share

Following independent work time, gather children together in the meeting area to talk about solving words in their reading.

▶ Invite a couple of children to share their experience with solving a tricky word. Project the pages from the children's books or write the sentences on a chart so that everyone can see.

Extend the Lesson (Optional)

After assessing children's understanding, you might decide to extend the learning.

▶ Continue to support this behavior in guided reading or during reading conferences. From *Prompting Guide, Part 1* (Fountas and Pinnell 2012), use prompts, such as this: *Read that again and get your mouth ready for the first sound.*

RML 4
SAS.U1.RML4

Reading Minilesson Principle
Look for a part you know.

Searching for and Using Meaning, Language, and Visual Information

You Will Need

▸ an enlarged text, such as *Pitter Patter* by Miriam David, from *Shared Reading Collection*

▸ chart paper and markers

Academic Language / Important Vocabulary

▸ word

▸ word part

Continuum Connection

▸ Begin to notice and connect features and parts of words: e.g., phonograms, first letter, word endings (p. 116)

Goal

Notice known parts of words and use them to help read the word.

Rationale

When you teach children to notice parts of words they know, you support them in learning how to solve unknown words while reading continuous text. A part means a letter or a cluster of letters. Children need to know that this is just one way to solve words as they read. Ultimately, they need to search for and use meaning, language, and print in an integrated way to achieve fluent reading.

Assess Learning

Observe children when they solve unknown words. Notice if there is evidence of new learning based on the goal of this minilesson.

▸ Do children look for a part of the word that they know and think about what would make sense to read a new word?

▸ Do they use the terms *word* and *word part* correctly?

Minilesson

To help children think about the minilesson principle, choose familiar texts and examples to demonstrate how to read words they don't know. Alternatively, use a text the children have not read before. Here is an example.

▸ Use *Pitter Patter* by Miriam David, or choose a familiar shared reading book (enlarged text). Turn to page 2 and begin reading, pausing before the word *then*. Point under the word.

> To figure out this word, I can look for a part I know. The word begins with a part you know: *the*. I see another part you know: the letter *n*. What is the word?

> What did you notice I did to figure out the word?

▸ Read the whole sentence.

> Does the word *then* make sense on this page?

> You can look for a part or parts you know to help you read a new word.

▸ Repeat this process with the word *that* on page 16. Use language such as *Look for a part you know* or *Look for a part that can help*. Children should recognize *th* as in *the* and the word *at*.

Have a Try

Invite the children to look for a known part in words with a partner.

▶ Point to the first word on page 16 (*Then*).

Turn and talk to your partner. This begins with an uppercase *T*. Do you see a part that can help you read this word?

▶ After children turn and talk, ask one or two children to describe what they did to read the word. Read the whole sentence together to confirm it makes sense.

Summarize and Apply

Summarize the learning and remind children what to do when they come to a word they don't know.

What did you learn today about how to read a word you don't know?

You can look for a part you know and think about what would make sense. What can we put on a chart to help remember this?

▶ Use children's suggestions or use the chart shown as a model.

When you are reading today, if you come to a word you don't know, look to see if there is a part that can help you.

Look for a part you know.

The + n = Then.

Share

Following independent work time, gather children together in the meeting area to talk about solving words.

▶ Invite a couple of children to share examples. Project the pages from the children's books or write the sentence on a chart.

Give a thumbs-up if you tried to read a word by looking for a part you know. Did anyone read a new word in a different way?

Extend the Lesson (Optional)

After assessing children's understanding, you might decide to extend the learning.

▶ Continue to support this behavior in guided reading or independent reading. From *Prompting Guide, Part 1* (Fountas and Pinnell 2012), use prompts, such as these: *Do you know a word that starts (ends) like that? Do you see a part you know?* Follow up with reinforcing language, such as this: *You used a part you know. You thought about a part you know.*

Section 3: Strategies and Skills

RML5
SAS.U1.RML5

Reading Minilesson Principle
Read the words you know quickly.

Searching for and Using Meaning, Language, and Visual Information

You Will Need

- an enlarged text, such as *Wiggles: Poems to Make You Wiggle Your Fingers and Toes*, from *Shared Reading Collection*
- highlighting tape (optional)
- chart paper and markers

Academic Language / Important Vocabulary

- words

Continuum Connection

- Locate known high-frequency words in print (p. 116)

Goal

Read high-frequency words quickly and easily.

Rationale

Some words appear frequently in oral language and in early texts. They are called high-frequency words. When you teach children to read words they know quickly, they have more attention for the meaning and language of the text. Fast, automatic recognition of a growing number of words supports fluent reading of the text.

Assess Learning

Observe children when they read aloud. Notice if there is evidence of new learning based on the goal of this minilesson.

- Do children read words they know quickly?
- Do you see evidence of a growing core of known words?
- Do they use the term *words* correctly?

Minilesson

To help children think about the minilesson principle, choose familiar texts and examples to provide an inquiry-based lesson about reading aloud. Here is an example.

- Use *Wiggles: Poems to Make You Wiggle Your Fingers and Toes* or choose a shared reading poem or book (enlarged text) that children have read or listened to. Turn to pages 2 and 3.

    In this poem, there is a word that you know well. The word *and* is on these pages many times.

- Invite a few children to come up and find the word *and* in the poem, asking them to mark it with highlighting tape, if available, or point to it.

    You know this word, so you can read it quickly. When you read a word quickly, it will help you read smoothly and you can think about what the writer is saying.

    Let's read it together. Follow along and read while I point. We won't use the hand motions this time.

Have a Try

Invite the children to apply the new thinking about reading aloud.

▶ Turn to page 10. Ask two children to come up.

The word *can* is on this page four times. Take turns pointing to *can* two times. Everyone else, look for *can* with your eyes.

Now look at page 11. Use your eyes to find *me*.

▶ Ask a volunteer to point to the word *me* two times. Point out that even though the two occurrences are different sizes, they have the same visual features.

Summarize and Apply

Summarize the learning and remind children to read words they know quickly.

Today you learned that it's important to read the words you know quickly. Let's make a chart to help remember this.

▶ Ask children to suggest several words they know how to read quickly and place them in the speech bubbles surrounding a person.

When you are reading today, be sure to read the words you know quickly.

Read the words you know quickly.

Share

Following independent work time, gather children together in the meeting area to talk about their reading.

▶ Invite a couple of children to share a word they read quickly. Project the pages from the children's books or write a few sentences on a chart.

▶ Remind children to remember to read words they know quickly the next time they read a book.

Extend the Lesson (Optional)

After assessing children's understanding, you might decide to extend the learning.

▶ Continue to support this behavior in guided reading or independent reading. From *Prompting Guide, Part 1* (Fountas and Pinnell 2012), use prompts, such as this: *Can you find _____?* Follow up with reinforcing language, such as this: *You read the words you know quickly.*

▶ Add high-frequency words to the chart or a word wall as children learn to recognize them and review them periodically.

Assessment

After you have taught the minilessons in this umbrella, observe children as they talk and write about their reading across instructional contexts: interactive read-aloud, independent reading and literacy work, guided reading, shared reading, and book club. Use *The Literacy Continuum* (Fountas and Pinnell 2017) to observe children's reading and writing behaviors across instructional contexts.

▶ What evidence do you have of new understandings related to searching for and using meaning, language, and visual information?

▶ When children come to an unknown word:

- Do they check the picture and think about what would make sense?
- Are they able to think about what would sound right?
- Can they reread the sentence and get their mouth ready for the first sound?
- Do they look for a part of the word that can help solve the new word?
- Do they read known high-frequency words quickly?
- Do they use terms such as *illustration, writer, predict, sound, or writer* when they talk about their reading?

▶ In what other ways, beyond the scope of this umbrella, are children searching for and using meaning, language, and visual information?

- Are they using language patterns close to oral language to search for and use information?
- Do they use simple sentence structures (subject and predicate with no embedded phrases or clauses) to search for and use information?
- Are children able to sustain searching for and using information over a short text?

Use your observations to determine the next umbrella you will teach. You may also consult Minilessons Across the Year (p. 51) for guidance.

Link to Writing

After teaching the minilessons in this umbrella, help children link the new learning to their own writing:

▶ In addition to reading high-frequency words quickly, it's also important to be able to write them quickly. Have children practice writing the high-frequency words they know, working over time to build up speed and fluency with their writing.

Minilessons in This Umbrella

RML1   Check your reading to be sure it makes sense.

RML2   Check your reading to be sure it sounds right.

RML3   Check the word to be sure it looks right.

Before Teaching Umbrella 2 Minilessons

Read and discuss shared reading texts that offer enlarged print (big books) so the children can participate in the reading. Use the selected texts from the *Fountas & Pinnell Classroom™ Shared Reading Collection* listed below or choose big books that include simple texts with supportive illustrations and engaging content, with the print and the illustrations clearly separated but closely matched in meaning. For shared reading, select texts beyond the difficulty level that most children can process in guided reading, so that shared reading can lead their processing competencies forward.

Shared Reading Collection

Molly's Leash by Susan Scott

Pitter Patter by Miriam David

Fly Away by Alina Kirk

As you read aloud and enjoy these texts together, help children

- discuss what the book is about,

- monitor their reading and demonstrate control of early reading behaviors, such as left-to-right directionality, return sweep, and word-by-word matching,

- demonstrate how to recognize and locate high-frequency words,

- demonstrate using the memory of repeated language patterns to monitor accuracy, and

- point out features of words (e.g., letters, beginnings, endings).

RML1
SAS.U2.RML1

Reading Minilesson Principle
Check your reading to be sure it makes sense.

Monitoring and Self-Correcting

You Will Need

- a big book that children have read and heard, such as *Molly's Leash* by Susan Scott, from *Shared Reading Collection*
- chart paper and markers

Academic Language / Important Vocabulary

- make sense
- try that again
- reread

Continuum Connection

- Reread the sentence to problem-solve, self-correct, or confirm (pp. 412, 418, 424, 430, 436)
- Cross-check one kind of information against another to monitor and self-correct reading (i.e., cross-checking meaning with visual information) (pp. 418, 424, 430, 436)

Goal

Use meaning to monitor and self-correct.

Rationale

Children need to know that what they read needs to make sense and when it doesn't they need to stop and fix it themselves or self-correct. Readers can self-monitor their reading to be sure what they read makes sense by asking themselves, "Does that make sense?" Self-correction behavior indicates the reader is noticing error and working to fix it. When the reader uses one kind of information and then checks it with another, he cross-checks. The goal is to help children learn to use flexible problem-solving actions to read accurately with independence and fluency.

Assess Learning

Observe children when they self-monitor their reading. Notice if there is evidence of new learning based on the goal of this minilesson.

- ▶ Do the children stop when their reading doesn't make sense?
- ▶ Are they able to cross-check information and reread to self-correct their errors?
- ▶ Do they use the terms *make sense, try that again,* and *reread* correctly?

Minilesson

To help children think about the minilesson principle, choose familiar texts and examples to demonstrate what to do when something doesn't make sense. Here is an example.

- ▶ Use *Molly's Leash* or choose another shared reading book or poem (enlarged text) that children have read and heard before.
- ▶ Read the title, and then open to pages 2 and 3.

  Think about this part of the story. What is happening? This says, "'Where is Molly's leash?' asked Mom." Is that right? Does that make sense with this story? Would Mom ask that?

  You can see in the picture they have their coats on and they are getting ready to take Molly for a walk. They need the dog's leash. So, Mom asks Jackson where the leash is. That makes sense.

- ▶ Turn to pages 4 and 5. Read the sentence, up to a key word that prompts checking information.

  "It's on the [pause]." What would make sense? "The leash is on the [pause]." Think about the story and think about what would make sense. Do you see that in the picture? Does it look right? Then, you might be right. You stopped and thought about the story. You read it again to be sure it made sense. You knew you were right.

▶ Reread the page, correcting the error.

"'It's not on the hook,' said Jackson." When your reading doesn't make sense, think about the story, and read it again to make it right.

Have a Try

Invite the children check meaning information with a partner.

▶ Turn to pages 6 and 7. Read the sentence up to the word *counter*.

Turn and talk to your partner. What do you think the word is? What would make sense?

▶ After they turn and talk, ask a few children to share their thinking and why.

Summarize and Apply

Summarize the learning and remind children to make sure their reading makes sense as they read.

What can you do to be sure your reading makes sense? Let's make a chart to help you remember what to do.

▶ Ask the children for ideas to go onto the chart, or use the sample shown.

When you read today, if what you read doesn't make sense you need to stop, think about the story, read the sentence again, and be sure it makes sense.

Share

Following independent work time, gather children together in the meeting area to talk about self-monitoring their reading.

When you read today, did you check to be sure your reading makes sense? What did you do?

Extend the Lesson (Optional)

After assessing children's understanding, you might decide to extend the learning.

▶ Remind children during guided reading and reading conferences that what they read has to make sense. Utilize prompts from *Prompting Guide, Part 1* (Fountas and Pinnell 2012), such as these: *Why did you stop? What did you notice? You said _____. Does that make sense? Could it be* [insert meaningful choices]? *You are nearly right. Try that again and think: What would make sense?* And reinforcing language: *You noticed that it didn't make sense.*

Check your reading
to be sure it makes sense.

Stop and think about the story.

Read the sentence again.

RML 2

SAS.U2.RML2

Check your reading to be sure it sounds right.

Monitoring and Self-Correcting

You Will Need

- a book children have read and heard, such as *Pitter Patter* by Miriam David, from *Shared Reading Collection*
- chart paper and markers

Academic Language / Important Vocabulary

- sounds right
- reread

Continuum Connection

- Use language structure to self-monitor and self-correct (pp. 412, 418, 424, 430)

Goal

Notice when something doesn't sound right and learn to self-correct.

Rationale

Children need to know that what they read must sound right. When children listen for what doesn't sound right, they can learn one way to self-monitor and self-correct. When they stop after an error, stop before a tricky word, or make multiple attempts or ask for help, they are self monitoring. When they work to fix the error for themselves, they self-correct.

Assess Learning

Observe children when they self-correct their read. Notice if there is evidence of new learning based on the goal of this minilesson.

- Do children ask themselves, "Does it sound right?"
- When something doesn't sound right, do the children stop or make further attempts or ask for help?
- Do they use the terms *sounds right* and *reread* correctly?

Minilesson

To help children think about the minilesson principle, choose familiar texts and examples to demonstrate self-monitoring and self-correcting. Here is an example.

- Use *Pitter Patter* or choose another shared reading book (big book) that children have read and heard.
- Read the title and then the first sentence on page 2, stopping after *sunny*.

  "It was a sunny" [pause]. Could the next word be *day*? Does it sound right and make sense? Let's check.

- Reread the sentence again, running your finder under the word *day*.

  "It was a sunny day." Now what did you notice? It sounded right and looked right. It also makes sense.

- Read the first sentence on page 4, stopping after the word *it*.

  Could the next word be *started*? Does it sound right and make sense? Let's check.

- Reread the sentence again, running your finger under the word *started*.

  "It *started* to rain." Now what did you notice? It sounded right and looked right. It also makes sense.

Have a Try

Invite the children to consider language structure with a partner.

▶ Read the first sentence on page 6 correctly.

"'May I come in?' squeaked the mouse." Think about the story. Now turn and talk to your partner about whether what I read sounds right.

▶ After they turn and talk invite a few pairs to share their noticings.

Now reread the sentence again to check it. "'May I come in?' squeaked the mouse." It has to make sense, too. When you read today, check your reading to be sure it sounds right.

Summarize and Apply

Summarize the learning and remind children to check their reading to make sure it sounds right as they read.

The words you read need to be words that make a sentence the way you would say it. Remember, we are thinking about how the sentences sound in English. Let's make a chart to help remember that what you read needs to sound right.

▶ Ask the children for ideas to go onto the chart, or use the sample shown.

When you are reading today, if something that doesn't sound right, stop and think about how it should sound in English. Then, you can reread the sentence and fix it up.

Share

Following independent work time, gather children together in the meeting area to talk about self-correcting while reading.

When you were reading today, did you read something that didn't sound right? Did you stop and try it again?

Extend the Lesson (Optional)

After assessing children's understanding, you might decide to extend the learning.

▶ Help children use problem-solving actions, such as monitoring, self-correcting, and searching for information (see the other minilessons in this umbrella) when you meet with them for reading conferences.

Check your reading to be sure it sounds right.

Stop and think about the story.

Think about what sounds right.

Section 3: Strategies and Skills

RML3

SAS.U2.RML3

Reading Minilesson Principle
Check the word to be sure it looks right.

Monitoring and
Self-Correcting

You Will Need

▸ a book children have read
and heard, such as *Fly Away*
by Alina Kirk, from *Shared
Reading Collection*

▸ sticky notes

▸ chart paper and markers

Academic Language /
Important Vocabulary

▸ makes sense

▸ try that again

▸ reread

▸ looks right

Continuum
Connection

▸ Use visual features of words to
self-monitor and self-correct
(pp. 412, 418, 424, 430, 436)

Goal

Notice when something doesn't look right and learn how to cross-check one kind of
information (visual information) with another to self-correct.

Rationale

Children need to know that they can use different kinds information (meaning,
language, print) to correct errors when their reading doesn't make sense, sound right,
or look right. Teaching children to cross-check what they know about sounds and
letters with the meaning of the story is one way they can self-correct.

Assess Learning

Observe children when they read. Notice if there is evidence of new learning based on
the goal of this minilesson.

▸ Can children monitor their reading by making sure it makes sense and looks right?

▸ Do they use the terms *make sense, try that again, looks right,* and *reread* correctly?

Minilesson

To help children think about the minilesson principle, choose familiar texts and
examples to demonstrate how to cross-check sources of information to self-monitor
and self-correct. Here is an example.

▸ Use *Fly Away* or another shared reading book (big book) that children have
heard and read. Turn to pages 2 and 3, and place a sticky note over the word
bird in the first sentence. Read page 2, stopping before the word *bird*.

"Look at the [pause]." I have to think about what would make sense in this
sentence. There is a bird in the picture: "Look at the bird."

The name of the bird is a parrot. Both *bird* and *parrot* would make sense.
What can I do to be sure I read the right word? What letter do you expect to
see first in *bird*?

▸ Uncover the first letter.

The word begins with *b*, so which is it? I'll read it again, saying that first
sound and thinking about what would make sense. "Look at the" /b/ *bird*.

Watch me check the first letter and the rest of the word.

▸ Run your finger left to right under bird and say the word slowly.

Now it makes sense and looks right, too.

▸ Repeat the process with pages 4 and 5, covering the word *cave* in the second
sentence with a sticky note and asking children to tell whether the word would
be *rock* or *cave*.

When you read, you need to think if it makes sense and looks right. If it doesn't, you need to stop and read it again. Be sure the word makes sense and looks right, too.

Have a Try

Invite the children to talk with a partner about being sure words make sense as they read.

▶ Read aloud page 8.

Listen as I read this page and check to see if what I read makes sense and looks right, too. Follow what I read with your eyes.

Could it be *ladybug* or *bug*? Which is it?

Summarize and Apply

Summarize the learning and remind children to be sure the words make sense and look right as they read.

Let's make a chart to help you remember what you learned today about what to do when your reading doesn't look right.

▶ Use children's suggestion or use the sample shown.

When you are reading today, ask yourself, "Does it make sense?" Then ask, "Does it look right, too?" You can run your finger under a word to check the first and last letter to be sure it looks right.

Share

Following independent work time, gather children together in the meeting area to talk about making sure words make sense as they read.

When you read today, did you notice something that didn't look right? What did you notice and how did you fix it?

Extend the Lesson (Optional)

After assessing children's understanding, you might decide to extend the learning.

▶ Refer to the charts in this umbrella to remind children how to self-monitor and self-correct their reading.

▶ During guided reading and reading conferences, use prompts from *Prompting Guide, Part 1* (Fountas and Pinnell 2012), such as these: *Why did you stop? What did you notice? You said _____. Does that look right? Check the first part of the word. Now check the last part. Does that word you said look like the word on the page?*

Check the word to be sure it looks right.

Stop and think about the story.

Think about what looks right.

Assessment

After you have taught the minilessons in this umbrella, observe children as they talk and write about their reading across instructional contexts: interactive read-aloud, independent reading and literacy work, guided reading, shared reading, and book club. Use *The Literacy Continuum* (Fountas and Pinnell 2017) to observe children's reading and writing behaviors across instructional contexts.

> ◗ What evidence do you have that children are using the meaning, language, and visual information to monitor and self-correct their reading?
>
> - Do they stop when their reading doesn't make sense?
> - Do they reread and self-correct their errors?
> - Do they stop and notice when their reading doesn't look right?
> - Do they reread the sentence and get their mouth ready for the first sound?
> - Do they stop when it doesn't sound right and reread to self-correct?
> - Do they use the terms *make sense, try that again, looks right,* and *reread* correctly when talk about monitoring and self-correcting their reading?
>
> ◗ In what other ways, beyond the scope of this umbrella, are the children monitoring and self-correcting?
>
> - Do they show increased fluency and reading stamina with longer and more complex text?

Use your observations to determine the next umbrella you will teach. You may also consult Minilessons Across the Year (p. 51) for guidance.

Link to Writing

After teaching the minilessons in this umbrella, help children link the new learning to their own writing:

> ◗ During interactive writing sessions and writers' workshop conferences, support children in checking to make sure that what they wrote makes sense, looks right, and sounds right. Encourage children to reread what they have written, using what they have learned in these minilessons, to self-monitor their writing by searching for and using meaning, structure, and visual information.

Minilessons in This Umbrella

RML1 Make your voice go down and come to a full stop when you see a period.

RML2 Make your voice go up when you see a question mark.

RML3 Read the sentence with strong feeling when you see an exclamation point.

RML4 Make the word sound important when you see bold or dark print.

RML5 Make your voice a little louder when you see a word in capital letters.

RML6 Put your words together so it sounds like talking.

Before Teaching Umbrella 3 Minilessons

Read and discuss books with a variety of punctuation marks and print features, such as bold print or words in all capital letters. Make sure your primary focus is to support the meaning and enjoyment of the books. Use shared reading books (big books) so that children can see the print as you read. For this umbrella, use the following texts from the *Fountas & Pinnell Classroom™ Interactive Read-Aloud* or *Shared Reading Collections,* or choose engaging big books from your own library.

Fun with Language

Having Fun with Language

Charlie Parker Played Be Bop by Chris Raschka

Max Found Two Sticks by Brian Pinkney

CREAK! Said the Bed by Phyllis Root

Exploring Animal Tales

The Little Red Hen by Paul Galdone

Animal Tales

Sharing Stories: Folktales

The Magic Fish by Freya Littledale

The Gingerbread Boy by Paul Galdone

Folktales

Rhythm and Rhyme: Joyful Language

Sleepy Bears by Mem Fox

The Importance of Friendship

Yo! Yes? by Chris Raschka

Understanding Feelings

Harriet, You Drive Me Wild! by Mem Fox

Shared Reading Collection

The Sleeping Giant by Barbara Gannet

The Big Race: An Aesop Fable adapted by David Edwin

Joyful Language

Friendship

Feelings

As you read aloud and enjoy these texts together, model fluent reading by

- changing the tone of your voice to reflect the meaning of the story and punctuation of the text, and

- emphasizing boldfaced or capitalized print to reflect meaning.

Shared Reading Collection

RML1
SAS.U3.RML1

Reading Minilesson Principle
Make your voice go down and come to a full stop when you see a period.

Maintaining Fluency

You Will Need

- several familiar books that have short sentences with periods, such as the following:
  - *The Magic Fish* by Freya Littledale, from Text Set: Folktales
  - *Sleepy Bears* by Mem Fox, from Text Set: Joyful Language
- projector and pointer or highlighter tape (optional)
- chart paper with large red period, labeled
- markers

Academic Language / Important Vocabulary

- period
- full stop

Continuum Connection

- Recognize and reflect some simple punctuation with the voice (e.g., period, question mark, exclamation mark) when reading in chorus or individually (p. 117)

Goal

Learn how a reader's voice changes when reading a sentence that ends with a period.

Rationale

When children identify periods and voice modulation in stories they hear read aloud, they develop deeper comprehension of the text because they are interpreting the writer's intended meaning. They gain skill and confidence with using periods as they read and write independently.

Assess Learning

Observe children when they read aloud. Notice if there is evidence of new learning based on the goal of this minilesson.

- ▶ Are children able to identify the periods on a page?
- ▶ Do they notice how a voice goes down and comes to a full stop at a period?
- ▶ Do they use the terms *period* and *full stop* correctly?

Minilesson

To help children think about the minilesson principle, demonstrate how to read a sentence that ends with a period. Here is an example.

- ▶ Show the cover of *The Magic Fish*. Copy the sentences from page 13 on chart paper (or project the page) so that children can see the periods. Point to the periods.

  Do you know the name of these marks? Listen carefully to how my voice sounds as I read a page from this story.

- ▶ Read the page, pointing to the words and periods, emphasizing how your voice goes down and stops after each period.

  What did you notice about my voice when I came to each period?

- ▶ Show the cover of *Sleepy Bears*.

  Listen to how my voice sounds as I read a page from *Sleepy Bears*. What do you think my voice will do when I come to the periods?

- ▶ Project or display page 4. Read the page, pointing to the words and periods.

  Did I read the sentences the way you expected?

  Authors put a period at the end of a sentence to let you know that the sentence has ended. That's why, when you are reading and you come to a period, you make your voice go down and come to a full stop.

Have a Try

Invite the children to think about punctuation with a partner.

▶ Continue projecting page 4 of *Sleepy Bears*.

Turn and talk about what you do with your voice when you see a period. Then, read the page to your partner. I will read it one more time and then you try.

▶ Read the page. Then allow time for children to talk and read.

Summarize and Apply

Summarize the learning and remind children to to think about what to do with their voice when they read a sentence that ends with a period.

What did you learn today about reading a sentence with a period?

▶ Write the principle on chart paper.

When you read today, notice the period at the end of a sentence. Bring your book when we come back together so you can share how to read a sentence that ends with a period.

Share

Following independent work time, gather children together in the meeting area to practice reading sentences that end with a period.

Turn to a partner. Choose a page from your book and point to the periods. Read the page and make your voice go down and come to a full stop when you see a period.

Extend the Lesson (Optional)

After assessing children's understanding, you might decide to extend the learning.

▶ Point out periods during shared reading of stories and informational books. Have children search for periods in poems and big books. Model how to read the sentences, and then have children join in and read chorally.

 Period

Make your voice go down and come to a full stop when you see a period.

RML2

Reading Minilesson Principle
Make your voice go up when you see a question mark.

You Will Need

- three or four familiar books that have short sentences with question marks, such as the following:
  - *The Little Red Hen* by Paul Galdone, from Text Set: Animal Tales
  - *The Magic Fish* by Mem Fox, from Text Set: Folktales
  - *CREAK! Said the Bed* by Phyllis Root, from Text Set: Fun with Language
- chart paper with large red question mark, labeled
- markers
- projector and pointer or highlighter tape (optional)

Academic Language / Important Vocabulary

- question mark

Continuum Connection

- Recognize and reflect some simple punctuation with the voice (e.g., period, question mark, exclamation mark) when reading in chorus or individually (p. 117)

Goal

Learn how a reader's voice changes when reading a sentence that ends with a question mark.

Rationale

When you teach children how to read punctuation, you help them reflect the meaning of the story in their voices, which contributes to comprehension.

Assess Learning

Observe children when they read aloud. Notice if there is evidence of new learning based on the goal of this minilesson.

- ▶ Are children able to reflect a question mark with their voices?
- ▶ Do children notice how a reader's voice goes up at a question mark?
- ▶ Do they use the term *question mark*?

Minilesson

To help children think about the minilesson principle, demonstrate how to read sentences that end with a question mark. Here is an example.

- ▶ Show the cover of *The Little Red Hen*.

  Do you remember how the hen in this story keeps asking the other animals to help?

- ▶ Copy the question from page 12 on chart paper (or project the page) so that the question mark can be clearly seen. Point to the question mark.

  What is this called?

- ▶ Title a chart Question Mark and draw the mark.

  As I reread some parts of this book, listen to how my voice sounds when I come to a question mark.

- ▶ Read the page, pointing to the words and the question mark.

  What did you notice about my voice?

- ▶ Continue reading a few other questions, asking children to identify question marks.

Have a Try

Invite the children to practice reading punctuation with a partner.

> Now think about another story you listened to, *CREAK! Said the Bed.*

❯ Write the question in the speech bubble on page 3 on chart paper (or project the page) and read the question.

> Turn and talk about what you noticed about my voice when I came to the question mark. Then practice asking Evie's question with your partner.

Summarize and Apply

Summarize the learning and remind children to think about how to read a sentence that ends with a question mark when they read.

> What do you do with your voice when you read a sentence that ends with a question mark?

❯ Write the principle on the chart.

> When you read today, notice if there is a question mark at the end of a sentence and make your voice go up. Bring your book when we come back together so you can share.

Share

Following independent work time, gather children together in the meeting area to practice reading sentences with question marks in groups of three.

> Did you find a question mark in your book? Share what you found. Try reading a page with a question mark and make your voice go up at the end.

Extend the Lesson (Optional)

After assessing children's understanding, you might decide to extend the learning.

❯ Talk about why authors use question marks in their writing.

❯ Have children draw pictures of themselves playing with friends. Assist them in adding one or more speech bubbles to the drawings with questions the friends might ask each other. Then have children share drawings in small groups, asking the questions and making their voices go up.

❯ During shared reading, point out question marks in poems and big books and have children read chorally reflecting the question mark with their voices.

RML 3

SAS.U3.RML3

Reading Minilesson Principle
Read the sentence with strong feeling when you see an exclamation point.

Maintaining Fluency

You Will Need

- three or four familiar books that have short sentences with exclamation points, such as the following:
  - *Harriet, You'll Drive Me Wild!* by Mem Fox, from Text Set: Feelings
  - *Sleepy Bears* by Mem Fox, from Text Set: Joyful Language
  - *Yo! Yes!* by Chris Raschka, from Text Set: Friendship
- chart paper with large red exclamation point, labeled
- markers
- projector and pointer (optional)
- sticky notes

Academic Language / Important Vocabulary

- exclamation point
- title

Continuum Connection

- Recognize and reflect some simple punctuation with the voice (e.g., period, question mark, exclamation mark) when reading in chorus or individually (p. 117)

Goal

Learn how to read sentences with exclamation points to reflect the meaning of the story.

Rationale

When you teach children how to read punctuation, you help them reflect the meaning of the story in their voices, which contributes to comprehension.

Assess Learning

Observe children when they read aloud. Notice if there is evidence of new learning based on the goal of this minilesson.

- ▶ Are children able to identify the exclamation points on a page?
- ▶ Do children notice how a voice changes at an exclamation point?
- ▶ Do they use the terms *exclamation point* and *title* when they talk with others?

Minilesson

To help children think about the minilesson principle, demonstrate how to read sentences that end with an exclamation point. Here is an example.

- ▶ Show the front cover of *Harriet, You'll Drive Me Wild!* by Mem Fox.

  How do you think the author wants you to read the title of this book?

  How did you know you should read that with strong feeling and voice?

  Mem Fox put an exclamation point to show you that Harriet's mom is frustrated and mad, so you need to make your voice sound excited.

- ▶ Display the prepared chart.
- ▶ Write the sentences from page 11 of *Sleepy Bears* (or project the page) so children can see the exclamation points.

  Here is a page from *Sleepy Bears*. Who can point to the exclamation points?

- ▶ Read aloud the page.

  What did you notice about the way my voice changed when I read the parts with the exclamation points? Why do you think the author put an exclamation point at the end of the sentence, "The circus is here!"?

- ▶ Record responses on the chart.

  Mother Bear is excited and happy about the circus. Let's read the first two lines together. Make your voice sound excited when you see the exclamation point.

Have a Try

Invite the children read sentences that end with an exclamation point.

▶ Show the cover of *Yo! Yes?* by Chris Raschka. Turn to the first page. Ask the children why they think Chris Raschka used an exclamation point when he wrote *Yo!*

> How does the author want you read this word?

> Chris Raschka uses periods, question marks, and exclamation points in this book. Let's read the story together. Remember to make your voice sound the way the author wants you to read it.

Summarize and Apply

Summarize the learning and remind children to think about how to read sentences that end with an exclamation point.

> What feelings might the author want to show with an exclamation point?

▶ Review the chart and add any new responses.

> When you read today, notice if there is an exclamation point at the end of a sentence. Read the sentence the way you think the author wants you to read it. Mark the page with a sticky note to share when we come back together.

Share

Following independent work time, gather children together in the meeting area to practice reading sentences with exclamation points.

> Give a thumbs-up if you found an exclamation point when you were reading. Who would like to read a sentence you found? Make your voice sound the way the author wants you to read it.

Extend the Lesson (Optional)

After assessing children's understanding, you might decide to extend the learning.

▶ Talk about why authors choose to use exclamation points in stories and how knowing about exclamation points helps you understand the story better.

▶ Use the recurring poem in *The Gingerbread Boy* to practice using exclamation points. Write the rhyme on sentence strips, teach children the words, and have them practice reading with expression.

Exclamation Point

loud   excited

strong   mad

happy

To get attention!

RML4
SAS.U3.RML4

Reading Minilesson Principle
Make the word sound important when you see bold or dark print.

Maintaining Fluency

You Will Need

- three or four familiar books that have some words in bold, such as the following:
  - *The Gingerbread Boy* by Paul Galdone, from Text Set: Folktales
  - *Charlie Parker Played Be Bop* by Chris Raschka, from Text Set: Fun with Language
  - *The Little Red Hen* by Paul Galdone, from Text Set: Animal Tales
- chart paper and markers
- projector and pointer (optional)
- sticky notes

Academic Language / Important Vocabulary

- bold print
- important
- louder
- author

Continuum Connection

- Recognize and reflect variations in print with the voice (e.g., italis, bold type, special treatments, font size) when reading in chorus or individually (p. 117)

Goal

Learn how a reader's voice changes to make words written in bold letters sound important.

Rationale

When you make children aware of ways that the author shows how to read certain words, such as using bold, or dark, print, you help them reflect the meaning of the story in their voices, which contributes to comprehension.

Assess Learning

Observe children when they read aloud. Notice if there is evidence of new learning based on the goal of this minilesson.

- ❱ Are children able to identify in bold print words on a page?
- ❱ Do the children change voice when reading a word in bold print?
- ❱ Do they use the terms *bold print, important, louder,* and *author*?

Minilesson

To help children think about the minilesson principle, demonstrate how to read aloud words in bold print. Here is an example.

> Listen again to this page from *The Gingerbread Boy*, when the gingerbread boy is eaten by the fox.

- ❱ Show (or project) pages 34–35 so that children can see the words. Turn the page and show pages 36–37.

  > What do you notice about how the letters have changed on this new page?

- ❱ Write *bold* on chart paper.

  > These words say He was all gone, but they are in bold, or dark, letters. Why did Paul Galdone put these words in bold print?

- ❱ Record responses.

  > Let's try reading the bold words the way the author wants them to sound.

- ❱ Project pages 1–2 of *Charlie Parker Played Be Bop* or copy the sentence with the bold print on chart paper.

  > What do you notice about some of the words on this page? How do you think the author wants you to read the words *be bop*, which are in bold print?

- ❱ Record responses on the chart.

  > Join in with me to read the words, using a little louder voice to show that the bold words are more important than the other words. You don't want to yell the word, just to put more stress on it.

Have a Try

Invite the children to practice reading words in bold print with a partner.

▶ Project page 17 of *The Little Red Hen* or copy the sentences with *Not I* on chart paper.

> Turn and talk about what you notice about the way Paul Galdone, the author and illustrator, decided to make the letters in the words *Not I* on this page. Also say the words *Not I* to your partner in a way that makes the words sound more important.

Summarize and Apply

Summarize the learning and remind children to notice words in bold print as they read.

> What did you learn today about reading words in bold or dark print?

▶ Write the principle at the top of the chart.

> When you read today, notice if there are any words in bold letters and mark the pages with a sticky note. Try to read the word the way the author wants you to make it sound.

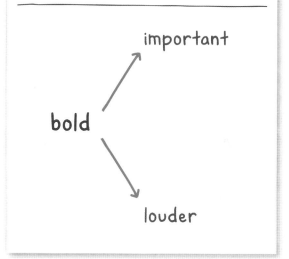

Share

Following independent work time, gather children together in the meeting area to practice reading words with bold or dark print.

> Who found a word in bold letters when you were reading? Share what you found with a partner. Try reading the words with bold letters, making your voice sound a little bit louder. Stress them to show that the words are more important.

Extend the Lesson (Optional)

After assessing children's understanding, you might decide to extend the learning.

▶ Talk about why authors choose to use bold words in stories and how knowing how to change your voice when reading words in bold print helps you understand the story better.

▶ Revisit *Charlie Parker Played Be Bop*, reading it as a poem, and have children join in on the words in bold print, especially the recurring words, *be bop*.

▶ Have the children make masks for the cat, the dog, and the mouse in *The Little Red Hen*. Then, children can act out the story, saying *Not I* the way the characters in the story would say it.

RML 5

SAS.U3.RML5

Reading Minilesson Principle

Make your voice a little louder when you see a word in capital letters.

Maintaining Fluency

You Will Need

- three or four familiar books that have some words in all capital letters, such as the following from Text Set: Fun with Language:
  - *CREAK! Said the Bed* by Phyllis Root
  - *Max Found Two Sticks* by Brian Pinkney
  - *Charlie Parker Played Be Bop* by Chris Raschka
- chart paper and markers
- projector and pointer (optional)
- sticky notes

Academic Language / Important Vocabulary

- capital letters
- author

Continuum Connection

- Recognize and reflect variations in print with the voice (e.g., italis, bold type, special treatments, font size) when reading in chorus or individually (p. 117)

Goal

Learn how a reader's voice changes to make words written in all capital letters sound important.

Rationale

When you make children aware of ways that the author shows how to read certain words, such as using all capital letters, you help them reflect the meaning of the story in their voices, which contributes to comprehension.

Assess Learning

Observe children when they read aloud. Notice if there is evidence of new learning based on the goal of this minilesson.

- Do children notice how a reader's voice changes when reading words in all capital letters?
- Do they use the words *author* and *capital letters*?

Minilesson

To help children think about the minilesson principle, demonstrate how to stress words that are in all capital letters. Here is an example.

- Show (or project) the cover of *CREAK! Said the Bed*.

  Which word is in all capital letters?

  As I turn each page, notice that the author, Phyllis Root, put some words in capital letters.

- Turn the pages so that children can see the words in all capital letters. Record the sound words on chart paper and have children practice reading the sentences with you the way the author intended them to sound.

  Why do you think Phyllis Root uses all capital letters for the sound words?

- Record responses on the chart.

- Project page 22 of *Max Found Two Sticks* or copy the sentence with bang on chart paper. Read the page, pausing before you read BANG.

  The next word on this page is bang, but it is in all capital letters.

- Record the word on the chart.

  How does the author want you to read this word? Why do you think the author wants you to read the word BANG a little louder, or make it sound important?

- Record responses on the chart.

Have a Try

Invite the children to think about words in capital letters with a partner.

▶ Project pages 15–16 from *Charlie Parker Played Be Bop* or copy the sentence with bang on chart paper.

The words on this page say *boppity, bippitty, bop bang*, but notice that the author has written one word in capital letters. What is the word?

▶ Record responses on the chart.

Turn and talk about how your voice sounds when you read the word *BANG* on this page. Why did the author make this word in all capital letters?

▶ Record noticings on the chart.

Summarize and Apply

Summarize the learning and remind children to add stress to words in all capital letters.

▶ Review the chart and write the principle at the top.

What did you learn about reading a word in all capital letters?

When you read today, notice if there are any words in all capital letters and mark the page with a sticky note. Bring your book to group share.

Share

Following independent work time, gather children together in the meeting area to practice reading sentences with words in all capital letters.

Give a thumbs-up if you found any words in all capital letters when you were reading. Who would like to read what you found?

Extend the Lesson (Optional)

After assessing children's understanding, you might decide to extend the learning.

▶ As you come across examples of words in all capital letters during interactive read-aloud, pause to ask the children how the author wants those words to be read.

▶ Talk about why authors choose to use all capital letters for some words in stories and how knowing how to change your voice when reading helps you understand the story better.

▶ Revisit *CREAK! Said the Bed* and using simple props or pictures of the items that make sounds in the story, such as a door and a bed, have children recite the sound words in a strong voice as they ask each other what each noise (door, bed, thunder) sounds like.

Make your voice a little louder when you see a word in CAPITAL LETTERS.		
Title	Words in Capital Letters	Why Capital letters?
CREAK! Said the Bed	CREEK SQUEAK BOOM	The author wants you to know how the door the bed, and the thunder sound.
Max Found Two Sticks	BANG	The author wants you to know that Max is playing the drum loudly.
Charlie Parker played be bop	BANG	The author wants to show that the music is louder.

Reading Minilesson Principle
Put your words together so it sounds like talking.

You Will Need

- familiar books with short sentences and punctuation, such as these *Shared Reading Collection* books:
  - *The Sleeping Giant* by Barbara Gannet
  - *The Big Race: An Aesop Fable* adapted by David Edwin
- chart paper and markers

Academic Language / Important Vocabulary

- words
- title

Continuum Connection

- Use phrasing, pausing, and word stress with intonation when reading in unison (p. 117)

Goal

Read fluently with phrasing so that the reading sounds like talking.

Rationale

Before children read independently at about level C, they are focused on matching voice to print—making sure that there is a one-to-one match between the words they are saying and the words they are reading. Once they move beyond that focus and are taught to break down sentences into meaningful phrases, their reading will begin to sound like oral language or talking, reflecting the writer's meaning and enhancing their understanding.

Assess Learning

Observe children when they read aloud. Notice if there is evidence of new learning based on the goal of this minilesson.

- Can the children read words together in phrases?
- Do they sound like they are talking when they read?
- Are they able to monitor their reading for phrasing?
- Do they use the terms *words* and *title* correctly?

Minilesson

To help children think about the minilesson principle, demonstrate how to read fluently with phrasing. Here is an example.

- Show the cover of the book *The Sleeping Giant*. Read page 2 in an unexpressive, staccato voice, pointing underneath each word.

  What did you notice about how I read the words on this page? I read each word separately. Listen to me read the same page again.

- Read page 2 again in a normal, expressive voice, pointing to each line and phrase appropriately.

  What did you notice about the way I read the words this time?

  I put my words together so that it sounds like talking. Look at these words. These words make sense together, so I read them together. Why is it important to do that? This makes your reading easy to understand. It sounds interesting.

- Show the cover of the book *The Big Race*. Read page 6.

  Listen to how I read the words on this page from *The Big Race*. What did you notice about how I read the words on this page?

  When you read, make it sound like you are talking. Your words almost touch each other when you say them.

Have a Try

Invite the children to read with phrasing.

▶ Continue reading the next four pages of *The Big Race*.

Let's read the next few pages together. I will read them first and then you try. Make sure that you put your words together so it sounds like you are talking.

▶ Point to each line as they read to support phrased reading.

Summarize and Apply

Summarize the learning and remind children to read so it sounds interesting.

What did you learn today about reading?

▶ Write the principle at the top of the chart paper.

What could we put on our chart to remind you to put your words together when you read?

When you read your books today, listen to how your reading sounds. Make sure that you put your words together so that it sounds like you are talking.

Share

Following independent work time, gather children together in the meeting area to practice reading sentences.

When you read today, did you put your words together to sound like you were talking? Turn and read one page to your partner.

Extend the Lesson (Optional)

After assessing children's understanding, you might decide to extend the learning.

▶ During guided reading, use prompts such as these from *Prompting Guide, Part 1* (Fountas and Pinnell 2012) to teach, prompt, and reinforce how children read:

• *Read it like this [model phrase units]. You need to listen to how your reading sounds. Listen to how I put my words together: [model phrase units].*

• *Put your words together so it sounds like talking. Try that again and put your words together. Are you listening to how your reading sounds?*

• *You put your words together. You made it sound like talking. You made your words almost touch each other that time.*

▶ Cut up familiar poems into phrases and place them in a pocket chart for children to reassemble and practice reading fluently.

Assessment

After you have taught the minilessons in this umbrella, observe your children as they talk and write about their reading across instructional contexts: interactive read-aloud, independent reading and literacy work, guided reading, shared reading, and book club. Use *The Literacy Continuum* (Fountas & Pinnell 2017) to observe children's reading and writing behaviors across instructional contexts.

▶ What evidence do you have of new understandings related to reading fluently?

- Can children identify periods, question marks, and exclamation points?
- Do children make their voices go down and stop when they see a period at the end of a sentence?
- Do children make their voices go up when they see a question mark?
- Do they show strong feeling in their voices when they see an exclamation point?
- Can they read words in bold print or capital letters and make them sound important?
- How do they talk about changes in a reader's voice depending on the type of punctuation, bold words, or capital letters in a story?
- Do they make their reading sound like talking?
- Do they use the terms *words, period, question mark, exclamation point, title, bold print, author, capital letters* correctly when talking about reading fluently?

▶ In what other ways, beyond the scope of this umbrella, are the children recognizing and applying rules of punctuation?

- Can children talk about why an author decided to use a particular type of punctuation to match the meaning of the words in other stories?
- Are children able to identify the reasons why an author chooses special types of writing, such as bold words or all capital letters in other stories?

Use your observations to determine the next umbrella you will teach. You may also consult Minilessons Across the Year (p. 51) for guidance.

Link to Writing

After teaching the minilessons in this umbrella, help children link the new learning to their own writing or drawing about reading:

▶ Encourage children to write or dictate sentences to correspond to their own drawings, using periods, question marks, exclamation points, bold letters, or capital letters to match the intent of the sentence.

Section 4 | Writing About Reading

Throughout the kindergarten year, children will respond to what they read in a reader's notebook. These lessons help children use this important tool for independent literacy learning. Kindergarteners will create drawings in response to texts, but as the year progresses, they will increasingly use writing, too. All opportunities for drawing and writing about reading support the children in thinking about texts and articulating their understandings.

4 Writing About Reading

Minilessons in This Umbrella

RML1   Collect your thinking in your reader's notebook.

RML2   Draw and write about yourself and the things you love.

RML3   Draw and write about your family.

RML4   Draw and write about your friends.

RML5   Draw and write about the things you like to do at home.

RML6   Draw and write about the things you like to do at school.

RML7   Draw and write about the places you like to go.

Before Teaching Umbrella 1 Minilessons

The minilessons in this umbrella introduce the idea of a reader's notebook to the children and are examples of how to teach children to use the first few pages of the All About Me section of *Reader's Notebook: Primary* (Fountas and Pinnell 2014), but any reader's notebook can be used (see p. 46 for more on using a reader's notebook). The goal is for children to have a consistent place to collect their thinking about reading. The information can serve as a foundation for reading and writing topics. Use the following texts from the *Fountas & Pinnell Classroom™ Interactive Read-Aloud Collection* text sets or use similar books about experiences familiar to your class.

Letters at Work: The Alphabet

   ABC, I like Me! by Nancy Carlson

The Importance of Kindness

   Lost! by David McPhail

Taking Care of Each Other: Family

   Jonathan and His Mommy by Irene Smalls

The Importance of Friendship

   Jessica by Kevin Henkes

   A Visitor for Bear by Bonny Becker

Learning and Playing Together: School

   Miss Bindergarten Gets Ready for Kindergarten by Joseph Slate

As you read aloud and enjoy these texts together, help children

- think about themselves, their families, and their friends, and

- understand that they can draw pictures and write about books they read.

The Alphabet

Kindness

Family

Friendship

School

Reader's Notebook

Reading Minilesson Principle
Collect your thinking in your reader's notebook.

Introducing a Reader's Notebook

You Will Need

- *Reader's Notebook: Primary* or a reader's notebook for each child
- chart paper and markers
- projector (optional)

Academic Language / Important Vocabulary

- notebook
- cover
- tab
- sections

Goal

Understand a reader's notebook is a special place to collect thinking about oneself and books.

Rationale

Children need to learn how to respond to reading in different forms for a variety of purposes and audiences. A reader's notebook is a place for them to explain more about themselves as authors, keep records of their reading lives, and share their thinking about books through drawing and writing. This lesson is based on *Reader's Notebook: Primary* (Fountas and Pinnell 2014), but you can use this lesson to guide the creation of a generic reader's notebook.

Assess Learning

Your goal is to observe children when they use a reader's notebook. Notice if there is evidence of new learning based on the goal of this minilesson.

- Do you have evidence from the children's talk and front cover drawings that they understand the purpose of a reader's notebook?

Minilesson

To help children think about the minilesson principle, introduce the idea of using a reader's notebook. Here is a sample lesson.

- Give each child a reader's notebook. Provide one or two minutes for children to look through the notebook.

    Look through your new reader's notebook. When you are finished, place the book down gently in front of you with the front up and put your hands in your lap.

    What do you notice about the reader's notebook?

- If the children are using plain notebooks, you will want to talk about what will go in the notebook. You might have them place colored sticky notes as tabs to mark the three sections.

    The reader's notebook has three sections, or parts. You will write or draw something a little different in each section. Open the front of the notebook and you will find an orange tab that says All About Me. What do you think you will draw and write about in this section?

    The next section has a blue tab. It says Books I Read. What do you think you will draw and write about here?

    Way at the back of the book, the green tab says Letters and Words. What do you see in this section?

Have a Try

Invite the children to talk about what they might draw.

▶ Sketch an enlarged version of the front cover on chart paper (or project the cover of your copy).

> Because your reader's notebook belongs to you, you can decorate the front cover with a special picture.

> You can draw a picture of yourself or you might draw a picture of books you love, people you like to read with, or things you like to read about. Turn and talk to a partner about what you plan to draw.

▶ After children have turned and talked, ask a few children to share with the whole class and draw their ideas on the chart. Another possibility is to give them a small picture of themselves and let them glue it on and decorate a "frame" with things they like.

Summarize and Apply

Summarize the learning about the reader's notebook.

> Today you learned that your reader's notebook is a special place to draw and write about your thinking.

> During reading time today, decorate the front cover of your reader's notebook. First, write your name on the cover like this.

▶ Model writing your name on the chart paper example. Decide if you want your children to also fill out the name of the school and the grade or you can have them filled out before you give the children the notebook.

> Once you have written your name and decorated the front cover, it will be your own special notebook. Stop drawing and writing when you finish the front cover. Be ready to share your drawing when we come back together after independent work time.

Share

Following independent work time, gather children in the meeting area with their drawings.

> Turn and talk with a partner about the drawing you made on your reader's notebook.

Extend the Lesson (Optional)

After assessing your children's understanding, you might decide to extend the learning.

▶ Have children integrate the use of a reader's notebook to collect their responses to books from interactive read-aloud and guided reading.

Reading Minilesson Principle
Draw and write about yourself and the things you love.

Introducing a Reader's Notebook

You Will Need

- a book about self-identity, such as *ABC I Like Me!* by Nancy Carlson, from Text Set: Alphabet
- chart paper prepared to look like the Me page in *Reader's Notebook: Primary*
- markers
- projector (optional)
- *Reader's Notebook: Primary* or a reader's notebook for each child

Academic Language / Important Vocabulary

- special
- reader's notebook

Continuum Connection

- Use a text as a resource for words, phrases, and ideas for writing (p. 172)

Goal

Draw and write to tell about oneself.

Rationale

When children draw and write about themselves in a reader's notebook, they communicate what makes them unique and special. As children share their thinking about themselves with their classmates, they become a member of a community of readers and writers who share interests and recommend books to each other.

Assess Learning

Observe children when they use a reader's notebook. Notice if there is evidence of new learning based on the goal of this minilesson.

- ▶ Do children draw and write in a reader's notebook about themselves and what they love?
- ▶ Do they approximate the spelling of unknown words?

Minilesson

To help children think about the minilesson principle, talk about how they can draw and write about what makes them special, the way an author writes about characters in a book. Here is an example.

▶ Show *ABC I Like Me!* Reread the first few pages of the book. Ask what the children notice the author told about in this book.

> In this book, you learned about what the pig, frog, and mouse like about themselves. The author also told you what the characters like to do. In your reader's notebook, you have a place to draw and write about yourself, just like Nancy Carlson wrote about the frog, pig, and mouse.

▶ If you are using *Reader's Notebook: Primary*, open to the orange tab and show the page labeled *Me*. Point to and say the word *Me*.

> On this page, you can draw and write about yourself. You will use just one page at a time to tell about yourself. Watch as I draw and write about me.

▶ Model for the children how they will draw and write in a reader's notebook, using a sketch of the page on chart paper (or projecting your own copy of the notebook).

> I want to tell about how I look. What could I draw?

> You know I love to read. What could I draw to show I love reading?

> What else do you know about me?

▶ Provide as many examples as you think your children will need to help them share about themselves.

Have a Try

Invite the children to talk with a partner about what is special about themselves.

> Look at how I filled in the Me page. Now think about your Me page. Think about what is special about you. Turn and talk to a partner about what you are going to draw and write on your page.

▶ After the partners have talked, ask a few children to share what they are going to put on their Me page.

Summarize and Apply

Summarize the learning and have children use a reader's notebook to tell about themselves.

> Today you learned that you have a special place in your reader's notebook to tell about yourself.

▶ Assist children in finding (or creating) the Me page. Show them the white square and lines where they will draw and write.

> Doing your best work, draw a picture to tell about yourself on your Me page. You can label your pictures or write about yourself on the lines under the drawing. If you don't know how to write any of the words, give them a try.

▶ Many children may not be writing conventionally yet. Encourage their attempts, knowing that as the year progresses, they will be able to produce more writing.

Section 4: Writing About Reading

Share

Following independent work time, gather children in the meeting area to share their drawing and writing.

> Turn and talk with a partner and share your drawing and writing about yourself on your Me page. Listen to your partner and answer questions about your page.

Extend the Lesson (Optional)

After assessing children's understanding, you might decide to extend the learning.

▶ If children are not yet writing, use interactive writing to add writing to their Me page. Or, quickly write what a child dictates.

▶ Provide additional reading minilessons to demonstrate how the children can add writing or labels to their drawings.

RML3
WAR.U1.RML3

Reading Minilesson Principle
Draw and write about your family.

Introducing a Reader's Notebook

You Will Need

- a book about family members, such as *Jonathan and His Mommy* by Irene Smalls, from Text Set: Family

- chart paper prepared to look like *My Family* page in *Reader's Notebook: Primary*

- markers

- projector (optional)

- *Reader's Notebook: Primary* or a reader's notebook for each child

Academic Language / Important Vocabulary

- family

- reader's notebook

Continuum Connection

- Use a text as a resource for words, phrases, and ideas for writing (p. 172)

Goal

Draw and write about families in a reader's notebook.

Rationale

Kindergarteners read many books about families. When they draw and write about their own families, they think about what is special about their families and make connections to books about families.

Assess Learning

Observe children when they use a reader's notebook. Notice if there is evidence of new learning based on the goal of this minilesson.

- Are children able to think of something to draw and write about their families and what they love doing together?

- Are children able to approximate the spelling of unknown words?

- Do they use the terms *family* and *reader's notebook* in conversation?

Minilesson

To help children think about the minilesson principle, talk about how they can draw and write about their family, just like an author does in a book. Here is an example.

- Show *Jonathan and His Mommy*.

  When we read this story, we learned all the things Jonathan likes to do with his mom. The author tells what the family likes to do together. You can tell about your family and all the things you like to do together in your reader's notebook, almost like Irene Smalls did in *Jonathan and His Mommy*.

- If you are using *Reader's Notebook: Primary*, open to the My Family page behind the orange tab.

  On this page, you can draw and write about things your family likes to do together. You will use just one page at a time to tell about your family.

- Model for the children how they will draw and write in a reader's notebook, using a sketch of the page on chart paper (or projecting your own copy of the notebook). Draw and write about what your family likes to do together.

  What did you learn about my family from my drawing and writing?

  Share some things your family likes to do together.

Have a Try

Invite the children to talk to a partner about their family.

> Look at how I filled in the My Family page. Now think about your My Family page. Think about what your family does together. Turn and talk to a partner about what you are going to draw and write on your page.

Summarize and Apply

Summarize the learning and have the children use a reader's notebook to tell about their family.

▶ Make sure each child has a notebook. Assist children in finding (or creating) the My Family page. Show them the white square and lines where they will draw and write.

> Doing your best work, draw a picture to tell about your family on your My Family page. You can label your pictures or write about your family on the lines under the drawing. If you don't know how to write any of the words, give them a try.

▶ Many children may not be writing conventionally yet. Encourage their attempts, knowing that as the year progresses, they will be able to produce more writing.

Share

Following independent work time, gather children in the meeting area to share their drawing and writing.

> Turn and talk with a partner and share your My Family page. Remember to listen to your partner and answer questions about your drawing and writing.

Extend the Lesson (Optional)

After assessing children's understanding, you might decide to extend the learning.

▶ If necessary, provide follow-up reading minilessons to teach children how to add details to their drawings.

▶ Model for the whole class or small groups how to label drawings and write simple sentences about their families.

▶ Use shared or interactive writing to demonstrate how to write labels or simple sentences about their drawings.

Section 4: Writing About Reading

Reading Minilesson Principle
Draw and write about your friends.

Introducing a Reader's Notebook

You Will Need

- a book about friendship that shows friends doing activities together, such as *Jessica* by Kevin Henkes, from Text Set: Friendship

- chart paper resembling the My Friends page in *Reader's Notebook: Primary*

- markers

- projector (optional)

- *Reader's Notebook: Primary* or a reader's notebook for each child

Academic Language / Important Vocabulary

- reader's notebook

- special

Continuum Connection

- Use a text as a resource for words, phrases, and ideas for writing (p. 172)

Goal

Draw and write about oneself and friends.

Rationale

Kindergarteners read many books about friendship and talk about how to respect others. When they draw and write about their friends, they find connections to characters and themes in the books they listen to and read.

Assess Learning

Observe children when they use a reader's notebook. Notice if there is evidence of new learning based on the goal of this minilesson.

- ▶ Are children able to draw something about their friends?

- ▶ Do they include labels or writing to explain what they like to do with their friends?

- ▶ Do they approximate the spelling of unknown words?

- ▶ Do they use the terms *special* and *reader's notebook*?

Minilesson

To help children think about the minilesson principle, talk about how they can draw and write about their friends, just like an author does in a book. Here is an example.

- ▶ Show the cover of *Jessica*. Invite children to notice pictures. Help children notice that each picture shows something that Jessica and Ruthie like to do together.

    In this story, you learned things Ruthie liked to do with her imaginary friend, Jessica. You have a special place in your reader's notebook to tell about your friends, almost like Kevin Henkes did in *Jessica*.

- ▶ If you are using *Reader's Notebook: Primary*, open to the orange tab turn to the My Friends page.

    On this special page, you can draw and write about your friends. You will use just one page at a time to tell about your friends.

- ▶ Model for the children how they will draw and write in a reader's notebook, using a sketch of the page on chart paper (or projecting your own copy of the notebook). Make sketches as the children respond.

    What do you like to do with your friends?

    When you draw and write about things you like to do with your friends, you show what is special to you about your friends.

Have a Try

Invite the children to talk with a partner about what they like to do with friends.

> Look at how I filled in the My Friends page. Now think about you're My Friends page. Think about what you and your friends like to do. Turn and talk to a partner about what you are going to draw and write on your page.

▶ After the partners have talked, ask a few children to share what they are going to put on their My Friends page.

Summarize and Apply

Summarize the learning and remind the children to use a reader's notebook to tell about their friends.

▶ Make sure each child has a notebook. Assist children in finding (or creating) the My Friends page. Show them the white square and lines where they will draw and write.

> Doing your best work, draw a picture to tell about your friends on your My Friends page. You can label your pictures or write about your friends on the lines under the drawing. If you don't know any of the words, give them a try.

▶ Many children may not be writing conventionally yet. Encourage their attempts, knowing that as the year progresses, they will be able to produce more writing.

Share

Following independent work time, gather children in the meeting area to share their drawing and writing.

> Turn and talk with a partner about what you drew and wrote on the My Friends page. Remember to take turns and listen to your partner.

Extend the Lesson (Optional)

After assessing children's understanding, you might decide to extend the learning.

▶ Use interactive or shared writing to demonstrate how to label or write about a drawing.

▶ Reference the My Friends page during interactive read-aloud or in other instructional contexts to support children in making connections and developing opinions about characters. Have them think about what they like about friends and if they could be friends with characters in their books.

My Friends

We like to play soccer.

Reading Minilesson Principle
Draw and write about the things you like to do at home.

Introducing a Reader's Notebook

You Will Need

- a book about family, such as *A Visitor for Bear* by Bonny Becker, from Text Set: Family
- chart paper prepared to look like the Things I Like to Do at Home page in *Reader's Notebook: Primary*
- markers
- projector (optional)
- *Reader's Notebook: Primary* or a reader's notebook for each child

Academic Language / Important Vocabulary

- special
- home
- reader's notebook

Continuum Connection

- Use a text as a resource for words, phrases, and ideas for writing (p. 172)

Goal

Draw and write about things one likes to do at home.

Rationale

When children draw and write about things they like to do at home, they communicate their interests and preferences. When they identify their interests, they will more easily select books that they will enjoy during independent reading.

Assess Learning

Observe children when they use a reader's notebook. Notice if there is evidence of new learning based on the goal of this minilesson.

- Do children draw and write about the things they like to do at home?
- Do they approximate the spelling of unknown words?
- Do they use the terms *special*, *home*, and *reader's notebook*?

Minilesson

To help children think about the minilesson principle, talk about how they can draw and write about what they like to do at home. Here is an example.

> Sometimes when you choose books from the classroom library for independent reading, you read about what the characters like to do at home.

- Show *A Visitor for Bear*.

> Do you remember some things that Bear liked to do at home? You might like to do some of the same things, and you can draw and write about that in your reader's notebook.

- If you are using *Reader's Notebook: Primary*, open to the orange tab turn to the Things I Like to Do at Home page.

> On this special page, you can draw and write about what you like to do at home. You will use just one page at a time to tell about that.

- Model for the children how they will draw and write in a reader's notebook, using a sketch of the page on chart paper (or projecting your own copy of the notebook). Make a sketch of what you like to do.

> What could I write to go with my picture?

> When you draw and write about things you like to do at home, you might get an idea for what you would like to read about.

Have a Try

Invite the children to talk with a partner about what they like to do at home.

> Look at how I filled in the Things I Like to Do at Home page. Now think about the same page in your reader's notebook. Turn and talk to a partner about what you are going to draw and write on your page.

▶ After the partners have talked, ask a few children to share what they are going to put on their Things I Like to Do at Home page.

Summarize and Apply

Summarize the learning and have children use a reader's notebook to tell about things they like to do at home.

▶ Make sure each child has a notebook. Assist children in finding (or creating) the Things I Like to Do at Home page. Show them the white square and lines where they will draw and write.

> Doing your best work, draw a picture to tell what you like to do at home. You can label your pictures or write about what you do at home on the lines under the drawing. If you don't know how to write any of the words, just give them a try.

▶ Many children may not be writing conventionally yet. Encourage their attempts, knowing that as the year progresses, they will be able to produce more writing.

Share

Following independent work time, gather children in the meeting area to share their drawing and writing.

> Turn and talk with a partner and share your drawing and writing about what you like to do at home. Remember to ask questions and listen carefully when your partner answers.

Extend the Lesson (Optional)

After assessing children's understanding, you might decide to extend the learning.

▶ Use interactive writing or shared writing to demonstrate how to add labels or writing to their pictures.

▶ Provide the opportunity during writers' workshop or in the writing center for children to write more or make books about the things they like to do at home.

Things I Like to Do at Home

I like to cook.

Reading Minilesson Principle
Draw and write about the things you like to do at school.

Introducing a Reader's Notebook

You Will Need

- a book about school, such as *Miss Bindergarten Gets Ready for Kindergarten* by Joseph Slate, from Text Set: School
- chart paper prepared to look like the Things I Like to Do at School page in *Reader's Notebook: Primary*
- markers
- projector (optional)
- *Reader's Notebook: Primary* or a reader's notebook for each child

Academic Language / Important Vocabulary

- school
- reader's notebook

Continuum Connection

- Use a text as a resource for words, phrases, and ideas for writing (p. 172)

Goal

Draw and write about the things one likes to do at school.

Rationale

A reader's notebook is a place for children to discover their interests and develop their reading identities. When children think and draw about what they like to do at school, they become more aware of their interests, which will help them to select books they will enjoy.

Assess Learning

Observe children when they use a reader's notebook. Notice if there is evidence of new learning based on the goal of this minilesson.

- ▶ Do children draw and write about the things they like to do at school?
- ▶ Are they able to explain their drawings to their classmates?
- ▶ Do they approximate the spelling of unknown words?
- ▶ Do they use the terms *school* and *reader's notebook* in conversation?

Minilesson

To help children think about the minilesson principle, talk about how they can draw and write about what they like to do at school. Here is an example.

- ▶ Show a few pages of *Miss Bindergarten Gets Ready for Kindergarten* to get children thinking about activities at school.

  Remember all of the things Miss Bindergarten got ready for the children? The children in her class did a lot of fun things in her classroom. You can draw and write about all the things you like to do at school.

- ▶ If you are using *Reader's Notebook: Primary*, open to the orange tab turn to the Things I Like to Do at School page.

  On this special page, you can draw and write about what you like to do at school. You will use just one page at a time to tell about that.

- ▶ Model for the children how they will draw and write in a reader's notebook, using a sketch of the page on chart paper (or projecting your own copy of the notebook). Make sketches in response to what the children suggest.

  What could I write to go with my picture?

  When you draw and write about things you like to do at home, you might get an idea for what you would like to read about.

  Notice that some of the things you like are the same as your friends and some things are different.

Have a Try

Invite the children to talk with a partner about things they like to do at school.

> Look at how I filled in the Things I Like to Do at School page. Now think about the same page in your reader's notebook. Turn and talk to a partner about what you are going to draw and write on your page. Make sure both of you have a chance to talk and that you listen to each other.

▶ After the partners have talked, ask a few children to share what they are going to put on their Things I Like to Do at School page.

Summarize and Apply

Summarize the learning and have children use a reader's notebook to tell about things they like to do at school.

▶ Make sure each child has a notebook. Assist children in finding (or creating) the Things I Like to Do at School page. Show them the white square and lines where they will draw and write.

> Doing your best work, draw a picture to tell what you like to do at school, just like I did. You can label your pictures or write about what you do at school on the lines under the drawing. If you don't know how to write any of the words, give them a try.

▶ Many children may not be writing conventionally yet. Encourage their attempts, knowing that as the year progresses, they will be able to produce more writing.

Share

Following independent work time, gather children in the meeting area to share their drawing and writing.

> Share what you drew and wrote about school in your reader's notebook. Remember to listen carefully to what your partner says. It's okay to ask a question about your partner's page. Be ready to share what you and your partner talked about.

▶ Invite several children to share with the whole group.

Extend the Lesson (Optional)

After assessing your children's understanding, you might decide to extend the learning.

▶ Use interactive writing or shared writing to help children write labels or simple sentences.

▶ Reference the Things I Like to Do at School page as children self-select books to encourage them to choose books about their interests.

Things I Like to Do at School

play | paint

I like to play.
I like to paint.

Section 4: Writing About Reading

Reading Minilesson Principle
Draw and write about the places you like to go.

Introducing a
Reader's Notebook

You Will Need

- a book that has different places, such as *Lost!* by David McPhail, from Text Set: Kindness
- chart paper resembling the Places I Like to Go page in *Reader's Notebook: Primary*
- markers
- projector (optional)
- *Reader's Notebook: Primary* or a reader's notebook for each child

Academic Language / Important Vocabulary

- special
- places
- reader's notebook

Continuum Connection

- Use a text as a resource for words, phrases, and ideas (p. 172)

Goal

Draw and write about places one likes to go.

Rationale

When children share their thinking about places they like to go, they identify and record their interests. Children need to learn how to choose and read about things that interest them. When they articulate their interests, the information will also support them in choosing topics they want to draw and write about.

Assess Learning

Observe children when they use a reader's notebook. Notice if there is evidence of new learning based on the goal of this minilesson.

- ⟩ Are the children able to draw and write about special places they like to go?
- ⟩ Are they able to talk about their drawing and writing?
- ⟩ Do they approximate the spelling of unknown words?
- ⟩ Do they use the terms *special*, *places*, and *reader's notebook*?

Minilesson

To help children think about the minilesson principle, talk about how they can draw and write about places they like to go. Here is an example.

⟩ Show *Lost!* Turn to pages that show the different places bear visited (for example, elevator in tall building, park, playground, library, forest).

In this book, the bear was lost, and the boy helped him find a home. As they looked for a home, they visited a lot of different places. What did you notice about some of the places they visited?

Bear liked some places but didn't like others. You have a special place in your reader's notebook to tell about places you like to go.

⟩ If you are using *Reader's Notebook: Primary*, open to the orange tab turn to the Places I Like to Go page.

On this special page, you can draw and write about places you like to go. You will use just one page at a time to tell about that.

⟩ Model for the children how they will draw and write in a reader's notebook, using a sketch of the page on chart paper (or projecting your own copy of the notebook). Make sketches in response to what the children suggest.

What could I write to go with my picture?

When you draw and write about places you like to go, you might get an idea for what you would like to read about.

Have a Try

Invite the children to talk with a partner about places they like to go.

> Look at how I filled in the Places I Like to Go page. Now think about the same page in your reader's notebook. Turn and talk to a partner about what you are going to draw and write on your page. Make sure both of you have a chance to talk and that you listen to each other.

▶ After the partners have talked, ask a few children to share what they are going to put on their own Places I Like to Go page.

Summarize and Apply

Summarize the learning and have children use a reader's notebook to tell about places they like to go.

▶ Make sure each child has a notebook. Assist children in finding (or creating) the Places I Like to Go page. Show them the white square and lines where they will draw and write.

> Doing your best work, draw a picture to tell where you like to go, just like I did. You can label your pictures or write about where you like to go on the lines under the drawing. If you don't know how to write any of the words, give them a try.

▶ Many children may not be writing conventionally yet. Encourage their attempts, knowing that as the year progresses, they will be able to produce more writing.

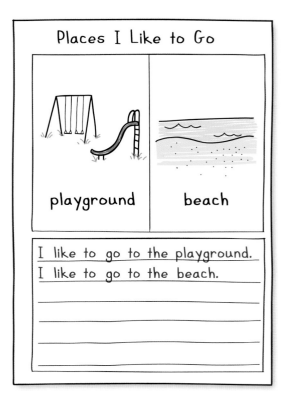

Share

Following independent work time, gather children in the meeting area to share their drawing and writing.

> Turn to a partner and share what you drew and wrote about where you like to go. Remember to listen to each other carefully. You may ask each other questions about the drawings.

Extend the Lesson (Optional)

After assessing your children's understanding, you might decide to extend the learning.

▶ Use interactive or shared writing to support children in adding labels or simple sentences.

▶ Reference the Places I Like to Go page of the reader's notebook when children self-select books to encourage them to choose books about their interests.

Assessment

After you have taught the minilessons in this umbrella, observe children as they talk and write about their reading across instructional contexts: interactive read-aloud, independent reading and literacy work, guided reading, shared reading, and book club. Use the *The Literacy Continuum* (Fountas and Pinnell 2017) to observe your children's reading and writing behaviors across instructional contexts.

▶ What evidence do you have of new understandings related to the All About Me section of *Reader's Notebook: Primary?*

  • Are children able to draw and write about themselves, their friends, and their family?

  • Do they identify their interests, drawing and writing about things they like to do and places they like to go?

  • Do they understand and use the terms *reader's notebook, tab, section,* and *special?*

▶ What other parts of a reader's notebook might you introduce to your children based on your observations?

  • Are children able to distinguish between fiction and nonfiction books?

  • How are they sharing their opinions about books?

  • Do you see evidence that they are drawing and writing about books they read in meaningful ways?

Use your observations to determine the next umbrella you will teach. You may also consult Minilessons Across the Year (p. 51) for guidance.

Link to Writing

After teaching the minilessons in this umbrella, help children link the new learning to their own writing.

▶ Provide opportunities for the children to write or draw more about family, friends, things they like to do at home or at school, or places they like to go during writers' workshop or as part of a writing center activity. Children can use something they drew and wrote in a reader's notebook as a starting point for further drawing and writing with more detail.

Minilessons in This Umbrella

RML1   Make a list of the books you love.

RML2   Make a list of the authors you love.

RML3   Make a list of the illustrators you love.

RML4   Make a list of the characters you love.

RML5   Write and draw to show things you like to read about.

RML6   Write and draw to show things you like to write about.

RML7   Use the lists in your reader's notebook to help you choose books.

Before Teaching Umbrella 2 Minilessons

The minilessons in this umbrella are based on *Reader's Notebook: Primary* (Fountas and Pinnell 2014), but any notebook can be used (see p. 46 for more on using a reader's notebook). It would be helpful to complete several author and illustrator studies (e.g., Eric Carle, Lois Ehlert) before starting the minilessons here.

These minilessons reference books from *Fountas and Pinnell Classroom™ Interactive Read-Aloud Collection* text sets Sharing Stories: Folktales, Taking Care of Each Other: Family, The Importance of Friendship, Noticing the Way the World Looks: Colors, and The Place Called Home as well as the following individual titles. Use any fiction texts with which children are familiar.

Kindness

Jamaica's Find by Juanita Havill

Lost! By David McPhail

School

Miss Bindergarten Gets Ready for Kindergarten by Joseph Slate

Look Out Kindergarten, Here I Come! by Nancy Carlson

Differences

Big Al by Andrew Clements

Animal Tales

The Little Red Hen by Paul Galdone

Animals

Elephants Swim by Linda Capus Riley

Actual Size by Steve Jenkins

Prepare children for writing in a reader's notebook by helping them

- talk about their favorite books,
- listen to and look at the illustrations in books by the same authors and illustrators, and
- share their opinions about what they like to read about.

Kindness

School

Differences

Animal Tales

Animals

Reader's Notebook

RML 1

WAR.U2.RML1

Reading Minilesson Principle
Make a list of the books you love.

Using a Reader's Notebook

You Will Need

- three or four favorite books, such as the following from Text Set: Kindness:
  - *Jamaica's Find* by Juanita Havill
  - *Lost!* by David McPhail
- chart paper prepared to look like the Books I Love page in *Reader's Notebook: Primary*
- markers
- projector (optional)
- *Reader's Notebook: Primary* or a reader's notebook for each child
- basket of class favorite books

Academic Language / Important Vocabulary

- author
- title
- reader's notebook

Continuum Connection

- Attempt to independently record text titles and authors in Reader's Notebook (may be drawings) (p. 172)

Goal

Be aware of favorite books and list the titles in a reader's notebook.

Rationale

When children use a reader's notebook to make a list of books they love, they identify their favorite books and learn to make lists as a way of remembering them.

Assess Learning

Observe children when they write and draw about books they read. Notice if there is evidence of new learning based on the goal of this minilesson.

- Do the children write the title and draw about a favorite book on the Books I Love page?
- Are they able to explain why they selected a particular book?
- Do they use the terms *author*, *title*, and *reader's notebook* in conversation?

Minilesson

To help children think about the minilesson principle, demonstrate how to write a list of favorite book titles. Here is an example.

- Show *Jamaica's Find*. Display the chart (or project the page from *Reader's Notebook: Primary*). Point to and say the words *Books I Love*.

  This is a special page in the reader's notebook. What do you think you could write and draw on this page?

  You can keep a list of the books you love in your reader's notebook. Watch as I write on the Books I Love Page in the reader's notebook.

- Write the titles and draw a sketch on chart paper to go with the book on the chart paper.

  What do you notice I wrote and drew on this page?

- Show *Lost!*

  Here is another book that I love. How should I add this book to the Books I Love list?

- Ask a volunteer to point to the title of the book and another to the place where you should write it. As you write, model checking each letter in the title.

  What did you notice about how I wrote the first letter in each word?

  What are some ideas for a drawing to go with this book?

- Using children's suggestions, add the drawing to the chart.

- If you are using *Reader's Notebook: Primary*, children can open to the orange tab and turn to the Books I Love page. If not, assist children in labeling a page *Books I Love* in a reader's notebook.

  On this page, you can make a list of the books you love.

Have a Try

Invite the children to talk about favorite books with a partner.

▶ Show covers of three or four more of the children's favorite books.

> Here are some books we have enjoyed together. Think about books for your Books I Love list. You might choose one of these to add to your list, or you might have another book you can add.

> Turn and talk to your partner about one of books you will put on your list.

Summarize and Apply

Summarize the learning and remind children to think about books they love to read.

> Review the chart with the children.

> What page in your reader's notebook did you learn about today?

> What can you write and draw on that page?

> Choose a favorite book you have read and put the title on your list. Pick one from the basket or choose one of your own. Bring your reader's notebook when we come back together so you can share your Books I Love page.

Share

Following independent work time, gather children together in the meeting area in groups of three to talk about books they love.

> Show what you wrote and drew on your Books I Love page. Talk about the book you picked and why you chose the book.

Extend the Lesson (Optional)

After assessing children's understanding, you might decide to extend the learning.

▶ Visit the school library with the children and ask the librarian about books that he loves and why. Children can share their Books I Love lists with the librarian.

▶ Record children talking about books they love. You may want to reference the reading minilesson on giving book talks in Section Two: Literary Analysis.

▶ Continue to have children add to their Books I Love lists during independent literacy work time. See the Section One: Management reading minilesson on using the reader's notebook icon.

RML2
WAR.U2.RML2

Reading Minilesson Principle
Make a list of the authors you love.

Using a
Reader's Notebook

You Will Need

- multiple text sets by the same authors, such as Text Set: Eric Carle or Text Set: Lois Ehlert
- chart paper prepared to look like the Authors I Love page in *Reader's Notebook: Primary*
- markers
- projector (optional)
- *Reader's Notebook: Primary*, or a reader's notebook for each child
- basket of books by favorite authors

Academic Language / Important Vocabulary

- author
- reader's notebook

Continuum Connection

- Recognize that an author or illustrator may write or illustrate several books (p. 28)
- Attempt to independently record text titles and authors in Reader's Notebook (may be drawings) (p. 172)

Goal

Be aware of favorite authors and learn to list their names in a reader's notebook.

Rationale

When you show children how to use a reader's notebook to list the names of their favorite authors, you encourage them to think about why they are drawn to certain books, and what they notice and enjoy about the author's writing style. They develop their tastes as readers.

Assess Learning

Observe children when they write and draw about authors they love. Notice if there is evidence of new learning based on the goal of this minilesson.

- Do children write the name of their favorite author and draw pictures on the Authors I Love page?
- Are they able to explain why they love an author?

Minilesson

To help children think about the minilesson principle, demonstrate how to write a list of favorite authors. Here is an example.

- Display the chart you prepared (or project the page from *Reader's Notebook: Primary*). Point to *Authors I Love* as you read the words with the children.

  What do you think you should write and draw on this page?

- Show one to two books by Eric Carle.

  I love Eric Carle's books, so I will put his name and a picture to remind me of his book in the reader's notebook. What do you notice about the first letter of each part of his name?

- As needed, point out that the author's name begins with capital letters and matches the way it looks on his book covers.

- Display several books by Lois Ehlert.

  I also love Lois Ehlert. Where should I add Lois Ehlert to my list?

- Have a child point to where you can add her name. Have another locate her name on a book. As you write the name, ask what they are noticing.

  What could I draw to show I love Lois Ehlert's writing?

- Make a sketch based on responses.

- If you are using *Reader's Notebook: Primary*, children can open to the orange tab and turn to the Authors I Love page. If not, assist children in finding and labeling a page *Authors I Love* in a reader's notebook.

  On this page, make a list of the authors you love.

Have a Try

Invite the children talk with a partner about authors they love.

▶ Show children a few books by authors they have studied or whose books they have read many times.

> Turn and talk to a partner about which authors you will add to your Authors I Love list. You may choose one of these authors, or you may have other ideas.

Summarize and Apply

Summarize the learning and remind children to notice the author's name when they read a book they love.

▶ Draw children's attention to the chart.

> What did you learn today about writing in your reader's notebook?

> During independent reading, choose a book by one of your favorite authors. You can choose from the books in this basket or others you have read. Write the name of the author in your reader's notebook. You can add a picture about the book you read. Bring your reader's notebook when we come back together so you can share your page.

Share

Following independent work time, gather children together in the meeting area in groups of three to talk about their favorite authors.

> Show the Authors I Love page in your reader's notebook to your group. Tell the author's name and why you like the author.

Extend the Lesson (Optional)

After assessing children's understanding, you might decide to extend the learning.

▶ Visit the web pages of favorite authors with the children to learn more about the authors. Share the information, such as photos, videos, and book-themed games.

▶ Write a class letter to a favorite author using shared or interactive writing.

▶ Teach children how to use the Authors I Love list as a resource for choosing books.

RML3
WAR.U2.RML3

Reading Minilesson Principle
Make a list of the illustrators you love.

Using a Reader's Notebook

You Will Need

- multiple text sets by the same illustrator, such as Text Set: Eric Carle or Text Set: Lois Ehlert
- chart paper prepared to look like the Illustrators I Love page in *Reader's Notebook: Primary*
- markers
- projector (optional)
- *Reader's Notebook: Primary*, or a reader's notebook for each child
- basket of books by favorite illustrators

Academic Language / Important Vocabulary

- illustrator
- illustration
- reader's notebook

Continuum Connection

- Recognize that an author or illustrator may write or illustrate several books (p. 28)
- Understand that an illustrator created the pictures in the book (p. 29)

Goal

Be aware of favorite illustrators and list the illustrators' names in a reader's notebook.

Rationale

When children use a reader's notebook to list the names of illustrators they love, you are encouraging them to think about the illustrator's craft and begin to think about why they love certain illustrations. You also help them understand how the illustrator and author work together.

Assess Learning

Observe children when they write and draw about illustrators they love. Notice if there is evidence of new learning based on the goal of this minilesson.

- ▶ Can the children write and draw about a favorite illustrator on the Illustrators I Love page?
- ▶ Are they able to share what they enjoy about a favorite illustrator?
- ▶ Do they use the terms *illustrator*, *illustration*, and *reader's notebook* in conversation?

Minilesson

To help children think about the minilesson principle, demonstrate how to write a list of favorite illustrators. Here is an example.

- ▶ Display the prepared chart of the Illustrators I Love page (or project the page from *Reader's Notebook: Primary*). Point to *Illustrators I Love* as you read the words with the children.

  Your reader's notebook is a place where you can write and draw about the books you like to read and look at. What will you write on this page?

  You can write the illustrators' names. You can also draw a picture on this page to help remember one or two of the illustrators. I'm going to try that with one of our favorite illustrators, Eric Carle.

- ▶ Display several books by Eric Carle. As you write, model how to find the illustrator's name and how to copy it.

  What should we draw for this illustrator?

- ▶ Make a quick sketch based on the children's responses.
- ▶ Repeat with Lois Ehlert.
- ▶ If you are using *Reader's Notebook: Primary*, children can open to the orange tab and turn to the Illustrators I Love page. If not, assist children in finding and labeling a page Illustrators I Love in a reader's notebook.

Have a Try

Invite the children to talk with a partner about illustrators they love.

▶ Show children a few books by illustrators they have studied or have read many times. Read the titles and illustrators' names.

> Here are some books with illustrations by illustrators we love. Think about which illustrator you would write on your Illustrators I Love page. Turn and talk to your partner about which one you will add.

▶ Ask several volunteers to share which illustrator they will list and why.

Summarize and Apply

Summarize the learning and remind children to notice the illustrator's name when they see illustrations they love.

▶ Draw children's attention to the chart.

> What did you learn today about writing in your reader's notebook?

> During independent reading, choose a book that has illustrations you love. You can choose from the books in this basket or others you have read. Write the name of that illustrator in your reader's notebook. You can add a picture about the book. Bring your reader's notebook when we come back together so you can share.

Illustrators I Love

Eric Carle
Lois Ehlert
Mark Pett
Grace Lin

Share

Following independent work time, gather children together in the meeting area to talk about the illustrators they love.

> Who would like to share an illustrator's name you wrote on your Illustrators I Love page?

> Why do you like that illustrator?

Extend the Lesson (Optional)

After assessing children's understanding, you might decide to extend the learning.

▶ Visit the web pages of favorite illustrators to help the children learn more about the illustrators' artwork.

▶ Notice and talk about the way favorite illustrators create their illustrations. Provide art materials so children can make illustrations using the same methods.

RML4
WAR.U2.RML4

Reading Minilesson Principle
Make a list of the characters you love.

You Will Need

- several familiar books with memorable characters, such as the following:
  - *Big Al* by Andrew Clements, from Text Set: Differences
  - *The Little Red Hen* by Patricia Siebert, from Text Set: Animal Tales
- chart paper prepared to look like the Characters I Love page in *Reader's Notebook: Primary*
- markers
- projector (optional)
- *Reader's Notebook: Primary*, or a reader's notebook for each child
- basket of books with memorable characters

Academic Language / Important Vocabulary

- character
- reader's notebook

Continuum Connection

- Notice and remember characters in simple narrative (p. 29)
- Identify characters in a story with labels (after drawing) (p. 173)

Goal

Be aware of favorite characters in stories and list the characters' names in a reader's notebook.

Rationale

When children use a reader's notebook to draw and write about favorite characters, they have an opportunity to reflect on why they connect with and enjoy characters in stories. This helps children to develop their reading interests and ability to articulate how they relate to characters. This connection to the characters will deepen children's understanding of the text. If you have already taught lessons on the pages about beloved books, authors, and illustrators, note the similarities with the Characters I Love page.

Assess Learning

Observe children when they write and draw about characters they love. Notice if there is evidence of new learning based on the goal of this minilesson.

- Can the children write a character's name and draw about it on the Characters I Love page?
- Are they able to tell why they love the character?
- Do they use the terms *character* and *reader's notebook* in conversation?

Minilesson

To help children think about the minilesson principle, demonstrate how to write a list of favorite characters. Here is an example.

- Display the prepared chart for the Characters I Love page (or project the page from *Reader's Notebook: Primary*). Point to the title as you read the words with the children.

  What do you think you will write and draw about on this page?

  Let's think about characters we have read about and make a list.

- Show *Big Al*.

  Who were the characters in this book?

- As they suggest characters, invite them to share why they loved those characters.

  Where can you find how to write the names of the characters?

  I am going to write the character's name on a line and make a label for my drawing.

- Invite a child to show where to find the characters' names. Model using the book to spell the name. Point out that sometimes a name is in the title and sometimes you have to look in the book.

- Repeat with *The Little Red Hen*.

▶ When completed, read the list and talk about what you could draw to go with the list. If you are using *Reader's Notebook: Primary*, children can open to the orange tab and turn to the Characters I Love page. If not, assist in finding and labeling a page in a reader's notebook.

Have a Try

Invite the children to talk with a partner about characters they love.

▶ Show children a few books from the book basket with characters they enjoyed reading or books with characters they have read many times.

> Think about one or two characters you plan to put on your Characters I Love list in your reader's notebook. Turn and talk to your partner about why you love those characters.

Summarize and Apply

Summarize the learning and remind children to think about characters they love.

▶ Draw children's attention to the chart.

> What did you learn today about writing in your reader's notebook?

> During independent reading, choose a book that has a character you love. You can choose from the books in this basket or others you have read. Write the name of the character in your reader's notebook. You can draw a picture of one or two of the characters you love. Bring your reader's notebook when we come back together so you can share.

Share

Following independent work time, gather children together in the meeting area in groups of three to talk about the characters they love.

> Show your Characters I Love page and share the name of a character on your list. Talk about why you love the character and what you drew.

Extend the Lesson (Optional)

After assessing children's understanding, you might decide to extend the learning.

▶ Have children coconstruct a poster or mural of favorite characters. Children can select their favorite character to draw, glue their drawings to the poster or mural, and label the drawings. Display the related books near the poster or mural.

▶ Have children role play their favorite characters from stories, thinking about how different characters would talk and act with each other.

RML 5
WAR.U2.RML5

Reading Minilesson Principle
Write and draw to show things you like to read about.

Using a Reader's Notebook

You Will Need

- several familiar books with memorable characters, such as the following from Text Set: Animals:
  - *Elephants Swim* by Linda Capus Riley
  - *Actual Size* by Steve Jenkins
- chart paper prepared to look like the Things I Like to Read About page in *Reader's Notebook: Primary*
- markers
- projector (optional)
- *Reader's Notebook: Primary*, or a reader's notebook for each child

Academic Language / Important Vocabulary

- title
- reader's notebook

Continuum Connection

- Draw (or use other art media) independently to represent information from a text (p. 172)

Goal

Be aware of favorite topics to read about and make a list of them in a reader's notebook to use for making good book choices.

Rationale

When children create and keep a list of things they like to read about, you help them develop an awareness of their particular reading interests. The list is a tool for them to use when selecting books that will keep their interest.

Assess Learning

Observe children when they write and draw about things they like to read. Notice if there is evidence of new learning based on the goal of this minilesson.

- Can children make a list of things they like to read about in a reader's notebook?
- Are they able to explain their choices for what they like to read?
- Do they use the terms *title* and *reader's notebook* in conversation?

Minilesson

To help children think about the minilesson principle, demonstrate how to write a list of reading interests. Here is an example.

- Display the prepared chart of the Things I Like to Read About page (or project the page from *Reader's Notebook: Primary*). Point to the title as you read the words with the children.

  What do you think you will write and draw on this page of your reader's notebook?

- Show *Elephants Can Swim* and *Actual Size*.

  Here are two books that I enjoyed reading. I learned things about animals in both books. I like to read about animals. What could I write and draw in my reader's notebook?

- Record children's responses on the chart paper.

  I also like to read books about friends, so I'll write and draw about that, too. When I want to choose a book to read, I can look at my list to help me choose a book that I will enjoy reading.

- If you are using *Reader's Notebook: Primary*, children can open to the orange tab and turn to the Things I Like to Read About page. If not, assist children in labeling a page *Things I Like to Read About*.

Have a Try

Invite the children to talk with a partner about things they like to read about.

> Think of some books you liked. What were they about? What do you like to read about? Turn and talk to your partner about something you like to read about.

▶ Ask volunteers to share their thinking. Add new ideas to the list.

Summarize and Apply

Summarize the learning and remind children to notice things they like to read about.

▶ Review the chart with the children.

> What did you learn today about writing in your reader's notebook?

> During independent reading, choose a book about something you enjoy reading about. You can choose from the books in this basket or others you have read. Write what you like to read about in your reader's notebook and draw a picture of it. Bring your reader's notebook when we come back together so you can share.

Share

Following independent work time, gather children together in the meeting area to talk about the things they like to read about.

> Give a thumbs-up if you wrote something on your Things I Like to Read About page.

▶ Ask two or three children to share something they wrote.

> Who else likes to read about _____?

Extend the Lesson (Optional)

After assessing children's understanding, you might decide to extend the learning.

▶ Continue to add to the class list of things children like to read about. If children have similar interests, suggest that they recommend books to each other about those common interests.

▶ Add new baskets to your classroom library and fill them with books that will appeal to children who like to read about the same things. Use interactive writing to make labels for them.

Reading Minilesson Principle
Write and draw to show things you like to write about.

Using a Reader's Notebook

You Will Need

- three or four familiar books that the children have enjoyed, such as the following:
  - books from the Text Sets: Eric Carle, Folk Tales, Family, Friendship, Colors, or Home
- chart paper and markers
- *Reader's Notebook: Primary*, or a reader's notebook for each child

Academic Language / Important Vocabulary

- reader's notebook

Continuum Connection

- Use a text as a resource for words, phrases, and ideas for writing (p. 172)

Goal

Be aware of favorite topics to write about and to make a list of them in a reader's notebook.

Rationale

When children recognize that authors have topics they like to write about, the children learn that they, too, can have topics they can write about. This will allow them to begin to think of themselves as writers with interests and ideas to share.

Assess Learning

Observe children when they write and draw about things they like to write about. Notice if there is evidence of new learning based on the goal of this minilesson.

- ▶ Can the children write and draw about things they like to write about on the Things I Like to Write About page?
- ▶ Are they able to explain to others what they like to write about?
- ▶ Do they use the term *reader's notebook*?

Minilesson

To help children think about the minilesson principle, demonstrate how to make a list of writing topics. Here is an example.

- ▶ Write the title *Things I Like to Write About* on chart paper.

    Authors often have different topics, or things, they like to write about.

- ▶ Show two to three of Eric Carle's books and help the children notice that he often writes about animals.

    Think about Eric Carle's books. What do you know that Eric Carle likes to write about?

- ▶ Show two to three of Paul Galdone's books (from Text Set: Folk Tales) and help children to notice that he retells many stories and animal tales.

    We have also read several of Paul Galdone's books. What does Paul Galdone like to write about?

- ▶ Invite children to tell some things they like to write about.

    What are some things you like to write about?

- ▶ As children share ideas, write their ideas on the chart and write the child's name next to the idea.

- ▶ Reread the list of ideas with the children. As you read each idea, ask for suggestions for what could be drawn in a reader's notebook to go with each idea. Add a quick sketch for one or two of the ideas.

Have a Try

Invite the children to talk with a partner about things they like to write about.

▶ Show three to four more books with different topics, such as family, home, friendship, or colors.

Turn and talk to a partner about ideas you will write on your Things I Like to Write About page and what you will draw.

▶ Ask children to share their ideas. Add new ideas to the class list.

Summarize and Apply

Summarize the learning and remind children to notice things they like to write about.

▶ Review the list you made with the children.

What is this list about?

How could you use this list when you write?

Choose one or more things you like to write about. They could be from this list, but you might have some other ideas. On the Things I Like to Write About page in your reader's notebook, write and draw pictures of things you like to write about. Bring your reader's notebook when we come back together to share.

Things I Like to Write About

Butterflies — Hikari

Things That Fly — Tyler

Family — Isaiah

Food — Imani

Share

Following independent work time, gather children together in the meeting area to tell what they like to write about.

Turn and talk with a partner to share what you drew and wrote. Listen to your partner and answer any questions.

Extend the Lesson (Optional)

After assessing children's understanding, you might decide to extend the learning.

▶ Display books by the same author. Talk about what the author writes about. Have a conversation about whether the books are about similar or different topics.

▶ Help children to understand how they can use the ideas on the Things I Like to Write About list to write books and stories.

RML7
WAR.U2.RML7

Reading Minilesson Principle
Use the lists in your reader's notebook to help you choose books.

Using a Reader's Notebook

You Will Need

- charts from previous minilessons (e.g., Books I Love, Authors I Love, Illustrators I Love, Characters I Love, Things I Like to Read About)
- 2–3 baskets of books by favorite authors
- basket of books with favorite characters
- *Reader's Notebook: Primary* or a reader's notebook for each child
- chart paper and markers

Academic Language / Important Vocabulary

- reader's notebook

Continuum Connection

- Recognize that an author or illustrator may write or illustrate several books (p. 28)

Goal

Use the lists in a reader's notebook to select books of interest.

Rationale

When you teach children how to use lists of their favorite authors, illustrators, characters, and topics to choose books, you help them consider their own tastes as readers. You encourage independence and provide them with a resource for making good book choices.

Assess Learning

Observe children when they choose books to read. Notice if there is evidence of new learning based on the goal of this minilesson.

- ▶ Are children using the lists in a reader's notebook as a resource for finding books?
- ▶ Are they making good book choices for themselves?
- ▶ Do they use the term *reader's notebook*?

Minilesson

To help children think about the minilesson principle, engage them in a discussion of how to use a reader's notebook as a resource for choosing books. Here is an example.

- ▶ Display the completed Authors I Love chart.

    I want to choose a new book to read, but I am not sure which one. One thing I can do is to look in my reader's notebook and turn to the All About Me section. I am going to look at the Authors I Love page. I see that one of the authors I love is Eric Carle.

    How might this help me choose a book from our classroom library?

- ▶ Guide children to notice that if they like a certain author, they might like to read other books by that author. If you have baskets in your classroom library organized and labeled by author, you can invite children to show which basket they might choose from.

    Since I know I like Eric Carle's writing, I will probably enjoy reading more books by him. I can choose an Eric Carle book to read from the classroom library.

- ▶ Repeat with the Characters I Love page.

Have a Try

Invite the children to talk about their lists with a partner.

▶ Quickly review the lists that were made in minilessons 1–5.

> Take a minute to look through the lists you have made in the All About Me section of your reader's notebook. Find a list that you think will help you choose a book you would enjoy reading.

> Turn and talk with a partner about how you can use the list to help you choose books in the classroom library. Let's make a chart to help you when you choose books.

Summarize and Apply

Summarize the learning and remind children to think about how to choose books they will like to read.

> Let's look at the chart. What does it help you do?

> Today, use one of the lists in your reader's notebook to help you choose a book from the classroom library. You might look for a book by an author or illustrator you love. You might choose a book that has a character you love or that is about something you really like to read about. When we come back together, you will share how you chose your book.

Share

Following independent work time, gather children together in the meeting area in groups of three to talk about how they choose books.

> Share the book you chose and which list in your reader's notebook helped you choose it.

Extend the Lesson (Optional)

After assessing children's understanding, you might decide to extend the learning.

▶ Involve the children in rearranging and labeling baskets of books in your classroom library to match some of the interests and preferences they have expressed in the All About Me section of a reader's notebook. For example, create and label a basket of books by a beloved illustrator, or organize all sports books into a basket labeled *Sports*.

▶ Encourage children during reading conferences to add to and reference the lists they have developed about their reading preferences.

Use the lists in your reader's notebook to help you choose books.

* Look in your reader's notebook.

* Find a book.

* Get the book and read!

Assessment

After you have taught the minilessons in this umbrella, observe your children as they talk and write about their reading across instructional contexts: interactive read-aloud, independent reading and literacy work, guided reading, shared reading, and book club. Use *The Literacy Continuum* (Fountas and Pinnell 2017) to observe children's reading and writing behaviors across instructional contexts.

▶ What evidence do you have of new understandings related to a reader's notebook?

- Do children talk about the books they love and share opinions about why they love them?
- Are they able to identify which authors and illustrators they love and why?
- Can they identify one or more of their favorite characters?
- Are they able to talk about things they like to read about?
- Do they share opinions related to what they like to write about?
- Are they able to use the lists they have developed through this umbrella to inform their book choices?
- Do children use academic language such as *author, illustrator, title*, and *character?*

▶ In what other ways, beyond the scope of this umbrella, are the children talking about what they enjoy about books, authors, illustrators, and characters?

- Are they applying the literary analysis minilessons you have taught in their oral and written responses to books?
- In what ways are they talking and writing about books?
- Are they ready to learn different ways to respond to fiction and nonfiction books in a reader's notebook? (See the Section Four umbrellas, Ways to Write About Fiction Books and Ways to Write About Nonfiction Books.)

Use your observations to determine the next umbrella you will teach. You may also consult Minilessons Across the Year (p. 51) for guidance.

Minilessons in This Umbrella

RML1 Tell about fiction books.

RML2 Tell about nonfiction books.

RML3 Make a list of your favorite fiction books.

RML4 Make a list of your favorite nonfiction books.

Before Teaching Umbrella 3 Minilessons

The lessons in this umbrella help children expand their ability to think, talk, and write about their reading in the Books I Read section of *Reader's Notebook: Primary* (Fountas and Pinnell 2014). This section is a place where children can tell about fiction and nonfiction books they have read or heard through writing or drawing and from that begin to understand their reading preferences. A blank notebook with space to draw and write can be used in place of the published version of *Reader's Notebook: Primary* (see p. 46 for more on using a reader's notebook). This umbrella can be taught as an entire set of lessons. However, you may decide to teach these lessons individually or in conjunction with related umbrellas in Section Two: Literary Analysis.

Use the following books from the *Fountas & Pinnell Classroom™ Interactive Read-Aloud Collection* text sets or select books that children have loved listening to, talking about, and sharing with others.

Learning How to Be Yourself

Harold Finds a Voice by Courtney Dicmas

Exploring Fiction and Nonfiction

Chickens Aren't the Only Ones by Ruth Heller

The Importance of Family

Jonathan and His Mommy by Irene Smalls

Exploring Fiction and Nonfiction

All Pigs Are Beautiful by Dick King-Smith

As you read aloud and enjoy books together,

- identify the title and author of each book,
- talk about their responses to books, and
- express opinions about books.

Be Yourself

Fiction and Nonfiction

Family

Exploring Fiction and Nonfiction

Reader's Notebook

Section 4: Writing About Reading

Reading Minilesson Principle
Tell about fiction books.

Introducing Writing About Reading in a Reader's Notebook

You Will Need

- chart paper prepared to look like the blue tabbed fiction Books I Read page from *Reader's Notebook: Primary*
- markers
- *Harold Finds a Voice* by Courtney Dicmas, from Text Set: Be Yourself
- projector (optional)
- one basket of familiar fiction books for each group of three to four children
- *Reader's Notebook: Primary* or a reader's notebook for each child

Academic Language / Important Vocabulary

- title
- author
- fiction

Continuum Connection

- Understand that fiction stories are imagined (p. 28)
- Attempt to independently record text titles and authors in Reader's Notebook (may be drawings) (p. 172)
- Draw (or use other art media) independently to represent information from a text (p. 172)

Goal

Learn how to use the Books I Read section of a reader's notebook to tell about fiction books.

Rationale

Children can tell about fiction books they have read through drawing and writing. You can teach children to use a reader's notebook as a place to share their thinking and keep a record of the fiction books they have read, by drawing and writing about those books. Early in the year, children may do more drawing than writing. As the year progresses, the amount of writing will increase.

Assess Learning

Observe children as they tell about books they have read or heard in a reader's notebook. Notice if there is evidence of new learning based on the goal of this minilesson.

- Is there evidence that the children understand what a fiction book is?
- Do children attempt to write the title and author of the book?
- Do they use the words *title, author,* and *fiction* when they talk about fiction books?

Minilesson

To help children think about the minilesson principle, demonstrate how to record fiction books in the Books I Read section. Here is an example.

- Show the prepared chart (or project the page from *Reader's Notebook: Primary*).

  Look at how the blue tab marks this section in your reader's notebook. This section, called Books I Read, is where you will write and draw about books you have read so that you can remember them.

  This page is labeled *Fiction: A fiction author tells a story.*

- Show *Harold Finds a Voice.*

  Here's a book we have read together. Is it fiction? How do you know?

  What could I draw and write to help me remember this book?

- Make a quick sketch. Then point to the word *Title.*

  This says *title.* What should I write here?

  I can copy the title from the book. Who can point to the title on the cover?

- Point to the word *Author.*

  This word is *author.* What does an author do?

  What should I write here?

  I can also copy the author's name from the book. Who can point to the author's name on the cover?

Have a Try

Invite the children to talk about fiction books in a small group.

 ▶ Divide the class into small groups of three to four children. Give each group a basket of familiar fiction books. These are books you have read to the children or used for shared reading.

    Talk to your group about which fiction book you will tell about in your reader's notebook.

Summarize and Apply

Summarize the learning and remind children to tell about fiction books in a reader's notebook after they read them or hear them.

 ▶ Review the chart with the children.

    What did you learn about this section of your reader's notebook?

    Today, on a page in your reader's notebook, tell about the fiction book you talked about with your group. Write the title and the author and make an illustration.

 ▶ Make sure each child has a reader's notebook. If you are not using *Reader's Notebook: Primary*, provide a Books I Read page for nonfiction that children can glue into a plain notebook. They can mark the section with a sticky note.

Share

Following independent work time, gather children together in the meeting area to tell about the fiction book they listed.

    Turn and talk with a partner to share your Books I Read fiction page. Listen to your partner and answer any questions.

Extend the Lesson (Optional)

After assessing children's understanding, you might decide to extend the learning.

 ▶ If children are not yet writing the title and author, look for opportunities to model where to find that information in books. Point out the use of capital letters.

 ▶ Create a class list of fiction books they have read or heard read. Children can use this as a resource when making their own lists of books.

 ▶ **Drawing/Writing About Reading** Provide minilessons to demonstrate how children can add writing or labels to their drawings.

RML2
WAR.U3.RML2

Reading Minilesson Principle
Tell about nonfiction books.

Introducing Writing About Reading in a Reader's Notebook

You Will Need

- chart from RML 1 in this umbrella
- chart paper prepared to look like nonfiction Books I Read page from *Reader's Notebook: Primary*
- markers
- projector (optional)
- familiar nonfiction book, such as *Chickens Aren't the Only Ones* by Ruth Heller, from Text Set: Fiction and Nonfiction
- one basket of familiar nonfiction books for each group of three to four children
- *Reader's Notebook: Primary*, or a reader's notebook for each child

Academic Language / Important Vocabulary

- title
- author
- nonfiction

Continuum Connection

- Record text titles and authors in a Reader's Notebook (and use drawings) (p. 174)
- Represent information from a text by drawing (or using other art media) or writing (p. 174)

Goal

Learn how to use the Books I Read section of a reader's notebook.

Rationale

Children can tell about nonfiction books they have read through drawing and writing. When you teach children to use a reader's notebook to share their thinking, they create a record of the nonfiction books they have read or heard read. Early in the year, children may do more drawing than writing. As the year progresses, the amount of writing will increase.

Assess Learning

Observe children as they tell in a reader's notebook about books they have read or heard read. Notice if there is evidence of new learning based on the goal of this minilesson.

- Is there evidence that the children understand what a nonfiction book is?
- Do children attempt to write the title and author of the book?
- Do they use the words *title, author,* and *nonfiction* when they talk about nonfiction books?

Minilesson

To help children think about the minilesson principle, demonstrate how to record nonfiction books in the Books I Read section. Here is an example.

- Show the chart from RML1 in this umbrella.

  In your reader's notebook, you told about a fiction book you read. You wrote the title and author. You drew a picture.

- Show the prepared chart (or project the page from *Reader's Notebook: Primary*).

  Today we are going to talk about another type of book you can tell about in your reader's notebook. Let's pretend this is my reader's notebook. The heading says *Nonfiction—A nonfiction author gives information.*

- Show the book *Chickens Aren't the Only Ones.*

  Is this a fiction book or a nonfiction book? How do you know that?

  What might I draw in my reader's notebook about this book?

- Draw a sketch on the chart paper from the children's responses.

  Who can point to the title of the book?

  Where should I write the title on this page?

- Record the title on the chart.

  Who can point to the author's name?

  Where should I write the author's name on this page?

- Record the author on the chart.

Have a Try

Invite the children to talk about nonfiction books in a small group.

▸ Divide the class into small groups of three to four. Give each group a basket of familiar nonfiction books—books that they have read or heard read in interactive reading or shared reading.

> Choose a book from the basket. Then talk to your group about which nonfiction book you will tell about in your reader's notebook.

Summarize and Apply

Summarize the learning and remind children to think about what they will write and draw in a reader's notebook.

▸ Review the chart with the children.

> What did you learn today about what you can write and draw in your reader's notebook?

> Today, you are going to tell about the nonfiction book you talked about with your group. Think about how you can tell about the book in your reader's notebook.

▸ Make sure each child has a reader's notebook. If you are not using *Reader's Notebook: Primary*, provide a Books I Read page for nonfiction that children can glue into a plain notebook.

Share

Following independent work time, gather children together in the meeting area to tell what they recorded.

> Turn and talk with a partner to share what you drew and wrote about a nonfiction book. Listen to your partner and answer any questions.

Extend the Lesson (Optional)

After assessing children's understanding, you might decide to extend the learning.

▸ If children are not yet writing the title and author, look for opportunities to model where to find that information in books. Point out the use of capital letters.

▸ **Drawing/Writing About Reading** Provide minilessons to demonstrate how children can add writing or labels to their drawings.

Reading Minilesson Principle
Make a list of your favorite fiction books.

Introducing Writing About Reading in a Reader's Notebook

You Will Need

▶ chart paper prepared to look like My Favorite Fiction Books page from *Reader's Notebook: Primary*, with about three fiction book titles listed

▶ markers

▶ projector (optional)

▶ *Jonathan and His Mommy* by Irene Smalls from Text Set: Family

▶ one basket of familiar fiction books for each group of three to four children

▶ *Reader's Notebook: Primary*, or a reader's notebook for each child

Academic Language / Important Vocabulary

▶ title

▶ author

▶ fiction

▶ favorite

Continuum Connection

▶ Attempt to independently record text titles and authors in Reader's Notebook (may be drawings) (p. 172)

▶ Make lists differentiating between fiction and nonfiction texts (p. 174)

Goal

Learn how to use to use a reader's notebook to list favorite fiction books.

Rationale

When children keep a list of their favorite fiction books in a reader's notebook, they create a useful reference tool for themselves. They can reflect on the book, use it to remember special parts of the books they love, and recommend books to others. You may need to save this lesson for later in the year when most children are doing some writing.

Assess Learning

Observe children when they list the books they have read or heard read. Notice if there is evidence of new learning based on the goal of this minilesson.

▶ Is there evidence from the children's talk and writing that they understand the purpose of the My Favorite Fiction Books page?

▶ Are children able to determine what a fiction book is?

▶ Do children add fiction titles to the appropriate page in a reader's notebook?

▶ Do they use the terms *title, author, fiction,* and *favorite* in conversation?

Minilesson

To help children think about the minilesson principle, demonstrate how and where to record favorite fiction books. Here is an example.

▶ Display the prepared chart (or project the page from *Reader's Notebook: Primary*). Read the titles.

> What is the same about these books? How do you know? Offer prompts as needed to help children realize that they are all fiction books.

> When you read a fiction book that you love, write the title and the author's name in this section of your reader's notebook, the way I listed some of my favorites here. The title of this part is My Favorite Fiction Books.

▶ Hold up *Jonathan and His Mommy*.

> I can look at the book to find out how to write the title and the author. Who can point to the title?

> Who can point to the author's name?

> What do you notice about the first letter in each part of the author's name?

▶ Repeat with the other books on the chart to reinforce the teaching, as necessary. (Save the chart for use in the next minilesson.)

Have a Try

Invite the children to talk about their favorite fiction books in a small group.

▶ Divide the class into small groups of three or four. Give each group a basket of familiar fiction books—books that they have read or heard read in interactive reading or shared reading.

> Look through the fiction books in the basket and choose one that you'd like to write on your list of favorites. Turn and talk to your group about which book is your favorite and why.

Summarize and Apply

Summarize the learning and remind children to remember where they can look for help in writing the title and author's name.

▶ Draw children's attention to the chart.

> What did you learn today about what you should write on this page?

> Today, you are going to write the title and author's name for the book you talked about with your group. Remember where you can look to help you with your writing.

▶ Make sure each child has a reader's notebook. If you are not using *Reader's Notebook: Primary*, provide a My Favorite Fiction Books page that children can glue into a reader's notebook or help them label a page.

Share

Following independent work time, gather children together in the meeting area to talk about their favorite fiction books.

> Who would like to share the title of one of their favorite fiction books?

> Did anyone choose the same fiction book?

Extend the Lesson (Optional)

After assessing children's understanding, you might decide to extend the learning.

▶ Encourage children to add titles to their list of favorite fiction books, including during interactive read-aloud and guided reading.

▶ During interactive read-aloud or shared reading, use interactive and shared writing to model recording lists of books.

> **My Favorite Fiction Books**
>
> Jonathan and His Mommy
> Lola at the Library
> A Visitor for Bear
> _____
> _____
> _____
>
> **My Favorite Nonfiction Books**
>
> _____
> _____
> _____
> _____
> _____
> _____

Reading Minilesson Principle
Make a list of your favorite nonfiction books.

Introducing Writing About Reading in a Reader's Notebook

You Will Need

- the chart from RML3, with about three nonfiction titles added
- markers
- projector (optional)
- *All Pigs Are Beautiful* by Dick King-Smith from Text Set: Fiction and Nonfiction
- *Reader's Notebook: Primary*, or a reader's notebook for each child
- one basket of familiar nonfiction books for each group of three to four children

Academic Language / Important Vocabulary

- title
- author
- nonfiction
- favorite

Continuum Connection

- Understand when a book is nonfiction (true information) (p. 30)
- Record text titles and authors in a Reader's Notebook (and use drawings) (p. 174)
- Make lists differentiating between fiction and nonfiction texts (p. 174)

Goal

Learn how to use a reader's notebook to list favorite nonfiction books.

Rationale

When children keep a list of their favorite nonfiction books in a reader's notebook, they create a useful reference tool for themselves. They can use this tool to reflect on books read, to remember special parts of a book, and to recommend books to others. You may need to save this lesson for later in the year when most children are doing some writing.

Assess Learning

Observe children as they list books they have read or heard read. Notice if there is evidence of new learning based on the goal of this minilesson.

- ▶ Is there evidence that children understand the purpose of the My Favorite Nonfiction Books page?
- ▶ Do you notice children choosing nonfiction books to add to the list?
- ▶ Can children articulate why they add certain nonfiction titles to the list?
- ▶ Do they use the words *title, author, nonfiction,* and *favorite* correctly?

Minilesson

To help children think about the minilesson principle, demonstrate how to list favorite nonfiction books. Here is an example.

- ▶ Display the prepared chart (or project the page from *Reader's Notebook: Primary*). Read the titles.

  What is the same about these books? How do you know?

- ▶ Offer prompts as needed to help children realize that they are all nonfiction books.

  When you read a nonfiction book that you love, write the title and the author's name in this section of your reader's notebook, the way I listed some of my favorites here. The title of this part is My Favorite Nonfiction Books.

- ▶ Hold up *All Pigs Are Beautiful*.

  I can look at the book to find out how to write the title and the author. Who can point to the title?

  Who can point to the author's name?

  What do you notice about the first letter in each part of the author's name?

- ▶ Repeat this process for other books to reinforce the teaching, as necessary.

Have a Try

Invite the children to talk about their favorite nonfiction books in small groups.

▶ Divide the class into groups of three or four. Give each group a basket of familiar nonfiction books—books they have read or heard read in interactive reading or shared reading.

> Look through the nonfiction books in the basket and choose one that you'd like to list in your reader's notebook. Talk to your group about which book is your favorite and why.

Summarize and Apply

Summarize the learning and remind children where they can look to help in writing the title and author's name.

> Today you learned that you have a section in your reader's notebook to write a list of your favorite nonfiction books.

> Today you will write in your reader's notebook the title of the book you told your group you liked. Point to the line where you will write the title of a favorite nonfiction book. You can look at the book to help you write the title.

▶ Make sure each child has a reader's notebook. If you are not using *Reader's Notebook: Primary*, provide a My Favorite Nonfiction Books page that children can glue into a reader's notebook or help them label a page.

Share

Following independent work time, gather children together in the meeting area to talk about favorite nonfiction books.

> Who would like to share what you wrote?

> How did you know how to write the title and the author's name?

> Did anyone else have the same book?

Extend the Lesson (Optional)

After assessing children's understanding, you might decide to extend the learning.

▶ Encourage children to add titles to their list of favorite nonfiction books during interactive read-aloud and guided reading.

▶ As you read during interactive read-aloud and shared reading, use interactive and shared writing to model recording lists.

My Favorite Fiction Books

Jonathan and His Mommy
Lola at the library
A Visitor for Bear

My Favorite Nonfiction Books

All Pigs Are Beautiful
Hats, Hats, Hats
Chickens Aren't the Only Ones

Assessment

After you have taught the minilessons in this umbrella, observe your children as they talk and write about their reading across instructional contexts: interactive read-aloud, independent reading and literacy work, guided reading, shared reading, and book club. Use *The Literacy Continuum* (Fountas and Pinnell 2017) to observe children's reading and writing behaviors across instructional contexts.

▶ What evidence do you have of new understandings related to responding to books they have read and listed in a reader's notebook?

- Do children list fiction and nonfiction books they know?

- Are they able to make a list of their favorite fiction books?

- Are they able to make a list of their favorite nonfiction books?

- Do they use the words *title*, *author*, *fiction*, and *nonfiction* when they talk about writing in a reader's notebook?

▶ In what other ways, beyond the scope of this umbrella, are they talking about and responding to both fiction and nonfiction books they know?

- In what ways are children sharing their thinking about books?

- Are they expressing opinions about books that could be shared in a book talk?

Use your observations to determine the next umbrella you will teach. You may also consult Minilessons Across the Year (p. 51) for guidance.

Grace Lin

Minilessons in This Umbrella

RML1 Tell the title and author when you share your thinking about a book.

RML2 Tell how a character feels.

RML3 Tell the story problem.

RML4 Tell where a story takes place.

RML5 Tell what a character is like.

RML6 Write a new ending for a story.

RML7 Think about all the things you can write about fiction stories.

Animal Tales

Nursery Rhymes

Before Teaching Umbrella 4 Minilessons

These minilessons may be taught sequentially as a unit or individually in conjunction with minilessons that support children in reading fiction texts. Skip any minilesson if children are not ready to engage with the principle. These minilessons are based on *Reader's Notebook: Primary* (Fountas and Pinnell 2014), but a reader's notebook can be any blank notebook with space for children to draw and write (see p. 46).

While you are teaching the minilessons in this umbrella, be sure that the children are reading fiction texts. Read and discuss books that have at least one of the following elements: characters with identifiable feelings, a clearly defined problem and solution, and a distinct setting. Use the following books from the *Fountas & Pinnell Classroom™ Interactive Read-Aloud Collection* text sets or choose similar books from your library.

Friendship

Family

Grace Lin: Exploring Family and Culture
Dim Sum for Everyone!
  by Grace Lin

Exploring Animal Tales
The Three Billy Goats Gruff
  by P. C. Asbjørnsen and J. E. Moe
The Three Little Pigs by Patricia Seibert

Sharing Stories and Songs:
Nursery Rhymes
Baa Baa Black Sheep by Iza Trapani

The Importance of Friendship
Jessica by Kevin Henkes

Taking Care of Each Other: Family
Where Are You Going, Little Mouse?
  by Robert Kraus

Sharing Stories: Folktales
The Elves and the Shoemaker
  by Paul Galdone

Living and Working Together:
Community
Fireman Small by Herbert Yee

Sharing Stories:
Folktales

Community

Reader's Notebook

As you read aloud and enjoy these texts together, help children
- identify the book title and the author's name,
- identify characters and the problem, and
- think about a new ending for a story.

Section 4: Writing About Reading

RML1
WAR.U4.RML1

Reading Minilesson Principle
Tell the title and author when you share your thinking about a book.

Writing About Fiction Books in a Reader's Notebook

You Will Need

- chart prepared to look like a Books I Read page from *Reader's Notebook: Primary*, with title and author's name in place
- a familiar fiction book, such as *Baa Baa Black Sheep* by Iza Trapani, from Text Set: Nursery Rhymes
- projector (optional)
- highlighter tape
- *Reader's Notebook: Primary* or a reader's notebook for each child

Academic Language / Important Vocabulary

- reader's notebook
- author
- title
- uppercase letter

Continuum Connection

- Attempt to independently record text titles and authors in Reader's Notebook (may be drawings) (p. 172)
- Draw (or use other media) independently to represent information from a text (p. 172)

Goal

Use the names of authors and titles of books when writing about reading.

Rationale

When you teach children to identify and record the title and author of books when writing about reading, they develop organizational and documentation skills. When they notice that an author has written more than one book they make connections among them and become aware of the author's craft and style.

Assess Learning

Observe children when they draw and write about stories they have read or heard. Notice if there is evidence of new learning based on the goal of this minilesson.

- Can children record the title and author of a book?
- Do children use uppercase letters for the title and author's name?
- Do children understand the terms *reader's notebook*, *author*, *title*, and *uppercase letter*?

Minilesson

To help children think about the minilesson principle, demonstrate how to write about a book in a reader's notebook. Here is an example.

- Display the prepared chart (or project the page from *Reader's Notebook: Primary*).

    There are lots of pages in your reader's notebook for writing about the books you read. In the part of your reader's notebook behind the blue tab, you will share your thinking about books by writing and drawing.

- Show the book *Baa, Baa, Black Sheep* and read what you wrote on the chart.

    What do you notice about what I wrote?

    On the Books I Read page, I wrote the title of the book next to the word *title*. I wrote the author's name next to the word *author*.

- Highlight the first letter of each word in the title and the author's name.

    Look at the first letter of each word in the title and the author's name. What do you notice?

    The first letter in each word begins with an uppercase letter. The title of a book and an author's name always begin with an uppercase letter.

- Add the directions to the chart. Point out the picture box.

    What do you think I will do in this box? I might draw a picture of the black sheep.

- Show the lined page opposite the page with the picture box.

    What might I do on this page? I can write my thinking about this story.

Have a Try

Invite the children to talk with a partner about what they will write in a reader's notebook.

 ▶ Show the book cover from another fiction book.

> Turn and talk with a partner about what you would write on the first line of the Books I Read page. Now talk with your partner about what you would write next. What type of letters will you use?

Summarize and Apply

Summarize the learning and remind children to tell the title and author of books they read in a reader's notebook.

> After you read today, write the title and author when you share your thinking about a book in your reader's notebook. Writing the title and author's name will help you remember and share the books you have read. Begin each name with a capital letter.

 ▶ Make sure each child has a reader's notebook. If you are not using *Reader's Notebook: Primary*, provide a Books I Read page that children can glue into a plain notebook. Assist children who are not yet comfortable with writing.

Share

Following independent work time, gather children together in the meeting area to talk about what they wrote on the Books I Read page.

> Bring your reader's notebook to group meeting. Turn and talk to a partner about the title and author of the book you read today. Point to the uppercase letters in the title and author.

Extend the Lesson (Optional)

After assessing children's understanding, you might decide to extend the learning.

 ▶ Create a bulletin board for displaying each of the books that children have read. On sentence strips, have the children write the title and author and draw a picture to add to the bulletin board.

 ▶ Have children vote on the favorite book and add the tally to the bulletin board.

 ▶ **Drawing/Writing About Reading** Have each child continue to use a reader's notebook that includes space for the title and author of each book.

Books I Read

1

Title: Baa Baa Black Sheep

Author: Iza Trapani

Write author's name.

Write title of book.

Section 4: Writing About Reading

Writing About Fiction Books in a Reader's Notebook

You Will Need

- chart paper prepared to look like Books I Read page from *Reader's Notebook: Primary*, with title and author, a picture, and one or two sentences filled in
- markers
- projector (optional)
- a familiar fiction book with a character exhibiting strong feelings, such as *Jessica* by Kevin Henkes, from Text Set: Friendship
- *Reader's Notebook: Primary*, or a reader's notebook for each child

Academic Language / Important Vocabulary

- reader's notebook
- author
- title
- character

Continuum Connection

- Infer characters' intentions, feelings, and motivations using text and pictures (p. 29)
- Draw or write about how a character might feel (p. 173)

Goal

Notice how a character in a story feels and draw or write about it.

Rationale

When children think about how a character feels, they can connect and empathize with the character. Noticing and understanding a character's feelings supports children in making authentic personal connections.

Assess Learning

Observe children when they draw and write about how characters feel in stories they have read or heard. Notice if there is evidence of new learning based on the goal of this minilesson.

- ▶ Can children draw and write about a character's feelings in a reader's notebook?
- ▶ Can they write something to go with the drawing?
- ▶ Do they understand the terms *reader's notebook*, *author*, *title*, and *character*?

Minilesson

To help children think about the minilesson principle, engage them in a discussion of characters' feelings and demonstrate how to write about them in a reader's notebook. Here is an example.

- ▶ Show the prepared chart (or project the page from *Reader's Notebook: Primary*) and the book *Jessica* by Kevin Henkes.

   Here is what I did after I read *Jessica* by Kevin Henkes. I wrote the title and the author's name on my reader's notebook page, using uppercase letters for the first letters in the title and the author's name.

- ▶ Point to and read the title and author.

   What else do you notice that I did?

   I drew a picture of Jessica and Ruthie. I also wrote something about them.

- ▶ Point out the drawing and read the two sentences.

   What do you notice that I drew and wrote about the characters? How do you think Jessica and Ruthie feel in my drawing?

Have a Try

Invite the children to talk with a partner about Ruthie.

▶ Show pages 13 and 14.

> Now let's think about how Ruthie feels at school. Notice Ruthie in these illustrations. Turn and talk about what you would write if you were telling about how Ruthie feels now in the story.

▶ Have a few children share what they would write or draw about Ruthie.

Summarize and Apply

Summarize the learning and remind children to notice how the characters feel as they read.

▶ Review the chart with the children.

> What did you learn today about what you can write and draw in your reader's notebook?

> Telling how a character feels helps you understand the character.

> While reading today, think about how the character feels and how you can write and draw about the character. Use your reader's notebook to show your thinking. If you don't know how to write a word, give it a try. Bring your reader's notebook to group meeting to share later.

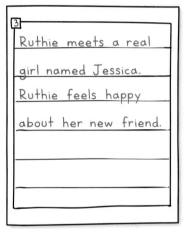

Share

Following independent work time, gather children together in the meeting area to talk about their reading.

> Turn and talk about the characters' feelings in your book. Read your writing to your partner and talk about your drawing.

Extend the Lesson (Optional)

After assessing children's understanding, you might decide to extend the learning.

▶ In a small group of three to four children, have the children play a game of Guess How I Am Feeling. Each child pantomimes a feeling and the other children guess what the feeling is.

▶ Have the children create a mask that expresses the character's feeling that they wrote about in a reader's notebook.

▶ **Drawing/Writing About Reading** In a reader's notebook, have the children draw and write about a feeling that is the same or opposite of what the character felt in the story.

Writing About Fiction Books in a Reader's Notebook

You Will Need

- chart paper prepared to look like Books I Read page from *Reader's Notebook: Primary*, with title and author, a picture, and one or two sentences filled in
- markers
- projector (optional)
- familiar fiction books with a clear problem, such as the following:
  - *Where Are You Going, Little Mouse?* by Robert Kraus, from Text Set: Family
  - *The Three Billy Goats Gruff* by P. C. Asbjørnsen and J. E. Moe, from Text Set: Animal Tales
  - *Reader's Notebook: Primary*, or a reader's notebook for each child

Academic Language / Important Vocabulary

- reader's notebook
- author
- title
- problem
- solution

Continuum Connection

- Tell about the important events of a story, after hearing it read several times and using the pictures in the text (p. 173)
- Write a summary that includes the story problem and how it is resolved (p. 173)

Goal

Write and draw about the problem in a fiction story and tell how it is solved.

Rationale

In thinking about what to write about the problem and solution, children naturally examine the relationship of the characters and the plot, developing a deeper understanding of the story's characters, plot, and structure. Consider teaching this lesson in conjunction with lessons about plot. (See Section Two: Literary Analysis.)

Assess Learning

Observe children when they draw and write about problems in stories they have read or heard. Notice if there is evidence of new learning based on the goal of this minilesson.

- Can children draw and write about the problem and solution in a story?
- Do they understand the terms *reader's notebook*, *author*, *title*, *problem*, and *solution*?

Minilesson

To help children think about the minilesson principle, engage them in a discussion about problem and solution and demonstrate how to write about them in a reader's notebook. Here is an example.

- Display the prepared chart (or project the page from *Reader's Notebook: Primary*). Point to and read the title and author. Show the cover of *Where Are You Going, Little Mouse?* by Robert Kraus.

  Look at my drawings. What parts of the story did I draw?

  I drew a picture of Little Mouse's problem and how he solved it. Listen to my thinking about Little Mouse's problem and his solution.

- Point to and read the sentences that you prepared.

  What do you notice about my thinking about Little Mouse's problem and his solution?

  I wrote who the character is, what the problem is, and how the character solves the problem. I can use these sentences to tell someone about *Where Are You Going, Little Mouse?*

Have a Try

Invite the children to talk with a partner about *The Three Billy Goats Gruff*.

▶ Show the cover of *The Three Billy Goats Gruff*.

> Think about the problem the three billy goats had and how they solved it. Turn and talk to a partner about what you could draw or write to show the problem the three billy goats had and how they solved it.

Summarize and Apply

Summarize the learning and remind children to think about the problem and how it is solved as they read.

> What have you learned that you can write in your reader's notebook? Look at the chart to remember.

> While reading today, think about the problem in the story and how it is solved. Think about who solved the problem and how the story changed after the problem is solved. Use your reader's notebook to write and draw to share your thinking. If you don't know how to write a word, give it a try. Bring your reader's notebook when we meet.

Share

Following independent work time, gather children together in the meeting area to talk about their reading.

> Turn and talk about the problem and solution that you drew and wrote about today. Show your partner the page in your reader's notebook.

Extend the Lesson (Optional)

After assessing children's understanding, you might decide to extend the learning.

▶ On drawing paper, have children draw a picture of a problem on one side. On the other side, have the children draw a solution. In a small group of three to four children, have one child show the problem and the others talk about a possible solution. The child shares the solution that was drawn. Repeat with the other children.

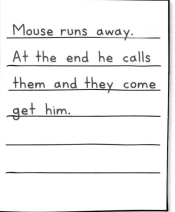

Section 4: Writing About Reading

Writing About Fiction Books in a Reader's Notebook

You Will Need

- chart paper prepared to look like Books I Read page from *Reader's Notebook: Primary*, with title and author, a picture, and one or two sentences filled in
- markers
- projector (optional)
- a familiar fiction book with a clearly identified setting, such as the following:
  - *Dim Sum for Everyone!* by Grace Lin, from Text Set: Grace Lin
  - *Where Are You Going, Little Mouse?* by Robert Kraus, from Text Set: Family
- *Reader's Notebook: Primary*, or a reader's notebook for each child

Academic Language / Important Vocabulary

- reader's notebook
- author
- title

Continuum Connection

- Recall important details about setting after a story is read (p. 28)
- Write a summary that includes important details about setting (p. 173)

Goal

Write and draw about where the story takes place to share thinking about fiction books.

Rationale

When children think about where the story takes place, they focus on the element of setting. An understanding of setting will deepen their understanding of the story. Consider teaching this lesson in conjunction with lessons on setting. (See Section Two: Literary Analysis.)

Assess Learning

Observe children when they write and draw about where stories they have read or heard take place. Notice if there is evidence of new learning based on the goal of this minilesson.

- Can children draw and write about where the story takes place?
- Do they use details from the story?
- Do they use the terms *reader's notebook, author,* and *title* correctly?

Minilesson

To help children think about the minilesson principle, engage them in a discussion about setting and how to write about it in a reader's notebook. Here is an example.

- Display the prepared chart (or project the page from *Reader's Notebook: Primary*) and show the cover of *Dim Sum for Everyone!* by Grace Lin. Point to and read the title and author.

  Today let's think about where a story happens, or where it takes place.

- Show the title and dedication pages and pages 1–2.

  Why do you think I drew many tables and chairs to show where this story took place? What else could I have put in my drawing to show that this story takes place in a restaurant?

- Point to and read the sentences.

  What did I write to tell about where this story takes place?

  I wrote that it takes place in a restaurant and they sell special food in the restaurant. What else could I have written to tell about where this story takes place?

Have a Try

Invite the children to talk with a partner about *Where Are You Going, Little Mouse?*

▶ Show the cover of *Where Are You Going, Little Mouse?*

Think about where this story happens, or takes place. Turn and talk about what you could draw and write to show where the story takes place.

▶ Call on a few children and discuss what to draw and write.

Summarize and Apply

Summarize the learning and remind children to think about where a story takes place as they read.

When you tell about where a story takes place what should you talk about? Where can you draw and write about it? Look at the chart to remember.

Today everyone will read a fiction story. Think about where your story takes place. Draw and write where your story takes place. Be sure to write the title and author of the book and use uppercase letters. If you don't know how to write a word, give it a try. Bring your book when we meet.

▶ Assist children who are not yet comfortable with writing.

Share

Following independent work time, gather children together in the meeting area to talk about their reading.

Turn and talk about where your story took place. Show your partner pictures in the book that helped you draw and write in your reader's notebook.

Extend the Lesson (Optional)

After assessing children's understanding, you might decide to extend the learning.

▶ Have children role-play a story but change the setting. For example, have them role-play the three little bears but have the bears living in a city.

▶ During interactive reading, generate a list of titles and settings on chart paper. After each reading, add to the list. Invite a few children to add a drawing for each addition.

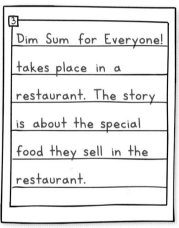

Section 4: Writing About Reading

Reading Minilesson Principle
Tell what a character is like.

You Will Need

- chart paper prepared to look like Books I Read page from *Reader's Notebook: Primary*, with title and author, a picture, and one or two sentences filled in
- markers
- projector (optional)
- a familiar fiction book with a character with clearly defined traits, such as these:
  - *The Three Billy Goats Gruff*, by P. C. Asbjørnsen and J. E. Moe from Text Set: Animal Tales
  - *Fireman Small*, by Wong Herbert Yee from Text Set: Community
- *Reader's Notebook: Primary*, or a reader's notebook for each child

Academic Language / Important Vocabulary

- reader's notebook
- author
- title
- character

Continuum Connection

- Infer a character's traits from story events (p. 29)
- Write a summary that includes important details about characters (p. 173)

Goal

Write and draw about what a character in a fiction story is like.

Rationale

When children think about a character's traits, they analyze how and why characters act the way they do. Being able to share their thinking about characters will deepen their understanding of elements of the story. Consider teaching this lesson in conjunction with lessons on characters. (See Section Two: Literary Analysis.)

Assess Learning

Observe children when they draw and write about characters in books they have read or heard. Notice if there is evidence of new learning based on the goal of this minilesson.

- Do children use details from the story when they draw and write about a character?
- Do they understand the terms *reader's notebook*, *author*, *title*, and *character*?

Minilesson

To help children think about the minilesson principle, engage them in a discussion about character traits and demonstrate how to write about them in a reader's notebook. Here is an example.

- Display the prepared chart (or project the page from *Reader's Notebook: Primary*) and show the cover of *The Three Billy Goats Gruff* by P. C. Asbjørnsen and J. E. Moe. Point to and read the title and authors' names.

  Today we are going to think about what the characters in stories are like.

- Read page 2. Point to the drawing of the troll.

  What do you notice about my drawing of the troll?

  What else could I draw to show my thinking about the troll in this story?

- Point to and read the sentences.

  What did I write about?

  Is there something else that I could have written to tell about the troll?

Have a Try

Invite the children to talk with a partner about *Fireman Small*.

> Now let's think about *Fireman Small* by Wong Herbert Yee. Let's look at Fireman Small in this story.

▶ Show pages in the book showing *Fireman Small* helping his community.

> What would you draw and write to tell about *Fireman Small*? Turn and talk to your partner about your thinking.

Summarize and Apply

Summarize the learning and remind children to think about the characters as they read.

> What can you draw and write about a character in a story? Where can you draw and write about it? Look at the chart to remember.

> While reading today, think about what the character is like in the story. In your reader's notebook, draw and write to tell what the character is like. If you don't know how to write a word, give it a try. Bring your book and reader's notebook to the group to share.

Share

Following independent work time, gather children together in the meeting area to talk about their reading in groups of three.

> First, show your partner your book and then talk about what the character is like in the story by telling about your drawing and reading your writing.

Extend the Lesson (Optional)

After assessing children's understanding, you might decide to extend the learning.

▶ Give each group three to four books that have been read recently. Have each child think about one character in one of the books. Have one child pantomime the character or say some words describing the character. The other children guess which book the character was in. Repeat with the other children.

▶ During interactive reading, generate a list of the names of different characters and their traits on chart paper. After each reading, add to the list. Discuss similarities and patterns. Invite a few children to add a drawing for each addition.

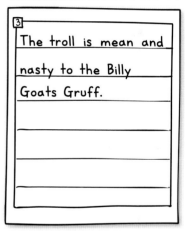

Books I Read

3

Title: The Three Billy Goats Gruff

Author: P.C. Asbjornsen and J.E. Moe

3

The troll is mean and nasty to the Billy Goats Gruff.

Section 4: Writing About Reading

Reading Minilesson Principle
Write a new ending for a story.

Writing About Fiction Books in a Reader's Notebook

You Will Need

- chart paper prepared to look like a page from *Reader's Notebook: Primary*, with title and author, a picture, and sentence filled in
- markers
- projector (optional)
- familiar fiction books, such as the following:
  - *The Elves and the Shoemaker* by Paul Galdone from Text Set: Folktales
  - *The Three Little Pigs* by Patricia Seibert, from Text Set: Animal Tales
- *Reader's Notebook: Primary*, or a reader's notebook for each child

Academic Language / Important Vocabulary

- reader's notebook
- author
- title
- characters
- ending

Continuum Connection

- Compose innovations on very familiar texts by changing the ending, the series of events, characters, or the setting (p. 173)

Goal

Compose innovations on very familiar texts by changing the ending.

Rationale

Children use a story's characters, setting, problem, and important events to predict an outcome. When they write an alternative ending to a story it prompts them to think about story elements and how they work together, and, to use their imagination.

Assess Learning

Observe children when they draw and write a new ending to a familiar story. Notice if there is evidence of new learning based on the goal of this minilesson.

- ▶ Can children draw and write a new ending to a story?
- ▶ Do they keep in mind the characters and events of the original story so the alternative ending makes sense?
- ▶ Do they understand the terms *reader's notebook*, *author*, *title*, *characters*, and *ending*?

Minilesson

To help children think about the minilesson principle, choose familiar texts and examples to use in modeling how to write a new ending for a story. Here is an example.

- ▶ Display the prepared chart (or project the page from *Reader's Notebook: Primary*) and show the cover of *The Elves and the Shoemaker* by Paul Galdone. Point to and read the author and title.

  Listen as I reread the ending of this book.

- ▶ Read to the end, beginning with "Quickly they took up . . ."
- ▶ Point to and read the alternative ending you wrote.

  Now listen to this ending: the elves went to find another family that needs help. What do you notice about what I wrote?

  Folktales have been around a long time and have been told in different ways. You can tell a folktale in a different way, too. You can write a new ending to a story, but remember to think about the characters and what they might do so the new ending makes sense. The elves helped the shoemaker, so I think it makes sense that they would go help someone else.

Have a Try

Invite the children to talk with a partner about *The Three Little Pigs*.

▶ Show the cover of *The Three Little Pigs*.

Think about the ending of this book, and then turn and talk to your partner about another way this book could end.

▶ After they turn and talk, call on a few children to discuss what they might draw and write in a reader's notebook.

Summarize and Apply

Summarize the learning and remind children to think about how else the story could end as they read.

When you write and draw a new ending for a story, what should you think about?

Today, read a fiction story from your independent reading books, or think about one of the animal tales or folktales we have read together. How could the story end differently? Draw and write a new ending in your reader's notebook. If you don't know how to write a word, give it a try.

▶ Assist children who are not yet comfortable with writing.

Share

Following independent work time, gather children together in the meeting area to talk about their drawing and writing.

Turn and talk about the new ending to your book. Show your partner your drawing and read the words you wrote.

Extend the Lesson (Optional)

After assessing children's understanding, you might decide to extend the learning.

▶ Have children role-play the new ending to a familiar story.

▶ **Drawing/Writing About Reading** Use interactive or shared writing to rewrite a story by changing the series of events, one or more characters, and/or the setting of the story.

Clothing Store

The Elves and the Shoemaker
Paul Galdone
The elves went to find another
family that needs help.

Reading Minilesson Principle
Think about all the things you can write about fiction stories.

Writing About Fiction Books in a Reader's Notebook

You Will Need

- charts from all previous minilessons in this umbrella
- chart paper and markers
- *Reader's Notebook: Primary*, or a reader's notebook for each child

Academic Language / Important Vocabulary

- reader's notebook
- author
- title
- problem and solution
- fiction
- character

Continuum Connection

- Tell important information about a text (p. 172)

Goal

Understand the different things to write about fiction books in a reader's notebook.

Rationale

Reviewing the different ways children can think about fiction stories will reinforce their learning and allow them to deepen their understanding of a story's characters, plot, and setting. Expressing their thinking through drawing and writing allows for different learning modalities and developmental levels.

Assess Learning

Observe children when they draw and write about stories they have read or heard. Notice if there is evidence of new learning based on the goal of this minilesson.

- ▶ Can children talk about the different things they can share about books through drawing and writing?
- ▶ Do they choose a way (or several ways) to tell about their reading?
- ▶ Do they understand the terms *reader's notebook*, *author*, *title*, *problem*, *solution*, *fiction*, and *character*?

Minilesson

To help children think about the minilesson principle, review ways to write about fiction stories. Here is an example.

- ▶ Use the charts from prior minilessons to review ways that children can share their thinking about fiction stories in a reader's notebook.

    What do you write first when telling about books?

- ▶ On chart paper, write *Title* and *Author*.

    When you write about a book, it's important to write the title of the book and the author's name.

- ▶ Show the charts for *Jessica* (RML2) and *Dim Sum for Everyone!* (RML4).

    What did I share about these two stories?

- ▶ Write *How a character feels* and *Where a story takes place* on the chart. Invite a volunteer to draw a happy face and another to draw a sad face. Invite a few volunteers to draw where a story could take place.

- ▶ Repeat with *Where Are You Going, Little Mouse?* and *The Three Billy Goats Gruff*.

Have a Try

Invite the children to talk with a partner what they will draw and write in a reader's notebook.

> Turn and talk to a partner about one thing from the chart you can put in your reader's notebook.

Summarize and Apply

Summarize the learning and remind children to think about what they could write about a story as they read.

> We have talked about different things you can write about fiction stories. Let's make sure we have them all on the chart.

▶ Have the children read the list together.

> Today everyone will read a fiction book. Choose one of the ways on the chart to write and draw about the story you read. If you don't know how to write a word, give it a try. Bring your reader's notebook to group meeting to share your thinking.

Share

Following independent work time, gather children together in the meeting area to talk share what they wrote and drew.

> Talk about your drawing with your partner and read the writing that tells about your thinking about your book.

> Think about the way you shared your thinking with your partner. Give a thumbs-up if your thinking was about a character's feelings.

▶ Repeat with the other items on the chart.

Extend the Lesson (Optional)

After assessing children's understanding, you might decide to extend the learning.

▶ After each interactive read-aloud, refer to the chart to revisit how children can write about fiction. If the book provides a new way to write about fiction, add to the list.

▶ **Drawing/Writing About Reading** Have children draw and write in a different way from before. If they wrote about the character's feelings, they might draw and write about where the story happened.

Things You Can Write About Fiction Stories

- Title and author

  | Jessica |
  | by Kevin Henkes |

- How a character feels

- Where a story takes place

- Problem and how it is solved

- What a character is like

Assessment

After you have taught the minilessons in this umbrella, observe children as they talk and write about their reading across instructional contexts: interactive read-aloud, independent reading and literacy work, guided reading, shared reading, and book club. Use *The Literacy Continuum* (Fountas and Pinnell 2017) to observe children's reading and writing behaviors across instructional contexts.

▶ What evidence do you have of new understanding related to ways for children to write about fiction books?

- Are children able to draw and write to show their thinking about different elements of fiction?

- Are children able to talk about the different ways of thinking about the elements of characters, problem and solution, and setting?

- Do they use the terms *reader's notebook, author, title, fiction, character, problem, solution,* and *ending* to talk about fiction?

▶ In what other ways, beyond the scope of this umbrella, are the children talking about other elements of fiction books?

- Are children beginning to see how to use their thinking about how a character feels, problem and solution, and setting in their stories?

- Can they think and talk about how the illustrations support their thinking about characters, setting, and problem and solution?

- When children read another book by the same author do they make connections about the author's style and the story elements?

Use your observations to determine the next umbrella you will teach. You may also consult Minilessons Across the Year (p. 51) for guidance.

Minilessons in This Umbrella

RML1 Tell the topic of a nonfiction book.

RML2 Tell something you learned from a nonfiction book.

RML3 Tell an interesting fact about a topic.

RML4 Think about all the things you can write about a topic.

Before Teaching Umbrella 5 Minilessons

These minilessons may be taught sequentially as a unit or individually in conjunction with minilessons that support children in reading nonfiction texts. Remember that a minilesson can be skipped if children are not ready to engage with the principle. The lessons are based on *Reader's Notebook: Primary* (Fountas and Pinnell 2014), but a reader's notebook can be any blank notebook with space for children to draw and write (see p. 46 for more on using a reader's notebook). Read and discuss nonfiction books with easily identified topics, interesting facts, and information that might be new to the children. Use the following books from the *Fountas & Pinnell Classroom™ Interactive Read-Aloud Collection* text sets or any nonfiction books that will interest your class.

The Place Called Home

Houses and Homes by Ann Morris

Sharing the Earth: Animals

Actual Size by Steve Jenkins

Exploring Fiction and Nonfiction

Chickens Aren't the Only Ones by Ruth Heller

Hats, Hats, Hats by Ann Morris

As you read aloud and enjoy these texts together, help children

- think and talk about the topic of the book, and

- notice and share new information.

Home

Animals

Fiction and Nonfiction

Reader's Notebook

Section 4: Writing About Reading

Reading Minilesson Principle
Tell the topic of a nonfiction book.

Writing About Nonfiction Books in a Reader's Notebook

You Will Need

- chart paper prepared to look like nonfiction Books I Read page from *Reader's Notebook: Primary*, with title, author's name, picture, and sentence in place
- markers
- projector (optional)
- familiar nonfiction books, such as the following:
  - *Houses and Homes* by Ann Morris, from Text Set: Home
  - *Actual Size* by Steve Jenkins, from Text Set: Animals
- 4–6 baskets of nonfiction books

Academic Language / Important Vocabulary

- nonfiction
- reader's notebook
- topic
- author

Continuum Connection

- Understand that a writer is presenting facts about a single topic (p. 30)
- Record text titles and authors in a Reader's Notebook (and use drawings) (p. 174)
- Tell important information about a text (p. 174)

Goal

Write and draw about the topic of a nonfiction book in a reader's notebook.

Rationale

When you teach children to write and draw about topics in nonfiction books, you help them understand that nonfiction books focus on a specific body of information. Thinking about the topic helps children build and increase their background knowledge about a topic.

Assess Learning

Observe children when they write and draw about the topic of a nonfiction book. Notice if there is evidence of new learning based on the goal of this minilesson.

- ▶ Are children able to identify and tell about the topic of a nonfiction book?
- ▶ Do the children use approximated spelling for unknown words?
- ▶ Do they understand the terms *nonfiction*, *reader's notebook*, *author*, and *topic*?

Minilesson

To help children think about the minilesson principle, engage them in a discussion about the topic of a nonfiction book. Here is an example.

- ▶ Display the prepared chart (or project the page from *Reader's Notebook: Primary*) and show the cover of *Houses and Homes*. Point to the title and author on the chart.

  I wrote the title of the book and the author's name in my reader's notebook before I started sharing my thinking. How do you think I knew how to write the title and the author's name?

- ▶ Show a few pages of the book and point to the drawings.

  Here is my thinking about this nonfiction book. What do you notice about my drawing? Why do you think I drew a lot of different houses?

  The picture I drew is of houses because this book is about different houses and homes around the world.

- ▶ Read and point to the sentence on the chart.

  Think about what I wrote about *Houses and Homes*. What do you notice about what I wrote?

  Houses and Homes tells about different houses all over the world.

Have a Try

Invite the children to talk with a partner about what they might draw.

▶ Show the cover of *Actual Size*.

> What can you tell from the title about this book? What could you draw and write to share your thinking about *Actual Size*?

> Turn and talk with a partner about what you could draw and write in your reader's notebook to share your thinking about *Actual Size*.

Summarize and Apply

Summarize the learning and remind children to think about the book's topic while they read.

> When you write and draw about a topic you show you understand what the book is about. Sometimes it will be easy to know the topic from reading the title, but sometimes you will need to read the book to discover the topic.

> Today when you read, choose a nonfiction book from these baskets. Think about the book's topic. Use your reader's notebook to draw and write about the topic. If you don't know how to write any of the words, give them a try.

Share

Following independent work time, gather children together in the meeting area to talk about their thinking about the nonfiction book and review the chart.

> Turn and talk about the topic of the nonfiction book you read today. Share with your partner your drawing and writing from your reader's notebook.

Extend the Lesson (Optional)

After assessing children's understanding, you might decide to extend the learning.

▶ Have children organize books in the classroom library by topics. Use interactive writing to create labels for the topics.

▶ Create a bulletin board to display nonfiction books children have read. Post sentence strips on which children have written or drawn the title, author, and topic.

▶ Have children vote on their favorite nonfiction book (from books you have read to them) and add the tally to the bulletin board.

Books I Read

Title: Houses and Homes

Author: Ann Morris

Houses and Homes tells about different houses. all over the world.

Section 4: Writing About Reading

<table>
<tr><td>

RML2

WAR.U5.RML2

</td><td>

Reading Minilesson Principle
Tell something you learned from a nonfiction book.

</td></tr>
</table>

Writing About Nonfiction Books in a Reader's Notebook

You Will Need

▸ chart paper prepared to look like nonfiction Books I Read page from *Reader's Notebook: Primary*, with title, author's name, picture, and sentence in place

▸ markers

▸ projector (optional)

▸ a familiar nonfiction book, such as *Chickens Aren't the Only Ones* by Ruth Heller, from Text Set: Fiction and Nonfiction

▸ 4-6 baskets of nonfiction books

▸ *Reader's Notebook: Primary* or a reader's notebook for each child

Academic Language / Important Vocabulary

▸ reader's notebook

▸ nonfiction

▸ information

Continuum Connection

▸ Gain new information from both pictures and print (p. 30)

▸ Reflect both prior knowledge and new knowledge from a text (p. 174)

Goal

Notice when you have learned something new from reading and write about it in a reader's notebook.

Rationale

When children process information they learned from a nonfiction book by writing and drawing about it, they understand the purpose of nonfiction, which is to inform. The ability to articulate new information demonstrates understanding of the text.

Assess Learning

Observe children when they draw and write about nonfiction books. Notice if there is evidence of new learning based on the goal of this minilesson.

▸ Are children able to identify information that they already know and information that is new?

▸ Can they draw and write something about the new information they learned?

▸ Do they use approximated spelling for unknown words?

▸ Do they understand the terms *reader's notebook*, *nonfiction*, and *information*?

Minilesson

To help children think about the minilesson principle, engage them in a short demonstration of using a reader's notebook to tell about what they learned when reading a nonfiction book. Here is an example.

▸ Display the prepared chart (or project the page from *Reader's Notebook: Primary*) and show the cover of *Chickens Aren't the Only Ones*. Point to and read the sentences.

> Here is my thinking after I read *Chickens Aren't the Only Ones*. What do you notice about what I wrote? I learned that *oviparous* is what you call anything that lays eggs. This was new information for me.

▸ Point to the drawing and read the labels.

> What do you notice about my drawing? My drawing matches what I wrote about.

Have a Try

Invite the children to talk with a partner about what they learned in a nonfiction book.

> Now turn and talk about something new you learned in *Chickens Aren't the Only Ones*. Tell your partner what you would draw and write to share your thinking about the new information.

▶ Have a few children share.

Summarize and Apply

Summarize the learning and remind the children to notice new information in a nonfiction book as they read.

▶ Review the chart with the children.

> What did you learn today about what you can write and draw in your reader's notebook?

> Choose a nonfiction book to read today. You can choose from these baskets. Then, in your reader's notebook, draw and write about something new you learned. If you don't know how to write any of the words, give them a try.

Share

Following independent work time, gather children together in the meeting area to talk about their drawing and writing.

> Turn and talk about what you wrote and drew in your reader's notebook. Read your writing to your partner and talk about what you learned.

▶ Ask two or three children to share what they talked about with their partner.

Extend the Lesson (Optional)

After assessing children's understanding, you might decide to extend the learning.

▶ Read aloud two books about the same topic. Talk with the children about what they learned that was the same in both books and what was different.

▶ **Drawing/Writing About Reading** Use interactive writing to create a list of new information learned in a nonfiction book.

Section 4: Writing About Reading

Reading Minilesson Principle
Tell an interesting fact about a topic.

Writing About Nonfiction Books in the *Reader's Notebook*

You Will Need

- chart paper prepared to look like nonfiction Books I Read page from *Reader's Notebook: Primary*, with title, author's name, picture, and sentence in place
- markers
- projector (optional)
- a familiar nonfiction book, such as *Actual Size* by Steve Jenkins, from Text Set: Animals
- 4–6 baskets of nonfiction books
- *Reader's Notebook: Primary* or a reader's notebook for each child

Academic Language / Important Vocabulary

- reader's notebook
- nonfiction
- information
- facts

Continuum Connection

- Identify and discuss interesting information in a text (p. 30)
- Show curiosity about topics (p. 30)
- Express opinions about facts or information learned (p. 174)

Goal

Draw and write about interesting facts from a nonfiction book in a reader's notebook.

Rationale

When children share their thinking about interesting facts in a nonfiction book, they demonstrate understanding of the information. Sharing their thinking deepens background knowledge of the topic of the book.

Assess Learning

Observe children when they draw and write about an interesting fact in a nonfiction book. Notice if there is evidence of new learning based on the goal of this minilesson.

- Are children able to identify facts in a nonfiction book?
- Are children able to draw and write about an interesting fact in a nonfiction book?
- Do the children approximate the spelling of unknown words?
- Do they understand the terms *reader's notebook*, *nonfiction*, *information*, and *facts*?

Minilesson

To help children think about the minilesson principle, engage them in a discussion of interesting facts in a nonfiction book. Here is an example.

- Show the cover of *Actual Size*. Show a completed chart of the Books I Read page (or project the page from *Reader's Notebook: Primary*). Point to and read the title and author on the chart. Then, point to and read the sentence.

  What do you notice about what I wrote?

  I shared a fact. A fact is a piece of information—something that is true. I thought this fact was very interesting. Look at the tooth I drew. What do you notice?

  It is huge!

Have a Try

Invite the children to talk about an interesting fact from a nonfiction book.

▶ Show a few pages of *Actual Size*.

> Who would like to share an interesting fact you could write and draw about in your reader's notebook?

▶ Repeat with a few more children.

> When people read the same nonfiction book, they can find different interesting facts.

Summarize and Apply

Summarize the learning and remind children to notice interesting facts as they read a nonfiction book.

▶ Review the chart with the children.

> What did you learn today about what you can write and draw in your reader's notebook?

> Choose a nonfiction book to read today. You can choose from these baskets. Then, in your reader's notebook, draw and write about an interesting fact in the book. If you don't know how to write any of the words, give them a try.

Share

Following independent work time, gather children together in the meeting area to share their drawing and writing.

> Turn and talk to a partner about the interesting fact you noticed in your nonfiction book. Show your partner your drawing and writing about your thinking in your reader's notebook.

Extend the Lesson (Optional)

After assessing children's understanding, you might decide to extend the learning.

▶ Create a class display of interesting facts the children have learned from their nonfiction reading. Have them add the title and author of the book along with an interesting fact they learned. Invite the children to post questions for others to encourage further inquiry.

Section 4: Writing About Reading

RML4
WAR.U5.RML4

Think about all the things you can write about a topic.

Writing About Nonfiction Books in a Reader's Notebook

You Will Need

- charts from RML1–RML3 in this umbrella
- chart paper and markers
- familiar nonfiction book, such as *Hats, Hats, Hats* by Ann Morris, from Text Set: Fiction and Nonfiction
- 4–6 baskets of nonfiction books
- *Reader's Notebook: Primary*, or a reader's notebook for each child

Academic Language / Important Vocabulary

- reader's notebook
- author
- title
- nonfiction
- topic
- facts
- information

Continuum Connection

- Tell important information about a text [p. 174]

Goal

Understand there are different ways to write about nonfiction books.

Rationale

When you review with children ways they can think about nonfiction books, you reinforce their learning and allow them to deepen understanding of the characteristics of nonfiction texts. When children express their thinking through drawing and writing, you allow for different learning modalities and developmental levels.

Assess Learning

Observe children when they draw and write in different ways about nonfiction books. Notice if there is evidence of new learning based on the goal of this minilesson.

- Are children able to talk about the different ways they can share their thinking about nonfiction books through drawing and writing in a reader's notebook?
- Do they approximate the spelling of unknown words?
- Do they understand the terms *reader's notebook*, *author*, *title*, *topic*, *information*, *nonfiction*, and *facts*?

Minilesson

To help children think about the minilesson principle, engage them in a discussion of ways to write about nonfiction books. Here is an example.

- Title a piece chart paper *Writing and Drawing About Nonfiction Books*. If you have taught the previous minilessons in this umbrella, use the charts from those lessons to prompt responses.

  We have talked about some ways that you can write and draw about nonfiction books in your reader's notebook. Let's make a list of those ways.

- Write the children's responses on the chart.

  Are there any other ways that you could show your thinking about a nonfiction book?

Have a Try

Invite the children to talk about ways to write about nonfiction books with a partner.

▶ Show *Hats, Hats, Hats*. Display some pages to review information.

> Think about how you could draw and write about this book. Turn and talk to a partner about what you might draw and write.

▶ Add any new thoughts to the chart.

Summarize and Apply

Summarize the learning and remind the children to think about how they could write about a nonfiction book that they read.

> We have talked about different things you can write about nonfiction books. Let's make sure we have them all on the chart.

▶ Have the children read the list together.

> Today everyone will read a nonfiction book. Then you will draw and write about the book. Choose one of the ways on the chart to write and draw about the book you read. If you don't know how to write any of the words, give them a try. Bring your reader's notebook to group meeting to share your thinking.

Writing and Drawing About Nonfiction Books

Topic

Something you learned

Interesting fact

Share

Following independent work time, gather children together in the meeting area to talk what they drew and wrote about a nonfiction book.

> Turn and talk to a partner about your drawing and read what you wrote.

> Give a thumbs-up if you shared your thinking about the topic (about something new you learned, an interesting fact).

Extend the Lesson (Optional)

After assessing children's understanding, you might decide to extend the learning.

▶ During interactive or shared reading, ask children to suggest something (e.g., an interesting fact) that could be recorded in a reader's notebook.

▶ Create a bulletin board of topics children have read about in nonfiction books. Encourage them to draw a picture of each topic.

Assessment

After you have taught the minilessons in this umbrella, observe your children as they talk and write about their nonfiction reading across instructional contexts: interactive read-aloud, independent reading and literacy work, guided reading, shared reading, and book club. Use *The Literacy Continuum* (Fountas and Pinnell 2017) to observe your children's reading and writing behaviors across instructional contexts.

▶ What evidence do you have of new learning about ways to tell and write about nonfiction books?

- Are children able to show their thinking about topics of nonfiction books in a reader's notebook?

- Do they approximate the spelling of unknown words?

- Do children share interesting facts and something new they learned from listening to or reading a nonfiction book in a reader's notebook?

- Are children able to talk about the different ways of thinking about nonfiction books?

- Do they use the terms *author, title, nonfiction, facts,* and *information* to talk about what they draw and write about nonfiction?

▶ In what other ways, beyond the scope of this umbrella, are the children talking about nonfiction books?

- Have they begun to think about writing and talking about the topics of nonfiction books in other content areas?

- When children read another nonfiction book by the same author, are they making connections across texts and can they write and draw their thinking in a reader's notebook?

Use your observations to determine the next umbrella you will teach. You may also consult Minilessons Across the Year (p. 51) for guidance.

Kindness

Fiction and Nonfiction

Minilessons in This Umbrella

RML1 Share your opinion about a book.

RML2 Share your opinion about authors you love.

RML3 Share your opinion about characters you love.

RML4 Write a letter to share your thinking about a book.

Before Teaching Umbrella 6 Minilessons

Animals

These minilessons teach children to share opinions about books, authors, and characters in a reader's notebook. Before teaching these minilessons, it would be helpful to introduce children to the sections of a reader's notebook. Conduct author and illustrator studies to help them develop knowledge of and preferences for different author and illustrator styles. Remember that a minilesson can be skipped if children are not ready to engage with the principle. These minilessons are based on the *Reader's Notebook: Primary* (Fountas and Pinnell 2014), but a reader's notebook can be any blank notebook with space for drawing and writing (see page 46).

Eric Carle

Use the following books from *Fountas & Pinnell Classroom™ Interactive Read-Aloud Collection* text sets or choose books that are familiar to your class.

The Importance of Kindness

Lost! by David McPhail

Jamaica's Find by Juanita Havill

Exploring Fiction and Nonfiction

All Pigs Are Beautiful by Dick King-Smith

Colors

Sharing the Earth: Animals

Actual Size by Steve Jenkins

Eric Carle: Exploring the Natural World

Does a Kangaroo Have a Mother, Too? by Eric Carle

Have You Seen My Cat? by Eric Carle

The Mixed-Up Chameleon by Eric Carle

Reader's Notebook

Noticing The Way the World Looks: Colors

Dog's Colorful Day by Emma Dodd

As you read aloud and enjoy these texts together, help children

- talk about their favorite books, characters, and authors, and
- share their opinions about books.

Reading Minilesson Principle
Share your opinion about a book.

Writing Opinions About Books

- chart paper prepared to look like Books I Read page from *Reader's Notebook: Primary,* with title and author, a picture, and one or two sentences filled in
- markers
- projector (optional)
- three or four familiar books, such as the following:
  - *Lost!* by David McPhail, from Text Set: Kindness
  - *Dog's Colorful Day* by Emma Dodd, from Text Set: Colors
- *Reader's Notebook: Primary* or a reader's notebook for each child

Academic Language / Important Vocabulary

- author
- title
- opinion
- reader's notebook

Continuum Connection

- Express opinions (interesting, funny, exciting) about texts (p. 173)

Goal

Express opinions about favorite books in writing and drawing and give an example to support opinions.

Rationale

When children use a reader's notebook to draw and write about books, they think about what they read and learn to express their opinions in writing. When they respond to the different aspects of a book, they demonstrate their understanding.

Assess Learning

Observe children when they share their opinions about books in a reader's notebook. Notice if there is evidence of new learning based on the goal of this minilesson.

- ▶ Do the children express an opinion about the book they read?
- ▶ Do children approximate the spelling of unknown words?
- ▶ Are they able to give a reason for their opinion about the book?
- ▶ Do they understand the terms *author, title, opinion,* and *reader's notebook*?

Minilesson

To help children think about the minilesson principle, engage them in a discussion of what it means to express an opinion about a book. Here is an example.

- ▶ Display the prepared chart (or project the page from *Reader's Notebook: Primary*). Show the cover of *Lost!*

  My opinion of the book *Lost!* is that it's a good book. I like this book because it has some funny parts. This is my opinion. An opinion is what you think about something.

  Your opinion might be that a book is interesting, exciting, or funny.

  What do you notice about what I did on this page? If you like a book, tell why you like it. What could I add to this page in my reader's notebook?

- ▶ Record responses on the chart paper.

Have a Try

Invite the children to talk with a partner about their opinion of *Dog's Colorful Day*.

▶ Revisit *Dog's Colorful Day*.

> Turn and talk to a partner about what you think about this book. What could you write and draw about in your reader's notebook?

▶ After time for discussion, ask a few pairs to share.

Summarize and Apply

Summarize the learning and remind children to notice their opinion of a book as they read.

▶ Review the chart with the children.

> Choose a book to read today. Then, in your reader's notebook, draw and write something to show your opinion of the book. Remember to write the title of the book and the author's name. You can look at the book to know how to write them. If you don't know how to write any of the words, give them a try.

> Bring your reader's notebook when we come together so you can share your opinion.

Share

Following independent work time, gather children together in the meeting area to share their opinion about a book they read.

> Turn and talk to a partner. Show and talk about what you wrote and drew in your reader's notebook.

> Did anyone read the same book as someone else? Did you have the same opinion?

Extend the Lesson (Optional)

After assessing children's understanding, you might decide to extend the learning.

▶ After reading aloud a book during interactive read-aloud or shared reading, ask children for their opinions of the book. Discuss how people can have different opinions of the same book.

▶ Schedule a regular time during independent literacy work for children to write in a reader's notebook. Create a list of ways they can write and draw about their reading.

Books I Read

2 Title: Lost!

Author: David McPhail

2 I liked the book because it was funny.

RML 2
WAR.U6.RML2

Reading Minilesson Principle
Share your opinion about authors you love.

Writing Opinions About Books

You Will Need

- chart paper prepared to look like Books I Read page from *Reader's Notebook: Primary*, with title and author, a picture, and one or two sentences filled in
- markers
- projector (optional)
- three or four books by a familiar author, such as Eric Carle
- basket of books by favorite authors children have read or heard
- *Reader's Notebook: Primary* or a reader's notebook for each child

Academic Language / Important Vocabulary

- author
- opinion
- reader's notebook

Continuum Connection

- Recognize that an author or illustrator may write or illustrate several books (p. 28)

Goal

Express opinions in writing about favorite authors and provide evidence for thinking.

Rationale

Children gain an understanding of authors by listening to and reading several books by the same author. When children use a reader's notebook to draw and write to share their opinion about an author, you encourage them to think about the author's craft, about who writes books, and about why they are drawn to certain books.

Assess Learning

Observe children when they share their opinion about an author they love in a reader's notebook. Notice if there is evidence of new learning based on the goal of this minilesson.

- Do the children write and draw about a favorite author in a reader's notebook?
- Are they able to tell why they love the author?
- Do they approximate the spelling of unknown words?
- Do they understand the terms *author, opinion,* and *reader's notebook*?

Minilesson

To help children think about the minilesson principle, engage them in a discussion to share their opinion about authors they love. Here is an example.

- Show the covers of several books by Eric Carle.

   You enjoyed listening to some of Eric Carle's books. Eric Carle is an author I love, so I wrote and drew about him in my reader's notebook.

- Display the prepared chart (or project the page from *Reader's Notebook: Primary*). Show the cover of *Have You Seen My Cat?*

   My opinion of Eric Carle is that I like his books. This is a page I made about Eric Carle. Why do you think I decided to draw a cat?

- Read the words on the lines.

   What do you notice about what I wrote? I wrote why I like Eric Carle's books. What else could I write on these lines?

- Add children's suggestions to the chart.

Have a Try

Invite the children to share an author they love with a partner.

▶ If children have made a list on the Authors I Love page, have them turn to the page as a reference.

> Think about an author you love and why. Turn and talk to a partner about the author and the things you could write and draw in your reader's notebook

▶ As needed, assist children to identify a favorite author and prompt conversation.

Summarize and Apply

Summarize the learning and remind children to write about authors they love and why they love them.

▶ Review the chart with the children.

> What did you learn today about what you can write and draw in your reader's notebook? Look at the chart to remember.

> Choose a book by an author you love. Draw and write about the author in your reader's notebook in the *Books I Read* section. If you don't know how to write any of the words, just give them a try. You can select an author from the books in the basket if you choose. Bring your reader's notebook when we come together so you can share your opinion.

Share

Following independent work time, gather children together in the meeting area to share their opinion about an author they love with a partner.

> Show the page in your reader's notebook about an author you love and share the special things you wrote and drew.

Extend the Lesson (Optional)

After assessing children's understanding, you might decide to extend the learning.

▶ Use this same lesson format to teach children to write about illustrators they love. Reference lists generated by children in the All About Me pages.

▶ Schedule a regular time during independent literacy work for children to write in a reader's notebook. Create a list of ways children can write and draw about their reading.

Books I Read
2 | Title: Have You Seen My Cat?
Author: Eric Carle

2 | I like books by Eric Carle.
I like Eric Carle because he asks questions.
I like how Eric Carle writes words in different ways.

Section 4: Writing About Reading

Reading Minilesson Principle
Share your opinion about characters you love.

Writing Opinions About Books

You Will Need

- chart paper prepared to look like Books I Read page from *Reader's Notebook: Primary*, with title and author, a picture, and one or two sentences filled in
- markers
- projector (optional)
- a familiar book with a strong main character, such as *Jamaica's Find* by Juanita Havill, from Text Set: Kindness
- basket of books that have favorite characters
- *Reader's Notebook: Primary* or a reader's notebook for each child

Academic Language / Important Vocabulary

- character
- opinion
- reader's notebook

Continuum Connection

- Draw or write about feelings such as empathy for a character (p. 173)

Goal

Express opinions in writing about favorite characters and provide evidence for thinking.

Rationale

Children get to know characters by listening to and reading a variety of books with vivid characters. When children use a reader's notebook to draw and write their opinion about characters, they connect the characters' experiences to their own lives and begin to think about why they are drawn to certain types of characters.

Assess Learning

Observe children when they share their opinion about characters they love in a reader's notebook. Notice if there is evidence of new learning based on the goal of this minilesson.

- ▶ Do the children write and draw about a favorite character in a reader's notebook?
- ▶ Are they able to tell why they love the character?
- ▶ Do they approximate spelling of unknown words?
- ▶ Do they understand the terms *character, opinion,* and *reader's notebook*?

Minilesson

To help children think about the minilesson principle, engage them in a discussion to share their opinions about characters they love. Here is an example.

- ▶ Show the prepared chart (or project the page from *Reader's Notebook: Primary*) and show the cover of *Jamaica's Find*.

    Here is a page I have made about Jamaica from the book you know, *Jamaica's Find*.

- ▶ Read the words and describe the drawing.

    What do you notice about what I wrote and drew?

    I wrote my opinion of Jamaica, and I wrote why I thought that about her. What other things about Jamaica could I write on these lines?

- ▶ Add children's suggestions to the page.

Have a Try

Invite the children to share an opinion about a character with a partner.

▶ Display a variety of books with characters the children have enjoyed.

> Here are some books with characters you enjoyed reading. Think about the characters you liked in these books. Choose one character you loved. Turn and talk to a partner about your opinion of that character.

Summarize and Apply

Summarize the learning and remind children to share an opinion about characters they love.

> Let's look at the chart to remind us of how we can share opinions.

> When you read today, choose a book that has a character you love. Draw and write your opinion of the character in your reader's notebook in the Books I Read section. If you don't know how to write any of the words, give them a try. Bring your reader's notebook when we come back together to meet so you can share.

Share

Following independent work time, gather children together in the meeting area to share their opinion about a character they love.

> Who would like to share the page from your reader's notebook about a character you love?

Extend the Lesson (Optional)

After assessing children's understanding, you might decide to extend the learning.

▶ Encourage children to self-select books with characters they enjoy reading about and talk about why they love the characters.

▶ Schedule a regular time during independent literacy work for children to write in a reader's notebook Create a list of ways children can write and draw about their reading.

> Books I Read
> ② Title: Jamaica's Find
> Author: Juanita Havill

> ② Jamaica is a good person.
> She gave the dog back.

Writing Opinions About Books

You Will Need

- *Reader's Notebook: Primary* or a reader's notebook for each child
- familiar nonfiction books, such as the following:
  - *All Pigs Are Beautiful* by Dick King-Smith, from Text Set: Fiction and Nonfiction
  - *Actual Size* by Steve Jenkins, from Text Set: Animals
- chart paper prepared to look like the Writing About Reading page in *Reader's Notebook: Primary*
- chart paper prepared with a letter to the class
- markers

Academic Language / Important Vocabulary

- reader's notebook
- letter

Continuum Connection

- Express opinions (interesting, funny, exciting) about texts (p. 173)

Goal

Compose a letter to share opinions about a book they love.

Rationale

Writing about reading supports children's understanding of the text. It requires them to think about what they read. Writing a letter about what they find interesting in a book helps them share an opinion with others. When they write a letter to the teacher, they have a real audience. If possible, write a one-sentence response to the child. This written conversation is similar to a one-to-one conference you might have.

Assess Learning

Observe children when they write a letter about a book. Notice if there is evidence of new learning based on the goal of this minilesson.

- ▶ Can children draw and write a letter about a book they read?
- ▶ Do they approximate the spelling of unknown words?
- ▶ Do they include the title of the book and something interesting about the book?
- ▶ Are they including the recipient and the sender in the letter?
- ▶ Do they know the terms *reader's notebook* and *letter?*

Minilesson

To help children think about the minilesson principle, engage them in a short demonstration of letter writing. Here is an example.

- ▶ Display the prepared charts (or project the pages from *Reader's Notebook*). Show the cover of *All Pigs Are Beautiful.* Point to and read the author and title.

   I am going to read you a letter I wrote to you about *All Pigs Are Beautiful.*

- ▶ Read the letter.

   What do you notice I did on this page?

- ▶ Invite a few children to share what they noticed. If necessary, guide the conversation with:

   What did I tell you about the book in my letter?

   One way to share your thinking about a book is by writing a letter to another person and drawing a picture. You can write about what you found interesting about the book.

Have a Try

Invite the children to talk about what they might write about *Actual Size* with a partner.

▸ Show the cover of *Actual Size* and a few pages if necessary.

> Turn and talk about writing me a letter about your thinking about *Actual Size*. What could you draw or write about?

▸ Ask a few children to share their thinking, guiding them with comments such as below, touching the parts of the letter on your chart as you review:

> So, you would write the date at the top and *Dear Mrs. S.* over here. Then, you would tell what you find interesting. Finally, you would sign the letter to let me know the letter is from you. I will read your letter.

Summarize and Apply

Summarize the learning and remind children to include the important elements of a letter in their writing.

> Writing a letter is a way to share your thinking about a book. Today, you thought about what you would tell me about *Actual Size*. Now you are going to write a letter. Include the date, my name, Mrs. S., the book title, and what you found interesting. Sign your name, so I know who wrote it. Bring your reader's notebook when we get together in group meeting.

Share

Following independent work time, gather children together in the meeting area to share their letters with a partner.

> Turn and talk to a partner. Read the letter you wrote and show your drawing.

Extend the Lesson (Optional)

After assessing children's understanding, you might decide to extend the learning.

▸ Provide more experiences for children to write letters to classmates, teachers, family, or friends about a book they love.

▸ Gather small groups of children to participate in interactive or shared writing of a letter about a book they have read.

Books I Read
2
Title: All Pigs Are Beautiful
Author: Dick King-Smith

2
March 12, 2019
Dear Class,
I read the book All Pigs Are Beautiful.
I think you will find this book interesting.
I didn't know that mud can
protect a pig from a sunburn!

From,
Your Teacher

Assessment

After you have taught the minilessons in this umbrella, observe children as they share their opinions about books while reading across instructional contexts: interactive read-aloud, independent reading and literacy work, guided reading, shared reading, and book club. Use the *The Literacy Continuum* (Fountas and Pinnell 2017) to observe children's reading and writing behaviors across instructional contexts.

▶ What evidence do you have of new understandings related to a reader's notebook?

- Can children share their opinions about books?
- Do they draw and/or write about their favorite parts of books to share their opinions in a reader's notebook?
- Are they able to identify which authors and/or characters they love and why?
- Do they draw and/or write in a reader's notebook to share their opinions about authors and/or characters?
- Are they able to share opinions about favorite authors and/or characters with others?
- Do they understand and use the terms *reader's notebook, author, title, opinion, letter,* and *character?*

▶ In what other ways, beyond the scope of this umbrella, are the children talking about what they enjoy about books, authors, illustrators, and characters?

- Have they begun to think about specific aspects that they enjoy?
- Do they talk about the different types of topics that authors choose to write about?
- Do they articulate which types of characters they enjoy reading about?

Use your observations to determine the next umbrella you will teach. You may also consult Minilessons Across the Year (p. 51) for guidance.

Glossary

alphabet book/ABC book A book that helps children develop the concept and sequence of the alphabet by pairing alphabet letters with pictures of people, animals, or objects with labels related to the letters.

animal fantasy A modern fantasy text geared to a very young audience in which animals act like people and encounter human problems.

animal story A contemporary realistic or historical fiction or fantasy text that involves animals and that often focuses on the relationships between humans and animals.

assessment A means for gathering information or data that reveals what learners control, partially control, or do not yet control consistently.

beast tale A folktale featuring animals that talk.

behaviors Actions that are observable as children read or write.

bold / boldface Type that is heavier and darker than usual, often used for emphasis.

book and print features (as text characteristics) The physical attributes of a text (for example, font, layout, and length).

character An individual, usually a person or animal, in a text.

chronological sequence An underlying structural pattern used especially in nonfiction texts to describe a series of events in the order they happened in time.

comprehension (as in reading) The process of constructing meaning while reading text.

conflict In a fiction text, a central problem within the plot that is resolved near the end of the story. In literature, characters are usually in conflict with nature, with other people, with society as a whole, or with themselves. Another term for conflict is *problem.*

cumulative tale A story with many details repeated until the climax.

dialogue Spoken words, usually set off with quotation marks in text.

directions (how-to) A procedural nonfiction text that shows the steps involved in performing a task. A set of directions may include diagrams or drawings with labels.

elements of fiction Important elements of fiction include narrator, characters, plot, setting, theme, and style.

elements of poetry Important elements of poetry include figurative language, imagery, personification, rhythm, rhyme, repetition, alliteration, assonance, consonance, onomatopoeia, and aspects of layout.

endpapers The sheets of heavy paper at the front and back of a hardback book that join the book block to the hardback binding. Endpapers are sometimes printed with text, maps, or design.

English language learners People whose native language is not English and who are acquiring English as an additional language.

expository text A nonfiction text that gives the reader information about a topic. Expository texts use a variety of text structures, such as compare and contrast, cause and effect, chronological sequence, problem and solution, and temporal sequence. Seven forms of expository text are categorical text, recount, collection, interview, report, feature article, and literary essay.

factual text See *informational text*.

family, friends, and school story A contemporary realistic text focused on the everyday experiences of children of a variety of ages, including relationships with family and friends and experiences at school.

fantasy A fiction text that contains elements that are highly unreal. Fantasy as a category of fiction includes genres such as animal fantasy, fantasy, and science fiction.

fiction Invented, imaginative prose or poetry that tells a story. Fiction texts can be organized into the categories realism and fantasy. Along with nonfiction, fiction is one of two basic genres of literature.

figurative language Language that compares two objects or ideas to allow the reader to see something more clearly or understand something in a new way. An element of a writer's style, figurative language changes or goes beyond literal meaning. Two common types of figurative language are metaphor (a direct comparison) and simile (a comparison that uses *like* or *as*).

fluency In reading, this term names the ability to read continuous text with good momentum, phrasing, appropriate pausing, intonation, and stress. In word solving, this term names the ability to solve words with speed, accuracy, and flexibility.

folktale A traditional fiction text about a people or "folk," originally handed down orally from generation to generation. Folktales are usually simple tales and often involve talking animals. Fables, fairy tales, beast tales, trickster tales, tall tales, realistic tales, cumulative tales, noodlehead tales, and pourquoi tales are some types of folktales.

font In printed text, the collection of type (letters) in a particular style.

form A kind of text that is characterized by particular elements. Mystery, for example, is a form of writing within the realistic fiction genre. Another term for form is *subgenre*.

genre A category of written text that is characterized by a particular style, form, or content.

graphic feature In fiction texts, graphic features are usually illustrations. In nonfiction texts, graphic features include photographs, paintings and drawings, captions, charts, diagrams, tables and graphs, maps, and timelines.

high-frequency words Words that occur often in the spoken and written language (for example, *the*).

humor / humor story A realistic fiction text that is full of fun and meant to entertain.

illustration Graphic representation of important content (for example, art, photos, maps, graphs, charts) in a fiction or nonfiction text.

independent writing Children write a text independently with teacher support as needed.

infer (as a strategic action) To go beyond the literal meaning of a text; to think about what is not stated but is implied by the writer.

informational text A nonfiction text in which a purpose is to inform or give facts about a topic. Informational texts include the following genres— biography, autobiography, memoir, and narrative nonfiction, as well as expository texts, procedural texts, and persuasive texts.

interactive read-aloud An instructional context in which students are actively listening and responding to an oral reading of a text.

interactive writing A teaching context in which the teacher and students cooperatively plan, compose, and write a group text; both teacher and students act as scribes (in turn).

intonation The rise and fall in pitch of the voice in speech to convey meaning.

italic (italics) A type style that is characterized by slanted letters.

label A written word or phrase that names the content of an illustration.

layout The way the print and illustrations are arranged on a page.

main idea The central underlying idea, concept, or message that the author conveys in a nonfiction text. Compare to *theme, message*.

maintaining fluency (as a strategic action) Integrating sources of information in a smoothly operating process that results in expressive, phrased reading.

making connections (as a strategic action) Searching for and using connections to knowledge gained through personal experiences, learning about the world, and reading other texts.

meaning One of the sources of information that readers use (MSV: meaning, language structure, visual information). Meaning, the semantic system of language, refers to meaning derived from words, meaning across a text or texts, and meaning from personal experience or knowledge.

mentor texts Books or other texts that serve as examples of excellent writing. Mentor texts are read and reread to provide models for literature discussion and student writing.

message An important idea that an author conveys in a fiction or nonfiction text. See also *main idea, theme*.

modern fantasy Fantasy texts that have contemporary content. Unlike traditional literature, modern fantasy does not come from an oral tradition. Modern fantasy texts can be divided into four more specific genres: animal fantasy, low fantasy, high fantasy, and science fiction.

monitoring and self-correcting (as a strategic action) Checking whether the reading sounds right, looks right, and makes sense, and solving problems when it doesn't.

mood The emotional atmosphere communicated by an author in his or her work, or how a text makes readers feel. An element of a writer's style, mood is established by details, imagery, figurative language, and setting. See also *tone*.

narrative nonfiction Nonfiction texts that tell a story using a narrative structure and literary language to make a topic interesting and appealing to readers.

narrative text A category of texts in which the purpose is to tell a story. Stories and biographies are kinds of narrative.

narrative text structure A method of organizing a text. A simple narrative structure follows a traditional sequence that includes a beginning, a problem, a series of events, a resolution of the problem, and an ending. Alternative narrative structures may include devices, such as flashback or flash-forward, to change the sequence of events or have multiple narrators.

nonfiction Prose or poetry that provides factual information. According to their structures, nonfiction texts can be organized into the categories of narrative and nonnarrative. Along with fiction, nonfiction is one of the two basic genres of literature.

nonnarrative text structure A method of organizing a text. Nonnarrative structures are used especially in three genres of nonfiction— expository texts, procedural texts, and persuasive texts. In nonnarrative nonfiction texts, underlying structural patterns include description, cause and effect, chronological sequence, temporal sequence, categorization, compare and contrast, problem and solution, and question and answer. See also *organization, text structure,* and *narrative text structure.*

oral tradition The handing down of literary material—such as songs, poems, and stories—from person to person over many generations through memory and word of mouth.

organization The arrangement of ideas in a text according to a logical structure, either narrative or nonnarrative. Another term for organization is *text structure.*

organizational tools and sources of information A design feature of nonfiction texts. Organizational tools and sources of information help a reader process and understand nonfiction texts. Examples include table of contents, headings, index, glossary, appendices, about the author, and references.

peritext Decorative or informative illustrations and/or print outside the body of the text. Elements of the peritext add to the aesthetic appeal and may have cultural significance or symbolic meaning.

picture book An illustrated fiction or nonfiction text in which pictures work with the text to tell a story or provide information.

plot The events, actions, conflict, and resolution of a story presented in a certain order in a fiction text. A simple plot progresses chronologically from start to end, whereas more complex plots may shift back and forth in time.

poetry Compact, metrical writing characterized by imagination and artistry and imbued with intense meaning. Along with prose, poetry is one of the two broad categories into which all literature can be divided.

predicting (as a strategic action) Using what is known to think about what will follow while reading continuous text.

principle A generalization that is predictable.

print feature In nonfiction texts, print features include the color, size, style, and font of type, as well as various aspects of layout.

problem See *conflict.*

problem and solution A structural pattern used especially in nonfiction texts to define a problem and clearly propose a solution. This pattern is often used in persuasive and expository texts.

procedural text A nonfiction text that explains how to do something. Procedural texts are almost always organized in temporal sequence and take the form of directions (or "how-to" texts) or descriptions of a process.

prompt A question, direction, or statement designed to encourage the child to say more about a topic.

Prompting Guide 1: A Tool for Literacy Teachers A quick reference for specific language to teach for, prompt for, or reinforce effective reading and writing behaviors. The guide is organized in categories and color-coded so that you can turn quickly to the area needed and refer to it as you teach (Fountas and Pinnell 2012).

punctuation Marks used in written text to clarify meaning and separate structural units. The comma and the period are common punctuation marks.

purpose A writer's overall intention in creating a text, or a reader's overall intention in reading a text. To tell a story is one example of a writer's purpose, and to be entertained is one example of a reader's purpose.

question and answer A structural pattern used especially in nonfiction texts to organize information in a series of questions with responses. Question-and-answer texts may be based on a verbal or written interview, or on frequently arising or logical questions about a topic.

reader's notebook A notebook or folder of bound pages in which students write about their reading. A reader's notebook is used to keep a record of texts read and to express thinking. It may have several different sections to serve a variety of purposes.

readers' theater A performance of literature—i.e., a story, a play, or poetry—read aloud expressively by one or more persons rather than acted.

realistic fiction A fiction text that takes place in contemporary or modern times about believable characters involved in events that could happen. Contemporary realistic fiction usually presents modern problems that are typical for the characters, and it may highlight social issues.

repetition Repeated words or phrases that help create rhythm and emphasis in poetry or prose.

resolution / solution The point in the plot of a fiction story when the main conflict is solved.

rhyme The repetition of vowel and consonant sounds in the stressed and unstressed syllables of words in verse, especially at the ends of lines.

rhythm The regular or ordered repetition of stressed and unstressed syllables in poetry, other writing, or speech.

searching for and using information (as a strategic action) Looking for and thinking about all kinds of content to make sense of a text while reading.

self-correcting Noticing when reading doesn't make sense, sound right, or look right, and fixing it when it doesn't.

sequence See *chronological sequence* and *temporal sequence*.

setting The place and time in which a fiction text or biographical text takes place.

shared reading An instructional context in which the teacher involves a group of students in the reading of a particular big book to introduce aspects of literacy (such as print conventions), develop reading strategies (such as decoding or predicting), and teach vocabulary.

shared writing An instructional context in which the teacher involves a group of students in the composing of a coherent text together. The teacher writes while scaffolding children's language and ideas.

sidebar Information that is additional to the main text, placed alongside the text and sometimes set off from the main text in a box.

small-group reading instruction The teacher working with children brought together because they are similar enough in reading development to teach in a small group; guided reading.

sources of information The various cues in a written text that combine to make meaning (for example, syntax, meaning, and the physical shape and arrangement of type).

speech bubble A shape, often rounded, containing the words a character or person says in a cartoon or other text. Another term for *speech bubble is speech balloon.*

story A series of events in narrative form, either fiction or nonfiction.

story about family, friends, and school A contemporary realistic or historical fiction text that focuses on the everyday experiences of children of a variety of ages, including relationships with family and friends and experiences at school.

strategic action Any one of many simultaneous, coordinated thinking activities that go on in a reader's head. See *thinking within, beyond, and about the text.*

stress The emphasis given to some syllables or words.

structure One of the sources of information that readers use (MSV: meaning, language structure, visual information). Language structure refers to the way words are put together in phrases and sentences (syntax or grammar).

style The way a writer chooses and arranges words to create a meaningful text. Aspects of style include sentence length, word choice, and the use of figurative language and symbolism.

subgenre A kind of text that is characterized by particular elements. See also *form.*

temporal sequence An underlying structural pattern used especially in nonfiction texts to describe the sequence in which something always or usually occurs, such as the steps in a process. See also *procedural text*, and *directions (how-to).*

text structure The overall architecture or organization of a piece of writing. Another term for text structure is *organization.* See also *narrative text structure* and *nonnarrative text structure.*

theme The central underlying idea, concept, or message that the author conveys in a fiction text. Compare to *main idea.*

thinking within, beyond, and about the text Three ways of thinking about a text while reading. Thinking *within* the text involves efficiently and effectively understanding what it is on the page, the author's literal message. Thinking *beyond* the text requires making inferences and putting text ideas together in different ways to construct the text's meaning. In thinking *about* the text, readers analyze and critique the author's craft.

thought bubble A shape, often rounded, containing the words (or sometimes an image that suggests one or more words) a character or person thinks in a cartoon or other text. Another term for *thought bubble* is *thought balloon*.

tone An expression of the author's attitude or feelings toward a subject reflected in the style of writing. For instance, a reader might characterize an author's tone as ironic or earnest. Sometimes the term *tone* is used to identify the mood of a scene or a work of literature. For example, a text might be said to have a somber or carefree tone. See also *mood*.

tools As text characteristics, parts of a text designed to help the reader access or better understand it (tables of contents, glossary, headings). In writing, references that support the writing process (dictionary, thesaurus).

topic The subject of a piece of writing.

traditional literature Stories passed down in oral or written form through history. An integral part of world culture, traditional literature includes folktales, tall tales, fairy tales, fables, myths, legends, epics, and ballads.

trickster tale A folktale featuring a clever, usually physically weaker or smaller, animal who outsmarts larger or more powerful animals.

understandings Basic concepts that are critical to comprehending a particular area of content.

visual information One of three sources of information that readers use (MSV: meaning, language structure, visual information). Visual information refers to the letters that represent the sounds of language and the way they are combined (spelling patterns) to create words; visual information at the sentence level includes punctuation.

wordless picture book A form in which a story is told exclusively with pictures.

writing Children engaging in the writing process and producing pieces of their own writing in many genres.

writing about reading Children responding to reading a text by writing and sometimes drawing.

Credits

Cover image from *A Bedtime for Bear*. Text copyright © 2010 by Bonny Becker. Illustrations copyright © 2010 by Kady MacDonald Denton. Reproduced by permission of the publisher, Candlewick Press, Somerville, MA.

Cover image from *A Fruit Is a Suitcase for Seeds* by Jean Richards, illustrated by Anca Hariton. Text copyright © 2002 by Jean Richards. Illustration copyright © 2002 by Anca Hariton. Reprinted with the permission of Millbrook Press, a division of Lerner Publishing Group, Inc. All rights reserved. No part of this excerpt may be used or reproduced in any manner whatsoever without the prior written permission of Lerner Publishing Group, Inc.

Cover image from *A Moose Is Loose* by Kana Riley. Copyright © 1995 by Houghton Mifflin Harcourt Trade Publishing. Reprinted by permission of Houghton Mifflin Harcourt Trade Publishing.

Cover image from *A Visitor for Bear*. Text copyright © 2008 by Bonny Becker. Illustrations copyright © 2008 by Kady MacDonald Denton. Reproduced by permission of the publisher, Candlewick Press, Somerville, MA.

Cover image from *Actual Size* by Steve Jenkins. Copyright © 2004 by Steve Jenkins. Reprinted by permission of Houghton Mifflin Harcourt Trade Publishing.

Cover image from *All for a Dime!* by Will Hillenbrand. Copyright © 2015 by Will Hillenbrand. Reprinted by permission of Holiday House.

Cover image from *All Pigs Are Beautiful*. Text copyright © 1993 by Foxbusters Ltd. Illustrations copyright © 1993 by Anita Jeram. Reproduced by permission of the publisher, Candlewick Press, Somerville, MA on behalf of Walker Books, London.

Cover image from *B Is for Bulldozer: A Construction ABC* by June Sobel. Text copyright © 2003 by June Sobel. Illustrations copyright © 2003 by Melissa Iwai. Reprinted by permission of Houghton Mifflin Harcourt Trade Publishing.

Cover image from *Baa Baa Black Sheep* written and illustrated by Iza Trapani. Copyright © Charlesbridge Publishing, Inc. All rights reserved. Used with permission of Charlesbridge Publishing, Inc. www.charlesbridge.com.

Cover image from *Big Al* by Andrew Clements with illustrations by Yoshi. Text copyright © 1988 by Andrew Clements. Illustrations copyright © 1988 by Yoshi. Reprinted with the permission of Atheneum Books for Young Readers, an imprint of Simon & Schuster Children's Publishing Division. All rights reserved.

Cover image from *Big Al and Shrimpy* by Andrew Clements with illustrations by Yoshi. Text copyright © 2002 by Andrew Clements. Illustrations copyright © 2002 by Yoshi. Reprinted with the permission of Atheneum Books for Young Readers, an imprint of Simon & Schuster Children's Publishing Division. All rights reserved.

Cover image from *Big Cats, Little Cats* © 2011 Bernette Ford. Permission arranged with Lee & Low Books, Inc., 95 Madison Avenue, New York, NY 10016.

Cover image from *Building a House* by Byron Barton. Copyright © 1981 by Byron Barton. Used by permission of HarperCollins Publishers.